ROMAN SUSSEX

ROMAN SUSSEX

MILES RUSSELL

The
History
Press

To M.P.

M.H. and R.R.

D.N.R. and J.A.R

D.R.R. and R.J.A.W.

B.E.R., M.E.R. and M.A.R.

Thank you all

First published 2006

Reprinted in 2014 by
The History Press
The Mill, Brimscombe Port,
Stroud, Gloucestershire, GL5 2QG
www.thehistorypress.co.uk

British Library Cataloguing in Publication Data.
A catalogue record for this book is available from the British Library.

ISBN 978 0 7524 3601 2
Printed and bound in Great Britain by
Marston Book Services Limited, Oxfordshire

CONTENTS

ACKNOWLEDGEMENTS

As I began writing this, the perhaps rather unexpectedly titled sequel to *Prehistoric Sussex*, I realised that I had actually started work on it some three decades before. This revelation came during the emptying of one of the many boxes of scrap paper that seem to spontaneously generate around the house in the most unexpected of places. In this I encountered a small, battered exercise book entitled *Roman Sussex; the life and times of people long ago*, which contained the thoughts and observations of an eight-year-old schoolboy by the name Miles Russell. Funny how things come full circle.

Over the last 30 years, since the writing of this first draft, my perspective on Rome and Roman Britain has been shaped through debate, discussion, excavation, survey, lectures, conference participation and, just occasionally, long heated arguments in the bar. I would like to thank all of the many people who have influenced my view over this time, from Patcham Middle School (where the word 'Roman' was first mentioned), via Patcham Fawcett Comprehensive, Varndean Sixth Form, UCL, the Field Archaeology and Oxford Archaeological Units to Bournemouth University and *Time Team*. You have all contributed, unwittingly or not, to the final feel of this *revised* book on Roman Sussex. I would also like to thank my parents and grandparents for tolerating my rather strange obsession with the ancient past, and encouraging me to investigate it in more detail.

For the purposes of this book, I am grateful to all those who generously allowed me to use their photographs and images, the majority being collected in 1999 during the preliminary research for *Prehistoric Sussex*. In particular I would like to thank Vanessa Constant, for redrawing some of the earlier figures used in the book, Barry Cunliffe and Oxford University, David Rudkin, John Manley, Hannah Crowdy, Emma Young, Barbara Alcock and Helen Poole of the Sussex Archaeological Society, Sally White, then of Worthing Museum, James Kenny and Chichester District Council, Andrew Woodcock and Martin Brown of East Sussex County Council, Mark Taylor and John Mills of West Sussex County Council, Henry Cleere, John Magilton, John Smith, John Funnel, Caroline Wells and Chris Butler. Special thanks must go to the Trustees of Bignor Roman Villa without whom this book would be so much the poorer.

I owe a great debt of thanks to Glynis Laughlin for reading endless draft copies of *Roman Sussex* and correcting my, sometimes random, thought processes. It goes without saying that any mistakes that remain are entirely my responsibility. I must thank her also for bravely combating the index monster and my wife Bronwen for calmly dealing with not just the glossary and index but also, perhaps more importantly, the real world outside the sanctity of my office. Special thanks to Linda Osborne, Ehren Milner and all in the A.I.P. office at Bournemouth University for their editorial and administrative assistance (and much-needed cups of tea). Thanks also to Peter Kemmis Betty, Laura Perehinec, Tom Sunley and all at Tempus for taking this project on and for believing that it might some day approach completion.

The book is respectfully dedicated to ten people: first, to Maurice Packham, my history teacher at Patcham Fawcett, for keeping my interest in the ancient past alive during the dark days of school. Secondly, to my lecturers at the Institute of Archaeology, now UCL, Mark Hassall and Richard Reece. Mark, for helping me to realise that one cannot understand Roman Britain without first understanding the inscriptions and Richard for teaching me that, whenever approaching archaeological evidence, one must keep an open mind at all times and question *everything*, even the most fundamental of assumptions. Thank you to David Rudling, for whom I worked throughout the 1980s on many exciting projects in Sussex, not least of all the villas of Arundel, Beddingham, Bignor and Goring, as well as Chanctonbury temple and the field systems and settlements of Thundersbarrow Hill and Eastwick Barn. Thanks must also go to Roger Wilson, first for writing the *Guide to the Roman Remains in Britain* (which was from its publication in 1975 was my own personal bible) and for the inspirational tour of Piazza Armerina in Sicily during the Easter weekend of 2004. It was this that made me realise that I could, and should, return to Roman archaeology and re-examine the evidence for Sussex. You may not all agree with the conclusions reached in this book, but without your influence it certainly could not have been written.

Lastly, and most importantly I should like to thank my parents for their constant guidance and support and, especially, Bronwen, Megan and Macsen who have coped with another massive disruption to their lives. You have all been kept awake at night by the heavy-handed sound of typing. Thank you. It will stop now. I Promise.

INTRODUCTION

The book before you now represents an attempt to explain the Romano-British heritage of a particular part of the British Isles. I have chosen the ancient county of Sussex for two reasons. The first is rather selfish, for I was born and grew up in Brighton and spent many of my early years visiting and exploring the county's Roman past. Secondly I feel that, if we are to understand the nature of Roman Britain (and indeed why the Roman Empire first looked towards Britain), then it is to Sussex that we must first turn.

THE LANDSCAPE

The modern county of Sussex is located on the south-eastern shore of Britain (1), facing out across the English Channel towards France. It is bounded along its north-eastern, northern and western perimeter by the counties of Kent, Surrey and Hampshire. Today Sussex covers an area of around 120km in length east to west, but is only 50km wide. Divided into two broad administrative zones from the late nineteenth century, the western half is governed from the city of Chichester, the eastern half from the market town of Lewes. Formal separation into discrete counties of East and West Sussex was not made until the restructuring of Britain's political map in 1974. More recently, devolution of local power into increasingly smaller units has meant that the towns of Brighton and Hove are a unitary authority, a sort of breakaway republic which is officially no longer part of the county. Tinkering with local government will no doubt continue throughout the twenty-first century and I have no desire to follow slavishly the vagaries of political fashion here. 'Sussex' is a neat and discrete geographical entity and therefore the essential discussion in this book will revolve around the limits of the county as defined prior to 1974.

The physical landscape of the county can be divided into three broad, if rather crude, blocks: the Weald (high and low), the South Downs and the coastal plain (2). The area of the Weald between the chalk ridges of the North Downs in Surrey and Kent and the South Downs of Sussex, has traditionally been forested, near total clearance for some areas only having been made possible within recent generations. The Weald itself comprises the heavy clays and alluvial (river-borne) silts and sands of

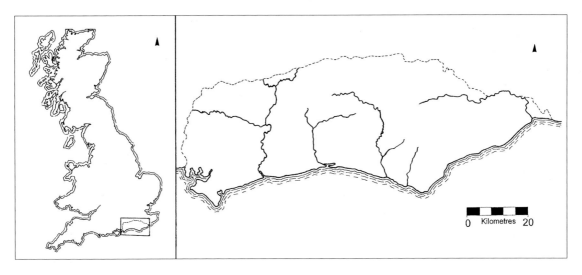

1 Sussex: location of study area

the Lower Weald, the sandy heathland of the North Weald and the still largely forested hills of the Sandstone Ridge.

The South Downs comprise an impressive chalk ridge which divides and separates the Weald from the coastal plain (*3*). Chalk is a white, permeable rock containing variable seams of nodular and tabular flint, a material used throughout the Prehistoric, Roman and medieval periods for tools and for use in building. The eastern limits of the Downs are dramatically marked by a series of cliffs ending at the internationally famous site of Beachy Head, just west of Eastbourne. The northern limits are characterised by a steep escarpment, which faces the sands, sandstones and clays of the Weald. To the south the Downs merge more gently into the coastal plain, the dip-slope being characterised by a network of dry valley systems. All major drainage flows southwards to the English Channel, the rivers Cuckmere, Ouse, Adur, Arun and Lavant dividing the Downs into a series of discrete blocks.

The flat expanse of the coastal plain to the south of the Downs is agriculturally fertile and probably represents the focus of settlement activity from the earliest of times. The coastline itself has changed dramatically over the course of the past 13,000 years, following the end of the last major ice age, with significant areas, from Selsey Bill in the west to the Beachy Head cliffs in the east, being lost to coastal erosion and marine transgression. Beyond the cliffs to Eastbourne, Hastings and Rye, where the Weald spills out into the sea, the opposite effect, that of soil accumulation, has incrementally added to the coastline, so that a series of important Roman and medieval harbours are now landlocked, whilst river estuaries and natural inlets have become clogged. The popularity of the coastal plain in recent years, especially with regard to tourism, has resulted in significant amounts of urban development with little or no useful periods of archaeological investigation.

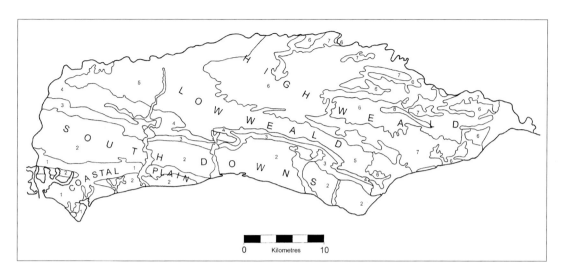

2 Sussex: plan to illustrate the geological make-up of the county and the relative positions of the coastal plain, South Downs and Low and High Weald: 1 = coastal plain (Eocene Beds); 2 = Chalk; 3 = Upper Greensand and Gault Clay; 4 = Lower Greensand; 5 = Wealden Clay; 6 = Tunbridge and Ashdown Sands; 7 = Wadhurst Clay; 8 = Purbeck Beds

3 The South Downs: the northern scarp slope of the chalk facing the Weald at Devil's Dyke, Fulking. *Author*

Sussex is a beautiful, dramatic and awe-inspiring county, despite the fact that little of it remains in anything like its original 'wild' state. Large areas have been modified, adapted and changed by human activity in some significant way. Agriculture has greatly affected the shape of the Downs and coastal plain, whilst deforestation and other land management schemes have altered the Weald. Modern development has also brought major change, from the simple enclosure of land behind ramparts, fences and hedgerows, to the wholesale destruction wrought by housing, road building and the rapacious demands of the train and aeroplane. Thankfully the complex urban sprawl of London has, to date, been kept at bay, although the Sussex towns of Crawley, Horsham, Worthing and Brighton are always threatening to burst at the seams and destroy vast swathes of the Weald and coastal plain in the process. Hideous road schemes and unnecessary out-of-town retail developments have in recent years hacked their indiscriminate way through the county. National Park status may help save some part of the chalk Downs, but how much of the Weald and coastal plain will be protected from the destructive hand of man in the immediate future is unknown.

ROMAN SUSSEX

The concept of 'Sussex' is, of course, a relatively new one and the borders that define it have no evident link to the topography, geography or geology. Those living in the area during the Prehistoric and Roman period had no concept of 'the county' and, in any case, were probably not constrained by the presence of frontiers, borders and administrative boundaries in the curious way that we are today. From a modern perspective, however, the county borders do provide a useful limit to a given study and, for the purposes of this narrative at least, they provide a handy cut-off point for the analysis of Romano-British life (4).

This book is not presented as an attempt to catalogue every single artefact and site that characterises and comprises Roman Sussex. If it is a basic site listing you are after then you are best to visit the National Monuments Record held by English Heritage in Swindon or the excellent Sites and Monuments Records (or Historic Environment Records as they are soon to be) of East and West Sussex County Council. Instead, like its companion volume *Prehistoric Sussex,* the archaeological and historic information presented here provides a single narrative attempting to explain the nature of human social development in a particular place at a critical period in British history. Much of the discussion will therefore attempt to place developments in Sussex within a wider geographical context for, as it will become apparent, one cannot understand Roman Sussex, without first understanding Rome itself.

The evidence presented in this book is gleaned from a variety of sources, Sussex being particularly lucky in having had an impressive amount of scientific research conducted upon its Roman archaeology. From the first exposure of the internationally

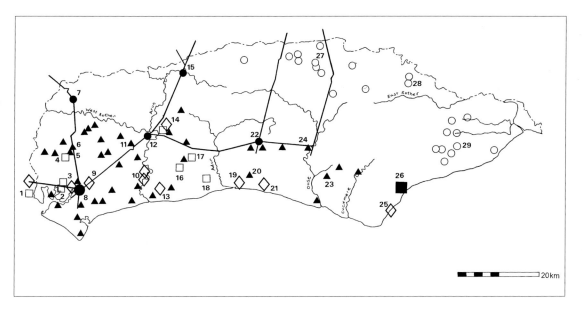

4 Roman Sussex: distribution of major sites. Blocked circles represent roadside settlements, open circles represent ironworking sites, squares are temples, diamonds are early villas/palaces, triangles are villas: 1 = Hayling Island (Hampshire); 2 = Bosham; 3 = Fishbourne; 4 = Bow Hill; 5 = Chilgrove 1; 6 = Chilgrove 2; 7 = Iping; 8 = Chichester; 9 = Westhampnett; 10 = Arundel; 11 = Bignor; 12 = Hardham; 13 = Angmering; 14 = Pulborough; 15 = Alfoldean; 16 = Muntham Court; 17 = Chanctonbury; 18 = Lancing; 19 = Southwick; 20 = West Blatchington; 21 = Brighton; 22 = Hassocks; 23 = Beddingham; 24 = Barcombe; 25 = Eastbourne; 26 = Pevensey; 27 = Garden Hill; 28 = Bardown; 29 = Beauport Park

famous Bignor mosaics by Samuel Lysons in 1811, to the detailed and dedicated work of the professional units, consultancies, local societies and volunteer groups of today, there is a wealth of high-quality material to draw upon. With this in mind, it is worth pointing out that interpretations drawn from this dataset are essentially impermanent. The wonderful thing about studying the past is that every new archaeological discovery and every new reading of the historical evidence, can force us to change our perspective totally. Other interpretations and readings of the primary data are certainly possible from information currently 'out there' in the public domain, either in popular books, academic accounts, museum displays, sites and monuments listings or the 'grey literature' of commercial archaeology. The archaeology itself is also visible in a great number of places, and I have appended a brief gazetteer to this book to act as a guide to the most accessible of monuments. If you have not done so already, I would urge you to seek out at least some of these.

I would also advise investigating the many archaeological groups, clubs, societies and museums that exist within Sussex. The Council for British Archaeology (Bowes Morrell House, 111 Walmgate, York, YO1 9WA) provides listings for all relevant groups, accessible via the internet at: http://www.britarch.ac.uk/index.html. The Sussex Archaeological Society, active in the examination and preservation of the county's past since 1846, is the primary port of call for anyone interested in further exploring the rich heritage of the area. The Society may be contacted at Barbican House, 169 High Street, Lewes, East Sussex, BN7 1YE, or via the web page at: http://www.sussexpast.co.uk. The Society also supports an incredibly informative website at http://www.romansinsussex.co.uk which contains comprehensive lists of the Roman sites, objects and museums as well as information for children, teachers and those in higher education.

There is much to discover out there: let us begin the journey.

1

FRIENDS, ROMANS, COUNTRYMEN

The third emperor of Rome, Gaius Julius Caesar Augustus Germanicus, better known to history as 'Caligula', spent the morning of 24 January AD 41 at the theatre, hurling fruit at the unprotected heads of fellow spectators. Despite having an upset stomach, derived from over-indulgence the previous day, Caligula was evidently enjoying himself. As master of the largest empire in the world he had the ultimate say in the daily lives of millions of men, women and children. Believing that his ancestors possessed divine origins, Caligula also had every reason to believe he was immortal. He could have had no idea that his life was at this point measured only in minutes.

As lunchtime approached, a number of the emperor's friends persuaded him that they should seek refreshment. In one of the narrow passageways that snaked out from the theatre, Caligula paused to watch a troop of young performers rehearsing for the afternoon show. Several of the imperial retinue, including the emperor's brother-in-law, Marcus Vinicius, and his uncle, Claudius, went on ahead, keen perhaps to get to the baths first. As Caligula watched the impromptu performance, the conspirators seized their chance.

Sources vary as to the exact order in which the fatal blows were delivered. The most popular account, provided later by the Roman historian Suetonius (Suetonius *Caligula*, 58), is that Cassius Chaerea, an officer in the elite praetorian guard, split the emperor's jaw with his sword, knocking him to the ground. The blow was severe but not fatal and Caligula, whilst sprawling on the floor of the covered passage, shouted that he still lived, something which, in retrospect, appears to have been a little unwise. The conspirators closed in, dispatching the First Citizen of Rome in a frenzy of stabbing to the chest and groin. Thus, noted the historian Cassius Dio, Caligula, after ruling 'three years, nine months, and twenty-eight days, learned by actual experience that he was not a god' (Cassius Dio, *Roman History*, LIX, 30).

The bloody assassination of the great grandson of Augustus, in a darkened tunnel beneath a theatre, marked a turning point, not only for Rome, but also in the history of the British Isles. As the conspirators turned their attention to the remaining members of the imperial family, one of Caligula's bodyguard, who to this point had not really earned his money, discovered the dead emperor's uncle Claudius cowering behind a curtain in the palace. Quickly hustled from the imperial house, Claudius was immediately taken to the praetorian barracks and, after an emergency meeting where no doubt the soldiers reflected that, without an emperor to protect, they were all unemployed, he was duly proclaimed as the successor to Caligula. Now in a position of absolute power Claudius had to prove his worth. Mindful that he was no great politician and possessed no claim to military prowess, Claudius desperately needed something to capture the hearts and minds of the senate and people of Rome. Like politicians of more recent years, what Claudius really needed was a war.

ROME AND BRITAIN

Britain provided a fantastic opportunity for the newly installed emperor to prove his military clout. First, from a propaganda perspective, the deified Julius Caesar, foremost warrior of Rome, had singularly failed to conquer the Britons during his two invasions of the island some 100 years earlier. If Claudius could win any kind of victory in Britain he would automatically be viewed by his people as being better than Caesar and, by implication, better than a god. Secondly, Claudius' predecessor Caligula had already been involved in some form of military intervention in the island (which could easily be downplayed by Claudius' spin-doctors) and ships, military units and provisions were probably all still in place. Thirdly, as all Claudius' predecessors had been aware, Britain was rich in grain, slaves and metals and there were plenty of harbours and anchor points already well known to the Roman army. A war in Britain would not only make sound political sense, but would also be economically viable if Rome could take direct control of all the Island's resources.

Britain, though geographically on the margins of the known, civilised world, had, in the past, often found itself very much at the centre of Roman power politics. The process had begun with the Greeks and Phoenicians who first encountered the inhabitants of the British Isles as they developed long distance trade networks across the Atlantic coast throughout the third and second centuries BC. This process of contact and documentation was greatly accelerated when the Roman Empire turned its attention to Gaul (modern France) during the mid-first century BC. Like the fictional Martians of H.G. Well's novel *War of the Worlds*, the Roman State now began to watch the Britons keenly and closely:

as men busied themselves about their various concerns they were scrutinised and studied, perhaps almost as narrowly as a man with a microscope might scrutinise the transient creatures that swarm and multiply in a drop of water … intellects vast and cool and unsympathetic, regarded this earth with envious eyes, and slowly and surely drew their plans against us. (Wells 1898, 7)

It was Julius Caesar who in 55 BC finally drew his up plans against Britain. Unlike the Martians in Wells' novel however, Caesar had not decided on an all out war of annihilation; no, what he had in mind was something altogether more devious.

GAIUS JULIUS CAESAR

Gaius Julius Caesar was a Roman general par excellence. He was also an opportunistic and callous bully who was instrumental in the death of the Roman Republic and the instigation of total rule by oppressive, militaristic autocrats. In 59 BC, already one of the most powerful men in Rome, Caesar obtained the governorship of Illyricum, Transalpine Gaul and Cisalpine Gaul, something that gave him authority over a broad swathe of territory from southern France through southern Italy to the Dalmatian coast.

Transalpine Gaul (literally 'Gaul beyond the Alps') provided Caesar with the springboard necessary for conquest, wealth and fame. In 58 BC he led his armies beyond the limits of the Roman Empire and into *Gallia Comata* ('Hairy Gaul'). He legitimised his actions by claiming Rome was at threat from the savage world of *barbaricum* and that only by striking first, could he save Roman territory, lives and investments. Playing on Rome's traditional mistrust and fear of those inhabiting the world north of the Alps, Caesar attacked the Helvetii, a Celtic people migrating westwards towards the pro-Roman Aedui tribe. Caesar hit the Helvetii as they marched. Of an estimated 370,000 tribespeople, only 130,000 survived. Evidently feeling that the death toll was not high enough, Caesar pursued the remnants of the tribe, slaughtering a further 20,000 men, women and children. He was not swayed by age, infirmity, sex or combat status; Caesar wanted merely to kill.

The next three years saw Julius Caesar's legions campaigning across Gaul, reaching the shores of Brittany in 56 BC and crossing the Rhine the following year. This Roman blitzkrieg was an amazing military achievement it is true, but at what ultimate cost were his actions to the indigenous population of Gaul? We have already noted the slaughter of the Helvetii, but this was only the first of many atrocities committed by Caesar. When, for example, in 57 BC, soldiers at his command attacked the Nervii tribe, some 60,000 were hacked down, whilst at Cenabum, the chief town of the Carnutes, he gave his men orders to kill all the inhabitants, some 40,000 men, women and children perishing in the process. Those who admire Caesar today as a great general, politician or statesman are missing the point somewhat.

The conquest of Gaul is a story of savagery and wholesale bloody carnage. Julius Caesar was a war criminal plain and simple; he was a man whose actions can easily be compared with more recent mass murderers such as Adolf Hitler, Joseph Stalin, Mao Zedong or Pol Pot.

Caesar's systematic, industrial slaughter of the Gauls was a callous piece of ethnic cleansing conducted purely to advance his own warped political agenda. The conflict that he began in Gaul lasted eight long years. When, in 52 BC, the last revolt against him ended in mass butchery at the hillfort of Alesia, Gaul lay broken: its great towns shattered, its population annihilated. 'By simple attrition' Barry Cunliffe has observed 'the strength of the Gauls and their desire to resist were worn away: hundreds of thousands were killed, hundreds of thousands were carried away to be sold in slavery and incalculable numbers were maimed' (Cunliffe 1988, 124).

As he cut a brutal swathe across Western Europe, Caesar hit on the masterstroke of documenting his version of events in a series of dispatches from the front line. Collectively these commentaries are known as the *Gallic Wars* and they are invaluable in providing clues to why Caesar acted in the way he did. Written entirely in the third person, as if Caesar were describing the exploits of another, the *Gallic Wars* provide a unique and totally Roman perspective on the worlds of Gaul, Germany and Britain at the end of the first century BC. Despite their value as an historical account, the commentaries are about as far away from a piece of objective reporting as one could possibly imagine. The *Gallic Wars* is a totally subjective official version of an unjust and unwarranted war, designed to show Caesar in the best possible light whilst simultaneously denigrating and demonising the enemy.

Despite Caesar's obvious historical distortion and cynical political spin, one part of the *Gallic Wars* is most useful to the student of Iron Age Britain: the account of Caesar's two incursions across the English Channel in 55 and 54 BC. Britain was viewed as a natural target by Caesar as no Roman general had ever left the known world to explore somewhere so alien and mysterious. Neither attack was intended to form the basis of a permanent conquest and, for that matter, neither were they particularly successful from a purely military perspective. The important point was that by intervening, however temporarily, in British affairs, Caesar had demonstrated that he could go anywhere and do anything. When reports of his exploits reached Rome, the senate considered them to be so great that they took the unprecedented step of granting 30 days public holiday.

CASSIVELLAUNOS AND MANDUBRACIUS

The first Briton that Caesar specifically mentions by name in the *Gallic Wars* is Cassivellaunos, whom he acknowledges to be his main adversary during the campaign of 54 BC. Caesar may never have met Cassivellaunos in person, and it is possible that the name is a garbling of a particular tribe, the Catuvellauni, who were prominent players during the later Claudian invasion of AD 43 (either that or the Catuvellauni were later named after the British king). Whatever the case, Cassivellaunos is portrayed as the villain of the piece, intimidating his neighbours and fighting an expansionist war of territorial acquisition across southern England. In the Roman mind, Cassivellaunos was public enemy number one: Al Capone to Caesar's Elliot Ness.

One British aristocrat that Caesar did have direct contact with during his campaigns was Mandubracius of the Trinobantes (or Trinovantes, who later occupied the area now largely covered by Essex). Mandubracius is an important figure in British history for he is the first Briton who seems to have embraced 'the protection of Caesar', having previously been ousted from power by Cassivellaunos. In 54 BC Mandubracius found himself in an excellent, and somewhat wholly unexpected situation: he needed Rome (to help restore him to power) as much as Rome needed him (to provide a secure base, food supplies and tactical information relating to enemy positions). At the end of the campaign, Caesar was able to leave Britain taking a number of British hostages (to ensure good behaviour in his absence), promises of protection money (euphemistically termed 'tribute') and the assurances that Cassivellaunos' tribe would 'not wage war against Mandubracius nor the Trinobantes'. Mandubracius was left as a British ally of the Roman State, someone who could enjoy special trade status and enhanced power and who could, in theory, rely on Caesar's protection in future times of trouble.

The concept of allied or client kings and queens was one which Rome found particularly favourable, for they provided the State with a degree of security along unstable frontiers. From a purely economic perspective, client kingdoms also provided Rome with the opportunity to make significant amounts of money through enhanced trading opportunities. Quite how Iron Age aristocrats such as Mandubracius first achieved positions of power, or how embracing that power was considered to be, is unfortunately not recorded. It is clear, however, that these British tribal 'kingdoms' were not fledgling democracies; power, be it political, economic, military, religious or hereditary, was the key to staying top dog in Late Iron Age Britain. The Roman State recognised the authority of the Iron Age elite, treating them as friends or enemies as and when the situation demanded. In Britain, the first named ally of Rome was Mandubracius, but many others were to follow.

THE DYNASTY OF COMMIOS

One allied king that Caesar made particular use of as mediator, nominal friend and translator during his British expeditions was an individual called Commios. Commios, an aristocrat from the Atrebates tribe in Gaul, eventually threw in his lot with the enemies of Caesar during the Great Gallic revolt of 52 BC. When this uprising was crushed, the Gallic king found himself in an unenviable situation: should he flee or submit to the mercy of Caesar? A failed attempt at assassination authorised by Labienus, one of Caesar's generals, helped him to make up his mind and Commios fled to continue the fight elsewhere. Finally, after years of bitter conflict with Rome, Commios came to terms with the Roman general Marcus Antoninus (Mark Antony).

> Commius … sent ambassadors to Antoninus, and assured him that he would give hostages as a security that he would go wherever Antoninus should proscribe, and would comply with his orders, and only entreated that this concession should be made to his fears that he should not be obliged to go into the presence of any Roman. (*Gallic Wars* VIII, 48)

Antony accepted that the Gallic king had possessed just cause for his past actions and permitted him to leave Roman territory unmolested. Commios could not of course be sent back to his own people, the Gallic Atrebates, but if he were to go anywhere then 'the fringes of the Roman world, where he knew people would have been as good as any location' (Creighton 2000, 61). Commios therefore left for Britain, a rehabilitated, if not entirely forgiven, former friend and ally of Caesar. The much-repeated theory that he fled, Roman soldiers snapping at his heels, would seem to be entirely without foundation (Creighton 2000, 59).

Coins bearing Commios' name were soon issued from Calleva, later the Roman town of Calleva Atrebatum (modern-day Silchester in Hampshire), suggesting that this was to become his principal seat of power. It is possible that there was a tribe already called the Atrebates in Britain and Commios merely joined them here, though it is far more likely that Commios and his followers set up a British 'Atrebatic confederacy' along similar lines to the tribe that he left in Gaul. This would in turn suggest that the name 'Atrebates' may have had a specific link to Commios and his family; perhaps as a dynastic, hereditary or family title. The iconography on the Commion coin series issued at Calleva demonstrate a clear affiliation to Rome (Creighton 2000), something one would expect from a fully rehabilitated former ally of the Roman State.

At least three individuals were later to claim direct descent (either politically or in terms of blood ties) from king Commios on a series of Late Iron Age coins recovered from central southern Britain. The individuals in question, Tincomarus, Eppillus and Verica, all styled themselves as the son of Commios and, as with their ancestor, all three used explicit Roman images on their coins. Verica, apparently the last in the line, also was keen to use the Latin term *Rex* (king), presumably as a way of demonstrating an ideological or political link with the senate and people of Rome.

Sometime after 30 BC, Tincomarus, whose coin series had previously extended along the western Thames, northern Hampshire and the southern coast of Sussex, was in Rome, together with one Dubnovellaunos, whose coin series had been largely restricted to Essex and eastern Kent. We know this because the names of both appear on the *Res Gestae*, a monumental statement dedicated by Augustus, grandnephew and principal heir of Julius Caesar. Both British kings are noted as 'seeking refuge', though from what is not recorded. It seems probable, however, that they were trying to persuade Augustus, the first emperor of Rome, to honour the promises and assurances of protection made by Caesar. Being a client king was a two-way process they would undoubtedly have reflected, and whoever had removed them from power really should be eliminated with the full military backing of Rome.

Later, the historian Dio Cassius (writing at the end of the second century AD), says that in or around AD 41 'a certain Berikos' was in Rome, bending the ear of the newly installed emperor Claudius. Berikos, who is usually equated with the British king Verica, 'had been driven out of the island as result of an uprising' and was in Rome primarily, so Dio informs us, to persuade Claudius 'to send a force there' (Dio Cassius *Claudius* LX, 19, 1). The circumstances that had deprived this descendant of Commios of power in Britain are sadly not described. It is interesting to note however, that the greatest concentration of his coins are to be found around Silchester in northern Hampshire as well as along the coastal zone of West Sussex. If the general distribution of these indicate the extent of political power that Verica wielded, then whatever the uprising entailed, it was presumably played out in this particular part of central southern Britain.

GAIUS OCTAVIANUS (AUGUSTUS)

Gaius Octavianus came to supreme power on 1 August 30 BC following the defeat of his rivals Mark Antony and Cleopatra at the sea battle of Actium. Actium marked the end of the civil war that had racked the Roman world following the assassination of Julius Caesar, in 44 BC, and it also emphatically marked the end of the Roman Republic. Octavian, the adopted son of Caesar, spent the next three decades after Actium subtly altering the Roman constitution and formalising his position at the heart of empire.

As *princeps,* Octavian was officially recognised as the 'First Citizen' of Rome. In the senate everyone was, theoretically at least, on an equal footing, but Octavian was now recognised as, to paraphrase George Orwell, being 'more equal' than his colleagues. As *pontifex maximus* (a title still held by the Pope today), Octavian became the chief priest of the Roman State. As consul he possessed supreme legal authority and as imperator he took command of Rome's legions, outranking all provincial governors in the process. His adoption of the name 'Augustus', a term resonant with religious, political and social connotations, helped to further confirm that he was 'more than human'. Throughout the stealthy acquisition of power, and perhaps mindful of the fate that befell Caesar, Augustus was careful to demonstrate that in everything he acted on behalf of the people. All official inscriptions bore the acronym SPQR for '*Senatus Populusque Romanus*' (the senate and people of Rome).

As overseer of empire and adopted son and heir to the estate of Julius Caesar, Augustus really needed to be seen as a successful general. Wars brought political prestige as well as the economic cost benefit of taking direct control of conquered resources (rather than having to deal through traders and middlemen). Grabbing land and territory for the State also brought significant additions to the slave market back at home. In the later years of the first century BC there was no real concept in the Roman mind of limiting conquest and defining static frontiers. The empire was in a state of continual expansion in all directions, only the severest of geographical or political constraints holding it back.

Throughout his early years in office, Augustus gave serious thought to emulating Julius Caesar by taking the war to Britain. In 34 BC Dio Cassius tells us that, though Augustus' plans for conquest appear to have been well developed, his advance towards Britain was halted by a revolt in the Balkans (Dio Cassius *Roman History* XLIX, 38). Evidently the idea of launching troops across the English Channel remained a potent one however, for in 27 BC we hear that Augustus:

> set out with the intention of leading an expedition into Britain, but on his arrival in Gaul he stayed there. For it seemed likely that the Britons would come to terms with him, and affairs in Gaul were still unsettled …. (Dio Cassius *Roman History* LIII, 22)

The following year Augustus remained:

> anxious for war against Britain since the peoples there would not come to terms …. (Dio Cassius *Roman History* LIII, 25).

Presumably the arrival of Tincomarus and Dubnovellaunos in Rome in, or shortly after, 30 BC provided the catalyst for Augustus' planned invasion. Something had evidently disturbed the status quo in Britain, ousting two pro-Roman monarchs, one of whom (Tincomarus) styled himself the son of Caesar's former ally Commios. Augustus was no doubt mindful of the prestige that had accompanied Caesar's wars in Britain and the damaging effect that a destabilised northern frontier would have, not only on trade, but also upon the still unsettled Roman province of Gaul. It is generally assumed that the plans for direct military intervention in Britain were eventually shelved by Augustus and, as trade between the Rome and Britain appears to have continued largely uninterrupted, that some sort of peace was established through diplomacy. Recent archaeological evidence unearthed from Sussex however, suggests that this was most certainly not the case.

FORTRESS FISHBOURNE

The late first-century palace at Fishbourne has rightly featured at the forefront of Roman studies since its discovery in 1960. The scale of the site is simply staggering (see chapter 6) and the mosaics, stonework, wall plaster and artefacts on display are, in the UK at least, second to none. There is, however, another side to Fishbourne that has only recently come to light. Fieldwork conducted by Alec Down in the 1980s and by David Rudkin and John Manley in the 1990s, to the east of the modern cover building and museum, have revealed evidence of a significant early Roman presence; evidence which seems to cast doubt on the accepted wisdom surrounding the invasion of Claudius in AD 43.

The excavations conducted by Rudkin and Manley between 1995 and 1999 concentrated on the area immediately facing the east wing of the palace (Manley and Rudkin 2003). Here the remains of a Mediterranean-style courtyard building (Building 3) were exposed, the dating and interpretation of which has caused some problems. One discovery that has perhaps surprisingly caused little controversy to date, but which could change our whole perception surrounding the Roman military in Britain, was found in a small trench, identified as Area B, to the north of the main dig.

Area B was placed specifically in order to answer two particular questions: how far north could a wall extending from the courtyard building be traced and how far did an east–west aligned ditch, originally located in the mid-1980s close to the current A27, travel towards the palace (Rudkin and Manley 2003, 80)? When excavated, Area B was found to have come down directly on top of the east–west ditch cut, which could now be demonstrated to have run for a distance of at least 90m. The ditch itself measured 3.5m in width and was 1.5m deep. Manley and Rudkin described the feature as being 'essentially V-shaped in profile with a possible 'cleaning slot' at the bottom' (2003, 80). There was no evidence to suggest the presence of a former rampart, though the restricted nature of the investigation meant that such evidence could easily have lain beyond the area of the trench.

Finds from the primary silts of the ditch and former ground surface through which the feature was originally cut, produced a quantity of local Late Iron Age ware and a smaller quantity of early Roman imports. The imported material comprised mainly red slip-ware and included an Arretine cup stamped on the base with the name MENA AVILI. Pottery stamps such as this can be traced to manufacturers and factory outlets around the empire and, more importantly, they can be tied to a specific date. The date of the Area B Arretine cup is between 10 BC and AD 10 (Manley and Rudkin 2003, 81). Of the remaining assemblage, which was unweathered suggesting rapid deposition after breakage, none of the vessels were any later than the Augustan period.

When use of the ditch came to an end, the feature was deliberately backfilled with clay soils presumably derived from the now abandoned rampart. Finds comprised tile, pottery, animal bone and marine shell. The pottery consisted of locally produced and imported wares, none of which were produced any later than *c.*AD 25-30. The profile of the ditch, its overall length, dimensions and form are all quite unlike the more irregular, flat-bottomed ditches of the Sussex Iron Age, and strongly suggest a Roman military origin. This, when combined with the observation that the ditch conforms to the same east–west axial alignment of all the early building sequences at Fishbourne, a Roman date, albeit any early one, seems difficult to refute.

Surprising though it may seem, pre-Claudian Roman pottery, such as that recovered from the Area B ditch, is not actually that uncommon from Fishbourne. In the 1960s, excavations beneath the palace site found a similar range of early first-century wares together with early first-century coins and pieces of military equipment all in association with a series of gravel roads and timber buildings. The buildings comprised two definite structures, one set between two parallel east–west aligned roads, the other lying along the northern edge of the upper most road. Traces of at least two further buildings were located, but the form and extent of these remain unknown (Cunliffe 1998, 25-31).

The first structure (Building 1) appeared to be the earliest of those recovered. Its footprint was formed by six roughly parallel trenches forming an area measuring 30.5m in length and 7.3m in width (5). A series of upright timbers, between 15 and 23cm in diameter, had formerly been embedded within these trenches forming a regular grid of vertical posts set 0.9m apart. The excavator, Barry Cunliffe, interpreted the remains as a granary (Cunliffe 1971). Granaries, or food storage buildings, were a regular and essential element of every Roman fort. Generally the internal floors of such structures were raised on stilts in order to permit the regular flow of air underneath the building (thus limiting the build up of damp conditions) and to deny easy access to rodents. The granary at Fishbourne appears to have had a tiled roof and traces of a covered loading bay were discovered along its northern side.

The second building was slightly larger and better defined than the first, its footprint being formed by a series of 0.9m diameter postholes, spaced at 2.4-2.7m intervals, forming a single structure covering an area of around 30.5 x 15.25m (6). As with Building 1, this structure appears to have functioned as a granary, the posts originally having supported a raised floor. Running along the northern limit of the building, an east–west aligned gravel surface flanked by two shallow drainage ditches was defined, possibly representing an ancilliary road. Dating for both timber granaries proved difficult to determine, though both could easily fit within a pre-Claudian timeframe, in line with the pottery recovered from the excavations there (Creighton 2001, 9). Certainly the pottery evidence suggested that Building 1 dated to before AD 20 and was therefore broadly contemporary with the ditch revealed in Area B by Manley and Rudkin. Because received wisdom states that the military structure found at Fishbourne cannot be earlier than AD 43, however, the evidence is usually taken to represent a post-invasion supply base issued with pottery that was 'well past its sell-by date'.

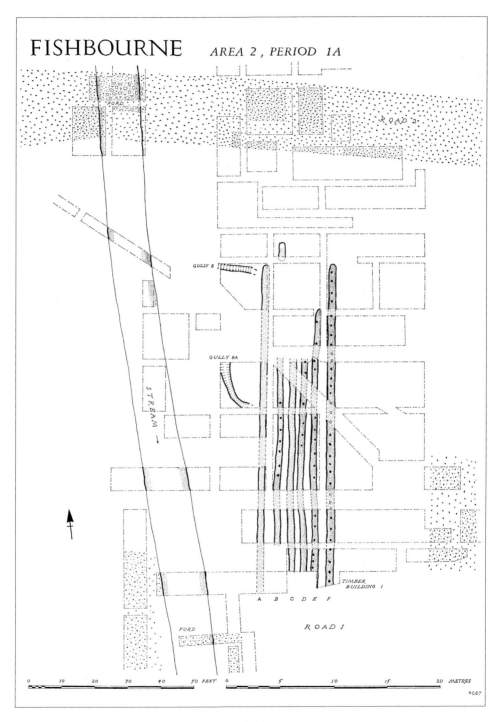

FISHBOURNE AREA 2, PERIOD 1A

5 Fishbourne, Timber Building 1, phase 1: six parallel foundation trenches marking the foundation of an early military granary together with a stream and gravel-surfaced roads.© *Institute of Archaeology, Oxford and Sussex Archaeological Society*

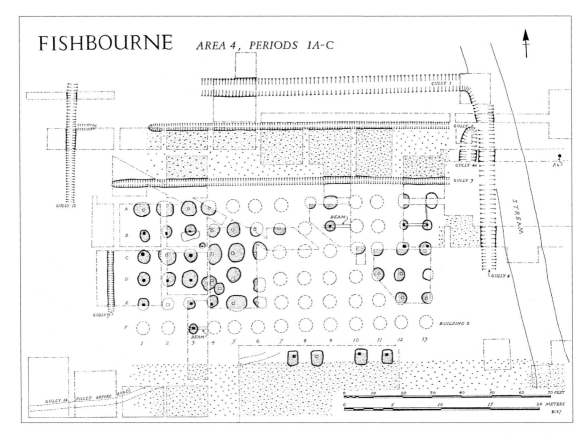

6 Fishbourne, Timber Building 2, phase 2: postholes marking the foundation of an early military granary together with drainage ditches, gravel-surfaced roads and a stream. © *Institute of Archaeology, Oxford and Sussex Archaeological Society*

Similar problems of archaeological interpretation, constrained by fixed historical parameters, also exist at Chichester. Here, beneath the remains of the medieval, Georgian and modern town, significant quantities of Roman military kit, including multiple fragments of plate armour, projectile weapons (*pilae*) at least one sword (*gladius*) and pieces of belt, buckle, shield and helmet fittings, have been found together with traces of timber buildings (e.g. Down 1981). As at Fishbourne, because we 'know' that the Roman invasion of Britain did not occur until AD 43 under the authority of the emperor Claudius, and we 'know' it was focused primarily on the landing site at Richborough in Kent, the remains recorded from Chichester 'must' therefore indicate part of a supply base initiated to support troop movements to the west in around AD 44. Needless to say, there is no definite evidence which may be used to support such a hypothesis and the material from Chichester could easily have derived from pre-Claudian (and pre-AD 43) activity.

Unfortunately, the pieces of kit uneartherd during (and since) the 1960s excavations at Fishbourne and Chichester, do not help refine the dating of a military presence any further. Although much of the material, especially a bronze legionary helmet dredged from Chichester Harbour in the nineteenth century (7 and 8), could happily be placed within the context of the very early first century AD (under the emperors Augustus or Tiberius), the problem with armour and weapons, from an archaeological perspective, is their longevity. Military equipment was constantly being patched-up, reworked and repaired rather than being replaced. Unless we are lucky enough to find a helmet, shield boss or sword with the name of a particular emperor engraved onto it, specific dates for the excavated material will continue to prove elusive.

7 Chichester Harbour: an early first-century bronze legionary helmet dredged up in the nineteenth century. The helmet has been badly damaged and has lost its cheek pieces but retains the neck guard designed to protect the back of the head from a sword or axe. The detached reinforcing strip may be an original piece or it may possibly have derived from another helmet. Fitted to the front of the helmet it would have provided some protection from a spear or glancing sword blow. A mollusc has attached itself to the crest. *Author with the kind permission of the Sussex Archaeological Society*

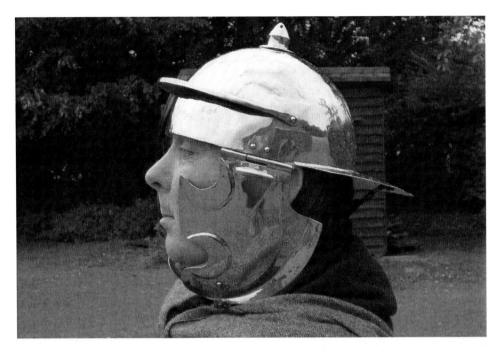

8 Chichester Harbour: a reconstruction of the bronze legionary helmet found in the nineteenth century, complete with cheek pieces and reinforcing strip. *Reproduced with the kind permission of John Smith*

A CONTEXT FOR FORTRESS FISHBOURNE?

The full extent and nature of military activity at Fishbourne will only be resolved by further fieldwork and it is likely that any new discovery will completely change our interpretation and perception of the site. That is the beauty of archaeology. New finds force old theories to be re-evaluated and rethought. New interpretations force the reassessment of old sources.

So how can the Fishbourne finds be interpreted? Could they simply be the product of long-distance trade and exchange? Of course we know there is a wealth of good evidence to support claims of significant trade contact between Britain and Rome throughout the last century BC and early years AD. Wine and oil storage vessels from the Mediterranean (known as amphorae) are found across the south and east coast of Britain from Essex through to Dorset and we have already noted that a number of British dynasts were styling themselves with Latin titles such as *Rex* on their coins. All this implies imperial patronage or at least a two-way process of trade whereby certain Britons bought into a Roman lifestyle whilst Roman traders acquired iron, gold, slaves and hunting dogs at a reduced price. Few have seriously suggested to date that Roman military involvement in Britain may have been more direct than this, but it is clear, that like it or not, there is now evidence that the Roman army was in Britain at least three decades before Claudius.

How can this be so? Why is there no ancient account of military forays into the uncharted lands of Iron Age Britain? Roman history, of course, creates its own problems. Something like 'the invasion' is an entirely one-sided (Roman) event within the literary sources, for we do not possess a British account. To make matters worse, classical writers were not as objective as we might hope a modern news reporter or journalist to be. Roman historians wrote for a Roman audience and most of the time they were writing in order to present a particular take on the past, using past events as a warning, morality tale or as propaganda. Most classical historians were also writing about periods that were very distant to them both in chronological and geographical terms. These were not freshly drafted reports and neither were they, in most cases, accounts by people who had actually been on the frontline witnessing the events as they unfolded.

The present consensus is that the invasion plans of Augustus came to naught and that Britain remained fiercely independent from Rome until the time of the emperor Claudius. The evidence from Fishbourne and from Chichester Harbour (9) as a whole would seem to contradict this. Roman troops were clearly stationed in Britain in some capacity during the early years of the first century AD. Perhaps they were here to protect friendly British kings from outside aggression or to protect Roman trade interests. Possibly they were here to appease Tincomarus and restore some sense of stability to the northern limits of the Roman world. Perhaps Augustus viewed a low-level provision of

9 Bosham: a view across Chichester Harbour in 2004. It was probably near here that the expeditionary (peacekeeping) forces of Augustus, Caligula and Claudius first landed

troops in Britain as only the first stage in a greater attempt at conquest and territorial acquisition. Certainly the provision of military outposts beyond the then limits of empire was a common enough feature elsewhere in the fledgling years of the Roman Super State; bases being found in Armenia, Egypt, Judea, Germany, and perhaps even Ethiopia and India. Under such circumstances it would perhaps be more difficult to understand why Rome would *not* have set up bases in Britain, certainly given the levels of commerce evident, than to believe that they would have left the Britons well alone.

In this, it is worth pointing out that Fishbourne is not unique and that other pre-Claudian forts may well have existed in Britain. At Colchester (*Camulodunum*) in Essex, for example, a small fort structure has been detected by aerial survey at Gosbecks, to the south of the modern town. When first recorded, archaeologists interpreted the fort as belonging either to the primary phase of military subjugation of the area (in AD 43/4) or to a phase of reconsolidation following the revolt of queen Boudica (AD 60/1). Unfortunately for both theories, the fort appears, on present evidence, to predate a section of the Iron Age defences of *Camulodunum*, a stratigraphic impossibility if no troops were in Britain before the accession of the emperor Claudius. Such an observation, the fort being earlier than the Iron Age earthworks, would suggest that the pro-Roman king of *Camulodunum*, Cunobelinus, constructed his *oppida* 'with a Roman-style fortlet right from the outset, dominating the southern entrance to the complex and protecting his own special enclave' (Creighton 2001, 9).

Whether this represented a defensive structure built 'in the style of' a Roman fort, or a military installation constructed by Rome in order to better protect (or watch over) a client king and establish some degree of control over the profitable network of trade, is, in the absence of detailed excavation and survey at Gosbecks, unknown. It is interesting to speculate, however, that the senate and people of Rome had established bases and billeted troops at both Fishbourne and Gosbecks in order to better protect their investments through a calculated display of intimidation and threatened force.

The annihilation of three Roman legions in the forests of Germany in the year AD 9 was a dramatic turning point in Augustus' foreign policy. The slaughter was a serious blow to Roman honour and prestige and seems to have put paid to Augustus' dreams of a northern European empire. If there were still troops at Fishbourne or elsewhere in Britain at this time, he may seriously have considered withdrawing them. The evidence from Fishbourne itself suggests that the military ditch was deliberately backfilled, or slighted, no later than AD 25. Perhaps troops in Britain returned to Gaul because either they were no longer needed or, more ominously, because their presence was no longer desired.

GAIUS CAESAR AUGUSTUS GERMANICUS (CALIGULA)

In AD 40 the third emperor of Rome, Gaius Caesar Augustus Germanicus, known to history by his nickname 'Caligula' (little boots), decided that like Augustus and Caesar before him, Britain was the ideal place to fight a triumphal war. Caligula's plans for conquest seem to have closely followed those of Caesar in that not just Britain, but also the area of Germany to the north of the Rhine, were both considered legitimate targets. Unfortunately the events of AD 40 are unclear, as history has not been kind to Caligula, and the Roman emperors that followed him were keen to downplay his achievements in architecture, diplomacy and the field of battle. The minutiae of court life were played out in the pages of later gossip columns and in the salacious detail of the Roman historian Gaius Suetonius Tranquillus. That is not to say that Caligula was a benign ruler whose life has been unfairly vilified, for it is clear that Gaius Caesar Augustus Germanicus was not a pleasant man to be around.

Born in AD 12 to Vipsania Agrippina, granddaughter of Augustus, and Augustus' adopted grandson, Germanicus Julius Caesar, Gaius became emperor on the death of his grand uncle Tiberius on 16 March AD 37. The citizens of Rome marked his accession with great celebration; the austere reign of his predecessor was at an end and the young son of the military hero Germanicus was now in town. Caligula seems to have maintained the support of the populace throughout his short reign. Indeed there was an immense outpouring of anger when his assassination was finally announced to the people. Aristocrats and senators felt differently: Caligula had made no secret of his contempt for them and many viewed his death as the ideal time to reinstate the republican constitution. Caligula was not, as many later writers would like to believe, simply insane, but he was something rather more sinister. Like Joseph Stalin, head of State in another 'evil empire', Caligula was 'morally neutral … and ultimately indifferent to the consequences of his actions on others' (Barrett 1989, 241).

Caligula's plan to emulate the deified Julius Caesar ended, so the overtly hostile traditions of Suetonius and Dio Cassius tell us, in fiasco. With his soldiers lined up on the Gallic coast 'in battle order' facing Britain, the emperor gave the order to 'gather shells and fill their helmets and the folds of their gowns' (Suetonius *Caligula* 46). This 'booty', Caligula claimed, represented 'spoils from the Ocean' to be transported to Rome as evidence of his great triumph over the sea. A *pharos* or lighthouse was erected on the shore 'as a monument of his victory' and to each soldier present the sum of 100 *denarii* was given with the words 'Go your way happy; go your way rich' (*Caligula* 46). Most modern writers have taken the view that Caligula's men had perhaps mutinied, not wishing to cross the English Channel, and were being humiliated for their disobedience. Others believe the event was a clear sign of Caligula's developing insanity. Some have even suggested that the shells may have been collected to act as ammunition for Roman catapults.

Our second source for this period, Dio Cassius, is also damning of Caligula's campaigns in the north noting that he had:

> … set out as if to conduct a campaign against Britain, but turned back from the ocean's edge, showing no little vexation at his lieutenants who won some slight success ….
> (Dio Cassius *Roman History* LIX, 21)

Despite Dio Cassius's contempt for Caligula, this short and often overlooked paragraph is intriguing for it implies that some officers under the emperor's command were actually involved in a successful action. Was this a landing, establishment of a defended beach-head, fighting or a combination of all three? Any landing may well have been designed to be small-scale, possibly as a precursor to larger invasion. As such, it would certainly have been played down by Caligula's successors. Given the distinctly garbled and overtly hostile accounts of Caligula's exploits, the truth of the matter is difficult to separate from the fiction, but the possibility of direct military involvement in Britain at this time should not be totally ignored.

A major achievement of Caligula's actions in Gaul and Britain, in fact the *only* one according to Suetonius, was:

> to receive the surrender of Adminius, son of Cynobellinus king of the Britons, who had been banished by his father and had deserted to the Romans with a small force. (*Caligula* 44)

Adminius is probably a later garbling (or mistranslation) of Amminus, the name of a British king issuing coins in eastern Kent in the AD late 30s or early 40s. If this is the same 'Adminius' that appears in Suetonius' history, then it would seem likely that he moved to Sussex prior to fleeing Britain altogether to the relative safety of Caligula. Coins stamped with an 'A' set within a star have been located from Chichester which seem to closely mirror the style of the Kent series and the only other contemporary textual account that we have of the man comes from an inscription found in Chichester itself (see chapter 4). Suetonius is damning of even this Amminus' defection, claiming that Caligula used the surrender to boast that 'the entire island had submitted to him'. As we shall see, this may not have been too far from the truth.

To understand the events surrounding the invasion of Britain in AD 43 by Caligula's successor, the emperor Claudius, we need to consider two prominent members of the British aristocracy of the time. Both men were kings whose reigns appear crucial to Roman success and central to their dominance over southern Britain and Sussex in particular. Their names were Tiberius Claudius Togidubnus and Gaius Sallustius Lucullus and the roles they played in the ascendancy of Rome will be examined in the next two chapters.

2

TIBERIUS CLAUDIUS TOGIDUBNUS

In the spring of AD 43, the emperor Tiberius Claudius Nero Germanicus swung his gaze towards the island of Britain and gave orders to bring it firmly into the orbit of Rome. Claudius, as we have seen in the previous chapter, was by no means the first Roman to involve himself in the affairs of Britain, contrary to the official version preferred by the emperor and his spin doctors. Caesar had fought a bloody path across Kent in 55 and 54 BC whilst Augustus appears to have had troops billeted in Chichester Harbour, ostensibly to protect trade interests, but also, perhaps, to quell the political instability that had resulted in the expulsion of a number of British kings and allies of Rome. The extent of Caligula's involvement in Britain remains unknown, as is the full nature of military deployment in the island at that time.

By AD 43 then, Britain and the Britons were both well known to the Roman Empire. Rome had been trading with certain Britons on a regular basis and interfering with their internal affairs for decades. A situation of calm stability was good for all parties. In peacetime, the Romans benefited from cheap metals, foodstuffs and slave labour, whilst some Britons grew fat on the proceeds of Roman trade and began to dominate not only their own lands but also those of their immediate neighbours. One such British magnate was Cunobelinus, whom the Roman historian Suetonius refers to as 'king of the Britons' (*Caligula* 44)

Cunobelinus (or Cunobelin) was an important figure in the Late Iron Age, and he is crucial to the way in which the Roman State perceived Britain. He would appear to have been king of the Catuvellauni, and therefore (perhaps) a descendant, in either politics or blood, of Caesar's great opponent Cassivellaunos. At some stage in the AD 30s he was minting coins in *Camulodunum* (modern-day Colchester), apparently the tribal centre of the Trinovantes for whom Caesar had specifically sought protection in 54 BC. It is quite possible that Cunobelinus (later immortalised by Shakespeare in his

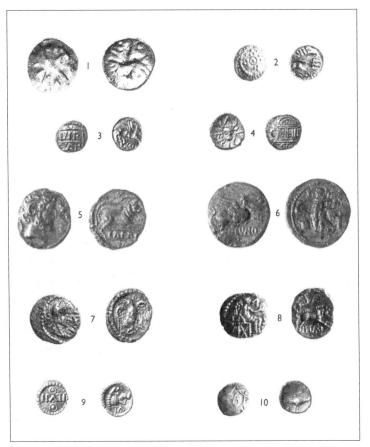

10 Chichester: Late Iron Age coins recovered from the north-western quadrant of the town 1968-75. The majority are of Catuvellaunian origin. 1 = Tincomarus; 2, 3 and 4 = Verica (note the monumental tomb or shrine on the reverse); 5 and 6 = Cunobelinus; 7, 8 and 9 = Epaticcus; 10 = Amminus.
© *Chichester District Council*

play Cymbeline) was continuing the expansionist wars of Cassivellaunos, gradually spreading his influence through eastern and southern Britain. The bulk of the pre-Roman Celtic coins recovered from Chichester and the surrounding areas appear to be of Catuvellaunian origin (e.g. Carson in Down 1978, 330-1), possibly reflecting a spread of influence into the south coast (10). Cunobelinus was in all probability the Iron Age equivalent of a Mafioso godfather, dangerous, strong, politically powerful and in control of all economic and financial transactions. Certainly the area around *Camulodunum* appears, in the last decade before Roman attack, to have been the premier importer of Mediterranean and exotic consumables. He was also, judging by the images appearing on his coins, an ardent supporter of Rome and may well, like other client kings of the period, have sent his children to Rome to be educated under the protection of the emperor (Creighton 2000).

The death of the king in the early AD 40s left a political void that seems to have been fought over by two of his surviving sons: Caratacus and Togodumnus. The instability following the demise of Cunobelinus and the subsequent interregnum, may have driven Verica, descendant of Commios and king of an area centred upon

Hampshire and West Sussex, to seek the protection of Rome (Dio Cassius *History of Rome* LX, 19). The flight of both Verica and Amminus (or Adminius) and their followers to the emperor provoked additional unrest, the historian Suetonius observing that Britain was 'in uproar at the time as a result of the Roman refusal to return certain fugitives' (*Claudius* 17). Within these turbulent times another figure appears: one who seems to have been critical to the success of the Claudian invasion and to the early years of occupation that followed. His name was Togidubnus.

TOGIDUBNUS

Unfortunately we do not possess a full and frank biography of Togidubnus and so what today is often discussed in relation to his life and achievements is really nothing more than speculation. Truth be told, we are not even sure of how to spell his name, variants of Cogidumnus, Cogidubnus, Togidumnus and Togidubnus all having been popular at some point in recent years. The current form 'Togidubnus' is derived from a consensus on the nature and acceptable form of Celtic names. Despite such seemingly intractable issues, there is still a reasonable amount that we may logically deduce about the status of Togidubnus for he is cited in two, very different, ancient historical texts.

In Chichester, a monumental Roman inscription names Togidubnus, giving him his full name and title (*11*), as well as apparently providing a specific geographical placement to his seat of power. The inscription was found in 1723, during the excavation of a cellar beneath the corner house on the northern side of Lion Street (at the point where Lion Street meets North Street), lying face up. A full version of the dedication, which survives today in fragmentary form, appears to have read:

NEPTVNO ET MINERVAE
TEMPLVM
PRO SALVTE DOMVS DIVINAE
EX AVCTOITATE TIBERI CLAVDI
TOGIDVBNI REG MAGN BRIT
COLLEGIVM FABRORVM ET QVI IN EO
SVNT DE SVO DEDERVNT DONANTE AREAM
PVDENTE PVDENTINI FILIO

and may be translated as:

To Neptune and Minerva, for the welfare of the Divine House by the authority of Tiberius Claudius Togidubnus, Great King in Britain, the guild of smiths and those therein gave this temple from their own resources, Pudens son of Pudentinus, donated the site.

11 Chichester: two different readings of the fragmentary 'Togidubnus Stone' found in 1723, dedicating a temple to Neptune and Minerva to the 'Divine House' of the Julio-Claudian dynasty. The top translation cites the main benefactor as being Tiberius Claudius Cogidubnus 'King and Imperial Legate in Britain', whilst the bottom suggests he was more likely to have been Tiberius Claudius Togidubnus, 'Great King in Britain'

The inscription formed the centrepiece of a classical temple dedicated to two very Roman deities, the god of the sea, Neptune, and the goddess Minerva, one of the three key deities of the Capitoline triad (the others being Jupiter and his partner Juno). Although not specifically dated, as no emperor is cited by name or title, mention of the 'Divine House' relates specifically to either the Julio-Claudian dynasty (as Caesar, Augustus and Claudius were all deified by the senate following their deaths) or to that of the Flavians (the same thing happening later to Vespasian and his son Titus). This means it must have been set up in the reigns of those immediately succeeding divine emperors, namely Claudius (AD 41-54), Nero (AD 54-68) or Domitian (AD 81-96). Given the form of the text and lettering, it has been suggested that the piece is more plausibly to have been made during either the reign of Claudius or Nero (Collingwood and Wright 1965, 26-7).

Addition of the names Tiberius and Claudius to Togidubnus's own tells us that not only was the he a fully paid-up Roman citizen, but more importantly that his sponsor for citizenship had been none other than Tiberius Claudius Caesar Augustus Germanicus, the emperor Claudius himself. Official recognition appeared to extend to further acknowledging him with the unusual but impressive title of 'Great King in Britain'. Earlier translations of the stone interpreted Togidubnus' title as REGIS LEGATI AUGUSTI IN BRITANNIA or King and Imperial Legate in Britain. This impressive, if unusual title, has since been widely discredited, although it is worth pointing out that another, slightly later, first-century sponsor of works in Chichester certainly possessed the title of Legatus Augusti (Gaius Sallustius Lucullus: see chapter 4).

Our second major source for Togidubnus is rather less complimentary, coming from the pen of the Roman historian Publius Cornelius Tacitus, who, writing at the end of the first century AD, says rather sneeringly:

> Certain states were handed over to king Cogidumnus – he in fact remained totally loyal down to our times – in accordance with the Roman people's old and long-standing policy of making even kings their agents in enslaving people. (Tacitus, *Agricola* 14)

The Cogidumnus of Tacitus' text is assumed to have been the Togidubnus of the Chichester inscription, the differences in spelling being either due to Roman misunderstanding or later scribal mis-transcription. So far, so good. The big problem with Togidubnus 'the Great' however, is that although he appears as an important figure in the years immediately after the conquest of southern Britain by Rome in AD 43, his background and his apparently swift rise to power, remain stubbornly obscure. Unlike other British kings in the first half of the first century AD, Togidubnus does not seem to have minted coins and does not appear to feature in any historical text relating to the initial stages of the Roman invasion. He seems to have quite literally sprung out of nowhere.

An elaborate background has been constructed for Togidubnus by modern historians in order to explain his sudden rise to the top of Romano-British society. Some claim he was the descendant of a British king, such as Dubnobellaunus, Tincomarus or Verica, who had fled the British Isles to the protection of Rome throughout the early half of the first century. Others have indicated that he may have been a minor aristocrat elevated by the Roman government as a quisling or puppet king. Possibly his loyalty to the senate and people of Rome throughout either the Boudican revolt of AD 60/1 or the Roman civil war of AD 69 may have resulted in his being rewarded with the construction of a large palace at Fishbourne, just to the south-west of modern Chichester.

There is, however, another solution to the problem of who Togidubnus was and why he was so important to the Roman cause. It is one that has far reaching implications for our understanding of the nature and causes of the Roman 'invasion' of Britain in AD 43.

TOGODUMNUS

Our only reliable source for the Claudian invasion is Dio Cassius, writing in the late second and early third century AD (over 100 years after the events he describes). Despite certain inconsistencies revealed in some of Dio Cassius' later texts, his oft quoted discussion of the events of AD 43 are important here not least because they provide a potential answer to the secret identity of Tiberius Claudius Togidubnus.

Dio Cassius' work is usually treated as a standard discussion of a major military invasion akin to the Normandy landings in France of 1944 or the Norman landings in England during 1066. The view has always been taken that in AD 43 a Roman general named Aulus Plautius landed in Kent with an immense army which included four legions (II, IX, XIV and XX), altogether comprising 20,000 soldiers, together with a similar number of second class ('expendable') auxiliary troops. Plautius' intention, it is usually believed, was to drive his army northwards across Kent and over the rivers Medway and Thames, scattering all opposition on the way. The Iron Age capital of *Camulodunum* (modern Colchester in Essex) was the Romans' ultimate objective; their target number one. Unfortunately, attractive though this theory undoubtedly is, Dio Cassius actually says nothing of the sort.

A careful rereading of his text shows that all Dio Cassius says on the invasion itself is:

> Aulus Plautius, a most respected counsellor, led an expedition to Britain, for a certain Berikos, having been driven out of the island by an armed uprising, had persuaded Claudius to send a force there. (Dio Cassius *Roman History* LX, 19)

Nowhere does Dio Cassius state that Plautius was leading a full-scale invasion and the assumption that four legions were involved is shown to be a piece of modern speculation. The four legion fiction is based on the observation that in AD 60 the II, IX, XIV and XX legions were all present in Britain and they must therefore have been so earlier. If one looks carefully at what Dio Cassius actually does say then there is evidence for only one legion being directly involved in the initial landings and their aftermath: the II. We know this because the then general of the II legion, Titus Flavius Vespasianus (later emperor), is specifically noted as taking part in at least one of the subsequent disputed river crossings. One legion (assuming it was complete and not operating as a small detachment) gives us a maximum accountable figure of 5,500 men for the preliminary stages of the AD 43 Channel crossing.

With regard to the landing itself, Dio Cassius observes that the troops:

> were carried across to the other side, having been divided into three sections in order not to hinder one another and to disembark section by section … They put into the island, no one opposing them. (Dio Cassius *Roman History* LX, 19)

Dio Cassius' description of the landings, in 'three sections' are not provided with specific geographical detail, nor (again) are the numbers of Roman soldiers involved mentioned. Unfortunately an unknown number divided by three remains an unknown number.

A forensic examination of Dio Cassius' text (such as that conducted by Louis Francis in 1991), indicates that what is being hinted at for AD 43 is not a full blown invasion (at least not at this stage), but an attempt to curtail civil unrest. Such unrest had presumably exploded following the death of king Cunobelinus, a pro-Roman dynast who ruled the much of what is now south-eastern England from his capital at Colchester. Britain, as a stable entity, was not only a valuable trading resource for Rome but was also important as a peaceful buffer protecting the northern shores of Rome's empire in Gaul. The anarchy that followed Cunobelinus' death must have threatened that stability. The key to resolving the unrest was to stop the king's descendants from squabbling over territory and return southern Britain to calm. Three descendants of Cunobelinus are specifically named in the Roman histories: Adminius (Amminus) who fled to Caligula in around AD 39; Caratacus and Togodumnus.

Events following the initial Roman landing seem to have gone well; Dio Cassius states that the two quarrelling parties led by the two most prominent surviving sons of Cunobelinus, Caratacus and Togodumnus, were brought to hand and the armed insurrection was put down. Negotiations followed and having restored order, Plautius was keen to return to the status quo and ensure that Caratacus and Togodumnus were sent back to their respective home territories. The shock and awe tactics of the Romans and their hope of a swift resolution to the British crisis unfortunately soon began to unravel. As Plautius oversaw the movement of one particular faction northwards, there occurred a series of skirmishes between them and Roman troops under his command.

As Plautius arrived at a major river (either the Medway in Kent or the Arun in Sussex) all attempts by the Roman troops to cross were thwarted by the enemy faction. At this point Plautius 'sent over a detachment of Celts who were accustomed to swim easily through rough water in armour'. The Celts are usually assumed to be a reference to auxiliary troops in the pay of Rome, but there is nothing to suggest this was the case. In fact, given what Dio Cassius says later, it seems more likely these are allied British troops. In other words we are seeing a series of events (such as occurred between Cleopatra VII and her brother Ptolemy XIII in Egypt during the late first century BC) where one native faction has allied itself to Rome whereas another has been identified as the aggressor.

A second point of conflict occurred as the Roman and allied troops approached the river Thames:

> Afterwards the Britons retreated towards the river Thames, where it discharges into the Ocean and, overflowing, forms a lake, stepping across easily and knowing precisely the firm and easy space to pass over but the Romans, following on closely, were foiled. However the Celts straight away swam across while others got across by a bridge a little way upstream, engaged with them from many sides and cut many of them down. But in the headlong pursuit of the remainder, chased them into swamps with no way out and many of themselves perished. (Dio Cassius *Roman History* LX, 20)

Following this, Dio Cassius notes:

> because of this action and also, at the same time, the destruction of Togodumnus, those Britons not greatly involved, but of a gentle and mild disposition, deemed it worthy to stand together at his side, against them. Plautius, becoming alarmed, advanced no further. (Dio Cassius *Roman History* LX, 21)

It is worth dissecting these two paragraphs in detail, for they are crucial to our understanding of what was to follow.

Within the battle itself, Dio Cassius is clearly once again indicating the difficulties experienced by the Roman troops (the II legion under Vespasian) and the aid received by their Celtic allies who 'straight away swam across' and pursued the enemy faction, chasing them 'into swamps' before being ambushed. At this point in the narrative, the conventional view is that Cunobelinus' son Togodumnus, who, it is usually believed, was co-ordinating the resistance against Rome, died and the remaining Britons (fighting against the Romans) were roused to avenge him. Unfortunately for this theory, this is not what Dio Cassius says. In fact the ancient historian does not state that Togodumnus died, or was even killed for that matter. What he actually talks about is 'the *destruction* of Togodumnus', which coming so soon after the description of Celtic allies being cut down in the marshes, can mean only one thing: Togodumnus was on the Roman side.

It is Togodumnus' army that is being *destroyed* by the enemy faction led (presumably) by his brother Caratacus and it is precisely this destruction which leads certain 'Britons not greatly involved' in the struggle 'to stand together at *his* (Togodumnus') side against *them*' (Caratacus army). The crucial thing about rereading this text is that not only do we see that Togodumnus was operating with Plautius, but more importantly he survived the ambush for the next thing the text states is that the Britons previously unaffected, now stood 'together *at his side*'. This implies a people joining the still living king rather than, as usually thought, warriors joining the fight to avenge his death.

At this point Plautius, 'becoming alarmed' at the obvious deterioration of events, sent word back to Rome for reinforcements. What began as little more than a peacekeeping mission to resolve a disputed succession had now degenerated into civil war. Interestingly, though Dio Cassius tells us little about the nature of these 'reinforcements' other than they included 'extensive equipment, including elephants, had already been got together for the expedition', he does later refer to 'legions'. Claudius had, it would seem, been fully prepared to take the credit for bringing peace to Britain through diplomatic means, but had also collected sufficient military reserves in case he needed to resort to force. At this point we can legitimately talk of an 'invasion', the reinforcements that Claudius was later to lead into Colchester comprising many of the military units that were later to garrison Britain. These reinforcements would presumably have taken the more direct route to Britain from Gaul, landing somewhere in Kent, the early military presence at Richborough being a prime candidate for the arrival of the emperor, his men, horses and elephants.

TIBERIUS CLAUDIUS TOGIDUBNUS

It is at this point in the narrative Togodumnus disappears. Soon afterwards, however, we start to hear about Tiberius Claudius Togidubnus. Given the general level of uncertainty already noted over the correct form of British names, I have no doubt that both men were in reality one and the same (see appendix 2). With Togodumnus/Togidubnus on Plautius' side at a time when Rome was desperately trying to save its trade investment in Britain, the whole situation remained salvageable. Togidubnus would have been vital to the Roman cause and would almost certainly have been well rewarded afterwards. Caratacus, Togidubnus' brother, however, remained a clear and present danger, continuing his fight against Rome into the early AD 50s.

As a king of the Catuvellauni, Togidubnus' power would almost certainly not have originally centred around Chichester and western Sussex. As joint heir to his father Cunobelinus' estate together with his brother Caratacus, the two brothers should theoretically have been based either at *Camulodunum* (Colchester in Essex) or *Verulamium* (St Albans in Hertfordshire), the two *oppida* over which Cunobelinus had claimed lordship. As *Camulodunum* became the chief target of Claudius' army, later having a legionary fortress implanted directly across it, whilst *Verulamium* became a *municipium* (a favoured town whose population was granted citizenship) we can only assume that it was in Hertfordshire that Togidubnus first reigned. Chichester and the lands that surrounded it could, in such a scenario, have been one of the cantons or states given to Togidubnus to repay his loyalty to Rome. Whatever the case, it would appear that Chichester soon became a favoured place amongst the Iron Age elite, the quantity and quality of palatial buildings established on land surrounding the town surpassing all other areas of Britain.

Identification of Togodumnus with Tiberius Claudius Togidubnus may also help to explain how and why he was given the title of 'Great King in Britain', for this is akin to the recognition given by the Roman State to his father Cunobelinus. It may also go some way to explain Tacitus' later caustic statement that the loyalty of king Togidubnus was in accordance with Rome's policy of 'making even kings their agents in enslaving people'. Tacitus wrote in praising terms about Caratacus, leader of the British resistance who, on his arrival in chains before the emperor Claudius in AD 51, spoke defiantly and with 'no downcast look, no appeal for mercy' (Tacitus *Annals* XII, 37). Claudius pardoned Caratacus, a calculated act designed to appeal to the masses. His brother Togidubnus, however, lived on in grand and luxurious splendour in Britain, not because he had bravely defied the Romans, but because he had wholeheartedly surrendered to them, an act that would not have appealed to Tacitus' view of the noble and honourable savage.

Tacitus' comment that Togidubnus remained loyal 'down to our times' could be taken as indicating that the Great King survived into very old age (Tacitus was writing after the reign of Domitian at some point in the AD late 90s or early 100s), or it could be a generalisation to suggest 'within living memory'. Whichever is the case it is probable, given the high level of early civilian architecture around Chichester in the late first century AD (see chapter 6) that Togidubnus or his descendants successfully weathered the storm of the Boudican revolt in AD 60/1. The revolt, led by the widow of the client king Prasutagus, who had ruled the Iceni tribe (modern-day Norfolk), was a serious set-back to Roman policy in Britain. Tacitus provides a detailed account of the causes of the revolt, as well as the horrors inflicted on the Romano-British population, the British defeat and inevitable reprisals that followed.

The revolt, which swept across southern Britain, resulted in the destruction of at least three early Roman towns (Colchester, London and St Albans) and cost the lives of thousands of men, women and children. Roman control over the province was seriously weakened and, at times, looked likely to be extinguished forever. This would have been an ideal time for Togidubnus, his friends, family and followers to distinguish themselves by proving their fidelity to the emperor. That Togidubnus was revered into the last decade of the first century AD, would suggest that he and his followers remained loyal to the Roman cause throughout the revolt. Given these considerations, the absence of Togidubnus from Tactitus' account of the uprising may at first appear rather curious. It could be that he had died before the revolt took hold, though the loyalty of his surviving family and friends in the face of a popular British uprising should still have been mentioned. More likely the non-appearance of Togidubnus in the story of the revolt had more to do with Tacitus' feelings towards the 'quisling king'.

The contempt that Tacitus felt for Togidubnus, and indeed many other British leaders, has already been noted. Caratacus was one of the few British kings to be praised by the Roman historian and this because Tacitus admired (and perhaps over-exaggerated) his sense of liberty and freedom, uncorrupted by the depravity and licentiousness of emperors. The Boudican revolt underlined all the problems that unchecked Roman imperialism could bring and it provided the perfect canvas on which Tacitus could endlessly moralise. The true hero of the Tacitean account of the revolt is the Roman governor Gaius Suetonius Paulinus who had been removed from the causes of the revolt (blamed on an over-zealous *procurator* Catus Decianus) whilst campaigning in North Wales. When news of the uprising reached him, Paulinus courageously rode back to London, reaching the city without his army but in advance of the rebels. Seeing the city could not be saved, he rejoined his army, chose a suitable site to fight the enemy and waited for almost certain death. In the battle that followed, Paulinus and his well-disciplined troops won a victory so complete, that the revolt collapsed overnight.

There is clearly no room in the dramatic story of the Boudican uprising, for a character like Togidubnus. Tacitus would perhaps not have been keen to advertise British involvement on the side of Rome, for this would not only have confused the storyline, blurring the distinction between good (Roman) and evil (British), but would also have seriously diluted the role played by Paulinus. In the story the governor is very much a classic hero in the solid, republican mould. He is courageous, steadfast and unyielding. At the end of the revolt, Tacitus is upset that Paulinus is recalled to Rome for being too harsh on the British survivors; worse his recall is due to the new *procurator* in Britain, one Gaius Julius Alpinus Classicianus, a man of Celtic stock.

Given the events of AD 43 and after, not to say his unyielding dedication to Rome, Togidubnus' role in the Boudican uprising must have been crucial to Roman success. As king whose territory included the Roman town of *Verulamium*, modern-day St Albans, Togidubnus' people had already been targeted by Boudica's army in an early example of ethnic cleansing. Togidubnus clearly had everything to lose and nothing to gain by the revolt of the Iceni and would have striven to ensure that the rebels were swiftly crushed. By holding the lands south of the Thames and containing the revolt to the north, Togidubnus would have ensured Roman investment in the province was saved. Given the armed forces available to the king in AD 43, it is evident we are not dealing with an effete Roman puppet, but a battle hardened veteran who enjoyed the popular support of his people. Whether he was able to deploy an army in support of Paulinus, as he had successfully done for Plautius, we will never know, but it is apparent that our understanding of the events of AD 60-1 is, if based solely on the account of Tacitus, severely flawed.

To better understand what happened once the revolt was crushed and how the process of Romanisation began again, we need to examine the evidence for a second prominent member of Romano-British society in Sussex: one Gaius Sallustius Lucullus.

3

GAIUS SALLUSTIUS LUCULLUS

Tiberius Claudius Togidubnus is not the only Romanised Briton to be specifically named from a Sussex context for evidence of a second was recorded from Chichester in 1658 by Samuel Woodford. Woodford, then finishing a Bachelor of Arts degree at Wadham College, Oxford, was compiling information for a book entitled *Inscriptionum Romano-Britannicarum Conllectio* which appears to have been intended as a list of all known Roman inscriptions from Britain. Unfortunately, as others have since noted (e.g. Haverfield 1895, 15-17), Woodford's manuscript frequently neglects to offer provenance for much of the inscribed stone and rarely supplies any useful comment or interpretation. Nevertheless, though it cannot be taken entirely at face value, the *Conllectio* supplies a wealth of information relating to material since defaced, mutilated or lost. The Chichester inscription represents one such piece that, since Woodford's record, has unfortunately faded back into obscurity. We do not know where within Chichester the stone was found, nor the context for its discovery, the only source for the *Conllectio* reference being one Henry Babbington. The inscription itself originally read:

I O M

PRO SALVTE

IMP CAES DOMITIANI

AVG

C SALLVSTIVS LVCVLLVS

LEG AVG

PR PR PROV BRITANNIAE

POSVIT

V S L M Q

which may be translated as:

To Jupiter Best and Greatest, for the Welfare of the emperor Caesar Domitianus Augustus, this was set up by Gaius Sallustius Lucullus, Legate of the emperor with praetorian powers of the province of Britain, who willingly and deservedly fulfilled his vow.

GOVERNOR OF BRITAIN

The Chichester inscription is important for a number of reasons. First, dedications and images to the emperor Domitian are generally rare across the empire. Caesar Domitianus Augustus, born Titus Flavius Domitianus, was the youngest son of the emperor Vespasian, and acceded to the imperial throne on the death of his brother Titus in AD 81. Despite his pedigree (both Vespasian and Titus had been deified by the senate), Domitian's reign was not a happy one, with many Stalinesque purges of the aristocracy occurring towards the end of his tenure. The list of misdemeanour, for which the increasingly paranoid emperor felt death was adequate punishment, included celebrating the birthday of a previous emperor, the giving of Carthaginian (North African) names to slaves and the inappropriate praise of particular Roman philosophers.

Following his assassination in AD 96, Domitian was removed from the collective memory of the Roman people through a process known as *damnatio memoriae*. This 'damnation of memory', authorised by the senate for those who had dishonoured the State, involved the removal, destruction or alteration of all official portraits and the erasure of the imperial name from all public works. The central concept behind *damnatio memoriae* was to eradicate every trace of a former citizen to the point that it would appear they had never lived. An indication of how such a process would have worked is given by George Orwell in his novel *1984*:

> Syme had vanished. A morning came, and he was missing from work: a few thoughtless people commented on his absence. On the next day nobody mentioned him. On the third day Winston went into the vestibule of the Records Department to look at the notice-board … It looked almost exactly as it had looked before – nothing had been crossed out – but it was one name shorter. It was enough. Syme had ceased to exist: he had never existed. (Orwell 1948, 67)

Damnatio memoriae was a punishment reserved only for those emperors who upset the senate and the leading aristocratic families during their life. Hence Caligula (AD 37-41), Nero (AD 54-68), Domitian (AD 81-96) and Commodus (AD 180-92), all men who openly attempted to curb the powers of the senatorial class, had their achievements expunged from the State archives, their names systematically erased and their images destroyed or hidden.

It is possible that the Chichester dedication had been buried or broken up shortly after Domitian's death during the empire-wide process of *damnatio*, but in the absence of any statement concerning its original context or relative completeness on discovery, this is impossible to state with certainty. It is also difficult to be precise about the date of the Chichester dedication. Domitian reigned from AD 81 to 96, but the inscription does not provide any clues as to which particular year the dedication was made. We can, however, be sure that the stone was not made before AD 84, as the Propraetorian Legate in Britain until that year was one Gnaeus Julius Agricola, father-in-law of the Roman historian Tacitus.

Dedications made by the Propraetorian Imperial Legate, or governor of a province are also generally rare, certainly in Britain, and when found usually relate to specific monumental building projects. The Legate of the emperor with praetorian powers was the most senior ranking official within any given province. Drawn from the highest level of Roman society, a governor was in control of the military organisation, civil infrastructure and judicial process of the province. His remit lasted a minimum of four years and he was directly answerable to the emperor. As a limiting factor against potential corruption, governors did not oversee monetary issues such as the balance of trade and collection of taxes for these were all the remit of another official known as a *procurator*.

The overall importance of the Chichester inscription is further greatly enhanced by the fact that the named governor, Gaius Sallustius Lucullus, is attested from an independent historical source, that of the Roman historian Suetonius. Unfortunately Suetonius gives us no background detail concerning the man Lucullus, but we learn that his fate was inextricably linked with Domitian, the man to whom he no doubt owed his career, then finally his life. According to Suetonius, Domitian:

> put to death many senators, among them several ex-consuls, including … Sallustius Lucullus, governor of Britain, for allowing some lances of a new pattern to be named 'Lucullean', after his own name…. (Suetonius *The Twelve Caesars: Domitianus* X)

So Lucullus fell foul of a despotic emperor for a seemingly trivial issue of naming of a new projectile weapon. Extreme though this may appear, it is clear, from the actions of many a twentieth-century dictator, that people have frequently (and sadly) died for less. It is possible that the story of the spear was one of those urban myths promulgated by people like Suetonius in order to underline the insanity of the emperor, but to some extent Domitian certainly had every right to feel insecure. People, amongst them aristocrats, senators, governors and generals, not to mention members of his own family, were frequently plotting against him. In January AD 89, for example, Domitian faced a revolt by the governor of Upper Germany, Lucius Antonius Saturninus. This was finally suppressed with the help from the armies of neighbouring provinces, but it appears to have left the paranoid Domitian feeling uncertain about the loyalty of other governors across Western Europe. It is possible that Lucullus had conspired with Saturninus, or perhaps Domitian merely suspected that he had (which would have been reason enough in the emperor's mind to have him executed). The story of the Lucullean lance could have been a trumped up charge or a later distortion of real events. Whatever the case, Gaius Sallustius Lucullus was removed from office with extreme prejudice and replaced by someone more to the emperor's liking.

Given what we have noted about the Lucullus stone, it is perhaps surprising that the inscription is not cited or referred to in any of the major historical works concerning Roman Britain. In fact the only real mention of it is in the standard text on Latin epigraphy, *The Roman Inscriptions of Britain* produced by R.G. Collingwood and R.P. Wright in 1965 (reprinted in 1995). Here the dedication (classified as RIB 2334) is consigned to the very end of the catalogue, in a section marked *Falsa* (Collingwood and Wright 1965, 734). Haverfield and Wright believed the inscription to be a forgery (strictly speaking the term 'hoax' would be more appropriate) based on the view first propounded by F. Haverfield in 1895 that all inscriptions derived from Henry Babbington ('a man I cannot trace': Haverfield 1895, 16) were forgeries.

It has to be said, on balance, that there is nothing in the wording, construction or phraseology of the Lucullus stone that screams 'hoax', in fact it would seem to be utterly genuine. Perhaps Haverfield doubted Woodford's original translation or that he felt that, in the absence of a secure context for the piece, that Babbington had created a piece of historical fiction. Without any form of independent verification for the stone's existence, it must be said that Haverfield's concerns were understandable.

SON OF AMMINUS

A point missed by Haverfield, Collingwood and Wright, however, was that evidence already existed to suggest that Babbington's find was indeed genuine. This evidence had surfaced in Chichester 165 years after the appearance of Woodford's *Inscriptionum Romano-Britannicarum Conllectio*. As with RIB 2334, the exact context for this second inscribed stone (*12*) does not appear to have been fully recorded (so we do not know whether it formed part of a pit fill, had been reused in a later building or was in any way close to its original position). It was dug up in 1823, beneath the floor of the house 'adjoining the Little Anchor Inn, North Street' (Collingwood and Wright 1965, 25). Since its discovery the piece has also suffered extensive damage, though a full record of its text (catalogued as RIB 90) was made in 1902. The dedication read:

GENIO S
LVCVLLVS
AMMINI FIL
D S P

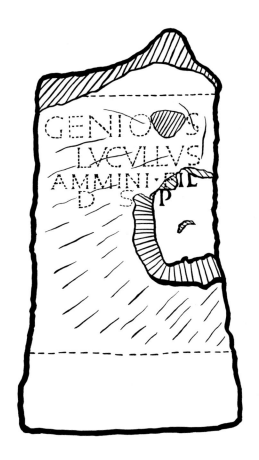

12 Chichester: the, now very much damaged, Lucullus altar found in 1823. The stone notes that he was the son of Amminus. © *Chichester District Council*

Which is usually translated as:

Sacred to the Genius (of the place) Lucullus, son of Amminus, set this up from his own resources.

It would perhaps be too heavy a strain on coincidence to have two ancient inscriptions made at the same time in the same town citing two separate individuals with the same name, especially as 'Lucullus' does not seem to appear anywhere else in the British Isles during the Roman period. As a side issue, it is unlikely that RIB 90 has been misread in the past, the S in the first line obviously standing for 'sacrum' or sacred and not 'Sallustius' (a break in surface between 'Genio' and the 'S' is also unlikely to have contained a G for Gaius). The alternative translation would simply have read: 'to the Genius (of the place), Gaius Sallustius Lucullus, son of Amminus, set this up from his own resources'. The positioning of the Lucullus altar, assuming it had not strayed far from its original location, at the very heart of Roman Chichester, would have further emphasised the importance of the donor for 'only a person of some local distinction would have been able to set up a large altar at this point' (Henig and Nash 1982, 245).

The discovery of a second Lucullus inscription from Chichester helps to validate the first. Had the discoveries been made the other way round, Babbington's find (RIB 2334) following the recovery of the Lion Street Altar (RIB 90), then doubts would have certainly arisen concerning the authenticity of the piece with Babbington being seen as a hoaxer, cashing in on the spectacular nature of the altar. By claiming a second piece dedicated by Lucullus, then equating him with the Sallustius Lucullus attested from the writings of Suetonius, would be the icing on the cake for an inveterate forger. The reality of the situation is very different for the dedication to Domitian was recorded prior to the Lion Street altar: crucially well before Babbington, Woodford or others could have made any link with an obscure governor of Roman Britain and the city of Chichester.

But of course Gaius Sallustius Lucullus was not an obscure governor and his association with Chichester becomes ever more interesting because of this. The Lion Street altar makes it clear that Lucullus was the son of someone with a good Celtic name: Amminus. Variants of this name occasionally crop up in Gaul, but there are only two other examples of this occurring in Britain: from the Late Iron Age coin series and from the writings of the Roman historian Suetonius.

Amminus is of course the Iron Age king who fled to the emperor Gaius Julius Caesar Germanicus (Caligula) in AD 40 (see chapter 2). The circumstances of his defection are unclear; all Suetonius tells us is that the Briton fled the wrath of his father 'Cynobellinus' and 'deserted to the Romans with a small force' (Suetonius *Caligula* 44). Later historians like Suetonius and Dio Cassius are scathing of Caligula's exploits on the northern shores of Gaul, but it is probable that elements of Caligula's army were actively campaigning in the island. The early coins of Amminus appear in Kent (Allen 1976), but later series occur solely in the area around Chichester (Henig and Nash 1982, 242). Could it be that it was here in western Sussex, that Amminus made his last stand before fleeing to the relative safety of Caligula? If it were, there is no evidence that he ever returned but his son did and it is interesting that it was in Chichester that Lucullus made his two dedications.

'Lucullus' itself is a good Roman name with a solid aristocratic pedigree. In historic terms it also possessed excellent historical associations, Lucius Licinius Lucullus being a former consul (not to say strict military disciplinarian) who as a general in the war against Mithridates, king of Pontus in the 70s BC, won a number of spectacular victories. It has been claimed that the name was chosen by the son of a Celtic king as Lucullus, whilst sounding 'ostensibly Roman, is probably a Celtic name derived from that of the god Lug, disguised in Latin form' (Birley 1979, 120). This is an intriguing proposition, but has no clear evidence to support it. Lucullus' first names, however, are far more informative.

As the son of an Iron Age prince (see appendix 2), Lucullus would have required an official sponsor in order to gain Roman citizenship. Togidubnus of course had the emperor Claudius, becoming Tiberius Claudius Togidubnus in the process. Lucullus' forenames tell us that he was supported in his quest for citizenship by a certain Gaius

Sallustius. The only candidate of sufficient status in the imperial court with this name was Gaius Sallustius Passienus Crispus. Sallustius Passienus Crispus was the adopted son of Gaius Sallustius Crispus (a wealthy aristocrat who acted as counsellor to the first emperor Augustus), and the great-great nephew and adopted grandson of Gaius Sallustius Crispus (the Roman historian Sallust). Sallustius Passienus Crispus, like his father and grandfather before, moved in powerful circles, becoming ever more intimately connected with the imperial family through marriage. First he wed Domitia Lepida the elder, granddaughter of Marcus Antoninus (Mark Antony) and Octavia (sister of Augustus) and later to Julia Vipsania Agrippina (Agrippina the Younger), sister of Caligula, sister-in-law of Tiberius, niece to Claudius and mother of Nero.

Gaius Sallustius Passienus Crispus was, by all accounts a witty orator and a wealthy and successful businessman. He was a prominent member of the imperial court, an influential member of the aristocracy. He was, in short, an ideal sponsor for a British prince. When Amminus fled to the relative safety of Caligula and the imperial court in AD 40, he would presumably have brought close members of his family rather than leave them to the tender mercies of his enemies. Was the young Lucullus with him? It is certainly possible. Amminus, seeking the protection of the Roman State, would likely have been made a citizen either by the emperor or by a close member of his inner circle. As a citizen of Rome, the British prince would have received the Roman forenames of his sponsor and any sons that he brought with him, or whom he had later, would almost certainly inherit the same. As Lucullus was Amminus' biological heir, we would expect the king, who fled Britain in AD 40, to have reinvented himself in Rome as Gaius Sallustius Amminus.

HEIR TO CUNOBELINUS

The important issue deriving from the two Lucullus stones unearthed in Chichester is this: at some point in the AD 80s the governor of Roman Britain was a Briton. Culturally Lucullus was very Roman, but ethnically, he was a descendant of British kings (see appendix 2). He had adopted a Roman name, was a fully paid-up member of Roman society, had the patronage of one of the most important families in the capital, and had (almost certainly), been brought up within the imperial court, speaking Latin and learning the ways of empire. Gaius Sallustius Lucullus, the son of Amminus and grandson of Cunobelinus, had finally made it big. His grandfather may have been recognised as 'King of the Britons' (Suetonius *Caligula* 44), and his uncle Togidubnus was officially credited as being a 'Great King of the Britons', but Lucullus had control of the whole island.

It may seem surprising that someone born a non-Roman (or whose immediate ancestors were from beyond the limits of empire) could achieve so much, becoming a Propraetorian Imperial Legate of one of the wealthiest provinces in the empire, but Lucullus' rise to prominence is not without parallel. A good example of the spectacular possibilities that promotion could bring in the Roman world is demonstrated, for instance, by the career of one Publius Helvius Pertinax. Pertinax was born in AD 126 in Alba, north-western Italy, the son of a freed slave. Until he was 34, he worked as a *grammaticus* (teacher of grammar), before deciding on a career change and joining the army. Meteoric rise through the military command structure (including a stint as a tribune in the VI Victrix legion stationed at York) eventually led to a variety of posts in civil administration. By the early AD 170s he was a member of the Roman senate and went on to hold the governorships of Upper and Lower Moesia (modern-day Bulgaria and Serbia), Dacia (Romania), Syria and finally Britain. He served as proconsul of Africa in AD 188 and as urban prefect of Rome the following year. On 31 December AD 192 the unpopular emperor Commodus was assassinated and Pertinax found himself acclaimed as his successor. If the son of a former slave could become governor of six provinces, a senator, a Legate, a consul, an urban prefect then finally emperor of Rome, why should it seem strange that the son of a British king should become governor of Britain?

The system of bringing up the children of allied kings in Rome was an old and established one. The children in question may have gone to Rome as hostages, to ensure the loyalty of their parents, or willingly as equals to be educated in the Roman way and benefit from the patronage of the imperial court. A system of imperial patronage and senatorial networking proved useful to people determined to make it good in the empire. A fine example of this is Marcus Julius Agrippa (Herod Agrippa), grandson of Herod the Great, who lived in the court of the emperor Tiberius, befriending both Caligula and Claudius, before returning to the east as governor of Judea in the early AD 40s.

The timing of Lucullus' appointment was crucial. In AD 84, the then governor of Britain, Gnaeus Julius Agricola, was recalled to Rome by the emperor Domitian. Agricola had served in Britain for an extended period of six years (the usual remit was only four) and, in that time, he had completed the conquest of Wales, subdued northern England and invaded Scotland. We know more about Agricola's time as governor than any other person to have held the post, for his son-in-law was the Roman historian Publius Cornelius Tacitus. Tacitus' work *Agricola* detailed the life and works of the great man, though some of what he says should be treated with caution as the historian was very keen to demonstrate that Agricola was one of the greatest of Roman military strategists. Tacitus, it is fair to say, is not the most objective of sources when it comes to his father-in-law.

A particular gripe of Tacitus that runs throughout the *Agricola* (like the name 'Worthing' through a stick of rock) is the feeling that his father-in-law had been recalled at the height of his powers and when the conquest of Britain was complete: 'Britain was conquered and immediately abandoned' he notes bitterly (Tacitus *Histories* I, 2). Domitian had done this, Tacitus felt, purely because he was jealous of Agricola's success and angered that the name of a mere governor was being 'raised above that of the emperor' (*Agricola* XXXIX, 4). There may well have been an element of truth in this, for Domitian was not the most stable of rulers, but also it could well have been felt back in Rome, that the British wars were proving far too expensive.

Agricola had been given the job of finishing the conquest of Britain by Domitian's father, the emperor Vespasian, but, six years on and with little economic gain evident from the prolonged fighting, Domitian probably had different priorities. Agricola had smashed the Caledonian armies sent against him at the battle of *Mons Graupius* (the site of which remains unknown) and the conquest of the north appeared complete. Domitian may have felt that the time was ripe to relieve the governor of his command and replace him with someone who better understood the Britons and could make the establishment of a Roman way of life more permanent. Someone who could speed up the Romanising process, stabilise the province and hasten economic returns. The war had been won, now Lucullus had to win the peace. Such considerations would have had no appeal to Tacitus. His father-in-law had been cheated of the public acknowledgement of his great victories and deprived of the rewards. That an ethnic Briton was put in post after Agricola would only have made the situation worse. As it was, of course, Lucullus did not live long enough to reap the full benefits of his position, for he was recalled and executed by the increasingly paranoid Domitian.

Lucullus' governorship undoubtedly saw the formalisation of major elements of the basic infrastructure of Roman Britain. Fledgling towns would have been encouraged and landowners provided with greater incentives to upgrade their lifestyle and become 'more Roman'. Additional people would have to 'buy into' the Roman way of life if the province as a whole was to succeed. Chichester may well have been Lucullus' favoured town, especially if his father Amminus had originally possessed land or power there. As with Togidubnus before, Lucullus' ultimate powerbase was probably centred elsewhere, but it is interesting to note that the main phase of palace building at Fishbourne and across the coastal plain of Sussex, occurred at just this time, within the reign of Domitian. In fact Fishbourne palace itself is (as we later shall see) a copy in miniature of Domitian's *Domus Flavia* on the palatine hill in Rome. Could this be where Lucullus planned to live out his golden years?

KING COILUS

There remains one last postscript to the story of Lucullus and it may be found buried deeply within two important early medieval texts. The first, and most famous, is the *History of the Kings of Britain*, an epic work compiled by Geoffrey of Monmouth in around AD 1136 which was intended to chronicle of the rulers of Britain from earliest times until the domination of the Saxons in the seventh century. The *History* contains much that is clearly fictional and, as a result, has often been ignored, or even derided, by modern historians. In his first chapter, however, Geoffrey claimed that the inspiration and primary source for the *History* was 'a very ancient book in the

British tongue' (*History of the Kings of Britain* 1, 1). Although he does not specifically say so, it is likely that this earlier text was the *Chronicle of the Early Britons*, or the *Tysilio Chronicle* as it is more commonly referred (Petrie 1917), a history written in the first half of the seventh century AD.

Today historians often steer well clear of both Geoffrey's *History* and the *Tysilio Chronicle*. Part of the reason is because they provide an unconventional and alternative, if not downright unusual, take on the Roman invasion of Britain in which there does not appear to be an occupation by a foreign power. Contrary to the view propounded by Roman historians such as Tacitus or Dio Cassius, Tysilio and Geoffrey describe Britain as 'a tribute-paying dependency, generally friendly to Rome, but autonomous' in which the line of British kings appears unbroken either side of AD 43 (Ashe 2000, 40). Of course, if Tysilio had been compiling his *Chronicle* from stories, legends or accounts originally generated within the first and second century world of southern Britain (as the rest of his work seems to imply) then the clear absence of a Roman conquering power does not seem at all strange. To members of the Catuvelluanian tribal aristocracy, such as Togidubnus, Amminus and Lucullus, the transition from native to Roman Britain would have appeared relatively seamless, a variety of ethnic Britons staying in (at least nominal) positions of power.

From the perspective of our story, perhaps the most critical part of Tysilio's *Chronicle* can be found in his description of events occurring late in the first century AD, a time when the Britons were ruled by a king called Coilus. Coilus, we are told:

> had been brought up in Rome, and such was his love for Rome that he did not withhold the tribute whilst he lived, though he could easily have done so' (*Tysilio Chronicle*, XXX).

Geoffrey of Monmouth elaborates on this, observing:

> 'He [Coilus] had been brought up from his infancy in Rome and, having been taught Roman manners, contracted a most strict amity with them. He likewise paid them tribute and declined to make them any opposition…by paying what was required of him, he enjoyed his kingdom in peace and no king ever showed greater respect to his nobility, not only permitting them to enjoy their own with quiet, but also binding them to him through his continual bounty and munificence' (*History of the Kings of Britain*, 18).

There can be little doubt that the Coilus appearing in the accounts of both Tysilio and Geoffrey was in fact Lucullus, Propraetorian Imperial Legate of the emperor Domitian. Although ignored by Tacitus, at least in the works of his that survive to this day, Gaius Sallustius Lucullus evidently remained a potent figure in the oral history of the British. His story may even have formed the basis for the legend of king Coel, the "merry old soul" of the popular children's rhyme: but that, as they say, is another story entirely.

4

THE REGINI

It has been apparent from the previous two chapters that the early story of Roman Sussex, and indeed of Roman Britain, is inextricably linked with two prominent, if at times overlooked, members of the native aristocracy. It is also linked with a town: Chichester, the ancient town of *Noviomagus*.

NOVIOMAGUS

The name *Noviomagus* is preserved from two ancient sources: the writings of the mathematician, astronomer and geographer Claudius Ptolemaeus (Ptolemy) and the anonymous author of a work known as the *Ravenna Cosmography*. We do not unfortunately possess a record of the town's name from a contemporary British source, either from inscriptions preserved from within Chichester itself, or from the tombstones finds discovered outside. This is a shame for, as we shall see, there has been some great dispute as to the full form of the name and of its meaning and translation.

Ptolemy worked in Alexandria in the early second century AD and his magnum opus, the *Geography*, was probably compiled between AD 140-150. The chief aim of the *Geography* was to present a 'graphic representation of the known world as a whole' (*Geography* I, 1). The 'known world' was divided into eight separate books, with Book II containing the full description of places in the British Isles. Not all places were cited by Ptolemy, only those he judged to be of specific importance, so a number of forts and small roadside settlements across southern Britain which are known archaeologically to have been in use at the time of the *Geography*'s compilation, are absent from the finished text. Unfortunately, as with so many other texts from the ancient world, we do not possess a complete and unadulterated *original* version of Book II, what has come down to the present day having been repeatedly transcribed (and sometimes garbled) by a variety of medieval copyists.

The *Cosmography* was compiled by a cleric (or clerics) in the Italian town of Ravenna shortly after AD 700. Although the text was set down some significant time after the collapse of Roman rule in Britain, it uses for its material a variety of disparate, earlier sources. Modern historians have been cautious of using the *Cosmography* too closely for, although the work is comprehensive, there are a great many obvious errors contained within it, as if the compiler (or copying scribe) was unfamiliar with the material. Despite the corruption of place names and the sometimes strange order of citation (ignoring a logical ordering), the *Cosmography* is a valuable source, as long as one is careful about how the information contained within it is used.

Two versions of Ptolemy's *Geography* record the name of the Roman town of Chichester as *Noeomagum* and also as *Noeomagus*, the latter noting that it served as a *polis* or capital of the *Regni* (Rivet and Smith 1979, 427). The *Cosmography* records the town as *Noviomagno* and as *Navimagno Regentium* (Rivet and Smith 1979, 427). It is difficult from these sources to gain a definitive view of the town's Roman name, which may in any case have changed over time. The first element seems to have plausibly been *Noviomagus*, something that could be translated as 'new town', 'new market' or 'new place'. There were a number of sites with the name *Noviomagus* on the continent, the modern towns of Nijmegen (Netherlands), Neumagen (Germany) and Noyon (France) all having ultimately derived from it (Rivet and Smith 1979, 427).

THE REGINI

The second element of Chichester's Roman name, recorded in the *Cosmography* as *Regentium*, has proved difficult to define with any certainty. If, as seems likely, Chichester was designed by the Roman State to act as a largely self-governing *Civitas* (tribal) town, then the term *Regentium* should apply to the tribal affiliation of the new urban centre. The problem is that *Regentium* is close enough to *Regnum* (the Latin for kingdom) to suggest that the full name of Chichester, as *Noviomagus Regnensium*, could have read: 'the new market of the people of the Kingdom'. Given that we know that Tiberius Claudius Togidubnus, the Great King in Britain who dedicated a temple in the town (see chapter 2), was at some point awarded 'certain states' in Britain by the emperor in recognition of his achievements (Tacitus, *Agricola* 14), could it be that the 'regnum' of Chichester was one such kingdom or tribal state? This is certainly possible. It is also possible that, as king Togidubnus appears to have been a member of the Catuvellauni tribe (based around modern-day St Albans in Hertfordshire), then 'the kingdom' could have been a separate territory created by Rome for the king and his family. Here the followers of 'Togidubnus the Great' could establish themselves on new land and with a new Roman legitimacy, building luxury Mediterranean-style homes on money provided by the emperor (see chapter 6).

Alternatively, the Regni, Rigni and Regini, noted in various readings of Ptolemy's Geography, could, like the Atrebates of *Calleva Atrebatum* (Silchester) or the Belgae of *Venta Belgarum* (Winchester) have actually been a separate and distinct tribal group at the time of the Roman conquest. Several modern writers have observed that, depending on the translation supplied, it is possible to suggest that *Noviomagus* was the tribal town of a people known as the Regini, a Celtic translation of which could mean 'the proud ones' (Jackson 1970, 78-9; Rivet and Smith 1979, 446; Down 1988, 28). If such an interpretation were correct it would suggest that Roman Chichester had originally been named *Noviomagus Reginorum* (Rivet and Smith 1979, 446), rather than the more usually suggested *Regnentium, Regnensium* or *Regnum*.

A big problem with all this is that our understanding of Late Iron Age tribal structure is poor to say the least and we possess no clear understanding of what the term 'tribe' actually means in the context of prehistoric Britain. Caesar, Tacitus and Dio Cassius talked in generalised terms of tribes and tribal leaders (princes, kings, queens, aristocrats etc.), but none provided specific information as to the nature of authority and social organisation in the Iron Age. The post-AD 43 Roman provincial government of Britain certainly respected (or created) tribal boundaries which helped to divide the island into a series of discrete, relatively autonomous tribal groups. Each group was, as we shall see, centred upon a brand new *civitas* capital, or tribal market, for the purpose of easier political control and tax collection. Unfortunately we just do not know whether or not these groupings reflected the real nature of political authority within pre-Roman society.

Most maps generated by modern historians and archaeologists in order to explain Late Iron Age Britain show that before the arrival of Rome, society was neatly segregated into a series of discrete, well-ordered tribes. The presumption is that each tribal zone probably possessed its own distinctive name, customs, culture and language. Such divisions unfortunately have the uncomfortable resonance of modern national or county borders and we possess absolutely no evidence to suggest that things were ever as clear-cut and ordered as this in prehistory. Fixed and impenetrable frontiers defining where one nation's brand of civilisation ends are a feature of modern, industrialised societies and not, as far as we can tell, the prehistoric communities of Iron Age Britain.

Although the Roman State was later to record the major tribal names, (such as the Atrebates, Iceni, Cantiaci etc.) and their tribal centres (*Calleva Atrebatum, Venta Icenorum* and *Durovernum Cantiacorum*), it is highly probable that they did not identify smaller groupings. There could, for example, have been other, far less significant, political groups or clans that were not legitimised within the new Roman order. Furthermore, it is debatable whether the people of a specific farming community within a particular tribal zone would have recognised their affinities to 'the greater tribe' or indeed to the leaders of that tribe. Social organisation and political structure within Later Iron Age Britain were probably far more complex and intractable than the Roman mind could effectively deal with, being used to the concept of 'the Senate and People' guided by 'the First Citizen', or emperor.

The real political map of Britain and the Britons was undoubtedly modified and simplified by the Roman State, which was happier with the concept of single tribes occupying single areas under the rule of individual leaders. The names given to tribes themselves could therefore merely reflect the names of a particular ruling dynasty or aristocratic lineage (as may be the case with Cassivellaunos and the Catuvellauni), at the time of first contact with Rome. Using such a model, various people of late twentieth-century Britain could legitimately have belonged to the tribe of 'Windsorites', 'Blairites' or 'Thatcherites' depending upon their political beliefs or social leaning. Iron Age tribes could simply have comprised those families owing allegiance to a particular political or economic leader, in much the same way as perhaps a medieval baron or post-medieval landowner.

We must also be careful of imposing too literal a translation, creating a series of apparently definitive tribal names and groupings in the process. A series of plausible names, such as the Iceni, Durotriges, Cantiaci, Atrebates, Trinovantes and Catuvellauni, are regularly mentioned and discussed in most modern texts on Roman Britain, but it is worth pointing out that these names are modern fabrications. In all cases they represent an attempt by modern linguists and historians to create a 'best fit' from a diverse mass of stone inscriptions, coin legends and corrupted Latin texts. A good example of this is a tribe that, in modern historical literature was always referred to as the Coritani. Discovery of a self-named coin issue has recently demonstrated that a more correct form of the tribal name may have been 'Corieltauvi', and this has since formed the new orthodoxy.

Unfortunately this rule of 'new discovery takes precedence' has not been consistently applied. The Iceni, for example, a tribe based in what is today Norfolk, clearly wrote Ecen, Eceni, Ec, Ecn or Ece on their coins (Rivet and Smith 1979, 373); never Icen, Iceni, Ic, Icn or Ice. 'Iceni' is a modern interpretation: a fiction. Similarly the established name 'Dobunni', a tribe credited with an area centred upon modern-day Cirencester (Rivet and Smith 1979, 339), are, given the literary and contemporary archaeological evidence, more likely have been the Bodunni. The 'Durotriges' of Dorset cite themselves as the Durotrages on more than one occasion (Rivet and Smith 1979, 352), whilst the 'Trinovantes' of Essex are always referred to in Latin texts as the Trinobantes (Rivet and Smith 1979, 475).

If we cannot be certain of the exact form that Iron Age tribal names originally took, can we be certain of their ethnic or cultural background. In short: were they Celtic? Well that depends on your understanding of the term 'Celt' and 'Celtic'. The words 'Celt' and 'Gaul' were terms that the Roman State applied to pretty much everyone they encountered across Western and Central Europe, regardless of attributes, cultural persuasion, language, customs, appearance or religious belief. As a consequence the term is not particularly useful if we wish to identify a particular ethnic grouping or to categorise a particular artefact, monument or site. Basically anything in Western Europe that pre-dates Roman or Greek influence may fairly be described as being 'Celtic'. Matters are complicated further by the Roman attitude towards 'the Celt'. Within the context of Roman social history, the Celt was the bogeyman, the barbarian at the gates, the ever-present threat to civilisation.

The Roman general Julius Caesar in particular played on this. The Gauls or Celts were, Caesar delighted in telling his audience, warlike and savage. They could not be reasoned with, they could not be trusted. They must be fought and they must be defeated. The threat must be neutralised and the enemy forcibly assimilated into the more civilised world of Rome. The wars fought by Rome against the Celts in Gaul were every bit as unyielding and brutal as those later fought across Europe by the conflicting ideologies of fascism and communism. The words 'Celt' and 'Gaul' became terms of Roman abuse: a bigoted shorthand meaning 'savage' or 'barbarian'.

Looking back at the pre-Roman communities inhabiting the area we now call Sussex, it is impossible to state categorically that these people were Celtic, let alone to assign them to a specific language group or ascribe ethnic origin. The Late Iron Age was a time that saw major changes in the archaeological record, both culturally and technologically. By implication, this is also a time of significant political and economic evolution, most of which was probably due to an increase in cross-channel trade, immigration and the introduction of wholly new cultural systems. No society is, after all, ever static. Cultural traits, fashions and ideas are forever changing, developing and evolving due to the processes of migration and interaction. Anyone who claims that British culture, now or in prehistory, was static, unchanging and wholly unaffected by immigrants bringing in new ideas, is either hopelessly naïve or offensively racist.

All we can really say, in the absence of any objective, contemporary anthropological data, is to say the people based around Chichester in the early first century AD were 'British' in the sense that they were resident in Britain at the time of the Roman invasion. Given the large-scale population movements noted by Caesar and others, it is inherently possible that much of the resident Iron Age population had not actually been born in Britain or were only first generation 'British'. Culturally most were north-western European, in that populations shared many of their distinctive traits across south-eastern Britain and northern France and Belgium. Even this definition is perhaps too rigid as, by the end of the first century BC, many people based along the coast of what is today Sussex were well on their way to becoming Roman.

LATE IRON AGE SETTLEMENT

In Sussex and across southern Britain, the most representative type site of the British Iron Age is usually thought to be the hillfort or defended hilltop enclosure. It seems to provide confirmation of the warlike sensibilities of Iron Age communities who were always feuding, brawling, fighting and stealing. Strong hilltop defences imply a very real fear of neighbouring communities and the desire to protect house and home. Or do they? The terms 'fort' and 'fortress' are emotive ones. They imply threats from abroad and the consequent need for constant defence. They suggest the presence of formidable armies roaming the field and yet it would seem that only a minority of the population lived, worked or worshipped in them. Most Iron Age settlements appear as relatively small-scale, close knit farming communities, trading, interacting and existing without the need to massively defend.

Warfare between the various Early Iron Age communities of southern England may have been endemic, in that there was a semi-permanent state of competition between tribes, clans or farming units, but rarely, if at all, would any group attempt to eradicate another. The total extermination of opposing cultural groups is something that may be defined as the modern, 'civilised' concept of war. Warfare between prehistoric societies more often took the form of competition. Competition helped foster alliances and enforce particular allegiances. It increased the desire amongst the leaders of particular communities for prestige goods and extreme dress items, and, ultimately more visually impressive forms of hilltop enclosure. Hillforts, then, could have less to do with a permanent state of hostilities, and more to do with the definition of a social heart of a specific clan group. Hillforts could be where organised gatherings met at particular times of the year. Places where people could come together for the purposes of trade, exchange, taxation, marriage, food distribution or religious ceremonies; places where the leadership of the tribe was reinforced and bonds of allegiance strengthened.

There are many varied and impressive forms of hillfort enclosure in Sussex. The majority of these sites, however, date from the Later Bronze and Early Iron Age (c.1000-100 BC) and not from the period under discussion here. Enclosures built towards the end of the Early Iron Age are referred to in the archaeological literature as developed hillforts, in that, though size and dimensions vary, a common theme was the intensification of impressive ramparts and entranceways. There are at least five developed hillforts in Sussex: Torberry, Cissbury, Caburn, Devil's Dyke and the Trundle. Unfortunately, excavation within the interior of these sites has been relatively limited and definite evidence of buildings is therefore scarce.

The main feature common to developed hillforts, especially the Trundle and Caburn, is the presence of large internal pits. Over 140 such pits have been located and archaeologically examined at the Caburn (13) during the course of excavations conducted between the 1870s and 1920s. These features came in a variety of shapes, including circular, rectangular and triangular, but all produced prolific quantities of artefacts suggesting some form of structured deposition. Given the nature of recording undertaken, it is sometimes difficult to be certain of the exact context of the finds, but it is apparent that a series of special deposits, including weapons, tools, pottery, coins, querns and disarticulated bone (both human and animal) were set down, often following broadly repeatable patterns of deposition. The domed interior of the Caburn is, furthermore, one of the county's more prominent landmarks, something which may have increased the significance of any deposition here (for

13 The Caburn: the earthwork remains of a developed 'hillfort' containing a dense mass of pits, now all backfilled. © *Sussex Archaeological Society*

any activity conducted within the interior would have been visible from a large proportion of the immediate landscape). Similar feelings may have been invoked at the Trundle where the basic internal pit assemblage and site location combine to overlook significant views of the chalk downs and coastal plain. Whatever was going on at these two sites, it does not appear to relate to any 'normal' idea of fortified settlement.

In Sussex, few of the large enclosures seem to continue beyond 100 BC and those that do concentrate solely within the Weald. At least six enclosure sites, namely Garden Hill, Hammer Wood, High Rocks, Philpots, Piper's Copse and Saxonbury, have been recorded here and the majority may be described as promontory forts, in that sections of their circuits are formed by a series of impressive rock outcrops. Evidence of ironworking, in the form of smelting furnaces, ovens, forging hearths and iron slag, has been found at Garden Hill, High Rocks and Saxonbury, suggesting that all these enclosures may have controlled (and protected) those engaged in the exploitation of natural iron ore deposits.

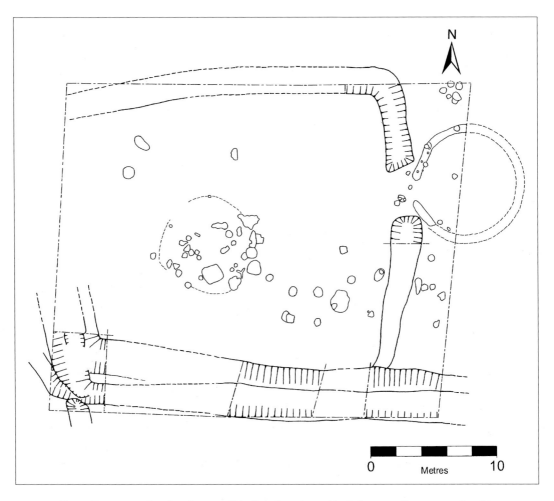

14 Copse Farm: an enclosed settlement of the Late Iron Age with timber roundhouses, metalworking area and at least one storage facility. Finds from the site suggested trade contact with the Mediterranean. *Redrawn from Bedwin and Holgate 1985*

Although enlarged hilltop enclosures disappear from most areas of Sussex from 100 BC, small enclosed farms and farmsteads remain. On the coastal plain, for example, a series of ditched enclosure sites, possibly representing defined fields or settlements, were examined at Copse Farm, Oving, between 1980 and 1983 (Bedwin and Holgate 1985). The occupation here comprised a rectangular enclosure with a simple, east-facing entrance (*14*). A circular spread of postholes, pits (some of which contained evidence of metalworking) and other features at the approximate centre of the enclosure appears to represent the remains of a substantial timber roundhouse. At least one four-post structure, possibly a storage structure, was also recorded from the interior, whilst a single-entranced ring gulley, defining the outer edge of a later house, was found blocking the enclosure entrance.

Copse Farm seems to have functioned primarily as a farm as the bones of cattle, sheep, pig and horse were found together with the carbonised remains of barley and spelt. The presence of both bronze and ironworking debris shows that industrial production had also been conducted. Distinctive forms of Mediterranean pottery storage containers, known as amphorae, further suggests that the farm owners possessed a liking for wine and that they benefited from a new, long-distance trade contact, possibly via a harbour or major inland market.

OPPIDA

As the hillforts of the Early Iron Age faded from most areas of south-eastern Britain, a new form of enclosure system developed. These systems are referred to in the archaeological literature as *oppida*. This is something of an unfortunate title, as it is derived from a term that Julius Caesar applied to almost every Iron Age enclosure, settlement or hillfort that he encountered during his campaigns across Britain and Gaul, regardless of location, extent or political affiliation. In fact Caesar never really defines what precisely he believes the term *oppidum* to mean. Given current archaeological considerations, the term probably has more valid application in France, Germany and Switzerland where certain Late Iron Age enclosures possess clear evidence of urban planning in the form of street grids, administrative centres, religious buildings, elite settlement and enclosing masonry walls.

There is nothing remotely comparable to continental *oppida* recorded from Late Iron Age Britain, though the term 'territorial *oppidum*' has at times been applied by archaeologists to a series of discontinuous linear earthworks found in areas where the hillfort appears to have died out. Territorial *oppida* are to be found in relatively low-lying areas of southern Britain and they often possess complex systems of banks and ditches that demarcate vast blocks of land. A notable example of the territorial *oppidum* can be found at Colchester in Essex, where an area of just over 32 sq km (*c*.12 square miles) was partially enclosed by a series of ramparts. There have been few extensive surveys of the interior, but it seems clear that only a few areas were in any way intensively inhabited. At Sheepen, to the west of the later Roman town, an area of Iron Age settlement associated with industrial activity, coin manufacture and exotic Roman imports has been located, while at Gosbecks and Lexden, to the south-west, a religious complex and major cemetery have been recorded (Hawkes and Hull 1947; Hawkes and Crummy 1995). Other *oppida* have been identified at St Albans in Hertfordshire, Silchester and Winchester in Hampshire and Chichester in West Sussex.

The Chichester *oppidum* comprises a network of ramparts (known as the Chichester Entrenchments or Dykes), which extend for an overall distance of 10km (east–west) x 4.5km (north–south), to the immediate north of the modern town (*15*). Some 15 separate earthworks have so far been identified, though later agricultural and urban

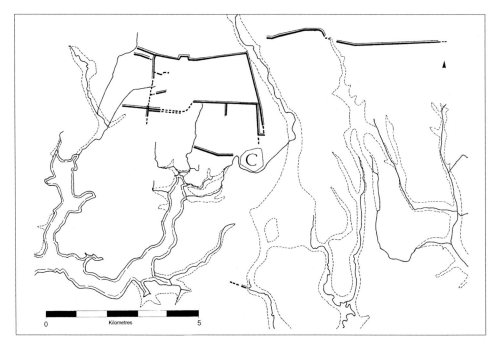

15 Chichester Entrenchments: plan of the system of earthworks to the north and west of Chichester (marked with a 'C'). *Redrawn from Cunliffe 1971*

development has almost certainly destroyed significant sections. In the area of Brandy Hole Copse, a local nature reserve on the northern outskirts of Chichester, the tree-covered rampart remains an impressive feature, standing to a maximum height of 3m in front of a largely backfilled ditch (*16* and *17*). Situated at the very southern edge of the South Downs, the entrenchments effectively cut off the neck of land between the main north–south river systems of this area from the Arun, via the Lavant and off towards Bosham Stream in the west. The entire coastal plain from Bognor Regis to Bosham, including Selsey Bill and the western limits of Chichester Harbour, was therefore separated by these earthworks from the lands to the north.

Dating the entrenchments has proved difficult. Limited excavations across the system to date have provided a restricted sample of material which confirms only a very general date in the Middle to Late Iron Age. The first, and so far only, detailed field survey of the system and its relationships was conducted by Richard Bradley between 1966 and 1967 (Bradley in Cunliffe 1971). In this, Bradley postulated that the entrenchments comprised three major phases of construction. The primary phase seemed to be marked by the most north-easterly stretch of rampart which followed a circuitous, contour-hugging route and demarcated land between the Arun, Lavant and the west (Bradley in Cunliffe 1971, 32). Later, straighter, sections of rampart intensified the enclosure of land to the immediate west of the Lavant, something that seems to indicate a more defensive purpose to the system (Davenport 2003, 106).

16 Chichester Entrenchments: a well-preserved, if tree-covered, section of north-facing bank and ditch at Brandy Hole Copse, Chichester. Note the later refortification of the ditch in the Second World War with anti-tank and glider traps. *Author*

17 Chichester Entrenchments: a well-preserved, densely tree-covered, section to the west of Brandy Hole Copse, north-west Chichester. *Author*

The sheer cost of constructing the entrenchments, at least in terms of labour, must have been immense. Richard Bradley has calculated that the total mass of gravel dug out in the course of cutting the ditches and building the ramparts would have been in the region of 340,000 tons and that the labour required to finish the system 'would be roughly equivalent to 1,500,000 man hours or the labour of 410 men working a 10-hour day every day for a year' (Bradley in Cunliffe 1971, 17). Even if the entrenchments were created in a series of stages over time, their building must have tied up a considerable body of the population.

Unfortunately no one has yet been able to supply a satisfactory answer as to why these earthworks may have been constructed in the first place. It is possible that they were designed to enclose the political heartland of the local tribe, clan or community. Studies of the ditch and bank system have, in the past, suggested that the centre of this territory may have been centred on Selsey Bill, where a large number of Late Iron Age coins have been found. This now appears highly unlikely (Davenport 2003, 106), and the real centre may now have been covered by modern Chichester. The sheer quantity of late Republican Roman imports recovered from excavations in and around Chichester certainly is suggestive of a focus of trade and political control but few definite structures have yet been found. The major problem here is that only limited areas of Iron Age activity have to date been exposed within the town. This, when compounded by the disturbance to early deposits caused by subsequent Roman, medieval and post-medieval development, means that we may never know where the chief settlement of the local Late Iron Age elite was concentrated.

The sheer size and scale of the Chichester Entrenchments suggest that they were designed to represent the boundaries of an important and powerful social group. Perhaps the *oppidum* may have represented the political formalisation of tribal authority, a monumental version of the linear ditch systems, or cross ridge dykes, of the Late Bronze and Early Iron Age, which defined more limited spaces along the South Downs. In this context the Chichester Dykes could be viewed as the late prehistoric equivalent of the Berlin Wall, the forty-ninth parallel or the demilitarised zone separating North and South Korea. But who in the Later Iron Age community would have had the political will or social need to create them? What was the threat to the security and well-being of the southern coast of Sussex deemed to have been?

Perhaps the local community felt afraid of the expansionist tendencies of their northern neighbours. Historically we know that a number of Late Iron Age kings from southern Britain, including Tincomarus and Verica, were seeking shelter in Rome at the beginning of the first century AD, so that theory may not be too wide of the mark. The fact that many of the hillforts of the Early Iron Age were not being refortified at this time however, could alternatively suggest that fear of attack (and the subsequent escalation of hostilities) was not in fact a major concern at least for the bulk of the population.

Only those with a vested interest in maintaining good relations with Rome may have felt the need to define the limits of their power in dramatic new ways. The control of trade with the Mediterranean, and of the profits that ensued, may have led some British leaders to better protect their investments with networks of defensive ramparts backed by displays of intimidation and force. A parallel for the development of power through the brutal control of business can perhaps be seen in the development of Mafia groups in America during the early half of the twentieth century. Here, the operation of small-scale criminal activities within New York led the more successful groups to gradually control significant areas of the city. By the time of prohibition in 1920, when the sale and consumption of alcohol was banned across the USA, the manufacture and distribution of bootleg beverages proved the perfect way for aspiring gangsters to develop their criminal empires. The exploitation of natural resources in return for Mediterranean consumables (such as wine) may have provided a similar route to the top for prehistoric entrepreneurs in Britain.

As with the royal houses of the British Iron Age, the control of business and the organisation of protection rackets in early twentieth-century America increasingly came under the control of a few powerful dynasties. In New York there were five prominent families dominating organised crime (the Bonanno, Colombo, Gambino, Genovese and Lucchese families), whereas in the later Iron Age of central and southern Britain there may have been 10 (the Atrebates, Belgae, Cantiaci, Catuvellauni, Corieltauvi, Dobunni, Durotriges, Iceni, Regini and Trinovantes). The conflicts that drove Tincomarus, Verica and Amminus out of Britain may therefore have been less about mere conquest and territorial acquisition and more to do with a struggle over resources and capital. Cunobelinus of the Catuvellauni based at *Camulodunum* (Colchester in Essex) seemed to believe that he was top dog in matters of trade with the Mediterranean, though other British rulers may have disagreed. If the leaders of Britain in the early first century AD can be equated with Mafia dons and their 'tribes' as well-developed organisations systematically exploiting certain resources, then central southern Britain may, at the beginning of the first century AD, have been in the grip of a protracted and costly turf war.

5

NOVIOMAGUS

Lying in the rain-lashed mud of a trench excavated through the compacted medieval and modern rubble of Chapel Street in Chichester was a sword. Made of iron and measuring a maximum of 520mm in length, the weapon had lost its hilt and scabbard, but still appeared in good shape, the 'slightly waisted', double-edged blade ending in a long V-shaped tip. This was a *gladius*, the primary weapon of the Roman legionary. Designed purely for stabbing, a single, powerful thrust, point first into the face or abdomen of an opponent, the purpose of the *gladius* was simply to maim or kill with a single blow. How many lives had been abruptly ended by the Chichester sword, we cannot say, although Graham Webster, who examined the piece, commented with evident relief, that it had the 'appearance of being unused' (Webster in Down 1981, 173).

You cannot escape the fact that the origins of Chichester are intimately associated with the Roman army. Pieces of military equipment, including helmet fragments, pieces of segmented plate armour and chain mail, throwing javelins, stabbing spears and decorative bronze fittings, have been recovered from all over the town in recent decades. The military were here all right, but what exactly were they doing?

THE ARMY

The quantity and quality of artefacts recovered from Chichester, combined with the possibility of military-style timber buildings (*18*) (e.g. Down 1981, 119-28) and at least one ditch 'of defensive proportions' (Down 1988, 14), strongly suggests a significant military presence which was almost certainly legionary in character. Representing the first professional field army in the ancient world, the legions were disciplined, well equipped, highly trained and motivated killing machines. You did not enter into a battle with a Roman legion and expect to win. The citizen-based

18 Chichester, Chapel Street: Area 3, Trench W, the partial foundations for a series of early Roman military buildings. © *Chichester District Council*

legions were not only the elite fighters of the Roman Empire however; they were also the primary engineers and builders. It was the legions who, within months of assimilating new territory into the empire, would set about creating the essential infrastructure of government: the forts, towns and roads. At Chichester, they could have been building all three.

The first stage of creating a classical-style town would have been to lay out a regular street grid. Intersecting at right angles, the grid was the basic skeleton of a new town. At the centre, where the two main highways (the *Cardo Maximus* and the *Decumanus Maximus*) crossed, the administrative brain (basilica) and economic heart (forum) of the new town were established. Army surveyors would have been critical to the planning of all towns in Britain, from the initial design phase, to the setting out and construction of buildings associated with local government. After this, it was up to the new civic authority to get the arteries pumping and flesh-out the street-based skeleton with private houses, public baths, shops, inns and other centres of social interaction. The presence of military units in 'Proto Chichester' could therefore merely indicate activity associated with the imposition of a Mediterranean-style politico-economic system on the native population. The army was there to create a 'New Market' in which the Britons could try self-government, albeit under the watchful eye of Rome.

An alternative view would be to suggest that the bulk of Roman military kit found in Chichester related to the construction of a fort, created during the initial days, weeks, months or years of the Roman invasion. But which one? We have already noted (in chapter 1) that there is significant archaeological evidence recovered from around the later palace site at Fishbourne, to suggest the presence of military units there before AD 25 (a good 18 years before the 'invasion' sponsored by Claudius). Many of the projectile weapons, decorative fittings and fragments of helmet and armour retrieved from Chichester could also have derived from a pre-AD 43 context. The main problem with establishing a precise date for ancient military equipment, as has already been noted, is that of longevity. Much of the Chichester assemblage could easily be placed within a late first-century BC or very early first-century AD (Augustan or Tiberian) time bracket as it could a mid-first-century (Claudian) one. Unless an inscription or dedication that specifically names an emperor is found in close association with such pieces, a definitive statement concerning the inception of Roman military activity at Chichester will remain frustratingly elusive. Only a new programme of archaeological fieldwork in the town will begin to provide us with an answer.

THE 'NEW MARKET'

Establishment of towns was essential if the people of Britain were to be integrated into the Roman Empire. The tribes, and more importantly their leaders, had to be fully Romanised, and working within the imperial system, if the new province were to function efficiently and effectively. To achieve this, the Roman State created a series of *civitates*, or cantons, which formalised the rather vague tribal identities of earlier periods, building a town at the centre of each. Here, all the major tribes identified by Rome in southern Britain, would be allowed to retain a certain degree of self-determination, but their place of regional assembly would now be in the town, under the careful scrutiny of the new Roman provincial government.

Two major types of town were created across southern Britain in the late first and early second century AD, the occurrence of both providing a clue as to the status of particular tribal groups. Winchester (*Venta Belgarum*), Silchester (*Calleva Atrebatum*) and Canterbury (*Durovernum Cantiacorum*) were all *Civitas* Capitals or tribal centres formalised by Rome. In most cases these new Roman towns were built close to, or directly over, a major Iron Age seat of power (or *oppida*), something which helped to ensure a relatively smooth transition from British to Romano-British administration. At Colchester in Essex, the Iron Age *oppida* of *Camulodunum*, perceived by the Roman State as a major centre of resistance during the events of AD 43, was replaced by the second major type of Roman town to be found in Britain: the *Colonia*.

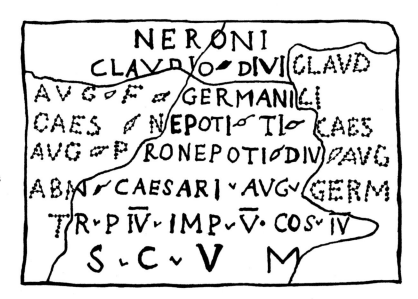

Coloniae, or 'colony-towns' were founded in freshly conquered enemy territory. Their purpose was to act as a model town (to help Romanise the natives) but also to perform as a military reserve, for premium space within the *Colonia* was allocated to soldiers approaching retirement age.

The situation occurring at Colchester, an *oppida* apparently belonging to the eastern branch of the Catuvellauni tribe, is in marked contrast to that of the western Catuvellauni, who were provided with a regional town at *Verulamium*, modern-day St Albans. *Verulamium* was accorded the status of a *municipium*, a self-governing community of Roman citizens. The disparity between the treatment of the eastern and western branches of the same tribe may have its origins in the way in which their leaders, Togidubnus/Togodumnus and Caratacus approached the arrival of Rome (see chapter 2). Caratacus actively campaigned against the Roman army, and was later hunted down in the mountains of North Wales. Togidubnus, however, sided with Rome and was well rewarded by both Claudius and Nero thereafter. It is probable that the followers or supporters of the pro-Roman Togidubnus were accorded high status in the *municipium* of St Albans, whilst their anti-Roman colleagues, originally operating from Colchester, became a conquered people.

That Chichester, *Noviomagus Regnensium* or *Reginorum*, was a *civitas* or tribal town of a people known as the Regni, Rigni, Regini (or simply *Regnum / Regnensium* – the 'people of the kingdom') seems tolerably certain (*colour plate 1*). It is difficult to know, however, what significance, if any, should be attached to the name *Noviomagus*. Does the application of the term 'New Market' refer to a new (Roman) capital built some significant distance from the old (Iron Age) one, or is this a 'New Market' in the sense of a 'shiny new town', built on top of, and directly replacing, its Iron Age predecessor? Both interpretations are certainly possible. *Noviomagus* was created on a block of level, well-drained land within the area enclosed by the Chichester Entrenchments, the linear earthworks defining the northern limits of a territorial *oppidum*. It may therefore be that the site for the town was specifically chosen in order to replace an existing centre of Iron Age regional power. The remains of such a centre, had it been in the path of the Roman property developers, are unlikely to have survived, although it should be noted that part of an Iron Age settlement has been found at the Cattlemarket site, close to the Eastgate (Down 1989, 55-83).

We do not know precisely when the decision to create the New Market was first made. The *colonia* at Colchester was under construction by AD 49, whilst evidence recovered from Silchester and St Albans suggest Romanised buildings in existence by AD 50 at least. Given that Chichester appears to have been one of the key tribal centres within the dominion of Tiberius Claudius Togidubnus, together with Silchester, Winchester, Bath and, almost certainly, St Albans, it is likely that urban development had also commenced here in the AD 50s. The first piece of evidence to provide an irrefutable date for Roman civic activity in Chichester comes from a monumental inscription found, then promptly lost, in 1740, at the corner of St Martin's and East Street. Thankfully a drawing had been made of the text. The stone (RIB 92), was in pieces when found (*19*), and, although a variety of different transcriptions have been offered, the current interpretation of the complete text reads:

NERONI
CLAVDIO DIVI
CLAVDI F GERMANICI CAES
ARIS NEPOTI TI CAES
AVG PRONEPOTI DIVI AVG
ABN CAESARI AVG GERM
TR P IV IMP V COS IV
S CV M

which may be translated as:

> For Nero Claudius Caesar Augustus, son of the deified Claudius, grandson of Germanicus Caesar, great-grandson of Tiberius Caesar Augustus, great-great-grandson of the deified Augustus, in his fourth year as tribune, five times declared general, in his fourth consulship, by decree of the senate the vow was deservedly fulfilled.

This dedication records a vow of loyalty made to the then imperial incumbent, Nero, citing his official name, full set of titles and descent from the deified Augustus. The fact that he was described as being chief general (*imperator*) for a fifth time, would place the dedication in AD 58 or early 59. From a modern perspective, the Nero inscription seems breathtakingly sycophantic, but for the people of *Noviomagus*, it was a critical dedication linking them directly to the divine Julio-Claudian family. This was a major statement and a key piece of civic identity and pride. It presumably formed part of a statue (possibly of Nero himself) or was placed in a prominent part of a major building.

The final line of the inscription, mentioning that 'by decree of the senate the vow was deservedly fulfilled' raises a number of issues. The abbreviation S.C.V.M. (*Senatus Consulto Votum Merito*) appears on a great number of official texts, and it is possible that the stone mason creating the inscription merely copied a basic formula without knowing (or realising) its true meaning. Given the importance of the message (that the good people of *Noviomagus* were fully integrated members of Roman society), it is perhaps unlikely that errors on this scale would have been made. It is possible that 'the senate' being referred to here is the Roman senate and that it was they who insisted that a permanent reminder of the loyalty vow be made. Far more likely, perhaps, is that 'the senate' appearing in the inscription is the senate of local government: a town council desperate to win the favour and consent of central government.

As a *civitas* capital, *Noviomagus* would have had its own council (*ordo*) or regional assembly that, to begin with, would theoretically have comprised elements of the native elite. In classical cities, membership of the *ordo*, limited by adherence to a strict property qualification, was restricted to 100, all of whom were male. Members, known as *decurions*, were eligible for a variety of official positions, the most prestigious of which was that of magistrate. Each year two magistrates, known as the *duoviri iuridicundo*, were elected to preside over judicial courts, organise religious festivals and supervise the running of the *ordo*. Magistrates were assisted by *duoviri aediles*, whose job it was to deal with public works and services, *quaestores*, who dealt with finance (including tax collection) and *censitores*, who managed the official documents of the canton, including all census records.

CIVIC BUILDING

With the site of the town decided and the street grid established (*20*), the first buildings to appear in *Noviomagus* would have been those associated with local government; the forum and basilica. The forum was essentially a large open courtyard surrounded by a covered walkway or colonnade which was designed to act as the economic heart of both the town and the region. It was the prestige market centre, the place to do business, to gather to hear proclamations and announcements and where tribal and civic identities could be subtly fused. The forum would contain all they key symbols of *Romanitas* including images taken from the Roman pantheon of gods (especially Jupiter) and portraits of the current head of State (or his honoured ancestors).

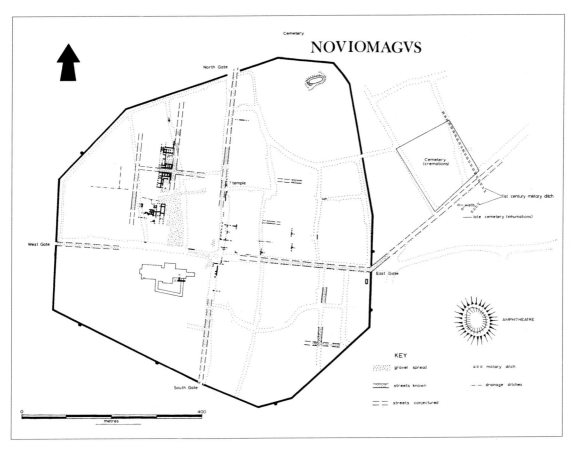

20 Chichester: plan of Roman buildings uncovered by the beginning of the 1990s. Note the incomplete nature of the known Roman street grid. © *Chichester District Council*

The basilica, which adjoined the forum, comprised a massive, apsidal-ended, fully covered rectangular hall, designed to act as the focal point of local government authority. As a key element in defining civic pride, the basilica was clearly intended to impress. In Britain, where few buildings had previously risen much above a single storey, the architectural impact of such a grand and monumental structure, must have been dramatic. The basilica created an ordered space in which the town council (*ordo*) could meet, where Roman (and tribal) justice was dispensed, rates of taxation calculated, the effectiveness of public services discussed and where the records, documents and legal papers relating to the region were stored. The blueprint for the forum and basilica complex, with its open courtyard backed by a covered administrative hall, can be seen in the *principia* or headquarters building found at the heart of all first- and second-century Roman forts. This would further seem to indicate that the design and initial layout of all new towns in Britain was overseen and co-ordinated by the military.

The location of the forum and basilica within the new town of *Noviomagus* is relatively easy to determine; less easy to demonstrate conclusively. The central area of the Roman town is now largely covered by the cathedral and the convergence of North, South, East and West Street at the market cross. Archaeological investigation within this area has, understandably, been rather limited, but what the discovery of certain features in West Street do permit is 'to indulge in informed guesswork' (Down 1988, 31). In 1940, the construction of an air-raid shelter through the cellar of the Dolphin and Anchor Hotel, exposed a substantial block of flint wall, running the length of the West Street frontage (Down 1981, 54). In 1980, the laying of a gas main along the northern edge of West Street, unearthed part of a large, east–west aligned stylobate (paved colonnade) and gutter whilst work at the junction of Chapel and West Street revealed 'paving slabs set in pink mortar' (Down 1981, 51-5; 1988, 31-4).

The substantial colonnaded building thus exposed, albeit partially, in West Street can, given its location in the town, only be that of the forum and basilica, the rest of which presumably lies beneath the Dolphin and Anchor (*21*). A further piece of evidence to support the identification is provided by a large piece of a monumental dedication to 'Jupiter, Best and Greatest, in Honour of the Divine House' found in 1935 during the excavation of foundations for the Post Office on the northern edge of West Street (Down and Rule 1971, 15). The stone was probably part of the base for a Jupiter column (see chapter 9), which is exactly the sort of feature that one would expect from within the forum precinct (Down 1988, 34).

Another major public building complex is known to lie beneath the site of the old Telephone Exchange in Chapel Street and the stores flanking West Street to the west of the forum. This time there can be no doubt as to the nature and identification of the structure, for this was the public bathhouse. Every Roman town would have had at least one major public bathing amenity, which, in the absence of public houses, night-clubs and casinos, would have acted as the foremost place of social interaction within the city. Roman bathhouses followed the same basic design throughout the empire; a range of rooms of varying temperatures which functioned in much the same way as a modern Turkish Bath or Swedish Sauna. Beginning in the unheated dressing room (*apodyterium*), the prospective bather entered the cold room (*frigidarium*) possibly to pause in a cold bath or have a quick shower (sometimes courtesy of a large bucket). Then he or she would move into the warm room (*tepidarium*) and be anointed with oils before finally progressing to the hot room (*caldarium*). Hot rooms possessed an underfloor heating system (hypocaust) comprising a floor raised on tiled stilts to allow the circulation of scaldingly hot air brought in via an exterior stokery or furnace. Allowing time to sweat profusely, the bather would scrape the oils from his or her body and wallow in the heat of the hot bath, before returning to the cold room and bath. Larger or more luxurious bathing complexes often possessed an exercise hall or yard (*palaestra*) or a hot dry room or sauna (*laconicum*). Most utilised the extensive availability of water to provide a flushing latrine.

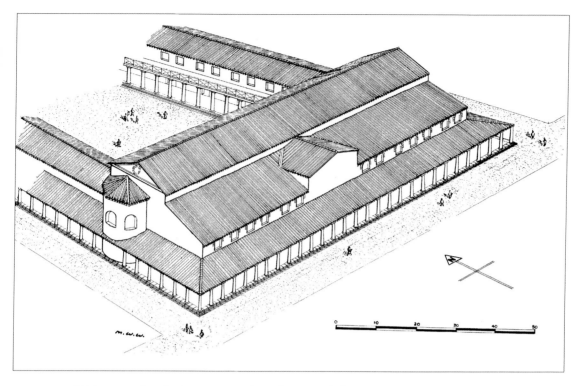

21 Chichester: an imaginative recreation drawn by Max Wholey of the monumental building known to exist beneath the Dolphin and Anchor in West Street, here interpreted as the basilica, with the open courtyard of the forum to the north. © *Chichester District Council*

The first hint of a bathing complex in Chichester was made in 1960, when building works on the northern edge of Morant's Store, later the Army and Navy Stores, unearthed part of a black and white mosaic and a fragment of apsidal wall, possibly part of a cold immersion bath. The mosaic is of particular interest for, although fragmentary, it possesses very close affinities with the late first-century geometric mosaics of the main palace phase at Fishbourne (chapter 6), possibly providing a link between the two sites (Down 1988, 36, 42). Fragments of relief-patterned tile recovered from the baths further suggest a connection between the building of the Chichester bathhouse and the primary phase of Fishbourne palace, something which at both sites could be in the region of AD 90-110 (Black 1987, 86). Between 1974-5, the northern end of the bathhouse was investigated (*22*), revealing a range of heated rooms (*caldaria*) and at least one warm room (*tepidarium*). Little evidence was recovered that might hint at the level of internal decoration within the baths, other than the mosaic already alluded to (Down 1978, 139-57). The baths were supplied by water pumped from a thickly walled cistern sunk into the natural gravels to the north-west of the complex. Water discharged from the bathhouse was carried away via a series of masonry-lined drains (Down 1978, 149-51).

22 Chichester, Tower Street, the apsidal end of room 1 in the public bathhouse. Note the much denuded remains of the hypocaust *pilae* (tile stacks) which once allowed hot air to circulate beneath a raised floor.
© *Chichester District Council*

The great Togidubnus inscription already discussed (chapter 3) from Chichester records the building of a classical-style '*Templum* to Neptune and Minerva'. Although the footprint of such a temple has yet to be securely identified within the confines of the modern town, it is likely that it was not far from where the inscription was first found, at the corner of Lion and North Street. Little archaeological investigation has been conducted here (perhaps understandably given that North Street is an important area of pedestrianised shopping), although limited work conducted during the late 1960s and 70s has suggested the presence of a major structure. In 1967, a service trench outside No. 70 North Street hit substantial tile-bonded foundation (Rule in Down and Rule 1971, 51-2), whilst in 1977 a 0.85m-wide stretch of what appeared to be the same wall was traced for a length of nearly 5m to the south (outside No. 71) during the cutting of a drainage trench (Down 1981, 23-6). Little can be said with regard to these brief pieces of intervention although it would appear likely that the walls sampled did indeed form the western frontage of the temple to Neptune and Minerva.

Apart from the bathhouse, the only other major centre of social interaction in Roman Chichester has been found to the south-east of the town where it is still (just) visible as an oval earthwork. This is the amphitheatre, where death was staged as a source of public entertainment. In the absence of an effective criminal justice system, the punishment of those who had transgressed the law, as decreed by the *ordo* or town council, would have taken place in the arena. The amphitheatre was therefore not just a place where gladiators fought or wild animals were hunted (both forms of sport were expensive and the bill would have landed at the feet of the presiding magistrates for the year), but where the townspeople could see wrongdoers receiving the full penalty of law. We may imagine that such events, when staged, proved extremely popular, a sad indictment of the human condition perhaps, but one only has to look at the crowds drawn to the public hangings of eighteenth-century England or the guillotining in post-revolutionary France, to realise that it was it was probably all too true.

Only very limited investigation of the Chichester amphitheatre has ever taken place, in 1935. This excavation demonstrated the overall dimensions of the original building, which measured 56.5m x 45.7m, the arena floor having been sunk 1.2m below Roman ground level. A bank of excavated soil piled up around the arena, and revetted by a masonry wall (to prevent collapse and, we may presume, to limit the chances of a criminal escaping), formed a secure base for a set of tiered seats. The masonry may well have been boarded over and covered in painted plaster On the basis of a limited finds assemblage, a constructional date of between AD 70 and 80 was proposed (White 1936).

Funding for major civic building projects within *Noviomagus* seems to have dried up some time in the mid-third century AD. Towards the end of the third century, a large amount of money was instead invested in a brand new construction work: town defences. The first long-distance perimeter to be set out at Chichester was, of course, the *oppida*, the ramparts of which comprised the Chichester Entrenchments. Some time in the first half of the first century AD, these had been superseded by a Roman military circuit, enclosing a far smaller area around, we may presume, an army sponsored trading post, advance fort or base camp (chapter 1). When, in the latter half of the first century, *Noviomagus* began developing over the area abandoned by the army, a defended perimeter perhaps seemed unnecessary (although it has been suggested that a large ditch found beneath the site of the Cattlemarket, by Eastgate, may have been part of a defensive work dating to the Boudican revolt of AD 60: e.g. Down 1988, 24-7). The defences constructed in the late third century were wholly different: a masonry wall, backed by an earthen rampart and fronted by at least two V-shaped ditches (Holmes 1962; Down and Magilton 1993), designed to fully enclose the *civitas* capital.

The wall was composed of a mortared flint core, the inner edge comprising more carefully coursed (and roughly faced) flint nodules (Down and Magilton 1993). The outer edge of the town wall circuit has been extensively robbed, and subsequently

23 Chichester: the site of the Friary Close bastion (external tower) under excavation in 1952. The original face of the Roman city wall is revealed as comprising small, well-shaped rectangular blocks of sandstone, a decorative building style known as *petit appareil*. © *Sussex Archaeological Society*

repaired, throughout the post-Roman and medieval periods, with few obvious traces of the original Roman face surviving. A clue as to the nature of the Roman wall surface was, however, discovered in 1952, during the demolition of an unstable projecting tower (or bastion) in the private garden of a house in Friary Close (Wilson 1957). Here it became apparent that the bastion was a later addition to the wall, its construction having preserved the original wall surface, protecting it from the attention of later stone robbers. The face, as revealed in 1952 (*23*) and again in 2003, was composed of small, well-shaped, regular sized, rectangular blocks of cream-grey coloured Malmstone, a sandstone derived from an outcrop of the Upper Greensand found at the northern foot of the South Downs (Kenny 2004). The stones were well coursed, being set in a light pink mortar. Such a style of building, known as *petit appareil*, is primarily decorative, and would not have enhanced the defensive capabilities of the town perimeter. Its use suggests that the wall was as much 'a justifiable demonstration of civic pride' as it was purely a protective measure (Kenny 2004, 23).

Those who designed and built the wall paid little attention to areas of settlement at the periphery of the town. Excavations conducted by John Holmes in the southern circuit in 1959 and by John Magilton by the west gate between 1987-8, have provided evidence of high-status structures, with painted plaster walls and mosaic floors, that were demolished at the time of the new development. That the buildings were domestic houses, and that they were still functioning right up to the arrival of the wall seems clear enough. What is unclear is why such buildings were not included within the new perimeter, a point noted by John Magilton:

> These may have been the homes of Chichester's wealthier citizens who preferred to live at a distance from the commercial centre but, if so, it is surprising that they apparently lacked the political influence to have their houses enclosed within the city's defences. (Magilton in Down and Magilton 1993, 108)

Despite the care and attention that had gone into the design and form of the wall, especially the neat and well-ordered facing stones, it would appear that it was an urgent necessity; one that needed to be built, irrespective of what, or whom, lay in its path.

What had happened to make the citizens of *Noviomagus* so keen to define the limits of their town in such a dramatic way? A probable answer can be found in the events of the later third century (chapter 11) when the coastal regions of Britain succumbed first to Saxon pirate infiltration, and then were later provided with a chain of new military installations designed to protect Britain from a re-invading Roman army. Britain, in the AD mid-280s, had become a rogue State, a breakaway province of the Roman Empire. The leader of the rebellion, a man called Carausius, appears to have modified existing harbour installations along the southern and eastern British coast, creating new strongly fortified establishments such as Pevensey in the process. The wall circuit of Chichester could easily fit into the earlier part of this timeframe, its construction reflecting the very real concern that the combination of Saxon attack and civil war, could threaten the very existence of town life.

Traces of at least five projecting towers, or bastions, are extant in the wall circuit of Chichester today. The two well-preserved examples, known as the Residentiary and palace Bastions, may still be seen in the south-western quadrant of the town (*24*), to the south of the Bishop's palace (Down and Magilton 1993, 125-6). A third tower, known as the Orchard Street Bastion, survives as a substantial, though detached, block of masonry in the private garden of a house in the north-western quadrant. Extensive analysis, research, survey and excavation conducted along the line of the wall over the past half century has demonstrated the former existence of at least 28 bastions (*25*), spaced at intervals of approximately 96m (Magilton in Down and Magilton 1993, 125-6).

24 Chichester: the Bishop's palace Bastion at the extreme south-western corner of the city wall in 2003. The walls still follow the line of the Roman circuit, but no Roman masonry is visible here. *Author*

Shorter interval distances occurred at the northern and western gates where towers were more closely associated with protecting points of entrance. The provision of towers represents an additional element of defence, allowing those inside to safely inspect the outer edge of the wall and clear it of potential attackers with bow or catapult fire. Dating evidence for the bastions has, to date, proved largely elusive. It is clear that they represent an addition to the original perimeter (none were bonded into the wall) and the assumption has always been that they were set up in the mid-fourth century (Magilton in Down and Magilton 1993, 125).

Four gateways originally punctured the masonry wall circuit of *Noviomagus*, guarding the roads from London (east gate), Chichester Harbour (south gate), Portsmouth, Winchester and the west (west gate) and Silchester (north gate). Unfortunately, very little is known about these structures, the northern, southern and western gateways being unceremoniously ripped down in the 1720s in order to improve access to the town (Down 1988, 54). During the 1780s, the east gate also succumbed to this extreme form of urban vandalism, but not before it had been recorded by a local artist by the name of Grimm. Grimm's woodcut of the eastern entrance to Chichester (*26*) shows a large, round-headed arched opening with a lesser arched passageway set immediately to one side. Late medieval housing dominates the upper storey and rearward side of the structure, but the large blocks of masonry evident in the arches would all seem to be Roman.

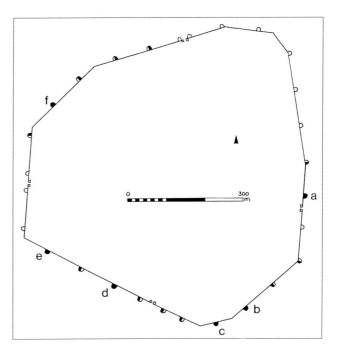

25 Chichester: plan compiled by John Magilton in order to show the distribution of surviving, inferred and speculative external towers in the city wall: a = Eastgate Bastion; b = Friary Close Bastion; c = Market Avenue Bastion; d = Residentiary Bastion; e = Palace Bastion; f = Orchard Street Bastion. *Redrawn from Down and Magilton, 1993*

26 Chichester: the east gate in 1782, just before its destruction, from a woodcut by Grimm. The two arches are clearly Roman, although the upper structure has been covered in medieval housing. © *Chichester District Council*

In basic form, the east gate at Chichester is similar to that of the somewhat vehicle-battered Newport Arch, in Lincoln, the only Roman archway to survive in Britain. The Newport Arch originally formed the north gate to Roman Lincoln (*Lindum*), and comprised a main central opening (for wheeled transport) flanked by two smaller (pedestrian) passages. No doubt Chichester east gate was designed to function in the same way. The stonework apparent in Grimm's illustration is substantial (assuming that the human scale is correct), the arches sitting on at least three enormous wedge-shaped supporting stones (*voussoirs*). This sort of monumental architecture is just what one would expect for the main gate greeting those travelling down Stane Street from the provincial capital in London.

TOWN LIFE

Away from the civic buildings, little is known about everyday domestic activity in Roman Chichester. Excavations conducted in the interior of the town have often been of restricted size and scale, Roman levels frequently being disrupted by later urban development. The first non-monumental buildings of *Noviomagus* appear to have been constructed primarily of wattle and daub, timber and thatch and, as a consequence, have rarely left a clear footprint in the archaeological record. Throughout the third and fourth centuries many timber structures were being rebuilt on a grander scale. A good example of this was excavated in 1984 at Greyfriars in North Street. Here a series of nine possible rooms, two with underfloor heating systems (*hypocausts*) were sampled. All had unfortunately been badly damaged by later activities (Down and Magilton 1993, 11-39). The house seems to have been laid out in the latter half of the fourth century AD, replacing a timber-framed structure of the early to mid-fourth century. A fragment of late third- or early fourth-century geometric mosaic, found to the south-west, at St Peter's in North Street, could conceivably be part of the same structure. The large, coarse *tesserae* used in the formation of the mosaic suggest that it was originally set within a corridor or possibly a private bathhouse (Neal in Down and Magilton 1993, 48-9).

Elsewhere in Chichester, the fragmentary remains of mosaic floors provide only a tantalising glimpse of the former splendour of houses and other buildings. Beneath the south aisle of the Cathedral, the north-western corner of a fine polychrome geometric mosaic, with a floral rosette design, of the late second or early third century AD was found in 1966 (Down and Rule 1971, 127-38), whilst a second polychrome mosaic, this time from the late third or early fourth century has been unearthed behind a shop fronting East Street (Down 1974, 99). The latter floor, referred to as the 'David Greig mosaic', had been badly damaged by later pit-cutting activity, but enough survived to suggest the presence of an extremely high-status house.

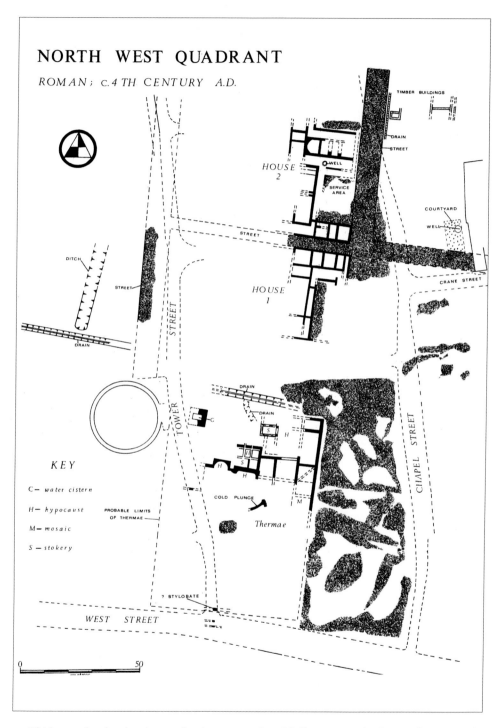

NORTH WEST QUADRANT

ROMAN; C.4TH CENTURY A.D.

TIMBER BUILDINGS

HOUSE 2

WELL

DRAIN

STREET

SERVICE AREA

COURTYARD

WELL

DITCH

STREET

STREET

CRANE STREET

HOUSE 1

STREET

DRAIN

TOWER STREET

CHAPEL STREET

DRAIN

DRAIN

C

S

H

H

S

H

COLD PLUNGE

M

KEY

C— *water cistern*

H— *hypocaust*

M— *mosaic*

S — *stokery*

PROBABLE LIMITS OF THERMAE

Thermae

? STYLOBATE

WEST STREET

0   50

27 Chichester: plan showing the two fourth-century private Mediterranean-style, Courtyard Houses with street grid uncovered in the Central Girls School site in Chapel Street and the public bathhouse behind West Street, as revealed in excavations conducted between 1969 and 1978. © *Chichester District Council*

At the Central Girls School site in Chapel Street, parts of two houses, flanking either side of an east–west aligned gravel street (27), to the north of the public baths have been unearthed (Down 1978). The final, fourth-century ground plan of the southern building (House 1), resembled a Mediterranean-style town house, with a rectangular courtyard surrounded by an ambulatory or corridor, and a range of rooms along the northern, western and possibly also southern sides. Mediterranean-style houses are characterised by an inward-looking plan, usually with four wings set around a central open space. Such houses were particularly suited to countries with a warm and sunny climate, permitting a good circulation of air and providing a shady and secluded area in which to relax. Provision of a courtyard also aided the separation and segregation of private and public space into discrete ranges. The northern range of House 1 at Chichester, which appears to have originally opened out onto the street, may have contained more public space, including reception rooms and perhaps an atrium, with more private space being allocated along the western and southern sides of the courtyard.

House 2, to the north of the gravel road, also reached its height in the fourth century AD. The ground plan of the final building, which seems to date to the mid-fourth century, suggests a courtyard facing onto the wider north–south aligned road, with rooms arranged along its northern, western and southern sides (Down 1978; 1981, 130-4). The northern range, which continued out of the excavated area, appeared to be a private bath suite, with a corridor and open courtyard (to another house?) to the north. The bath suite comprised an apsidal room at its western end, which Down interpreted as a *tepidarium* or warm room (Down 1978, 119), bordering a heated room, with a polychrome mosaic and hypocaust, and two further rooms, with tessellated floors, the easternmost fronting the street. A room in the southern range (third from the eastern end) was provided with a hypocaust and may originally have functioned as a *triclinium* or dining room. The overall scale of the foundations for House 2, measuring 1m in width and over 1m deep, appeared excessive for a single-storey building and may indicate the presence of an upper floor. Although not fully excavated, the scale of House 2 is ambitious, being conducted by someone 'who could command considerable resources' (Down 1981, 134).

By the later years of the fourth century, House 2 found itself operating under a very different set of circumstances. Holes in the tessellated floors were poorly repaired with tile, whilst daub, plaster and domestic rubbish appeared to be accumulating in the northern range. Alec Down, who excavated the site, painted a particularly evocative picture of the southern courtyard in its final phase:

> the whole of the service area at this time must have been quite malodorous, especially in the summer. Much of the domestic food debris, including thousands of oyster shells, had accumulated on top of the gravel surface of the courtyard and combined with the smell from the cesspits would have created a stink quite unacceptable to twentieth-century nostrils. (Down 1981, 134)

Some evidence for the industrial and economic life of *Noviomagus* has been recovered from fieldwork conducted both within the town and from 'the suburbs' that developed along the major highways. In Chapel Street, excavations conducted beneath the Central Girl's School, found that here industrial processes had commenced in the mid-first century AD. Two pottery kilns, generating a variety of products from coarse ware bowls, platters and cooking pots, to fine ware beakers, bowls and jars were found, although the possibility exists that they were established to service the military rather than the occupants of the fledgling town (Down 1978, 57, 210). Associated with the kilns was evidence for enamelling and possible bronzeworking (hearths and pits with small crucibles), again dating to the mid-to-late first century AD. Another late first-century area of metalworking, this time involving iron-ore smelting, has been recorded from the St Peter the Less site in North Street (Wacher 1974, 437-8) whilst a large amount of iron forging seems to have been conducted in the area of the Cattlemarket, to the immediate south east of the town during the fourth century (Down 1988, 78).

The areas of first-century manufacturing activity in *Noviomagus* could have been related to the 'guild of smiths' recorded from the inscription to Togidubnus' great temple of Neptune and Minerva (RIB 91: see above). Quite what the guild entailed, and who was eligible for entry, is unclear but they may well have been a collection of artisans working in the new building projects of Chichester and the surrounding area (such as the Proto Palace at Fishbourne). Such work would have proved extremely lucrative to the budding metalworker, mosaicist, glass blower or potter, and we might imagine that these people were hired in from a range of firms, elsewhere in the empire, in order to make the dreams of king Togidubnus (and later governor Lucullus) a reality.

Insect remains, including both grain and flour beetles, recovered from the waterlogged conditions of a Roman well at the Cattlemarket site suggest that this area was used for milling and the storage of grain during the later fourth century AD (Gelling in Down 1989, 239-40). Some of this grain may have been stored in granary-type timber buildings with floors raised on stilts or posts. A significant quantity of dung beetles indicate the presence of grazing animals or livestock, whilst a study of the faunal remains provided evidence for the slaughtering of cattle and sheep, with on-site secondary butchery (the cutting up of carcasses into joints of meat: Down 1989, 82). The presence of butchery waste seems to have provided an attractive environment for scavengers, dog-gnawed bone (together with the remains of the dogs themselves) being retrieved from a variety of refuse pits. Scattered hearths, cesspits and postholes suggest the presence of artisan's homes (Down 1989). All this produced a lively image of a busy and vibrant community:

> a settlement outside the town where sheep and cattle were driven in from the outlying
> districts for sale and/or slaughter; where farriers plied their trade and shod horses and
> gelded cattle and where the forging of iron tools and other implements and the storage
> of grain and the milling of flour took place. Down 1989, 82)

The location for this settlement was a crucial one: outside the eastern gate of the town, connecting directly with Stane Street and the large agricultural estates beyond, a point not lost on the Victorian leaders of Chichester, who established their own cattle market on exactly the same spot in the early 1870s (Down 1989, 83). Suburbs also appear to have developed outside the northern and southern gates to *Noviomagus* (Down 1988, 38).

THE PEOPLE OF *NOVIOMAGUS*

We know almost nothing about the citizens of Roman Chichester. Of the total population that must have been born, lived, worked and died in *Noviomagus*, very few have survived in the archaeological record; less still have been found and recovered in time, prior to their unrecorded destruction at the hands of the ever-developing modern city. In 1993, only 431 former residents of the town had been recorded in the form of 338 cremations and 93 inhumations (Down and Magilton 1993, 87). A few more bodies have since been found, but, even when combined with the unknown quantity retrieved from early archaeological and antiquarian explorations (e.g. Down and Rule 1971, 89), the overall percentage of population for Roman Chichester remains minute.

At least four cemeteries are known to have existed beyond the limits of the Roman town (under Roman law it was illegal to bury the deceased inside the town perimeter), clustering outside the north gate, east gate (St Pancras and Neddlemakers/Hornet sites) and west gate. The discovery of a skeleton with 'a large number of silver coins in a pot' in 1817 just outside the south gate may hint at a further area of burial in this area (Down 1988, 59). Over 300 cremations and nine inhumations have now been recovered from the St Pancras cemetery (*28*), spanning the period AD 70 to the early third century (Down and Magilton 1993, 87), with a further 16 inhumations having been retrieved from the Needlemakers/Hornet site to the immediate south and south-west. Cremation appears to have formed the earliest burial type in the St Pancras cemetery (Down and Rule 1971). A variety of depositional forms and grave goods were recorded by Alec Down during the course of the excavations at St Pancras, one curious observation being that all artefacts set down with the deceased, including hairpins, brooches, needles and pottery vessels, appeared to have been damaged or broken prior to burial. 'The pattern is too regular to be coincidental and it seems that only articles which were ritually 'killed', or were unsuitable for use by the living, were acceptable as grave goods' (Down 1988, 62).

The different forms of burial rite noted at St Pancras included:

(i)   single vessel deposition (cremation in the urn)

(ii)   deposition in or with a wooden box containing a combination of drinking vessels, food, footwear and sometimes jewellery, lamps and/or, lampholders (*29*)

28 Chichester: cremation deposits within the St Pancras cemetery (Area 4, Trench G) as revealed in 1965. © *Chichester District Council*

(iii)   deposition in a tiled cist

(iv)   deposition of drinking vessels in a crescent or semicircular shape with the cremation scattered in-between

(v)   deposition with or in an inverted vessel

(vi)   deposition in a vessel with a coin

Although the popular modern stereotype of Roman burial is the placement of a coin with the deceased (either with the cremation or in the mouth of an inhumation), ostensibly to pay Charon, ferryman to the underworld, few of the burials found around Chichester appear to have respected this concept, with only six out of the 326 cremations burials from St Pancras (and only one inhumation in the Westgate cemetery and one in the Needlemakers) registering the custom. None of the Needlemakers inhumations (*30*) appeared to predate the mid-to-late fourth century. Two of the bodies may possibly have been decapitated prior to burial (Down 1981, 95).

Excavations conducted across the cemetery in the former gardens of the Theological College in the area of Westgate in 1985 and 1987 revealed two main phases of deposition. The earliest phase seems to have represented by crouched inhumations (the body lying on one side with the knees brought up towards the chin). These were generally on a north–south alignment and may date to the third century AD. In the second phase of deposition, which possibly occurred in the mid-fourth century, the recorded burial rite appeared fairly consistent, with east–west aligned bodies on their backs in an extended position, hands resting in the pelvis area. Few grave goods could be identified, much of the pottery associated with the skeletons possibly having been deposited in the form of grave backfill. The presence of nails, especially in those graves approximating an east–west orientation, suggested the former presence of timber coffins whilst non-nail burials may presumably have been deposited in shrouds. Two high-status bodies were buried in lead coffins. The positions of the later graves appear to have been carefully planned in rows, with little or no areas of intercutting (Down and Magilton 1993, 76-7). In order to achieve this successfully, each grave plot may well have been marked on the surface. It is possible that some or all of the later inhumations recovered from the Westgate site were Christian, an east–west alignment being the major feature of burial within this religion. In the absence of clear supporting archaeological evidence however, this must remain speculative (Down and Magilton 1993, 84-5).

Our only other evidence for the population of Roman Chichester, aside from the physical remains of the deceased, comes from those individuals specifically named on monumental inscriptions. We have already noted two of the more prominent benefactors of *Noviomagus*, Tiberius Claudius Togidubnus and Gaius Sallustius Lucullus, cited on three major dedications, only two of which survive

29 Chichester: an inhumation (burial No. 193) disturbing earlier 'box burial' cremation (No. 194) from the St Pancras cemetery excavated in 1965. 194 has been deposited with an urn, a flagon, three plates, three dishes (two of high status Samian), a beaker, an iron lampholder, an iron spike and a pair of hobnailed sandals. The inhumation is lying on its right side, knees drawn up in a crouched position. © *Chichester District Council*

to this day. Togidubnus no doubt helped the early development of Chichester (as well as Silchester, Winchester and Bath) during the reign of the emperor Nero, and sponsorship of great works such as the building of the, still unlocated, temple to Neptune and Minerva. Lucullus, on the other hand, probably oversaw the major redevelopment of the city, formalising the street grid and establishing the forum, basilica, public baths and amphitheatre, all of which date to the time of his rise to power in the late first century AD. Whether his father, Amminus, mentioned in the inscription from the Little Anchor Inn in North Street, ever returned to the Chichester area after Claudius' annexation of southern Britain in AD 43, we shall probably never know (see chapter 3).

Another mid-to-late first-century benefactor of *Noviomagus* is specifically named as 'Pudens son of Pudentinus' who 'donated the site' on which Togidubnus' great temple was built. Sadly we know nothing about him, his connections to *Noviomagus*

30 Chichester: two fourth-century inhumations from the Eastgate, Needlemakers cemetery. The fully articulated skeleton (burial No. 13) was originally in a coffin and had a coin of Constantine I, minted between AD 330-37, in the skull (presumably to pay Charon). The deposition of No. 13 disturbed an earlier grave (No. 14), removing the right leg. This was eventually replaced in the grave fill of burial 13 (to the left of the photograph). © *Chichester District Council*

31 Chichester: tombstone of
Boudicca Aelia Cauva, aged 36,
found near to the south gate in
1833. © *Chichester District Council*

or how he ended up owning land there. It is possible that Pudens was a local
business magnate, profiting from heightened Roman activity in the area, or was an
expatriate making it rich in the newly acquired province. Given that he possessed
land in Chichester, and was able to donate at least some of it to Togidubnus for
the construction of his temple (and was keen to have that fact recorded on a
monumental inscription), it is probable that Pudens held office as a city councillor
(*decurion*) serving on the *ordo*, possibly even as one of the annually elected *duoviri
iuridicundo*. His name sounds plausibly Roman and, as such, it will have effectively
masked any tribal or ethnic background.

Four further individuals are cited, albeit partially, in the monumental inscriptions
of Chichester. A backfilled pit from the Needlemakers site, just outside the east gate
produced a fragmentary text telling us that '…us the Treasurer' set the dedication
to 'the Mother Goddesses of the Homeland' at 'his own expense' (chapter 9: Down
1988, 23). Sadly, the treasurer's name is lost. It is further difficult to know what he
may have been treasurer of, or indeed from which 'homeland' the mother goddess
was ultimately derived. Whatever his background, the treasurer was clearly wealthy
and was no doubt hoping that, as with Pudens, a religious dedication may increase
his local political standing. By recording the fact on an inscribed stone, he was
further advertising his generosity to the good people of *Noviomagus*.

Three tombstones, all broken up and reused in the town fortifications of Chichester
during the later third century (when building stone was at a premium), provide an
extremely fragmentary, but tantalising glimpse into the lives of the more ordinary
citizens of the town. Two examples of sandstone were found close to the south gate
(which may further point to the former presence of a cemetery in this area). The
first (*31*), discovered in 1833 (RIB 94), bears part of an inscription reading:

...CCA AELIA
...CAVVA
FIL AN XXXVI

which has been translated and expanded (Collingwood and Wright 1995, 28) to:

Boudicca Aelia Cauva, daughter of...aged 36

or possibly:

Boudicca Aelia of the Cauvan tribe...aged 36

The expansion of '...CCA' to 'Boudicca' is obviously speculative. To be fair though, the missing element of the text related to a feminine Celtic name and Boudicca certainly fits. Nothing is known of a specific 'Cauvan' tribe, but given what has already been noted about tribes and clan names (chapter 4), it is possible that a Cauvan group did exist in the area, simply not appearing in later Roman geographical listings. More likely perhaps, Cauva was a personal, ethnic name (British or Gallic) that survived the Romanising process.

Another partial inscription (RIB 95), representing two thirds of a tombstone (*32*), the left side of which was decorated, reads:

CATIA...
CENSORIN...
AN XXIII...

Which may be translated as:

Catia Censorina, aged 23 years

or alternatively:

Catia, wife (or possibly daughter) of Censorinus aged 23

Loss of the right third of the inscription means that we are uncertain as to Catia's full name or whether she was related to a 'Censorinus', as either daughter or wife. Both names are solidly Roman however, so 'Catia Censorina' would have been a perfectly acceptable name for a young lady moving within late first-century Romano-British society in *Noviomagus*. The loss of text also means we that we cannot be sure whether Catia was 23 or 24 when she passed away (a fourth 'I' could have been removed). Whatever the case, it is clear that the lives of both Catia and Boudicca Aelia were both cut short at a tragically early age.

Above: 32 Chichester: tombstone of Catia Censorina, aged 23, found near to the south gate in 1833. © *Chichester District Council*

Right: 33 Chichester: tombstone of an unknown porter (*atriarius*), aged 85, found within the makeup of the south-eastern sector city wall in 1809. Now lost. © *Chichester District Council*

The third piece of a Roman tombstone (RIB 93) was found in 1809, during the removal of a section of town wall in the south-eastern sector of Chichester (Collingwood and Wright 1995, 27). Lost for 80 years, the stone was discovered for a second time, slightly worse for wear, in the gardens of the Bishop of Chichester. Unfortunately it has since disappeared again, but thankfully a record was made at the time of its rediscovery (*33*):

...M
...NUS AT
...ARIUS
...LXXXV

which has been translated and expanded to read:

To the gods of the Underworld, ... nus the porter, aged 85 years

As with the treasurer of 'the Mother Goddesses of the Homeland' dedication, the name of the deceased in this tombstone is frustratingly incomplete. His job description is also difficult to decipher, although *atriarius* or 'porter' seems a fair bet from the fragmentary evidence. His age, at 85, is one of the longest life-spans recorded from a tombstone anywhere in Britain and shows, despite the sad evidence recorded from the tombs of Catia Censorina and Boudicca Aelia Cauva, that it was possible to live a long and prosperous life in the New Market town of the Regini.

6

PALACES

On the arid stretch of tarmac that is the A27, a small, brown tourist sign points to a welcome oasis of calm, just to the south of bustling modern Chichester. Having negotiated the roundabout, the visitor's car glides on through a pretty Sussex village and eventually to a 1960s housing estate and the ultimate destination: 'Fishbourne Roman palace'.

Fishbourne represents one of the great success stories of British twentieth-century archaeology. Late in 1960, a mechanical digger, excavating a trench for a water main through an area of pasture to the north of Fishbourne village, hit something solid and came to a juddering stop. The driver, inspecting the front bucket of his machine, realised that he had just dug his way through a mass of stone, brick and tile. News of the discovery was relayed to the chief engineer and thence to members of the Chichester Civic Society. 'We were incredulous', Barry Cunliffe was later to recall, 'for the rubble clearly came from a substantial Roman building constructed of fine squared, greensand blocks, with plastered and painted walls and mosaic floors' (Cunliffe in Manley and Rudkin 2003, 1). Slowly, realisation dawned that this was not the usual, 'run of the mill' Roman building, but something really quite exceptional.

Roman remains had been sporadically recorded from the Fishbourne area since at least 1805, when a tessellated pavement and the base of a column were found during the construction of the Bull's Head. In 1812, 'more subterranean remains' were found, whilst in 1929, a 'quantity of Roman material' was recovered from the nearby Rectory. In 1936, a mosaic was found close to the line of the current A259. Fishbourne was evidently the site of some importance in the Roman period but, prior to 1961, no one had even considered that 'all the fragments belonged to a single structure' (Cunliffe 1998, 12).

Trial excavations swiftly followed, developing into a larger term project of investigation, which lasted until 1969, a full report being published with commendable speed two years later. By this time the land upon which the Roman remains lay had been acquired by Ivan Margary on behalf of the Sussex Archaeological Society, with a view to erecting a cover building and preserving the remains from road building and housing development. From its opening in 1968, Fishbourne Roman palace has become one of the largest and most successful tourist attractions of southern England.

FISHBOURNE: THE 'PROTO PALACE'

In AD 60, the revolt of queen Boudica, which had threatened the very existence of the fledgling Roman province of Britain, ended following a pitched battle between the rebellious tribes and the remnants of the Roman military garrison (the *XIV Gemina* and *XX Valeria* legions). Throughout the winter of AD 60/61, all traces of the insurgency were hunted down by the vengeful Roman administration, Tacitus noting dryly that 'any tribe that had wavered in its loyalty or had been hostile was ravaged with fire and sword' (Tacitus *Annals* XIV, 38).

One tribe that had not wavered in its loyalty, and which indeed seems to have been deliberately targeted by Boudica in an early form of ethnic cleansing, was the western Catuvellauni whose tribal capital was the city of *Verulamium* (modern-day St Albans). As already noted (in chapter 2), Togidubnus of the Catuvellauni must have played a significant role during the revolt, protecting Roman (and his own) interests and holding all the lands to the south of the Thames. Togidubnus may well have engaged the army of Boudica on the field of battle, repeating his actions against Caratacus when bringing aid to the first governor of Britain, Aulus Plautius, in AD 43. Unfortunately, Togidubnus' combat status during the revolt is unknown, though as he apparently 'remained loyal' down to the latter decades of the first century AD (Tacitus *Agricola* 14), it is likely that his role in helping to suppress the rebellion was significant (contrary to the version that Tacitus relates in the *Annals*). Whatever the reality of the story, it is interesting that within a few years of the revolt having been crushed, a series of wealthy civilian houses were being constructed across West Sussex, an area largely unaffected by the uprising. Perhaps it was now, following the reclamation of southern Britain by Rome, that the followers of Togidubnus, having weathered the storm, were honoured by (or gave themselves) the name Regini: 'the proud ones.'

The best known, and certainly better investigated, of all the early Roman building projects of this period in Sussex is the so-called 'Proto Palace' at Fishbourne, a structure that underlies the south-eastern quadrant of the later 'palace proper' visible today. The Proto Palace comprises a substantial, stone-built Courtyard House of a type familiar in the Roman Mediterranean (*34* and *colour plate 2*). Its construction necessitated the tearing down of all existing timber buildings on the site, some of which were of military origin, levelling the ground surface and the diversion of at least one stream. Sadly, it has not been possible to excavate all of the building, as much of it lies beneath the modern A259 and the houses which front it, but of the small area investigated, it has been possible to calculate that its footprint measured at least 58m x 46m.

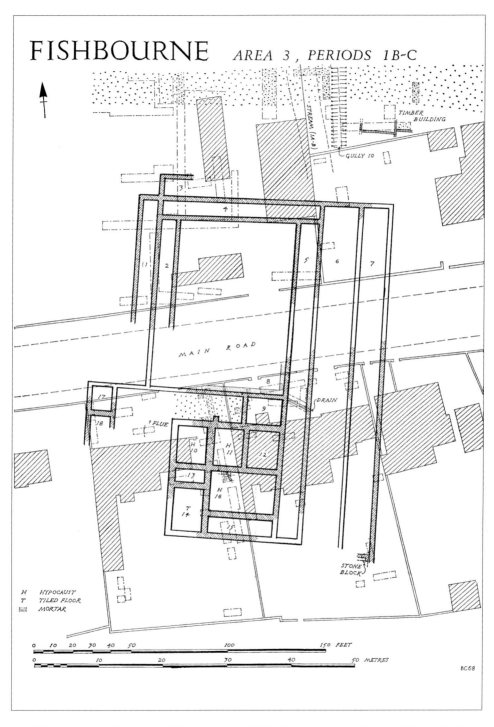

FISHBOURNE *AREA 3, PERIODS 1B-C*

TIMBER BUILDING

GULLY 10

STREAM (1A-B)

3

4

1

2

5   6   7

MAIN ROAD

8

17

DRAIN

18

9

FLUE

H 10   H 11   12

13

H 16

T 14   15

STONE BLOCK

H   *HYPOCAUST*
T   *TILED FLOOR*
     MORTAR

0 10 20 30 40 50   100   150 *FEET*

0   10   20   30   40   50 *METRES*

BC68

34 Fishbourne: plan of the Proto Palace, a substantial Mediterranean-style Courtyard House built in the mid AD 60s. The plan remains incomplete due to the presence of modern houses and a road.
© *Institute of Archaeology, Oxford and Sussex Archaeological Society*

Building works appear to have begun for the structure in the mid-AD 60s (Cunliffe 1971, 58), within a few years of the Boudican revolt. An alternative constructional date for the Proto Palace of AD 75-80 has, however, also been proposed (Black 1987, 84-5). Building works across the site as a whole would certainly have taken some time and it is possible, from a conception in the mid-AD 60s, that construction and alteration was ongoing some 10 years later. When complete, the main building appears to have comprised four major elements: a courtyard or garden surrounded by a colonnade, a bathhouse and two separate domestic ranges (along the eastern and westernmost sides: Cunliffe 1998, 41-2). Little is known about the use, function and full extent of the majority of rooms within the Proto Palace, with the obvious exception of the built space at the south-eastern corner. The suite of rooms established here appear to have been designed as a bathhouse, possessing a hot range, including three possible *caldaria* heated by *hypocausts*, a *tepidarium*, a *frigidarium* and a cold immersion bath. Much of its basic plan appears to have been retained within the later 'palace proper'.

Although the Proto Palace was incorporated into the later, larger structure, its building materials being cannibalised for the redevelopment, much can still be said about the style and form of the early phase. Rubble from the rebuild shows that the primary building possessed an exquisite level of interior décor. Fragments of painted plaster indicate the former presence of a 0.9m-high blue/black dado overlaid with floral designs in yellow, green and white. Above this, the wall plaster was separated into rectangular panels of blue, red and yellow on a blue/green background overlaid with a further series of floral designs in white, yellow and red. The whole effect was topped off by a painted cornice. Some walls appear to have been further subdivided by stucco pilasters of fluted design (Cunliffe 1998, 44).

No floor levels survived intact from this early phase, though fragments incorporated within the building rubble of later phases, suggest a range of predominantly black and white mosaics and simple pavements (*35*) composed of large pieces of cut stone (*opus sectile*). Many different varieties of stone were used in the building, including marble from eastern Gaul and Italy, siltstones from the Sussex Weald and Purbeck Marble, probably from Dorset. Large pieces of ornamental stone, reused as the packing for timber posts in the later building, show that parts of the Proto Palace possessed columns capped with Corinthian capitals (*36*). A further fragment of carved stone, this time the face of a young man (see below) further hint at the level of decoration attained by this building.

All this represents one of the earliest examples of Roman interior décor yet recovered from a domestic site in Britain. We do not know much about how, if at all, the interiors of Late Iron Age houses were decorated, but expansive use of colour on the walls, solid decorative floors and ornate stonework were clearly all new to the domestic structures of the British Isles. To someone brought up at the heart of the Roman world, such things would have appeared normal, but to the indigenous Briton, whose contact with Rome had been through trade and exchange or through a more violent form of interaction on the battlefield, such a repertoire of material would have been mind-blowing.

35 Fishbourne:
pieces of cut stone
(*opus sectile*) from
the floors of the
Neronian Proto
Palace. © *Institute
of Archaeology,
Oxford and Sussex
Archaeological
Society*

The Proto Palace, though undoubtedly formidable, was only one of a number of
buildings set out at Fishbourne in the mid-AD 60s (*37*). To the immediate north-
east of the main range lay a substantial stone-built structure known, somewhat
unromantically, as 'Building 3' (Manley and Rudkin 2003). Building 3 comprised
a quadrangle of rooms arranged around a rectangular courtyard. Dating evidence
suggested a major building phase in the latter half of the first century AD, though
the origins of the structure may have been in an earlier period. To the north-west
of the Proto Palace lay Building M1, an enigmatic and apparently unfinished
structure which seems to mirror certain aspects of design apparent in the later
'palace proper' (Cunliffe 1998, 46-7). Neither Building 1 nor 3 make much sense
from the incomplete areas exposed to date, although 1 may represent an additional
domestic range, possibly with a large entrance hall, whilst 3 may have served in an
administrative capacity or as a shrine.

Left: 36 Fishbourne:
a Corinthian capital,
reconstructed from
smashed fragments
reused in later building
works, from the top
of a column originally
forming part of the
Proto Palace. © *Institute
of Archaeology, Oxford
and Sussex Archaeological
Society*

Below: 37 Fishbourne:
an as yet incomplete
plan of the buildings of
the Proto Palace phase,
constructed between
the mid-AD 60s and late
AD 80s. *Redrawn from
Manley and Rudkin 2003*

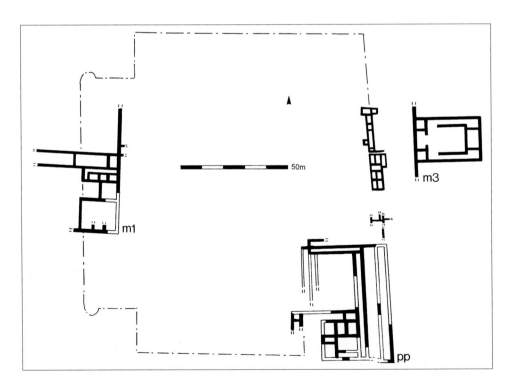

The area covered by this civilian building project was evidently massive, but how can this early phase of Roman architecture in West Sussex be interpreted? A potential clue may be offered by a building development being undertaken in Rome at precisely the same time as that of the Fishbourne complex: the *Domus Aurea*.

NERO AND THE *DOMUS AUREA*

The *Domus Aurea*, or 'Golden House', is the name given to the complex of buildings designed by the architects Severus and Celer for the emperor Nero following the great fire that swept Rome in AD 64. The fire, which Tacitus described as being 'more terrible than any other that has struck Rome in terms of the violence of the flames' (Tacitus, *Annals* XV, 38) burned for well over a week and devastated a large area of the city. Of Rome's 14 districts, three were completely destroyed whilst a further seven were badly damaged. Nero, who had been out of the city when the fire had started, returned to find part of his new imperial residence, the *Domus Transitoria*, ablaze. Taking shelter with his retinue, the emperor 'dressed up in theatrical clothes' and proceeded to sing 'of the destruction of Troy' (Suetonius, *Nero* 38), an act which perhaps understandably did not endear him to later Roman historians. When the flames finally abated, Nero helped to coordinate the relief effort and then, in what turned out to be a public relations catastrophe, cleared an area of around 80ha within the old city centre on which he planned to build his new home from Rome.

The sheer extravagance of the project was truly shocking. Nero retained the more modest buildings of his imperial predecessors on the Palatine, but in the *Domus Aurea* he created an artificial rural idyll in the very heart of the city. The building project commissioned by the emperor comprised, not a single great house or palace, but 'an imposing agglomeration of luxurious villas, bath buildings and pleasure spots' (Segala and Sciortino 1999, 13) set across the Esquiline and Caelian hills and the entire valley between them. The whole was aesthetically scattered across an artificial parkscape, a humanly constructed landscape of forests, sacred groves, colonnades and an ornamental lake which was 'more like a sea than a pool' (Suetonius *Nero*, XXXI, 1). The former heart of the city was gouged out by this rustic folly; the reality of town life replaced by a garish fantasy. Like all aristocratic families in Rome, the emperor now had his town house and rural retreat, but 'where Nero beat them all was in convenience' (Ball 2003, 6).

And what of the buildings themselves? Those structures in which the emperor chose to entertain his guests were 'overlain with gold and studded with precious stones and mother of pearl' scoffs Suetonius, adding:

> all the dining rooms had ceilings of fretted ivory, the panels of which could slide back
> and let a rain of flowers or perfume from hidden sprinklers, fall down upon his guests.
> (Suetonius *Nero* XXXI, 2)

Little of this grand design survives, later emperors choosing to ignore, and then finally demolish the houses of Rome's foremost megalomaniac. One section, known as the Esquiline Wing (or the 'Pavilion of the Oppian Hill') survived only because its rooms were filled with rubble in the AD 70s so that the ground level could be raised in order to build the great Flavian Amphitheatre, known to history as the Colosseum. The buried remains of the Esquiline Wing lay forgotten until the end of the fifteenth century. When the subterranean structure was finally explored, the painted walls of Nero's palace caused quite a stir. Among the frequent visitors to the site were the Renaissance artists Perugino, Ghirlandaio, Pinturicchio, Filippino Lippi and Raphael, all of whom were inspired by the freshness of the paintwork, the dramatic use of colour and texture and the breathtaking beauty of the design.

The rich internal schemes of the *Domus Aurea* were further supplemented by a range of Hellenistic sculptures, generated through the 'brutal pillaging' of Greece by Nero (Pliny, *Natural History*, XXXIV, 48). Among the statues looted by the First Citizen of Rome were various representations of Alexander the Great (to whom Nero felt a natural affinity), from Ephesus and a range of pieces hacked from a monument dedicated to Attalus I from the Acropolis in Pergamun. The pieces removed from Pergamun are of particular interest, for they were part of a victory group designed to commemorate the defeat of the Galatians by king Attalus in around 230 BC. The Galatians, a vigorous Celtic people, were originally depicted at the very moment of their defeat, committing a mass act of suicide. Two of the more famous pieces from the group show a Celtic noblemen, his cloak flung back over his shoulder, plunging his sword through his heart (via his clavicular cavity) having just slit the throat of his wife. A second, and no less famous piece, universally referred to as 'the Dying Gaul', depicts a mortally wounded Celtic warrior, naked but for his gold neck ring or torc, collapsing in agony onto his shield. The significance of Nero's acquisition of these pieces has never fully been addressed, but it is evident that, three years on from the humiliating events of the Boudican revolt in Britain, Nero was keen to relish his victory over the Celtic people.

The uprising led by queen Boudica in AD 60/1 had levelled at least three Roman cities, crushed a legion (the *IX Hispana*) and resulted in the deaths of many thousands of citizens, provincials, officials and natives. The whole of Rome's investment in Britain had been at stake and, had it not been for the swift action of the governor, Suetonius Paulinus, combined with the vital intervention of king Tiberius Claudius Togidubnus (as argued in chapter 2), the loss of Britain would have been inevitable. If the revolt had succeeded, then the political fallout for Nero and his advisors would have been severe, for many in Rome had already noted that a primary grievance of the British rebels had been the rapaciousness of the emperor and his delegated officials. At the end of the revolt, many of the British leaders, Boudica included, took their own lives rather than risk capture (Tacitus *Annals* XIV, 37), mirroring the final actions of the defeated Galatians. How Nero must have enjoyed overseeing the installation of the Pergamun figures within the *Domus Aurea*. Their setting, probably in the Octagon Suite, the main banqueting hall of the Esquiline Wing (Segala and Sciortino 1999, 41), would have been an eternal monument to his victory over the forces of evil. The graphic scenes of Celtic defeat, humiliation and death would artistically mask just how close Nero himself had been to catastrophe.

A final element in the concept of the *Domus Aurea* was an immense statue, the *Colossus Neroni,* which stood in the great atrium on the Velian Hill. The Colossus was a representation of the sun god Sol (Helios) inspired, in all probability, by the Colossus of Rhodes, formerly one of the Seven Wonders of the Ancient World. The figure, designed by the Greek sculptor Zenodorus, stood over 35m in height and dominated the main entrance to the rural palace complex. Cast in bronze, the figure stood nude, apart from a crown of solar rays (each measuring around 6m in length) and held a globe in its left, slightly outstretched hand. What worried the Roman elite about the Colossus, was not so much the extravagance of the statue, but the arrogance of the statement, for Nero had his own facial features replace those of the sun god. To many, this was the ultimate statement of absolute power; the final act of an egotistical madman.

FISHBOURNE AND THE *DOMUS AUREA*

Although the *Domus Aurea* in Rome and the buildings that comprise the earliest phase of civilian building at Fishbourne are of vastly differing scale, it is clear that both possess the same central conceit: a range of Romanised buildings scattered aesthetically across a rural setting. The internal decoration evident in Fishbourne's Mediterranean-style Courtyard House, the Proto Palace, is also clearly influenced by that of Nero's grand design in Rome, right down to the use of marble, ornate capitals, black and white tessellated floors and richly decorated wall plaster. This is, perhaps, unsurprising given the strong links, already noted (chapters 2 and 3) between the British and Roman aristocracy.

Unfortunately we do not know, as yet, the full extent of building works at Fishbourne. Despite this, it is evident that the complex, and it is important to remember that the primary phase comprises far more than just the Courtyard House known as the Proto Palace, was probably designed as a rural retreat, like the villas of the Roman elite and the *Domus Aurea* of Nero. The occupant of such a rural home would have been an important member of the new Romano-British elite whose normal daily routine was probably centred upon the city; in this case the developing urban sprawl of nearby Chichester. Unlike Nero's pleasure dome, set around an artificial lake, the Fishbourne villa complex faced out across Chichester Harbour, a setting still found desirable by today's multimillionaire property developers. 'Who then', to paraphrase a modern piece of daytime television, 'would have lived in a house like this?'. Was it designed as the official residence of a Roman administrator, built in order to lessen 'the barbarian horrors of Britain' (Reece 1988, 8), or the rural retreat of a well-Romanised Briton?

There is a clear indication of Nero's delight over the defeat of Boudica in his use of dead and dying Celtic figures within the *Domus Aurea*, and it is highly likely that his pleasure, not to say sense of relief at victory, may have spilled over into rewarding those members of the native elite who had not sided with the rebels. The wealth and extravagant levels of expenditure displayed within the first major civilian phase at Fishbourne, could very well be the direct result of such imperial patronage. We have already noted a dedication made by an ethnic Briton called Tiberius Claudius Togidubnus to the 'Divine House' (almost certainly the Julio-Claudian house of Nero) in Chichester (RIB 91). To this may be added the discovery of a fine gold signet ring (*colour plate 3*) inscribed with the name Tiberius Claudius Catuarus, recovered from an excavation to the immediate east of the Fishbourne site (Tomlin 1997). In the first century AD, only Roman citizens of the highest rank were permitted to wear gold rings, and only with the explicit permission of the emperor. We do not know who Catuarus was, but he has a Romanised Celtic name and was presumably of equivalent social standing to Togidubnus.

Togidubnus and Catuarus, both of British descent, were evidently of sufficient power, position and status within Roman society, to commission the building of the Proto Palace. Only the discovery of an inscription from Fishbourne saying something akin to '*Hic habitat Togidubnus*' or '*Hic habitat Catuarus*' would settle the matter of ownership from an archaeological perspective (cf. Reece 1988, 8).

HEADS OF STONE

Aside from the 'Togidubnus inscription' (RIB 91) and the vow of loyalty made by 'the senate' of *Noviomagus* to Nero, set up in AD 58 or 59 (RIB 92), two further links between the Proto Palace development of Fishbourne and the emperor Nero Claudius Caesar Drusus Germanicus are worth noting here. The first is a life-sized marble head of a young man (*38*) found during the course of the 1961-69 excavations at Fishbourne. The head has been very badly damaged in antiquity, with only part of the face, comprising the right ear, right cheek, the lower right eyelid, lower nose (the tip of which is missing), mouth, chin (part of which is also missing), and small areas of the neck, right temple and hair surviving. Enough is present, however, to demonstrate that this was a sensitive and highly accomplished piece created by a sculptor who was undoubtedly a master of his game.

We must assume, unless the sculpture was an on-site portrait commission, that the head was part of a larger piece, a full, three-dimensional, freestanding figure. The sculpture had been decapitated, the head being smashed into pieces, fragments being unceremoniously dumped into the disturbed foundations of the palace proper. As a Mediterranean import, the figure would undoubtedly have been expensive, something that makes its treatment and final place of repose appear all the more unusual. Was this destruction and burial of the head something that occurred when

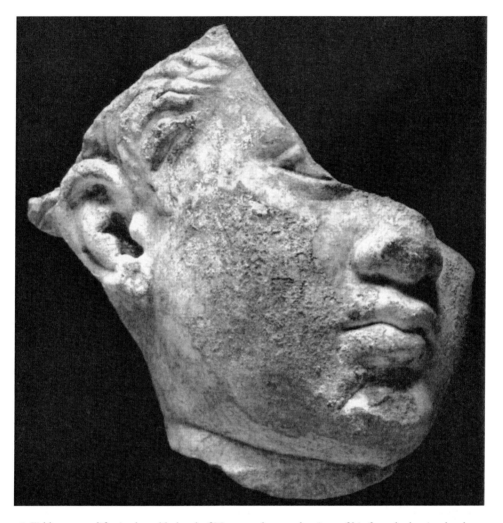

38 Fishbourne: a life-sized marble head of Nero, aged 14, at the time of his formal adoption by the emperor Claudius in AD 51, found during the course of the 1961-69 excavations. The image, which formed part of the Proto Palace phase, has been forcibly removed from the body and smashed, probably during the process of *damnatio memoriae*, which followed Nero's death in AD 68. The pieces were then symbolically reused in the foundations of the later palace. © *Institute of Archaeology, Oxford and Sussex Archaeological Society*

the palace site was being robbed, following its fiery demise in the later third century AD? Possibly. It is perhaps more likely that the piece represented an architectural detail from an earlier constructional phase of the palace and was simply broken and reused during the huge redevelopment of the site in the later first century. In this, the head would have been treated in much the same way as the Corinthian capitals of the Proto Palace which were discovered smashed and dumped in the post-packing of the palace period gardens (Cunliffe 1971b, 11-14).

The image is an intriguing one and the style suggests a life-like portrait of a very real individual, rather than an idealised image of a god or mythological figure. In the initial analysis of the head, Jocelyn Toynbee observed that 'the rounded cheeks, the full, curving lips, and the unformed features, especially as seen in profile, are definitely suggestive of early youth' (Toynbee in Cunliffe 1971b, 156). Who then was the portrait of? Few recognisable features survive to be able to make a firm identification. Toynbee noted that the artistic treatment was suggestive of a young man from the imperial, Julio-Claudian family, though she could not see why the owner of the Proto Palace 'would have wished to adorn it with the portrait of a child who was still at so undeveloped a physiognomic stage, unless he were his own offspring' (Toynbee in Cunliffe 1971b, 156).

In recent years the hypothesis has developed from Toynbee's comments concerning the 'offspring' of the palace owner towards the view that: *if* Fishbourne palace had been designed for king Togidubnus then the young man depicted in marble *could be* a portrait of his son and, *if* so, then the sculpture *may* provide a clue as to the appearance of the king himself. This is an intriguing and attractive hypothesis, but unfortunately is also an entirely self-perpetuating one based upon a near total absence of hard fact. Toynbee's initial view concerning the possible representation of a younger member of the imperial house is one that has unfortunately not been developed for, in the case of the Fishbourne Proto Palace, there is indeed every reason why the owner would have wished to adorn it with a portrait of a child, especially if that child was the adopted son and heir to the divine emperor Claudius.

Our view of the emperor Nero Claudius Drusus Germanicus is an unflattering one. Suetonius, in his *Lives of the Twelve Caesars* observed that Nero:

> was about average height, his body marked with spots and malodorous. His hair was light blond. His features were regular rather than attractive. His eyes were blue and somewhat weak. His neck was over thick, his belly prominent, and his legs very slender ... He was utterly shameless in the care of his person and in his dress, always having his hair arranged in tiers of curls, and during the trip to Greece also letting it grow long and hang down behind; and he often appeared in public unshod and in a dining-robe with a handkerchief bound about his neck. (Suetonius *Nero*, 51)

Suetonius was undoubtedly exaggerating the more unpleasant side of the Nero's character, as one would expect for an emperor who, after death, was declared an enemy of the Roman people. Having said that, it is clear that the later portraits of Nero, on coins or in stone, all show the marked effects of a debauched existence; a lifestyle of overfeeding and under exercise. The Nero that we see from AD 64 until his death, aged only 32, in AD 68 is heavy in the face, with prominent chins and a thick neck. We may wonder why he permitted the use of such images, for modern dictators, politicians and celebrities usually prefer to be portrayed as eternally youthful and athletic, even if the reality is very different. To the ancient mind, however, obesity was frequently used as an obvious signifier of wealth, luxury and success. An over-fleshy image of the First Citizen would have clearly and effectively communicated his god-like status to the Roman people.

Nero's early official portraits, however, are quite unlike those produced in the final years of his life. The man we see staring out from images produced at the time of his official adoption by the emperor Claudius in AD 51, when Nero was just 14 years of age, are slender and boyish

> with a coiffure of long comma shaped locks parted near the centre of the forehead, lengthy sideburns curl in front of the ears. The facial features are smooth and regular. Well formed, almond shaped eyes, with crisply delineated upper and lower lids are set beneath straight brows. The nose is aquiline. The mouth consists of full upper and receding lower lip. The chin is rounded and the ears protrude from the head. (Varner 2004, 46)

Two of the best-known examples of the teenage Nero are preserved in the Museo Nazionale d'Antichita in Parma and the Musee du Louvre in Paris. Both stone representations show a placid, toga-wearing youth, arms slightly outstretched. The eyes, nose, ears and hairstyle are all instantly recognisable as Nero, though there is no indication of the monster to come. A third version of the younger Nero, possibly manufactured at the time of his accession to the imperial throne in AD 54, has been recorded from Britain. The head, this time made of bronze, was recovered from the river Alde at Rendham, near Saxmundham in Suffolk in 1907 and is now on prominent display in the British Museum where it is misidentified as 'a representation of the emperor Claudius'. That it is not Claudius, is plain to see (Varner 2004, 72-3), and it is interesting to observe that, as with the majority of images of Nero throughout the empire, the Suffolk example had been decapitated and mutilated before being dumped in a river; the axe blow to the back of the neck (and jagged tear around the throat), clearly tells the story of a forcible removal.

The marble head from Fishbourne would, after the Saxmundham head, appear to represent the second portrait of Nero as a young man recovered from Britain. The 'rounded cheeks' and 'full, curving lips' observed by Toynbee (Toynbee in Cunliffe 1971b, 156) exactly match the features of the teenage heir of Claudius on display in Parma, Paris and London, as do the rounded lower face, slightly protruding ears, curving locks of hair and almond-shaped eyes. The reuse of the head in the redesigned palace at Fishbourne suggests that, as with the Corithian capitals already described (see above) that the image of the youthful Nero had originally formed part of the Proto Palace phase. Whether it had graced the atrium of the main domestic structure or one of the other buildings of the early phase (such as the enigmatic 'Building 3': Manley and Rudkin 2003), is ultimately impossible to say.

The Fishbourne head has been forcibly removed from the body whilst substantial blows to the head have fragmented the image, further damage being inflicted upon the nose and chin. This seems to follow very closely the process of *damnatio memoriae*, a post mortem mutilation inflicted upon Nero Claudius Drusus Germanicus and everything he was associated with. Following his death in AD 68, Nero was declared a *hostis* (hostile element) by the senate; an evildoer whose life and deeds required purging from collective memory of the Roman people. His monuments were rededicated, his name removed from inscriptions and his image overthrown. The destruction of a sculpture of the young *princeps* (First Citizen) would be totally in line with such an empire-wide practice. The dumping of the smashed fragments into the foundations of a new palace, which swept away all trace of the Nero-inspired early phase, would probably further be seen as an entirely appropriate fate for the disgraced emperor.

The second monumental head from the Chichester / Fishbourne area is perhaps more exciting, not to say explosive, for it seems to expressly link the design phase of the Fishbourne Proto Palace complex with that of the *Domus Aurea* in Rome. The head is just larger than twice life-size and has nearly been battered into oblivion (*39*). It was recovered from the margins of Chichester Harbour, 'in the area of Bosham churchyard' at some point prior to 1804 (Chichester HER CD2053). The piece is, at the time of writing, hidden away in a corner of the downstairs gallery in the small, but rather excellent, District Museum at the end of Little London in Chichester. Most visitors to the museum pass by without comment, which is a shame for the piece is nothing less than one of the most important archaeological discoveries from the Roman province of Britain.

The head is clearly an imperial portrait, no other member of Roman aristocracy would have the gall, or possess the relevant permissions, to record their own features in such a way. This was a dramatic statement of status and prestige; a colossal symbol of power. That the face is male, and that it probably once formed part of a full, free-standing piece, seems clear enough, but which emperor, or relative of emperors, is being depicted? Vespasian (AD 69-79) is at times cited as the inspiration, whilst more recent analyses have suggested Trajan (AD 98-117: e.g. Henig 2002, 51, 55). Although damage to the nose and lower face is bad, enough survives of the hairstyle, facial proportions and nature of the eyes, to make a clear and unambiguous identification. Once again it is Nero.

This particular example of the emperor Nero Claudius Drusus Germanicus is an example of imperial portraiture dating to the later half of his reign, as he matured from his post-adoption, boyish persona, but before the excessively fleshy emperor of his final four years. This is third main portrait type of the fifth man to hold the title of *princeps*, a style which can securely be placed as originating between the years AD 59-64 (Varner 2004, 48). The face is thickset and heavy, the lips registering the faintest hint of a smile. Despite the loss of his 'aquiline nose', his eyes are well formed and 'almond-shaped' betraying the crisply delineated lids. The hair is luscious and full, comprising:

> locks which are carefully arranged over the forehead in parallel curves moving from left to right … locks grow long on the nape of the neck and are swept forward. Long sideburns still curl in front of the ears. (Varner 2004, 48-9)

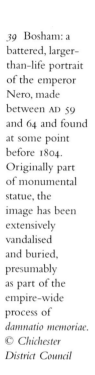

39 Bosham: a battered, larger-than-life portrait of the emperor Nero, made between AD 59 and 64 and found at some point before 1804. Originally part of monumental statue, the image has been extensively vandalised and buried, presumably as part of the empire-wide process of *damnatio memoriae.* © *Chichester District Council*

It is the coiffure that is the most distinctive and recognisable aspect of the Bosham head. The long curling locks of hair that frame the forehead, flick out over the ears and descend the nape of the neck (*40*) are all unmistakably those of the more mature Nero. Good parallels for the style and physiognomy of the Bosham head may be found in surviving examples of later Neronian portrait preserved in the Museo Palatino in Rome, the Glyptothek in Munich and the Worcester Art Gallery in Massachusetts, USA (Varner 2004, fig 82-4).

As with the Fishbourne head, the damage sustained to the face of the Bosham Nero is clear enough: great force has been applied to the nose and chin in an intentional act of vandalism designed to render the face unrecognisable. As a consequence of the *damnatio memoriae* that followed Nero, few well-preserved portraits of the *princeps* survive across the empire, most having been defaced, mutilated or otherwise damaged. Many of those heads that were not smashed or cast out were reformed into the likeness of later emperors. In the British Museum resides a head of Nero

40 Bosham: the colossal stone portrait of Nero from the side. The sculpture may originally have stood in Chichester or at Fishbourne (during the Proto Palace phase) or alternatively it may have been intended as a British version of the *Colossus Neroni*, which stood in the great atrium of the *Domus Aurea* on the Velian Hill in Rome. © *Chichester District Council*

which was recovered from the North African city of Carthage in the mid-1830s, a cast of which today takes pride of place in the museum of Fishbourne. The image is almost unrecognisable as that of the fifth *princeps*, the features having been recarved into the face of Vespasian (AD 69-79). The curling locks of hair across the temple and around the ears and neck, however, are not those of the later emperor and they betray the original source material. The Bosham head was not modified or recarved, rather it seems to have been detached from the body of the imperial statute and buried: an act of *damnatio memoriae* widely repeated elsewhere across the empire.

The identification of a 'colossal statue' of the emperor Nero close to the site of the Fishbourne Proto Palace building project raises a number of issues, not least of all the possibility of a Fishbourne/Bosham colossus akin to that in the formal atrium of the *Domus Aurea* in Rome. A monumental statue to the adopted son of the deified Claudius would not be out of place in this part of Britain, especially if, as already indicated, the Proto Palace development at Fishbourne was intended to mimic the opulence of the grand imperial house. A larger than life statue of Nero situated close to the entrance of the broad open waterways of Chichester would also be appropriate, the original Colossus of Rhodes, upon which the *Colossus Neroni* was based, being designed to guard the approaches to an important Mediterranean harbour.

Unfortunately, the exact context of the Bosham head remains elusive, details surrounding the nature and causes of its discovery being vague, cursory and insubstantial. It is worth noting, however, that the area around Bosham abounds in unusual sculpture, a head of Caligula, a finger from a larger than life statue, a stone torso and a number of unusual altars having been recovered in the last few hundred years (Chichester HER; Kenny 2004). The torso, rebuilt into the structure of Bosham Manor House is particularly worthy of note here for, although it appears to be of different geological type from the Bosham head (and seems to be of a slightly smaller scale), the features portrayed, a cloak fixed to a military cuirass (breastplate), is very similar in style to that beloved of the more athletically posed Neronian figures (e.g. Varner 2004, figs 88 and 89). At the very least it represents another example of an imperial statue of the first or early second century AD derived from a restricted geographical area.

FISHBOURNE: THE PALACE

Whatever the intent and extent of the early phases of civilian building at Fishbourne, one thing is clear: the project was never finished. The Proto Palace was still new and the western structural range (M1) was not completed much above foundation level, before construction was halted and a new and more daring design phase was initiated.

At some stage before the finalisation of the grandiose villa-complex at Fishbourne, the architectural plans were torn up, the existing buildings swept away, and a more extravagant building project undertaken (41 and *colour plate 4*). Curiously, though large areas of the palace site have been archaeologically examined, agreement on a date for the inception of building activity has proved elusive. Barry Cunliffe has drawn attention to the coin assemblages found immediately beneath the primary phase floor levels for, although large numbers of these belonged to the reign of the emperor Vespasian (AD 69-79), none appeared to have been minted after AD 73 (Cunliffe 1971; 1998, 49). AD 73 therefore provides a neat *terminus post quem*, or 'date after which' the site must have been created. The question is how long after AD 73? Many of the coin series appeared to be 'relatively unworn', suggesting that they may not have been long in circulation prior to burial beneath the palace structure. Pottery, especially the imported, high-status Samian wares, also appear to point towards a date 'in the second half of the 70s' (Cunliffe 1998, 49), whilst coins of Vespasian's son Domitian (reigned AD 81-96) recovered from the final phases of construction suggested that certain finishing touches were being conducted by the early 80s.

Ernest Black, in his reanalysis of *The Roman Villas of South-East England* (1996), suggested that the postulated phasing for the construction of the Fishbourne palace was far too early. Looking again at the material recovered from the excavation, Black suggested that although the artefacts provided a useful *terminus post quem* for the building of the palace, they did not, rather crucially, indicate a precise date for the actual commencement of building works (Black 1987, 84-5). Examining the relief-patterned tile used in the construction of the 'palace proper', Black further noted that they were identical to the designs used in the construction of the baths (*thermae*) at Chichester. If, he postulated, it could therefore be taken that palace and urban bathing complex were built at the same time, then 'the date of the construction of

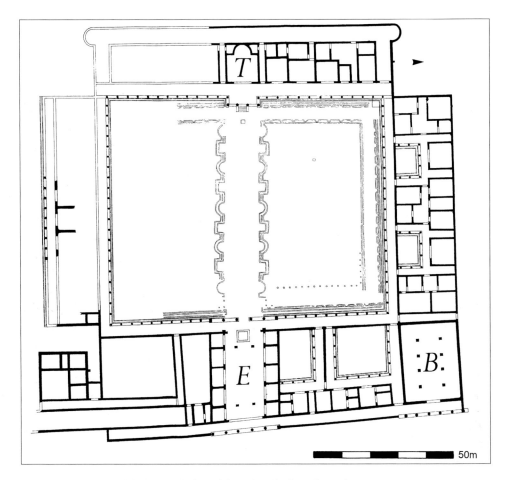

41 Fishbourne: a simplified ground plan of the palace, built in the early AD 90s, a copy in miniature of the emperor Domitian's *Domus Flavia* in Rome. The eastern (public) range is shown at the bottom of the plan, with the grand entrance hall (E) at the centre and the aisled basilica (B) at the extreme bottom right. The apsed *triclinium* (T) is at the centre of the west wing, with the northern guest wing, arranged around two small courtyards, at the right of the figure. The courtyard is shown with ornamental bedding-trenches, whilst the incompletely understood southern (private?) wing is on the far left. *Redrawn from Cunliffe 1971*

the *thermae* then provides a date for the palace' (Black 1987, 86). In Black's model, both the Chichester baths and the primary phase of the 'palace proper' at Fishbourne belonged to the period AD 90-110.

There may yet be a middle way. It has already been noted (at the end of chapter 3), that the palace in Sussex is not entirely without precedent in the Roman world. Although at 4ha (10 acres), Fishbourne represents one of the largest civilian building projects north of the Alps, a 'piece of Italy transplanted into a distant, newly conquered province' (Wilson 2002, 70), there exists, in Rome itself, a structure which matches Fishbourne in basic plan, design and, interestingly enough, in date.

DOMITIAN AND THE *DOMUS FLAVIA*

In AD 81, the Roman emperor Titus Flavius Sabinus Vespasianus, son of the deified Vespasian, died in office. During his brief reign as First Citizen of Rome, Titus had proved himself a capable enough leader, but now the imperial throne was claimed by his brother, Titus Flavius Domitianius Augustus, known to history as the emperor Domitian. Domitian's reign, like those of Caligula and Nero before, was not a popular one and would later be used as an example of the corruption of absolute power. His increasingly despotic style of leadership, and ever more paranoid suppression of the senatorial class, made few friends amongst the aristocracy of Rome and, despite attempts to court the favour of the army, Domitian was finally assassinated in AD 96.

Though regarded by many as an unstable and paranoid tyrant, Domitian oversaw the completion of some of Rome's great architectural projects. The Arch of Titus, the Stadium in the Campus Martinus and the Temple of Vespasian all belonged to the early part of his reign, whilst projects left uncompleted at his death included a new forum set between the Forum of Augustus and the Temple of Peace (finished by his successor Nerva in AD 97) and the redevelopment of an large area between the Capitoline and Quirinal (completed by Trajan between AD 104 and 110). The two greatest architectural achievements of Domitian's reign, however, were the Flavian Amphitheatre, the great circus of death known to history as the Colosseum, and the creation of a new and opulent imperial residence, the *Domus Flavia* (42).

From the outset, Domitian had wanted a house worthy of his status as both First Citizen of Rome and the son of the deified Titus Flavius Sabinus Vespasianus (Vespasian). Keen to distance himself from the blatant excesses of the Julio-Claudian dynasty, Domitian had been unwilling to occupy Nero's Golden House, and neither had he shown much enthusiasm for Titus' home, the *Domus Tiberiana*, or for his father's former residence in the Gardens of Sallust. Instead, he commissioned the architect Rabirius to design and build a home on the Palatine Hill, a location possessing significant associations with the first emperor Augustus, and also with Romulus, the legendary founder of the eternal city.

The eastern ridge of the Palatine was chosen for the project, Rabirius first overseeing the creation of a level platform through the cutting of a great step into the hill, and the piling of excavated material out to the north. Construction of the building proper began soon after Domitian's accession, the completed structure being inaugurated in AD 92. So great was the achievement of Rabirius in creating a home fit for an emperor, that not only was it to remain the imperial residence for the next three centuries, but it also gave the world a new term: 'palace', derived from the hill through which it was so dramatically positioned.

The 'business end' of the *Domus Flavia* was set around three official rooms: an entrance hall or throne room; an apsed hall or basilica; and a *lararium*, or shrine to both the household gods and to the ancestral spirits of the Flavian family (in particular his deified father and brother). The entrance hall, measuring 30 x 37m, was

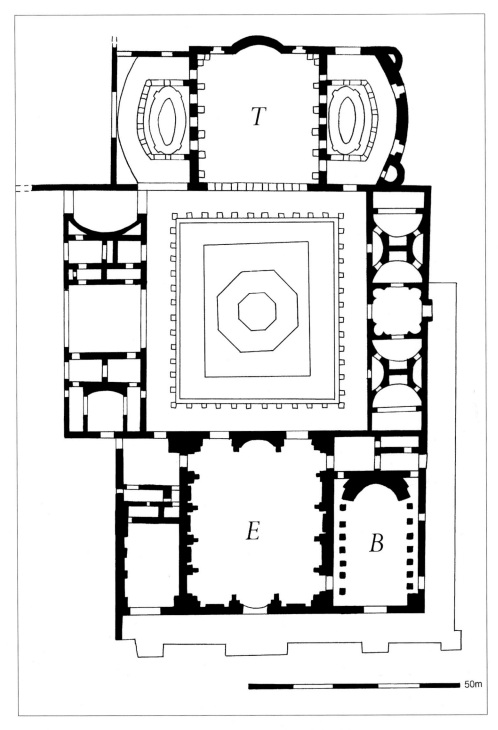

42 Rome: a simplified ground plan of the *Domus Flavia*, the palace of the emperor Domitian, inaugurated in AD 92. Note the positions of the entrance hall (E), aisled basilica (B), central courtyard and apsed *triclinium* (T). *Redrawn from Sear 2000*

1 Chichester: an imaginative creation of *Noviomagus*, looking south-east (with the Isle of Wight in the distance), in around AD 100 painted by Mike Codd. Note the amphitheatre in the foreground, temple, forum and basilica and public baths in the centre and, in the background, the newly developing site of Fishbourne Palace.
© *Chichester District Council*

2 Fishbourne: an imaginative recreation of the Proto Palace, a Mediterranean courtyard house with bath suite attached. © *Sussex Archaeological Society*

3 Fishbourne: the Catuarus Ring. Note that the name of Tiberius Claudius Catuarus has been reversed, presumably to act as a seal-stamp. © *Sussex Archaeological Society*

4 Fishbourne: an imaginative recreation of the palace, with the entrance hall, basilica and bath suite in the foreground, the *triclinium* in the background, at the other side of the courtyard. Note that the sea is no longer thought to have been this close to the building. © *Sussex Archaeological Society*

5 Fishbourne: a partial recreation of the formal gardens in the central courtyard of the Palace, taken in 2004, prior to the redevelopment of the museum and cover buildings. *Author*

Left: 6 Fishbourne: the mosaic in room N21, one of the few floors to display colour in the primary phase of the palace. The small white-edged diamond visible in the top right of the photograph may be the signature of the mosaicist. Note how the floor is subsiding into earlier (poorly backfilled) features. © *Sussex Archaeological Society*

Below: 7 Fishbourne: detail of the border to a mosaic in room N7 showing a double-arched gate set within a crenellated town or fortress wall. © *Sussex Archaeological Society*

Above: 8 Fishbourne:
fragments of painted plaster
from the western internal
courtyard of the north wing
(above) and from in front
of the apsed *triclinium* of the
west wing (below).
© *Institute of Archaeology,
Oxford and Sussex
Archaeological Society*

Right: 9 Fishbourne:
a fragment of painted
plaster depicting either a
colonnaded villa fronting
the sea (akin to the
Fishbourne palace) or a
stately barge or imperial
trireme. © *Institute of
Archaeology, Oxford and
Sussex Archaeological Society*

Left: 10 Fishbourne: a late first- or early second-century mosaic of Medusa overlaying an earlier one of black and white geometric design from room N13 in the north wing. © *Sussex Archaeological Society*

Below: 11 Chilgrove 1: a recreation of the fragmentary geometric mosaic recorded in room 6. © *Chichester District Council*

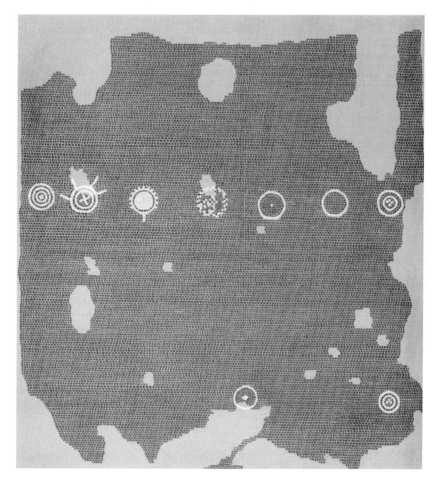

Right: 12 Chilgrove 2: the enigmatic floor recorded in room 7 of the Aisled Building (2). © *Chichester District Council*

Below: 13 Bignor: an imaginative recreation of the villa complex, when it was thought to comprise a single phase of development, painted by Alan Sorrell. Note the apsidal ended audience chamber (room 3) at the bottom right, flanked by its own private courtyard. *Reproduced with kind permission of the Tupper family, Bignor villa, West Sussex*

14 Bignor: the ornamental basin with fountain at the southern end of room 7, the *triclinium* or dining room. *Reproduced with kind permission of the Tupper family, Bignor villa, West Sussex*

15 Bignor: the Ganymede and Jupiter (as an Eagle) mosaic at the northern end of room 7. *Reproduced with kind permission of the Tupper family, Bignor villa, West Sussex*

16 Bignor: the geometric mosaic from room 6. *Reproduced with kind permission of the Tupper family, Bignor villa, West Sussex*

17 Bignor: a coloured etching of room 3, the apsidal-ended audience chamber containing the Venus and Gladiators mosaic, being exposed for the first time in 1812, painted by Richard Smirke. *Reproduced with kind permission of the Tupper family, Bignor villa, West Sussex*

18 Bignor: detail of Venus from the mosaic in room 3. Note that part of the upper portion of the nimbus has been restored. *Reproduced with kind permission of the Tupper family, Bignor villa, West Sussex*

19 Bignor: detail of the fighting cupids panel in room 3 showing the *secutor* and *retiarius* advancing. *Reproduced with kind permission of the Tupper family, Bignor villa, West Sussex*

20 Bignor: detail of the dolphin panel surviving in room 26b. The TER may indicate the signature of the mosaicist. *Reproduced with kind permission of the Tupper family, Bignor villa, West Sussex*

21 Bignor: detail of the geometric design of the north corridor (room 10). *Reproduced with kind permission of the Tupper family, Bignor villa, West Sussex*

22 Bignor: coloured drawing of room 33 shortly after its exposure in 1812 by Samuel Lysons. Note the damaged four seasons mosaic, steps leading up to the higher level of the northern corridor and the surviving areas of painted wall plaster. *Reproduced with kind permission of the Tupper family, Bignor villa, West Sussex*

23 Bignor: detail of Medusa from the centre of the mosaic in room 56, the *apodyterium* or changing room of the southern bath suite. *Reproduced with kind permission of the Tupper family, Bignor villa, West Sussex*

24 Fishbourne: detail of the central roundel of the redesigned room N7 depicting Cupid on a Dolphin. © *Sussex Archaeological Society*

25 Fishbourne: detail of a sea-panther from the Cupid on a Dolphin mosaic in room N7. © *Sussex Archaeological Society*

26 Highdown: a decorated early fifth-century glass goblet from grave 49. © *Worthing Museum and Art Gallery*

27 Patching: a selection of the late fourth- and early fifth-century silver coins recovered in the hoard.
© *Worthing Museum and Art Gallery*

28 Patching: the 23 late fourth- and fifth-century gold coins and two gold rings recovered in the hoard.
© *Worthing Museum and Art Gallery*

the largest of the three rooms, and possessed a throne in a shallow apse set within the rear wall. Here the emperor, in all his majesty, would have sat to meet with, listen to and accept the deference of official guests and visitors. Marble columns lined the side walls of the throne room, framing a series of niches, which presumably contained images from the Roman pantheon of gods or from the Flavian past.

The great basilica was to the immediate north of the entrance hall/throne room. Presumably designed for official gatherings and meetings whereby delegations could seek an audience with specific members of the palace staff, the basilica could be independently accessed from the outside, without the need for entering through the State throne room or from the more private areas behind. Two parallel settings of eight columns ran the length of the hall, terminating before a large and deep apse within which the emperor or, perhaps more likely, his delegated representative, would meet and greet. The *lararium*, to the south of the main entrance hall/throne room, was by far the smallest of the three official rooms in the range.

Doors to the rear of the throne room provided access to a large open courtyard surrounded by a column-lined passage or portico. Overall, this probably gave the appearance of a cloister walk within a later medieval monastic establishment. At the centre of this open courtyard was an ornate, octagonal fountain. The northern wing of the palace could be entered from the centre point of the courtyard, via an octagonal vestibule, which gave access to two discreet, though undoubtedly lavish, guest apartments. The southern side of the courtyard opened out towards the *Domus Augustana*, the older and perhaps more private wing of the palace, whilst the western range contained areas of reception and entertainment, focused around a monumental *triclinium* or dining room.

The *triclinium* was almost as grand and impressively decorated as the primary throne room or entrance hall. A wide and shallow apse, consciously mirroring that housing the throne in the entrance hall, was set into the rear wall of the area of dining, whilst two elaborate oval fountains flanked the northern and southern sides and presumably provided a 'visual and aural accompaniment to the meal' (Sear 2000, 150). The eastern edge of the *triclinium*, which faced the remainder of the palace, was effectively screened from the central courtyard by a series of six monumental columns made of Egyptian granite.

FISHBOURNE AND THE *DOMUS FLAVIA*

As with the *Domus Flavia*, the entrance hall to the Fishbourne building, set centrally within the east wing, was the single largest room in the whole complex (*43*). Measuring 24.4 x 32m, the internal space of the hall was divided into a main area, flanked along the northern and southern walls by two rows of five cubicles or alcoves, framed by supporting columns. Nothing is known of the contents of these alcoves, though they may presumably have contained statuary (Cunliffe 1998, 82). The easternmost cubicles

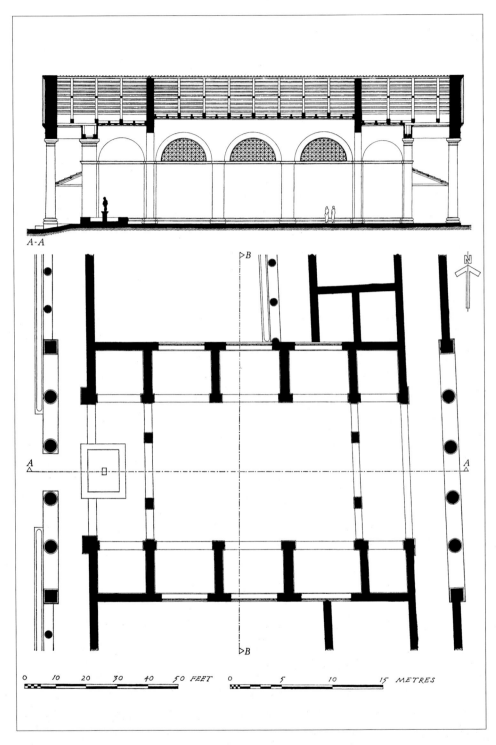

A·A

43 Fishbourne: an imaginative elevation of the grand entrance hall of the palace from an original drawing by Nigel Sunter. © *Institute of Archaeology, Oxford and Sussex Archaeological Society*

facing the main entrance, may conceivably have held porters or some other form of security force designed to control access to the interior (Manley 2003, 129).

Wall footings running the width of the hall, along its eastern and western ends, further divided the internal space. The western footing suggested the former presence of a 'screen wall', comprising a central arch flanked by two lesser arches (Cunliffe 1998, 82), an effect that added considerably to the architectural detail of the large hall. The two side arches provided direct access to the interior of the palace, via the internal courtyard, whilst the central arch framed a squared stone feature. In the *Domus Flavia*, this particular point of the entrance hall was occupied by an apse containing the imperial throne; at Fishbourne the space appears to have been used to house an ornamental pool, possibly containing a fountain. Whether or not this was the original function of the stone pediment at Fishbourne is debatable. It is possible that a throne, seat or statue formed the primary focal point of the hall, the pool being developed under the auspices of later owners (see below).

To the north of the entrance hall, and separated from it by a range of rooms and private apartments, was an aisled hall measuring 21.3 x 27.5m (*44*). As with the basilica in the *Domus Flavia*, the room at Fishbourne was divided into a central 'nave' and two side aisles by a series of columns that supported parallel arcades. The Fishbourne arcades comprised two rows of four columns set directly onto blocks of limestone measuring 0.3m in thickness and 0.9m square (Cunliffe 1998, 83). As with the *Domus Flavia*, the basilica here could be accessed independently from the rest of the palace via a monumental external entrance flanked by a huge colonnade. The structured independence of the hall, combined with its relative isolation from the north and east wings, suggests that this room was intended for semi-public assemblies and meetings between the outside world and representatives of the palace staff (Cunliffe 1998, 84; Manley 2003, 129-30).

There is no immediate parallel at Fishbourne for the third official room, the *lararium*, set in the front facing, 'business end' of the *Domus Flavia*, unless a specifically religious function was performed by Building 3, discovered in 1995-9, to the immediate east of the palace entrance hall (Manley and Rudkin 2003). At Fishbourne, the space to the south of the entrance hall appears to have been largely occupied by the main bath suite, itself a redevelopment of the former Proto Palace, or earlier domestic range (see above). Unfortunately, archaeological examination here has not been as complete as that undertaken across the northern half of the palace, due to the presence of the road and private houses of modern Fishbourne.

Of the remaining rooms contained within the east wing of the Fishbourne palace, those set between the entrance hall and the great basilica deserve further attention. Here, two colonnaded courts of differing scale fronted the central courtyard (*45*). Behind them, against the main east-facing external wall of the palace, a group of 11 rooms were arranged. The range appears to have been divided into at least four discrete blocks consisting of: E3 and adjoining rooms E1 and E2; E6 and adjoining rooms E4 and E5; E9 and adjoining rooms E10 and E11; and a stand-alone room E7 separated

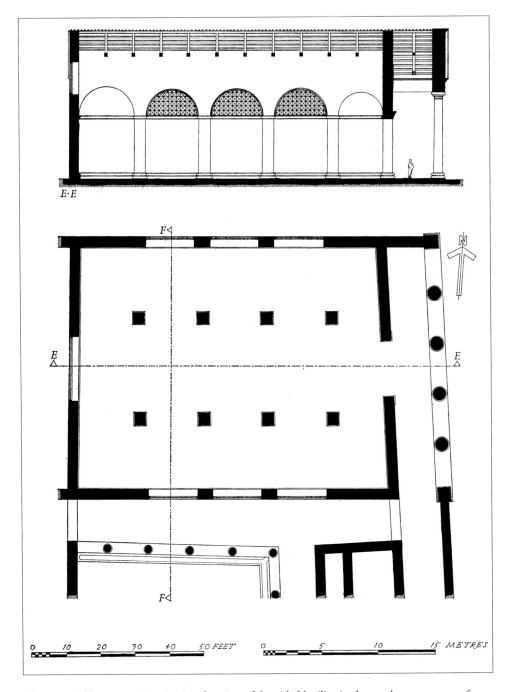

Above: 44 Fishbourne: an imaginative elevation of the aisled basilica in the north-west corner of the palace, from an original drawing by Nigel Sunter. © *Institute of Archaeology, Oxford and Sussex Archaeological Society*

Opposite: 45 Fishbourne: plan of the 'administrative offices' in the east wing, between the entrance hall and aisled basilica. © *Institute of Archaeology, Oxford and Sussex Archaeological Society*

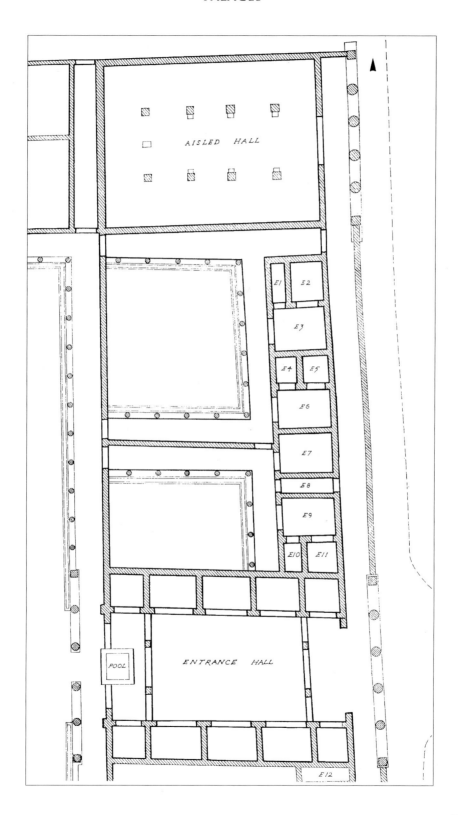

AISLED HALL

E1
E2
E3
E4
E5
E6
E7
E8
E9
E10
E11

POOL

ENTRANCE HALL

E12

46 Fishbourne: the bedding trenches in the formal garden area of the central courtyard. The stone-lined cuts running diagonally across the bedding trenches represent modern land drains. © *Institute of Archaeology, Oxford and Sussex Archaeological Society*

from rooms to the south by an east–west aligned corridor (E8). These rooms were the least well appointed in the palace and it is possible that they represented workspaces or administrative offices divided into two discrete zones, E1-6 with access to/from the northernmost internal courtyard and E7-11 with access to the smaller southerly court. If these were intended as officials' lodgings or administrative rooms, then the internal courtyards and corridor (running the length of the northern half of the east wing) would have helped keep both visitors and lesser staff or officers 'out of sight as far as possible and away from the more dignified parts of the palace' (Smith 1997, 176).

The eastern wing of the Fishbourne palace thus described, led directly to a large open courtyard. This courtyard was divided in two by an ornamental pathway 12.2m wide, linking the entrance hall directly to the staterooms of the western wing. A series of colonnaded walks defined the northern, eastern, western and, presumably, southern limits of this courtyard space. Bedding trenches, dug it is thought for an ornamental hedge, were arranged alongside the path, in parallel arrangements of matching recesses, presumably in order to incorporate an arrangement of statues or other features (*46* and *colour plate 5*).

Access to the north wing was obtained via two sets of paired entrances, placed either side of two small, internal courtyards (*47*). These two courtyards formed the central focus for three major units of accommodation. Suites of rooms, accessed directly from a hallway are sometimes referred to as being of *medianum*-type (Manley 2003) and such units can be identified throughout the northern wing. The westernmost *medianum*-type apartment was formed by two paired rooms (N1 and N2) linked by a corridor or concourse (N5). The middle range comprised a suite of three rooms (N9, N10 and N11) linked via a corridor (N14) to a paired set (N12 and N13), whilst the eastern range consisted of a paired set (N18 and N22) linked by a squared service room (N19) to a larger suite of three (N20, N21 and N23). In all these cases it is possible that the smaller spaces represented bedrooms, whilst the larger were used as living rooms or reception areas (Manley 2003, 130-1). In addition to the two internal courtyards, the three discrete blocks of apartments also appeared to have shared access to a set of two enlarged rooms set along the north wall (N7 and N16). These may have served as dining rooms or meeting chambers that were both separated and sound-insulated from the main domestic ranges.

Few of the rooms were not significantly modified in later periods, though in some cases enough survived from the primary phase to allow an interpretation of the original internal décor. In the majority of cases, solid floors were decorated with complex geometric designs in a combination of black and white *tesserae* (*48*), occasionally with the odd splash of red or blue (*colour plate 6*). One design of particular interest was revealed in room N7 in 1980, following the lifting of a later floor depicting a cupid on a dolphin (see chapter 8 for a discussion on this piece). The earlier mosaic, executed primarily with black and white *tesserae*, was composed of 16 square panels, each with a different internal pattern of interlocking geometric designs (*colour plate 7*). Surrounding this was a border depicting a crenellated town or fortress wall, with two double-arched gates (at the northern and southern margins), a set of single-arched gates (at the east and west) and a tower in each corner. Such a design is so far unique in Britain, though parallels are known from first-century AD sites in Gaul (Cunliffe 1998, 69). It would be interesting to know if this floor, which was set in one of the two main dining rooms in the north wing, was a purely artistic device, or whether it was intended to represent either the (as yet unwalled) new town of *Noviomagus* or to convey the former military history of the Fishbourne site and of its role in the initial phases of conquest.

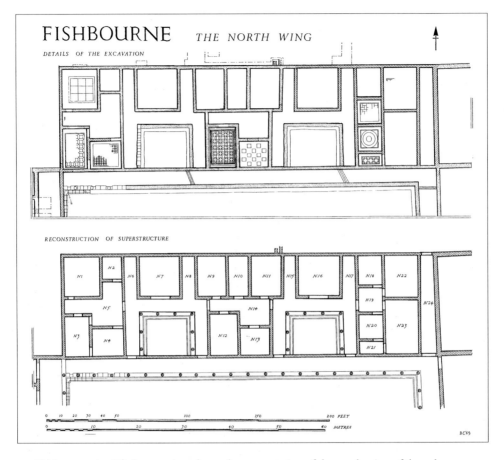

FISHBOURNE   THE NORTH WING

DETAILS OF THE EXCAVATION

RECONSTRUCTION OF SUPERSTRUCTURE

47 Fishbourne: simplified excavation plan and reconstruction of the north wing of the palace.
© *Institute of Archaeology, Oxford and Sussex Archaeological Society*

Internal walls throughout the north wing were plastered and painted with a variety of designs, frequently combining large rectangular panels and a rich use of colour (*colour plate 8*). A well-preserved sample recovered from room N9 demonstrated the 'rich, almost overbearing nature of the mock marble painting' (Cunliffe 1998, 72), whilst a sizeable fragment recovered from the infill of a later ditch preserved an amazing scene depicting what appears to be a colonnaded villa fronting the sea (*colour plate 9*). Such images are known from a number of Italian sites of the first century AD (and in particular at Stabiae where a lively harbour scene was preserved within a building destroyed by the eruption of Vesuvius in AD 79: Cunliffe 1971, 57; 1998, 80), although it is tempting to suggest that the influence here might have been the Fishbourne palace itself. An alternative suggestion, that the piece from Fishbourne shows a stately barge or trireme, may also be possible. Evidence recovered from later demolition deposits suggest that some rooms in the primary phase possessed stucco mouldings, decorated with birds and fruit (*49*), which were placed high on the walls, possibly at the interface between wall and ceiling.

48 Fishbourne: the complex, black and white geometric design forming the mosaic in room N12 of the north wing. © *Institute of Archaeology, Oxford and Sussex Archaeological Society*

49 Fishbourne: a fragment of decorative, moulded stucco from the interface of wall and ceiling from the north wing of the palace. © *Institute of Archaeology, Oxford and Sussex Archaeological Society*

The arrangement of the north wing to create 'a series of private environments based on small colonnaded courtyards, cut off from the main building except for small communicating doors' (Cunliffe 1971, 150) is an intriguing one which raises the question of how this domestic range was originally intended to be used. Barry Cunliffe suggested that the organisation of space within the wing might indicate discrete blocks of accommodation set aside for the use of important visitors (Cunliffe 1971, 150), whilst Ernest Black has argued in favour of separate residential areas for more than one high-status family (Black 1987, 28-9). Both suggestions are plausible.

The western range of the palace at Fishbourne contained areas of reception and (we may presume) public entertainment. Unfortunately, as the entire wing was constructed upon a raised platform, making it dominate the complex, later plough attrition has proved particularly damaging and few of the original rooms survived in anything like their original condition. As with the western range of the *Domus Flavia*, the central focus of this wing at Fishbourne was a large, apsed room set on the main east–west axis opposite the entrance hall (*50*). This space may, by analogy with the *Domus Flavia*, have functioned as a *triclinium* or dining room. Although nowhere near as spacious as the monumental *triclinium* of the palace in Rome, the Fishbourne example, measuring 9.5 x 10.7m with a 6.1m diameter apsed recess, was clearly one of the most important enclosed spaces in the entire building (*51*).

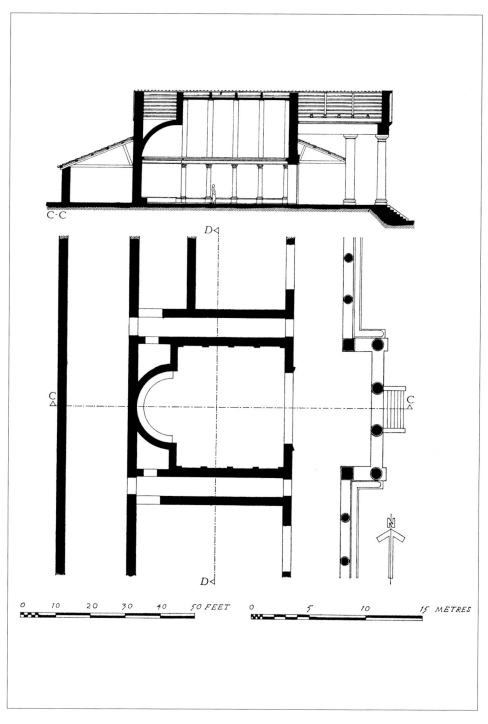

50 Fishbourne: an imaginative east to west elevation of the great, apsidal-ended *triclinium* (dining room) in the west wing from an original drawing by Nigel Sunter. © *Institute of Archaeology, Oxford and Sussex Archaeological Society*

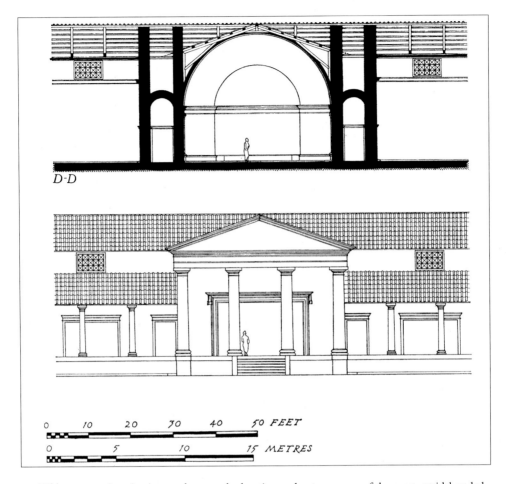

51 Fishbourne: an imaginative north to south elevation and entranceway of the great, apsidal-ended *triclinium* (dining room) in the west wing from an original drawing by Nigel Sunter. © *Institute of Archaeology, Oxford and Sussex Archaeological Society*

Sadly, due to the relentless pressure of post-Roman ploughing, little of the interior décor has survived to the present day. Cunliffe has argued convincingly that the room possessed a vaulted roof, the interior of which was covered with stucco, 'raised ribs' painted white to contrast with the vivid blue, purple and red background (Cunliffe 1998, 56-7). Only small fragments of the original floor were preserved, but enough to show the fine quality of the piece, the tiny white, yellow, black and red *tesserae* suggesting a mosaic which would originally have surpassed all others in the palace. Traces of a timber bench were found running along the length of the apsed wall at the rear of the *triclinium* (Cunliffe 1971, 88). This may have served either as a form of 'throne' or head table for the palace owner or as a curved dining couch (*stibadium*) where guests could sit and watch dancers or other entertainers who occupied the middle space of the room during more elaborate meals (Manley 2003, 130).

To the north of the central apsed *triclinium* lay W11 (*52*), an area which appears to have been a *hypocauston*, a small room 'which had the function of heating rooms adjacent to them indirectly' (Black 1987, 49). The room, which was itself fed with heat from W12 (a stoke-room) may have been designed to heat either W11 or W8, both comparatively small, but presumably important spaces which could have been in use 'for fairly long continuous periods' (Black 1987, 51). This in turn would suggest offices, a library or, perhaps more plausibly, bedrooms. A bedroom suite positioned so close to the main dining area and insulated from it by narrow east–west aligned, mosaic floor-covered corridor (W13) (*53*), would in turn indicate a high-status apartment, possibly one designed for the head of the household (Black 1987, 51; Manley 2003, 130). Given that W8 opened directly onto the colonnaded garden, whilst W10 could be accessed only via its own private corridor, the latter is perhaps more likely to have functioned as the bedroom of the palace owner or high ranking official, whilst W8 may have served as an important state room.

Of the high-status apartment itself, comprising rooms W7 and 10, both accessed via corridor W9, and W11 beyond, little survived other than the floor plan. Room W10 appeared to have been relatively simple, as one would perhaps expect for private sleeping quarters, being floored with a thick layer of pink mortar laid on a concrete screed. A pink mortar floor also graced W11, the walls of which had been plastered and painted predominantly in red and white with areas of greeny-blue. rooms W7 and 8, which both opened directly out onto the central colonnaded courtyard, appear to have both possessed mosaics, only that in W8 surviving to any great degree. Here the design comprised a simple, if rather fussy, black and white geometric design, the only colour being provided by the yellow and red tendrils that coiled along the eastern and western extremities (*54*). Such a design, it has been suggested, would have proved perfectly acceptable in a frequently used room where it may well have been 'partly obscured by furniture' (Cunliffe 1998, 61).

A further major block of accommodation, akin to the *medianum*-type apartments in the north wing, was positioned at the northern limits of the west wing. Here W3 seems to have acted as a link room or concourse, being floored with a complex black and white geometric mosaic. The mosaic in room W6 was subdivided into two broad and unequal elements: a largely geometric design, or 'carpet', which covered the main part of the space and a 'mat' or smaller area of chequer-work running along the western wall by the door. This division was created, it has been claimed, to ensure that 'a person entering through the door in the north-west corner would walk out onto the mat and would be able to obtain a clear view of the entire carpet' (Cunliffe 1998, 58). W6 appears to have been floored with a mosaic that possessed a set of border tendrils akin to that already observed in room W8. The walls of the rooms in the northern apartment of the west wing were plastered and painted, the paintwork in W3 being deliberately speckled in order to imitate marble.

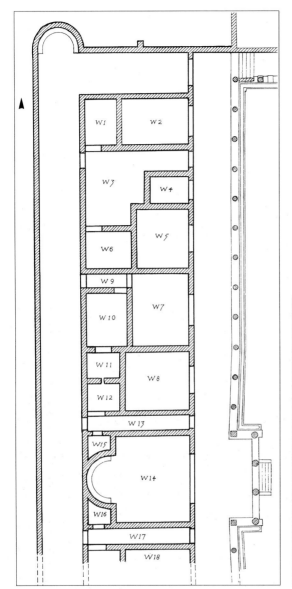

Left: 52 Fishbourne: simplified plan of rooms in the northern half of the west wing. © *Institute of Archaeology, Oxford and Sussex Archaeological Society*

Below: 53 Fishbourne: the simple, black and white mosaic of corridor W13, separating the main dining area from the master bedroom. Significant parts of the floor have been worn away and crudely repaired using pink mortar.
© *Institute of Archaeology, Oxford and Sussex Archaeological Society*

Other apartments clearly lay to the south of the *triclinium* in the west wing. Although the full nature of these has yet to be determined, enough of the ground plan has been revealed to show that 'the two halves of the wing were not symmetrically arranged' (Cunliffe 1998, 63). Limited investigation conducted between 1987 and 1988 in the back gardens of houses fronting the A259 have revealed part of another two mosaics: a black and white geometric floor and an example from a corridor of similar design to that revealed in W13 to the north of the *triclinium* (Cunliffe, Down and Rudkin 1996).

All the apartments in the wing were connected to an impressive, 5.2m wide, apse-ended, north–south aligned corridor or ambulatory that seems to have run the entire length of western range. The excavated northern apse was lined internally with a stone-built, plaster-coated bench that had been painted red. Floor levels had been entirely erased, though the lack of *tesserae* from this area may indicate that the space had originally been mortar floored (Cunliffe 1971, 89; Rudkin 1988, 28). Surviving quantities of wall plaster suggested that the walls had originally possessed a pink dado, splashed with black, brown and white (so as create the impression of marble), with white panels, framed in red and yellow, above. Cunliffe noted that the corridor, in its location, design and basic form 'cannot fail to call to mind the *hippodromos* of Domitian's palace in Rome' (Cunliffe 1971, 92). The *hippodromos*, or 'race course', could have been designed as a monumental exercising area or a space along which 'the owner and his advisers' could walk and discuss matters of a private nature, away from the prying eyes and ears of the palace complex (Manley 2003, 130-1).

54 Fishbourne: a small fragment of mosaic in room W5 at the northern end of the west wing. The coiling tendril design is very similar to that recorded in W12. © *Institute of Archaeology, Oxford and Sussex Archaeological Society*

Very little is known about the extent and nature of the south wing at Fishbourne, most of which presently lies buried beneath the A259. This is particularly unfortunate given that the relationship between the bath suite of the Proto Palace and the later complex, at the extreme south-eastern edge of the palace, remains lost to us. Limited investigation conducted within the gardens of private houses bordering the road, have, however, provided a tantalising glimpse of what may have been contained there. Excavations conducted in the garden of a house to the south of the modern road in 1967 revealed the substantial footings for a south-facing colonnade or stylobate. This discovery is important for it suggests the first major break in the 'architectural syntax' of the Fishbourne palace. Elsewhere across the complex, the primary view was inwards, to the central courtyard or to the private courts in the northern and eastern ranges, but the southern range was provided with an external vista. Here the residents could 'turn their backs on the politics of the palace' and gaze out 'across the southern garden towards the waters of Chichester Harbour' (Manley 2003, 132). Evidence of a range of external features beyond the walls of the southern wing may represent the slight traces of a terraced garden, perhaps akin to those of the grand Mediterranean villas, which landscaped the view and presented it in a more organised and structured way (Manley 2003, 132).

FISHBOURNE PALACE IN CONTEXT

The preceding discussion has demonstrated how the palace at Fishbourne mirrors the key architectural features of the *Domus Flavia,* (central courtyard, public range containing a large entrance hall and aisled basilica, an impressive *triclinium*, a private range and a guest wing arranged around a series of discrete apartments) built by the architect Rabirius for the emperor Domitian. The term 'palace', as frequently applied to the main phase of building at Fishbourne is therefore an entirely appropriate one for the *Domus Flavia* was the original 'palace' building, constructed at great expense through the Palatine Hill in Rome. Obviously the *Domus Flavia*, as the residence of the divine Flavians, takes architectural precedence over the Fishbourne complex, an observation which helps refine the date of the Sussex site.

Domitian's palace was commissioned shortly after his accession to the imperial throne on the death of his brother Titus in AD 81. Although plans for an imperial residence on the Palatine may have been circulating earlier than this, foundations for the palace at Fishbourne are unlikely to have been set out before the start of construction in Rome, and probably not before the completion of works, and the inauguration of the *Domus Flavia*, in AD 92. Given that Domitian's palace would possess empire-wide architectural impact only on its completion, and that to commence work on a copy before the *Domus Flavia* was finished would almost certainly incur the wrath of a paranoid emperor (afterwards it would seem more a case of sincere flattery), the main phase at Fishbourne is unlikely to predate the period AD 85-90.

Who then could the Sussex palace, the *Domus Flavia* in miniature, have been built for? It is rare that an archaeological site and a historical person can be linked with any degree of certainty and attempts to do so are often fraught with problems, ambiguities and confusion. The chronology and sequence for Fishbourne, even in its revised state, does however tie in with a number of historically attested figures. Tiberius Claudius Togidubnus and Tiberius Claudius Catuarus have already been mentioned with regard to the primary phases of major civilian development at Fishbourne. Togidubnus is cited from an inscription in Chichester, Catuarus from a gold ring found from close to the palace. If we accept that building work for the Sussex palace did not commence before AD 90 (at the earliest) and that both men were ethnic Britons who owed their position and status to the emperor Claudius for service to Rome before and during the events of AD 43, then they would both certainly of an advanced age by the time the foundations were being laid. If Togidubnus were in his early 20s when first noted as a potential successor to his father, king Cunobelin, in AD 43, then he would be in his early 70s at the time of Fishbourne's dramatic redevelopment. We know next to nothing about the age or status of Catuarus, though he could conceivably have been Togidubnus' kinsman (Cunliffe 1998, 108), possibly a brother, cousin or even a son. Given that the main phase of building work at Fishbourne used the *Domus Flavia* as an architectural blueprint, being constructed at a time when the emperor Domitian was on the ascendant, then a third candidate for occupancy of the Sussex house appears.

In Chichester, we have already noted the discovery of two monumental dedications set up on behalf of Gaius Sallustius Lucullus (chapters 3, 4 and 5). Lucullus, son of Amminus and grandson to Cunobelin, reached the pinnacle of his career when, in the AD mid-80s, he became Propraetorian Imperial Legate, governor of the province of Britain. Lucullus owed his position as governor to Domitian and his status as a member of the Catuvellaunian royal house to his blood ties to Cunobelin. His family had served the emperors Caligula, Claudius and Nero well during the formative years of Rome in Britain and had no doubt forged links with the later emperor Vespasian, father of Domitian, when he had served in Britain as commander of the II Augusta during the events of AD 43 and 44. Given Lucullus' ethnic background, political history and status (holding the most important of provincial offices), then his candidature as palace owner would appear a strong one. If Togidubnus (and/or Catuarus) had been the owner of the Proto Palace with its links to Nero and the Julio-Claudians, then it is likely that he did not live to see the rise to power of his nephew Lucullus and the modification of his rural retreat into the palace fit for the imperial elite.

SOUTHWICK PALACE

The villa at Southwick should also be more properly referred to as a palace for it is a smaller version of the main phase of building work at Fishbourne; another *Domus*

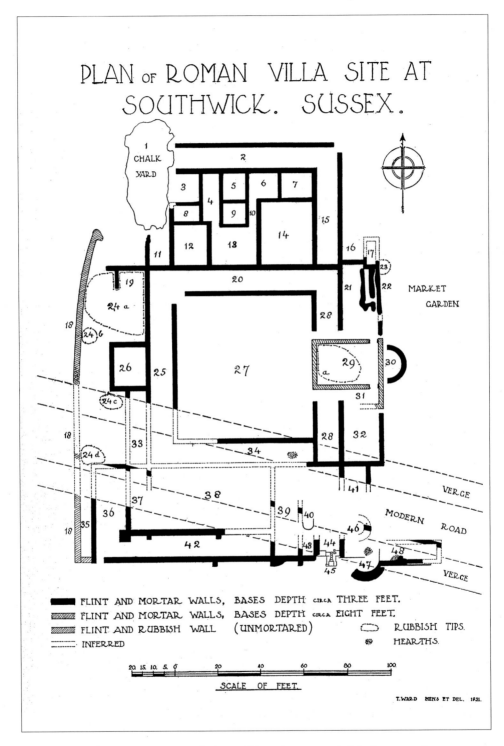

PLAN of ROMAN VILLA SITE AT SOUTHWICK. SUSSEX.

1 CHALK YARD

2

3   5   6   7

4

8   9   10

15

12   13   14

16   17

11

23

19   20   21   22   MARKET

GARDEN

24 a

28

18

24 b

26   25   27   29   30

a

31

24 c

18

28   32

33   34

24 d

41

VERGE

38

37   39   40   MODERN   ROAD

36

46

18   35

42   48   44   48

45   47

VERGE

FLINT AND MORTAR WALLS, BASES DEPTH circa THREE FEET.
FLINT AND MORTAR WALLS, BASES DEPTH circa EIGHT FEET.
FLINT AND RUBBISH WALL (UNMORTARED)   RUBBISH TIPS.
INFERRED   HEARTHS.

20 15 10. 5. 0   20   40   60   80   100.

SCALE OF FEET.

T.WARD MENS ET DEL. 1931.

55 Southwick: ground plan showing all phases of the palace as revealed during excavations conducted in 1931. © *Sussex Archaeological Society*

Flavia in miniature (55). Unlike Fishbourne however, the story of the Southwick palace is a sad one. In contrast to the favourable treatment meted out to its relative, the tale of Southwick is one of neglect, missed opportunities and unthinking vandalism. It is also the story of a major piece of fieldwork conducted by a determined and heroic group of amateur archaeologists in the face of rapacious urban development. That we can say anything at all about the building at Southwick is thanks mainly to the unstinting efforts of two men: Messrs E.F. Salmon and Samuel E. Winbolt. Throughout the 1920s it was E.F. Salmon who collected information on the site and drew attention to its proposed destruction and it was he, together with Samuel Winbolt, who planned and co-ordinated a large-scale piece of rescue archaeology in order to salvage, what was then, the most sumptuous Roman villa building in Britain.

The first recorded discovery of Roman remains at Southwick was in 1815, when a James Rooke reported having seen 'pavements exposed' (Winbolt 1932, 13). No record of the nature or design of these pavements appears to have been made, an unfortunate state of affairs when one considers the quality of the Fishbourne floors already alluded to. In 1847, members of the Sussex Archaeological Society meeting in Shoreham, were treated to a display of 'Roman Pottery, Mosaic etc., from the Roman Villa at Southwick, belonging to Mr N. Hall' (Winbolt 1932, 13). Hall seems to have cleared at least four rooms in the Roman building, the walls of which were covered in blue-painted wall plaster. The display to the Archaeological Society was reported in the first edition of the Sussex Archaeological Collections, with a note to the effect that the Committee hoped 'to publish some details on a future occasion', but sadly the occasion never arrived. The plans, drawings and details of the mosaic, together with all the finds recovered prior to 1847, disappeared without trace, something which Winbolt observed was 'inexplicable and, indeed, hardly creditable' (Winbolt 1932, 13).

In 1930, the palace field was sold for housing development. In January of 1931, Winbolt and Salmon obtained permission to excavate but, before they could start, a road was smashed through the southern half of the complex, a sorry state of affairs mirrored in the unhappy relationship between Fishbourne palace and the modern A259. A small core team, supplemented by 'enthusiastic voluntary workers', began work at Southwick in March 1931 and, over nine short weeks, cleared an extensive area. The following year, ground to the north of the new road was purchased by the Sussex Archaeological Trust and the future of the site seemed secure. Maintenance, however, proved difficult and plans to expose the building more fully and erect a form of cover, came to nothing. In 1953, faced with ever mounting financial problems, the Sussex Archaeological Trust committed a most lamentable, short-sighted and opportunist act, and sold the land. Within the space of a year, new development had further scoured out the Roman levels, leaving very little for future generations. Further indignities were to follow for a large proportion of the original site archive, maintained under the auspices of Hove Museum, was 'given away during local government reorganisation in 1974' (Rudling 1985, 73).

Despite the evident horrors that have befallen the Roman building at Southwick, it is clear that this was a structure of national importance; one that helps provide a key to our understanding of early Roman life in Sussex and something that further helps to put the palace of Fishbourne into context. When Southwick was in the process of being excavated in the 1930s there was nothing to compare the discovery with, the full extent and nature of Fishbourne palace at this time being unknown. Winbolt struggled with the recorded ground plan of the building, observing in the 1932 report that, although in area covered Southwick was not as great as certain recorded villas in southern England, it appeared 'unique in regularity and completeness of plan' (Winbolt 1932, 22). Later, in an account published within the *Victoria County History*, Winbolt seemed to be favouring a more complex sequence of building phases and development (Winbolt 1935, 27). The reality of the situation at Southwick is probably a combination of the two: a single unitary plan established late in the first century AD, with subsequent remodelling and alteration.

It was not until the discovery and examination of the Roman palace at Fishbourne that the ground plan of the Southwick building begin to make sense (*56*). Barry Cunliffe was the first to notice the similarities in structural form between the two sites (Cunliffe 1973, 74) and Ernest Black, in his study of *The Roman Villas of South-East England*, was able to conclude that Southwick was indeed 'a copy, on a smaller scale of the period 2 palace at Fishbourne' (Black 1987, 102). The main axis of entrance hall through courtyard to apsed dining room (*triclinium*) as seen at Fishbourne palace is duplicated at Southwick, albeit the Southwick site clearly faced west, not east as at Fishbourne. The primary phase *triclinium*, which was narrowed in a later period, measured approximately 10m x 8m, the entrance hall being around 4.9m square (Winbolt 1932, 16). Little can be said about the internal nature of the *triclinium*, as it was so substantially rebuilt in later periods, but the walls of the secondary development were 'covered with a thick rendering of cream-coloured plaster' (Winbolt 1932, 18). The curious arrangement of structural features defining rooms 17 and 22 to the north of the *triclinium*, were interpreted by Winbolt as comprising, at least in part, the remains of a latrine (Winbolt 1932, 17). Black, in his reassessment of the site, suggested that 17 was more likely to represent a *praefurnium* or furnace supplying a hypocaust to the west whilst 22 may actually be part of a corn-drying oven belonging to a later phase (Black 1985, 102).

To the south of the entrance hall lay what is almost certainly the remains of a large basilical hall of the type noted from both Fishbourne and the *Domus Flavia*. This room was heavily modified during a secondary phase of development, when the space was subdivided into a smaller units (36, 37, 38 and 42), but the basic plan of a large rectangular hall divided into a central nave and two side aisles by a set of columns supporting parallel arcades, is clear enough. Bases for two of the columns in the southern arcade survived beneath the later dividing wall between rooms 38 and 42. Together these suggest the maximum span between columns in either arcade was 21ft at the eastern and western ends of the hall and 28ft at the centre. The position

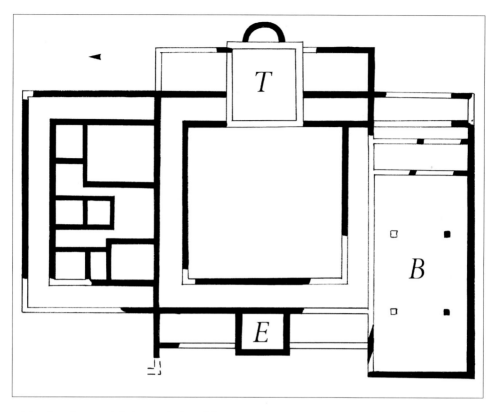

56 Southwick: a simplified ground plan of the primary-phase palace, built in the early AD 90s, another copy in miniature of Domitian's *Domus Flavia* in Rome. The entrance hall (E) at the centre of the western range is shown at the bottom of the picture, with the aisled basilica (B) at the extreme bottom right (south). The apsed *triclinium* (T) is at the centre of the east wing, with the northern private or guest wing, arranged around a single small courtyard, is at the left of the drawing. It is not known whether there were any ornamental features in the central courtyard. *Redrawn from Winbolt 1932*

of the basilica at the extreme southern margins of the Southwick palace indicates the same degree of structural independence as evidenced at Fishbourne and in the *Domus Flavia* and may suggest that this too was designed for meetings between the outside world and representatives of the palace staff.

The north wing of the Southwick palace contained a range of living quarters which, as with the north wing at Fishbourne, was arranged into discrete areas. Here the two main blocks (rooms 3, 8 and 12; rooms 7 and 14) were separated by a corridor surrounding a combined room (5 and 9) which, as at Fishbourne, may have served as communal space or a form of guest *triclinium*, and a small, private courtyard (13). Unfortunately, of the artefacts and architectural details recovered during the course of the excavations, few appear to have been specifically identified to context, meaning that it is now almost impossible to describe the internal décor of specific rooms, nor to ascertain potential function from the material assemblage.

In the 'south-east room of the north block' (room 14), the largest internal space within the wing, Winbolt noted large quantities of finely cut *tesserae*, eight of which were of glass applied with gold leaf (Winbolt 1932, 24-5). Three more examples of this exceptional artefact type were recovered across the palace during later excavations (Rudling 1985, 82-3). Gold-on-glass *tesserae* are 'not common in this country during the Roman, or for that matter, any other period' (Rudling 1985, 83) and their presence here provides good evidence of a lavish piece of expenditure. It is a great tragedy that there is no extant record of the mosaic contained within room 14 (though it could conceivably have been largely intact during the first exposure of the site in 1815), for it would almost certainly have rivalled the finest floors recorded from the British Isles.

Little could be said concerning the structural nature of the southern wing which lay beneath the road built in 1930. To the south of the road verge, Winbolt identified a well-built, tile and concrete *praefurnium* which fed a hypocaust in the room immediately to the north (under the road). Tantalising fragments of building revealed in the course of pipe laying beneath the road, included at least two apsed walls and a piece of *opus signinum* (concrete) floor. These presumably represent the area of the original bath suite to the palace (Winbolt 1932, 21-2).

Re-examination of the material assemblage recovered from Southwick by Ernest Black in the 1980s has revealed the presence of a particular form of roller-stamped tile from a collection of early die patterns known as the 'London-Sussex' group (Black 1987, 12-3). Tiles of this kind were found at Fishbourne in the baths of the Proto Palace and were reused in later modifications, all of which provides a further link between the Southwick and Fishbourne building projects. Given the evidence of the surviving pottery and coin assemblages recorded from Southwick, a constructional date for the palace in the later half of the first century AD seems likely. Given the duplication of ground plan evident between Southwick, Fishbourne and the *Domus Flavia*, that date can plausibly be further restricted to around, or shortly after, AD 92.

Southwick and Fishbourne are not the only sites in Sussex where the recorded artefactual assemblages, namely tile, coins and pottery, suggest dates in the final years of the first century AD for the initial stages of construction. Roman structures sampled at Pulborough, Angmering, Eastbourne, Brighton, Arundel and Langstone (in Hampshire) have all produced evidence indicating activity contemporary with the palaces of Fishbourne and Southwick, whilst finds recovered from Westhampnett near Chichester, are also suggestive.

PULBOROUGH

The first evidence to suggest significant Roman activity at Pulborough was found in the early nineteenth century (Horsfield 1835), though the reported circumstances of the discovery are frustratingly vague. The Reverend Cartwright traced the outline of a series of Roman rooms in 1817 which formed 'the foundations of a quadrangle' measuring 46m north x 60m west (Page 1905, 25). The quadrangle, or courtyard, was surrounded by a series of rooms in which fragments of large tile and *tesserae* were found, whilst the walls had been decorated with 'straw coloured' wall plaster (Praetorius 1911, 1). Cartwright does not record the presence of any floors, though the finding of *tesserae* may indicate that subsequent ploughing has destroyed any potential mosaics.

In 1907, during the planting of a garden hedge, two parallel Roman walls were found running for a distance of some 42m (Praetorius 1911, 1). Messrs C.J. Praetorius, a Fellow of the Society of Antiquaries, and H. Price began a small investigation of the Roman masonry in locating a third wall, forming what appeared to be a second corridor, which terminated in an apse with a substantial buttress. A suite of rooms was revealed within the area defined by the north–south wall and the two east–west corridors. The full extent of these structures remains unknown. Unfortunately neither Praetorius nor Price appear to have recorded the extent of their investigations at Borough Farm, though the occasional reference to oblique trenches cut between walls (Praetorius 1911, 2 and figure 1) seems to indicate that both men adopted the simple procedure of wall-chasing. Not all rooms were fully cleared nor defined, as is evident from Praetorius' plan where unexcavated or suspected walls are represented as dotted lines.

At least one of the rooms uncovered possessed a mosaic floor suspended above a hypocaust, only the hypocaust tiles having survived the ravages of post-Roman agriculture (Praetorius 1911, figure 2). The hypocaust had been heated from the room to the immediate east. The relatively small size of the heated space suggests that it was not originally a *triclinium* or dining area, nor a space for entertaining or other forms of communal gathering. Ernest Black has suggested that a similar arrangement within the Flavian palace at Fishbourne indicates that the heated room there (W10) was probably the bedroom (*cubiculum*) of the owner (Black 1987, 49). It is possible that the heated room uncovered by Praetorius and Price at Pulborough was also a bedroom, or possibly an office or library (Black 1987, 51).

A small room in the western half of the range contained 'a great quantity of floor *tesserae* … comprising some two or three thousand small cubes of chalk and a smaller number of cubes made from sandstone and red tile' (Praetorius 1911, 2). *Tesserae* surviving in Worthing Museum and Art Gallery today indicate that not all of these pieces were as loose as described, some areas surviving as discrete sections of mortared floor. The wall plaster at Pulborough was very well preserved, Praetorius noting that the predominant colours were 'blue, red, yellow, cream and a turquoise blue' (Praetorius 1911, 8). Tantalisingly 'in several cases the design was of a floral character, while other pieces were painted or splashed to imitate marble or had panels with coloured borders' (Praetorius 1911, 8). Sadly, despite the quality of preservation recorded in 1909, none of these pieces survive to this day. The internal walls themselves were noted as being in very good condition and evenly built with faced stone (Praetorius 1911, 5).

Given that so little of the Pulborough building was revealed in 1909, and that no serious consideration was made at the time with regard to chronology and phasing, it would perhaps be unwise to speculate too much on room layout and function. It is worth noting, however, that the basic arrangement of features here, when combined with the nature and distribution of finds, would seem to indicate that the site is comparable with the west wing at Fishbourne, a range which contained the master bedroom, apsed dining room, private quarters and an apsidal-ended corridor. The presence of an apsidal corridor at Pulborough, linking the heated room with the rest of the range, is certainly suggestive of the Fishbourne example and the *hippodromos* of the *Domus Flavia*, but cannot be taken any further at this stage.

BRIGHTON AND ANGMERING

Evidence to suggest the presence of significant Roman activity in the area of Preston Road in Brighton first came to light in 1876 when a series of pits, part of a wall and two burials were disturbed during the construction of new housing (57) (Toms and Herbert 1926, 3-4; Kelly and Dudley 1981, 70). Further parts of a building were unearthed the following year as work commenced on the construction of 90-96 Preston Road. The partial outline of at least seven rooms was traced at this time. Some of the walls, which survived to just above floor level, were plastered and painted in panels and bands of blue, red, crimson, purple, green and yellow. Large numbers of loose *tesserae*, predominantly white, grey, red and black, were found during the course of the examination, together with the larger part of a mosaic. This floor, recorded from room 1, measured 14 x 15ft 6in and was of 'geometrical design, whereon circles about a yard in diameter' were observed, each circle enclosing 'a star-shaped device' (Toms and Herbert 1926, 13). Sadly no drawing of the complete design appears to have survived, although the description sounds uncannily like a number of the mosaics recorded from the period 1 palace at Fishbourne. Further (unspecified) mosaics of 'red grey and white in colour' were revealed in August 1877 (Kelly and Dudley 1981, 71).

Additional excavations conducted under difficult conditions in 1926, 1962-3 and 2002 have unfortunately not added a great deal to the ground plan of the main building, although a variety of other features (including burials, walls, pits, wells and possible floors) have been recovered from the immediate vicinity. One discovery worthy of particular note was that of a funerary box containing a variety of grave goods including pottery, glassware, an iron lampholder and two pipe-clay portrait busts. The busts may have been manufactured in Central Gaul, in the later half of the first or very early second century AD. Measuring less than 14cm in height, the pieces portray the heads and upper shoulders of two females which have been interpreted 'as ornaments rather than devotional figures' (Kelly and Dudley 1981, 83).

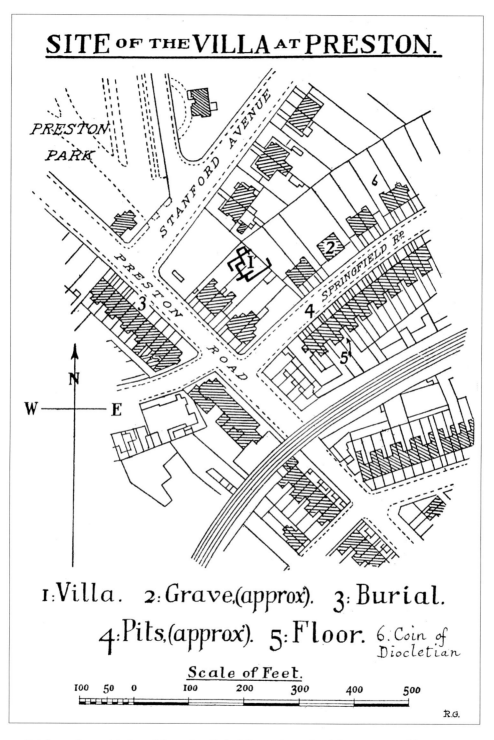

SITE OF THE VILLA AT PRESTON.

PRESTON PARK

STANFORD AVENUE

PRESTON ROAD

SPRINGFIELD R.

N
W — E

1:Villa. 2:Grave,(approx). 3:Burial.
4:Pits,(approx). 5:Floor. 6.Coin of Diocletian

Scale of Feet.
100 50 0   100   200   300   400   500

R.G.

57 Brighton: the partial plan of the early villa building and associated features exposed in 1926.
© Brighton and Hove Archaeological Society

141

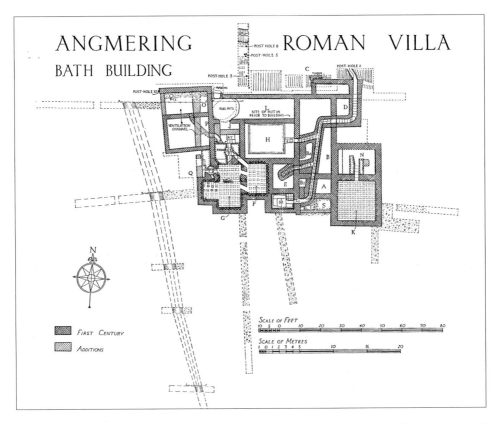

58 Angmering: plan of the early bathhouse revealed during excavations conducted between 1937 and 1939. © *Sussex Archaeological Society*

The ground plan of the domestic range at Angmering has yet to be recorded, though an elaborate and structurally independent bathhouse has been extensively examined (58). The detailed excavation of the bathing suite began in 1937 and continued until the outbreak of hostilities in 1939. During this time the majority of the building was exposed, revealing the full panoply of bathing requirements including a cold room (*frigidarium*), cold immersion baths, warm room (*tepidarium*), hot room (*caldarium*), a hot steam room (*sudatorium*) and other heated areas (Gilkes 1999). Dating the site has proved difficult; though it is clear it comprised a variety of distinct constructional phases, the earliest of which may have commenced in the later half of the first century AD (Black 1987; Gilkes 1999, 64-5). Certainly a number of flue tiles found in the walls of rooms F, G and K appear to date from the period AD 90-110 (Black 1987, 84-6) and the building could be comparable with the main phases of construction at both Southwick and Fishbourne. Oliver Gilkes has suggested that domestic activity on the site may have dispersed, each discrete group being set within its own separate enclosure (Gilkes 1999, 65-8). Until further work is conducted at the site, the full nature and extent of the Angmering complex must remain unknown.

ARUNDEL, EASTBOURNE AND OTHERS

Evidence to suggest other areas of significant early Roman domestic activity in Sussex has been recovered from excavations at Arundel (Tarrant Street and Shepherds Garden), Eastbourne and from the area surrounding Westhampnett church, where late first-century Roman tile has been incorporated into the medieval building (Black 1987; Rudling 1998, 44). Unfortunately the exact nature of the Westhampnett site is unknown, whilst urban development has covered (and almost certainly largely obliterated) the building in Tarrant Street, Arundel. An additional site to the west of Chichester, at Langstone in Hampshire, overlooking Hayling Island, almost certainly belongs to this early group and excavations conducted there appear to have produced evidence of a structure not unlike that recorded from Southwick (Gilkes 1998).

Another early Roman structure, akin to those noted above, may lie at Bignor, beneath the remains of the later villa complex. The main sequence of Bignor villa is well documented (Aldsworth and Rudling 1995), large areas of it having been investigated since the site was first discovered in 1811 (see chapter 8). One area that remains poorly understood, however, is the primary phase of activity, a series of 'diagonal walls', representing a building earlier than, and misaligned with, the main villa, having first been exposed by Samuel Lysons in the early nineteenth century. The plan of the 'diagonal walls' has never been fully resolved, although it is clear that the area that they originally covered was extensive (Aldsworth and Rudling 1995, 181). The fragmentary plan is suggestive of a range of rooms set around a large, central courtyard, akin to the Mediterranean-style of the main domestic range in the Fishbourne Proto Palace and the artefacts recovered from all phases of investigation at Bignor certainly hint at some form of activity here in the late first or early second century (e.g. Aldsworth and Rudling 1995, 110-1). The full extent and nature of this constructional phase is, as yet, unknown, but must remain a key priority for future work.

The complex noted from beneath the streets of Eastbourne is also poorly understood, although large areas have been investigated on a number of occasions, in 1712, 1841, 1848, 1853 and 1879. The first area to be examined comprised a possible sunken bath and an adjoining mosaic of white *tesserae* with a double line of red and brown *tesserae*. After excavation the bath and mosaic were unfortunately left exposed to the mercy of the weather and souvenir hunter. When Dr Jeremiah Milles passed by the site in 1743 he observed that both features were 'now entirely destroyed, so that one can only see the bed of plaster in which the mosaic was fixed; everybody that came to see it took pieces of it, and no care was taken to preserve it.' (Milles quoted in Sutton 1952, 4). Interestingly, Milles also noted that from the area of the bath to the sea 'and, as I am told all the way to Eastbourne, which is about a mile further, they find foundations of Roman walls' (Milles quoted in Sutton 1952, 4).

Clearly the area of archaeological interest at Eastbourne was a significant one. In 1841 a 'mosaic pavement' was found when the Roundhouse, a building threatened by coastal erosion, was demolished whilst the construction of a sea wall to the south west in 1848, some 91.5m to the south of the 1712 mosaic, revealed the foundations of a substantial structure eroding from the cliff edge. The main feature here appeared to be a corridor, traced for a distance of over 68.6m, paved with 'tile and cream coloured stone'. In 1853, the bases of 'two large columns' were unearthed during building work in Grand Parade, whilst further foundations and floor levels relating to the main structure were uncovered in 1879. Sadly, given the sporadic and poorly recorded nature of these early exploratory diggings, combined with the rapacious nature of Eastbourne's urban development, it is not known how all these areas were related, or even if they were in any sense contemporary. The length of the corridor revealed in 1848, and nature of rooms observed, is however highly suggestive, comparing favourably with the main phase of the palace at Fishbourne. Similarities between the finds from the two sites, especially that of the flue tile (Black 1987), provides a further link between the two structures.

As with Fishbourne, it is impossible to say with any certainty who lived in the palace at Southwick or in the other early buildings recorded at Pulborough, Angmering, Westhampnett, Arundel, Brighton, Eastbourne or Langstone. The chronology, sequence and form of Fishbourne, as noted above, plausibly ties the site to the ascendancy of Gaius Sallustius Lucullus, governor of Britain in the late 80s or early AD 90s, and the majority of these early sites can confidently be said to be the same. This was a period of substantial effort on behalf of central government to better Romanise key players in the province through the development of new civilian building projects and (probably) increased financial incentives. This process seems to have begun in earnest under the auspices of Lucullus' predecessor, the governor Gnaeus Julius Agricola. The Roman historian Tacitus specifically highlighted this process and provided an insight to the methods used:

> Agricola gave private encouragement and public aid to the building of temples, courts of justice and dwelling-houses, praising the energetic, and reproving the indolent …
> He likewise provided a liberal education for the sons of the chiefs, and showed such a preference for the natural powers of the Britons over the industry of the Gauls that they who lately disdained the tongue of Rome now coveted its eloquence. Hence, too, a liking sprang up for our style of dress, and the toga became fashionable. Step by step they were led to things which dispose to vice, the lounge, the bath, the elegant banquet. (Tacitus *Agricola* 21)

The paragraph ends with a typical piece of Tactitean cynicism when he observes that: 'all this in their ignorance they called civilisation, when it was but a part of their servitude' (Tacitus *Agricola* 21).

The movers and shakers of the developing Roman province seem to have ploughed their money into developing new homes from Rome on the south coast in Sussex. Whether these *nouveau riche* sprang from the surviving Iron Age aristocracy (as Lucullus), or were simply those who, whatever their ethnic origins, were keen to exploit the province and settle down, we will probably never know, but the probability that they were Britons on the make seems likely. Every society throughout history throws up its 'newly rich'; a class of people who generate a substantial amount of money and who then endeavour to spend it as swiftly and conspicuously as possible. Indeed, the social systems of late first-century Chichester and Fishbourne may have been akin to that of post-Soviet, late twentieth-century Russia where the term 'novyi Russkiy', or New Russian, is applied with contempt to the prominently successful. New Russians flaunt their wealth through the acquisition of expensive homes and gaudy western status symbols. Often viewed as arrogant, tasteless and lacking in cultural refinement, New Russians are frequently treated with suspicion by those who feel that they attained their wealth thorough dubious, illicit or downright criminal means. 'New Britons' of the later first century AD may well have been the same.

FISHBOURNE AND SOUTHWICK: A CHANGE OF PLAN

The removal from power of Lucullus by Domitian seems to have ushered in a period of change to the palace at Fishbourne. The man for whom the copy in miniature of the *Domus Flavia* had been designed was now dead and the great political experiment of the Flavian dynasty in Britain was over.

The execution of Cunobelin's grandson and Propraetorian Imperial Legate of Britain meant that the original palace, which may not yet have been complete, now faced an uncertain future. With the governor gone, the buildings at Fishbourne would presumably have been confiscated by the State to be retained in Imperial hands, passed on to other officials or to be bought up by and surviving members of the Catuvellauni/Regini household untainted by the imperial smear campaign. Alternatively, the State apartments and palatial splendour of the Fishbourne complex could have been made available at a 'knock down price' to an up and coming member of the new commercial elite; the British *nouveau riche*. Whatever the case, the basic structure and design of the Fishbourne palace, a range of high-status apartments linked to a monumental *triclinium*, entrance hall and bath suite, was now probably both uneconomical and politically untenable.

Whoever acquired Fishbourne palace in the early years of the second century AD, they immediately initiated a major change in design (59). The first alterations came with the modification of the great aisled hall. The hall or basilica, such a prominent feature in both the *Domus Flavia* and the primary layout of the Fishbourne palace, was presumably no longer required and a bath suite was unceremoniously inserted through the room and against the northern edge of the east wing. It has been noted (e.g. Cunliffe 1998, 111) that at the time this bathing complex was added, the suite in the south-eastern corner of the palace, built over the remains of the Proto Palace, was still in 'good working order'. The apparent duplication of bathing establishments

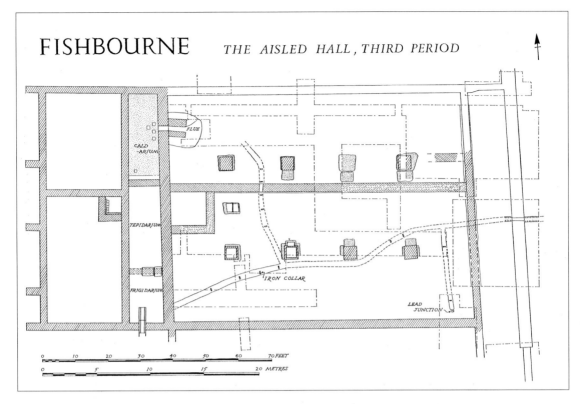

FISHBOURNE *THE AISLED HALL, THIRD PERIOD*

FLUE

CALD-ARIUM

TEPIDARIUM

FRIGIDARIUM

IRON COLLAR

LEAD JUNCTION

| 0 | 10 | 20 | 30 | 40 | 50 | 60 | 70 FEET |

| 0 | 5 | 10 | 15 | 20 METRES |

59 Fishbourne: interpretative ground plan of the early second-century bathhouse and exercise hall inserted into the aisled basilica. © *Institute of Archaeology, Oxford and Sussex Archaeological Society*

in the northern and southern wings of the palace may therefore suggest that the building had now been subdivided between at least two separate owners, each of whom desired their own access to a private bath. Such a theory could tie in with the theory that the concept of single occupancy use of the complex died with Lucullus late in the first century.

The new baths were established on fairly simple lines, three new rooms being created in the former passageway that had previously separated the basilica from the rest of the north wing. The northernmost room of this new suite was given an underfloor heating system or hypocaust, fed directly from a furnace and stokehole built to the east, in an area previously part of the main hall. This new room was, in all probability, intended to serve as the *caldarium* (hot room). The newly formed middle room was, if the interpretation is correct, a *tepidarium* (warm room) the heat for it deriving from the hypocaust of the adjoining *caldarium*. A small plunge bath, floored with tile and rendered in red mortar, was set into the centre of the room's west wall. The most southerly room was, via a process of elimination, almost certainly the *frigidarium* (cold room), although the possibility remains that this could have functioned as a latrine, a large central drain feeding from here into the palace gardens.

At the same time the bath suite was being inserted, the aisled hall was being reduced in width from 20m to around 11.6m, the southernmost arcade now serving as a centrally placed row of roof supports. The new rectangular-shaped building that emerged from the ruins of the basilica may, thanks to its proximity to the baths, be interpreted as a *palaestra* or exercise facility where a prospective bather could first build up an impressive sweat. The insertion of a possible drinking fountain (or wash basin) within the south-eastern corner of the modified hall may increase the likelihood of such a suggestion.

Quite why it was felt necessary to reduce the hall so drastically in size ands scale remains unclear, although Cunliffe speculated that the weight of the original roof may have caused structural problems which led to a complete rethink and redesign (Cunliffe 1998, 113). Whatever the reasons, it was clear that by the early years of the second century AD, the basilica or assembly room was no longer considered a necessary part of structure. New ownership meant a new design for life. A provincial governor and descendant of kings would presumably have been keen to emulate the style of the emperor and possess a basilica. Secondary owners would not have felt the same desire to emulate so closely the style of the imperial family and neither would they have countenanced, nor required, such a flagrant waste of premium floor space. The basilica was remodelled and its functionality dutifully increased.

Further additions to the original design of the palace, perhaps indicating that the 'official or semi public functions at the site were now at an end' here (Cunliffe 1988, 115), included evidence to suggest that the centrally-placed formal gardens were beginning to fade away and that parts were now being used to dump domestic waste.

Small-scale modifications can also be detected in room N13, at the very centre of the north wing, between the two open courtyards. Here a new mosaic was set directly over the heavily worn geometric design. The new work managed to compress the head of Medusa into the central roundel and surrounded this with at least eight roughly octagonal panels each side possessing a distinctive form of leaf or flower design (*colour plate 10*). The face of Medusa, her hair a writhing mass of snakes with wings set above her crown, though now badly damaged, is instantly recognisable. Analysis of the *tesserae* in the mosaic has demonstrated that most of the red pieces used were cut from Samian pottery, the high-class table ware of Romano-British society. None of the pieces yet identified appear to post-date AD 90-100, providing a tight *terminus post quem*, or date after which the mosaic must have been laid. Could this represent one of the last pieces of building work in the palace proper, prior to the death of Gaius Sallustius Lucullus and the subdivision of the complex? Certainly the choice of motif would have been appropriate, the story of Medusa being intimately entwined with both Neptune and Minerva, the two deities to whom Togidubnus dedicated a temple in the nearby town of Chichester (see chapter 10).

As the palace of Fishbourne underwent drastic modification, a similar process of change seems to have begun at Southwick. We have already noted that the

Southwick complex was a smaller version of Fishbourne which copied the basic division of private and public space set around an entrance hall, *triclinium* and central courtyard. As with its larger cousin, significant alterations to the Southwick ground plan commenced shortly after the removal of Gaius Sallustius Lucullus from office, at some point in the late first or very early second century AD. A small bath suite, mirroring the addition to the northern wing of Fishbourne, was inserted into the north-eastern corner of Southwick, whilst in the east range, the structure of the *triclinium* was drastically modified, possibly for the addition of an underfloor heating system (Black 1987, 103-4). The large basilica at the south-western corner of the Southwick palace also appears to have been substantially altered at this time. Whether there were similar changes to the structural integrity of the remaining early Roman buildings suggested at Angmering, Pulborough, Arundel, Eastbourne, Langstone and others, remains to be seen.

7

ROADS AND ROADSIDE SETTLEMENT

The town of *Noviomagus* and the palaces and early villas of the successful native elite, were only part of the new order developing across Sussex and the south-east in the latter half of the first century AD. In order to keep the peace, as well as ensuring the economic viability of the new territory, central government required rapid and continual access to the agricultural estates, ironfields and centres of civilian population. The harbours, ports and river-based trade centres that characterised the exchange network of pre-Roman Britain were maintained, and in some instances updated and improved, but Rome needed a more efficient system of inland communications. A cross-country network of roads was therefore swiftly laid out across the hitherto largely impenetrable landscape of lowland Britain.

TRANSPORT INFRASTRUCTURE

Evidence of the communications network imposed by Rome upon the landscape of Sussex remains clear to this day. Drive out from Pulborough northwards along the A29, and you cannot fail to be impressed by Stane Street, a dead straight length of road bulldozing its way through the rural landscape: a classic piece of Roman military engineering. More impressive perhaps are the physical remains of Stane Street, preserved on the South Downs close to Bignor Hill, some 9.5km north-east of Chichester, in an area ignored by later road planning authorities. Here the road is easily traceable as a prominent linear earthwork, measuring 17.7m in width and still standing 1.2m high (*60*), running through Nore Wood and up to The Gumber.

For nearly 1.6km, two flanking ditches are visible on either side of Stane Street, giving the road an overall width of around 26m (*61*), a distance which Ivan Margary

60 Stane Street: a section of the road, showing *agger* and western flanking ditch (beneath modern footpath), preserved on the South Downs close to Bignor Hill, 9.5km to the north-east of Chichester. *Author*

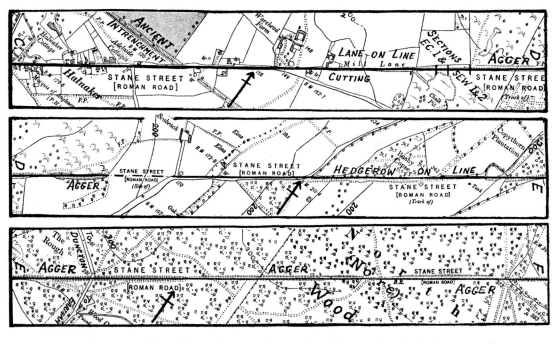

61 Stane Street: part of Ivan Margary's 1948 survey showing the route taken by the Roman road through Halnaker and on towards Bignor Hill. © *Sussex Archaeological Society*

62 Stane Street: aerial view of the road *agger* as it runs through Nore Wood, taken early in the 1940s. The arrows indicate the position of the flanking ditches. © *Sussex Archaeological Society*

observed 'was a standard measurement for first-class roads, perhaps to demarcate a zone for the highway' (Margary 1948, 51). The embankment that sits clearly between these ditches, becoming more pronounced as one heads north towards the crest of the Downs (*62*), is known as the *agger*. Generally, the *agger* was a broad, slightly cambered bank which supported and raised the road above ground level. Composed from material excavated from the side ditches or from nearby quarries, the *agger* was usually, although not exclusively, metalled 'with the best material that could be obtained locally' (Margary 1948, 18). Such material could include flint, gravel, sandstone or, in the case of more easterly roads constructed within the vicinity of the Wealden ironworking sites, cinder and iron slag (*63*). For the major highways, of which Stane Street was one, the metalled surface would have been rammed down into a series of well-compacted layers.

The designers and builders of Roman roads were not hindered by concerns of where to place their highways. In order to function effectively, central government needed a network of direct, reliable thoroughfares linking all the major towns, forts and harbours and road developers therefore aimed for straightness. Modern worries about the environmental impact of major building works were not shared by the ancients and neither was the Roman State really all that concerned about the location of existing settlements, for farms and villages could all be relocated. It was undoubtedly the army that set the pace and direction of the first road network in

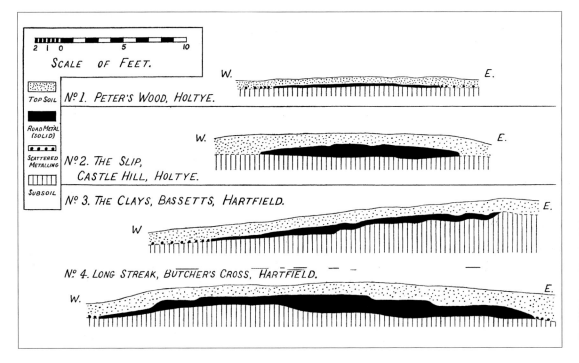

63 Holtye and Hartfield: sections recorded by Ivan Margary through the London – Lewes highway showing the extent of iron slag and cinder road metal. © *Sussex Archaeological Society*

Britain, linking their forts with the emerging towns, farms and areas of metalworking, creating the supply lines necessary to maintain order in the new province, and the army was not to be questioned (nor sadly halted by any form of road protest).

The major highways through Roman Sussex have all been identified and plotted on the ground, much of the work being conducted by one man: Ivan Margary. Margary made the study of the Roman roads in south-eastern England his life's work, publishing many detailed and authoritative works charting the route taken by these ancient thoroughfares. Margary's fieldwork was exhaustive, analysing maps, place names, local traditions, aerial photographs, land documents and archaeological findspots, as well as conducting his own field surveys and excavation. In his book *Roman Ways in the Weald*, first published in 1948, Margary recorded the telltale signs to be aware of when attempting to establish the alignment of a previously unknown road:

(1)   A straight length of modern road suddenly turning off to continue as a normally winding one, but the straight line going on as a line of hedges or a lane.

(2)   A line of hedgerows accurately straight for a considerable distance, though be aware of old estate boundaries which sometimes do this.

(3)   Lengths of parish and county boundaries, sometimes.

(4)   A straight modern road suddenly making a detour and then resuming the original line. Derelict remains may be found within the detour.

(5)   A modern road, originally straight and with very wide verges, now warped by the enclosure of small plots, first on one side and then on the other, which make it appear winding. Such a road is nearly always old, and derelict remains may be found within the bends.

(6)   Changes of alignment were usually made on high ground, so that straight modern roads doing this may be suspected.

(7)   High ground was preferred for strategic reasons, so that a suitable ridge is a very likely place on which to find a Roman road alignment. If the ridge is winding, the road may curve along it like a ridgeway. (Margary 1948, 31-2)

Having identified a possible road on a map, aerial photograph or other document, Margary then went on to explain the ways in which a detailed ground survey or limited excavation could help confirm or deny the existence of a potential Roman road.

Margary's work was, for its time, literally ground breaking and many of his detective techniques have been adopted and adapted by the fieldworkers and archaeological surveyors of today. Not all of the routes he described and documented, however, have been proved by excavation and, as David Rudling has already noted, caution should be exercised concerning some of the identified routes that were not part of the official highway system linking forts and towns (Rudling 2003, 114). Having said that, without Ivan Margary's efforts, we would be much the poorer in our understanding of the Roman road network in Sussex and the south-east.

The major route-way, as already noted, was that of the Chichester to London road, known since early medieval times as 'Stane Street'. It would be wrong, however, to think of Stane Street as a road that was, in its earliest incarnation, specifically designed to link the towns of Chichester and London. Stane Street did of course *eventually* connect the two cities, but, from the outset, the basic alignment of the road suggests that it may have fulfilled an entirely different objective. The original alignment of the highway is clear enough: a dead-straight line running from Dell Quay in Chichester Harbour, to the river Arun at Hardham, just below modern-day Pulborough.

Sporadic fieldwork around the Pulborough and Hardham has indicated the presence of a significant area of Later Iron Age and Early Roman activity. Indeed, the considerable quantities of Late Iron Age pottery, which include late first-century BC/ early first-century AD Roman amphorae and fine wares, recovered to the immediate north-east of the town (in association with a range of rectangular enclosure ditches: Cunliffe *et al.* 1996, 17, 135-6; Caroline Wells pers. comm.) would appear to hint at an important trading post. Such a trade centre, established at the northern limits of the tidal range of the river Arun, would probably have been thriving by the latter years of the Roman emperor Augustus (Cunliffe *et al.* 1996, 17). The significance of the area may further be highlighted by the observation that the river Arun represents one of the few rivers in Roman Britain for which a Latin name has been recorded: the *Trisantona* (Rivet and Smith 1979, 45).

Dell Quay, at the opposite end of the Stane Street alignment from Hardham to the south-west, is where road meets the sea and, we may presume, where it plugged directly into the cross-channel trade network to Gaul and beyond. There is no indication that the road, at the time of its initial laying out, joined the city of *Noviomagus* to anything. Indeed the town seems to have been a later addition to the already existing road line (James Kenny pers. comm.), necessitating a wide detour into the later developing urban centre. Neither was Stane Street initially heading for London, for this direction required a change in orientation from the Hardham/Pulborough area. We may also assume that *Londinium* as a concept did not exist much before the AD mid-50s, and its significance as a provincial capital did not emerge until long after the Boudican revolt of AD 60/1. Only after its initial design was established was Stane Street realigned and modified in order to connect Chichester, the town of the Regini, to that of the London, later capital of the province. All this suggests an early route, designed to connect two important harbours or centres of Late Iron Age and Early Roman sea trade. Quite how early however, is on present evidence impossible to say.

Other key route-ways extended out from Chichester, the road leaving the town from the north, eventually reaching Silchester, the Roman city of *Calleva Atrebatum*. As with Stane Street, the alignment of the Roman highway suggests that Silchester may not have been the primary destination, that possibly being Iping, to the north of the West Sussex river Rother. The road exiting Chichester from the west presumably headed out towards the enlarged natural harbours of Portsmouth and the Solent, also serving to link Chichester with Winchester, the *civitas* capital of *Venta Belgarum*.

Additional highways in Sussex have been recorded from the east, two important routes being those connecting London to Lewes and London to Brighton (Margary 1948, 93-123; 124-64). No major areas of Roman settlement, excepting villa sites, are known in either the Brighton or Lewes area, and it seems reasonable to assume that these highways were intended to provide a swift means of transportation between the provincial capital and the ironfields and natural rivers of the Weald. Roads did not, of course, provide the only means of transporting Wealden iron, and the presence of tiles stamped with the identification mark of the *Classis Britannica*, or British Fleet, at ironworking sites such as Beauport Park, near Hastings (chapter 10), implies significant involvement in iron production. Harbours and fleet bases may well have existed at Bodiam, on the East Sussex Rother and at Pevensey on the coast (chapter 11). A major east–west thoroughfare, known today as the 'Greensand Way', also lay to the north of the chalk Downs, linking the Hardham/Pulborough area (and Stane Street), via Hassocks, to the Lewes and Brighton to London roads.

64 Worthing: early
fourth-century
milestone dedicated
to Constantine I.
*Author with kind
permission of the Sussex
Archaeological Society*

Distance along these main roads would have been calculated in miles (*milia passuum*: literally 'one thousand paces'), the Roman mile being shorter than its modern equivalent. Milestones, basically an upright pillar of stone carrying distance information such as the relative mile number, were often established along major Roman highways, especially in Italy and in those lands bordering the Mediterranean. In Britain, such stones often were more simply inscribed with the names of emperors, under whose patronage or authority (we may assume) repairs were conducted. One such milestone (*64*), found in Worthing (RIB 2220), carries the inscription:

...DIVI

CONSTANT...

PII AVG

FILIO

which some have translated as:

> ... son of the deified Constantius Pius Augustus

This unfortunately rather uninformative text does not supply us with a fixed date for the inscription. It could refer either to a son of Flavius Valerius Constantius (Constantius I), full emperor of the West AD 305-6 or his grandson Flavius Julius Constantius (Constantius II), emperor of the East AD 337-61 (adding the West to his domain from AD 353). The house of Constantine had particular resonance in Britain, Constantius I dying whilst on campaign in York, his son Flavius Valerius Constantinus, later Constantine I (also known as 'Constantine the Great') being proclaimed successor to empire there in AD 306. Given the rather limited use of titles supplied on this stone, it may plausibly be suggested that the emperor being referred to was indeed Caesar Flavius Constantinus Pius Felix Invictus Augustus (Constantine I) son of Caesar Gaius Flavius Valerius Constantius Augustus (Constantius I), putting the stone's erection at some point between AD 307 and 337. Sadly, we will probably never be able to identify the original position that the milestone occupied prior to its discovery. It could have been removed from either Stane Street (to the north) or have come from a coastal road, the precise route of which has now been lost.

MANSIONES

Two of the major road arteries, running north-east from Chichester along Stane Street and the more circuitous route running north-north-west from Chichester to Silchester, were associated with a series of rectangular earthwork enclosures at Hardham, Alfoldean, Iping and Neatham (in Hampshire). All four sites (Hardham and Alfoldean on Stane Street and Iping and Neatham on the Silchester road) have at times been referred to as *mansiones*.

Officially a *mansio* was a place, station, or more specifically a building, provided by the Roman State, for the use of official travellers, military personnel, messengers and tax collectors. *Mansiones* were the Roman equivalent of an elite service station, a cross between a motel and a post-medieval coaching station. *Mansiones* were set at regular distances along the main highways of empire by the provincial or local (*civitas*) governments. On Stane Street, Hardham was established some 15 Roman miles to the north-east of Chichester, with Alfoldean a further 12 Roman miles, and the potential sites at Dorking and Ewell a further 11.5 and 10 Roman miles respectively. From Ewell the final stretch into London was just 14 Roman miles (Black 1995, 14).

As a building, a *mansio* itself can be identified in the archaeological record as a structure with a repeating series of internal spaces (bed and reception rooms), a communal dining area and latrines, all set around an enlarged courtyard, with stables and a bathhouse. The level of interior décor within *mansiones* varied considerably, much like a modern hotel, from the basic shared 'bed-and-breakfast' style accommodation, to the high-status single occupancy rooms reserved for the wealthy or the travelling administrative elite. Inns, hostels, taverns and other, potentially less reputable establishments, would also probably have been set up along major thoroughfares, together with *mutationes*, the Roman equivalent of the modern garage, where a traveller could conceivably repair their transport, re-shoe a horse or find a complete replacement.

The site at Alfoldean was first noted in 1810, with further investigation being conducted throughout the late nineteenth and early twentieth centuries. Few of these 'probings' seem to have been recorded in any great detail; although work conducted in 1912 allegedly unearthed a mosaic (Belloc 1913, 250) or tessellated floor. The first detailed work commenced between 1922 and 1923, under the direction of Samuel Winbolt (65). The exploration focused upon the interior of the enclosure, Winbolt unearthing a range of substantial buildings, foremost among which was a structure confidently interpreted as the 'officers quarters' (Winbolt 1923, 92). Unfortunately, it is difficult to establish a coherent plan of the building from the record supplied, probably due to extensive post-Roman stone robbing and agricultural disturbance, although the discovery of red, white and blue *tesserae*, *opus signinum* (mortar floor), roof tile, floor tile, painted wall plaster and window glass does suggest a significant and elaborate building (Luke and Wells 2000, 94-5). Excavation and survey conducted in 2005 during the course of the Channel 4 television programme *Time Team*, revealed more of the masonry first exposed by Winbolt, suggesting that, instead of 'officers quarters', the building would appear to have been a substantial, courtyard *mansio* with a bathhouse to the north (Black 1987, 122; Neil Holbrook pers. comm.).

An extensive civilian settlement developed to the south of the Alfoldean enclosure. It is possible that, having set out both the road and the stopping-off-point, that settlers were actively encouraged by the *civitas* authorities to establish themselves around the new *mansio* (Black 1995, 94), in much the way that a civilian settlement (or *vicus*) often grew around semi-permanent army bases. Little is known about the nature and form taken by the Alfoldean settlement, though it would appear to have replaced a rural farming centre belonging to the later Iron Age (Mike Luke pers. comm.). With the road and *mansio* in place, there was a major realignment of the settlement, a series of land plots being set at right angles to Stane Street, extending for over 600m along the road, south from the river Arun. The plots were defined by shallow gulleys and trackways, the street frontage available varying between 68-131m (Luke and Wells 2000, 80). A variety of round, square and rectangular buildings were set within the land parcels defined at no more than around 10m from the edge of the highway. Artefacts recovered during the course of fieldwalking and 2005 trial excavations suggest a relatively high standard of living in the settlement, which seems to have flourished 'at least into the early fourth century AD' (Luke and Wells 2000, 99).

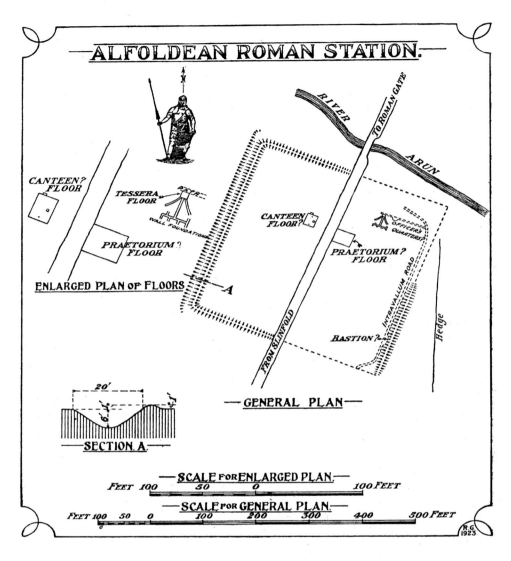

65 Alfoldean: a surface survey and excavation plan of the enclosure compiled by Robert Gurd for Samuel Winbolt in 1923. The interpretation of Officers' Quarters, *Praetorium* and canteen floor are not followed today, the buildings to the east of the road seemingly all forming part of a well-appointed *j157* with bathhouse. © *Sussex Archaeological Society*

Alfoldean, Hardham, Iping and Neatham were all surrounded by an extensive series of earthworks, defining military-style square or rectangular enclosures with rounded corners (the classic 'playing-card shape' beloved by Roman forts of the first and second centuries AD). The dimensions of the Sussex enclosures were all broadly similar, Hardham measuring around 100 x 100m, Alfoldean 125 x 125m and Iping 110 x 100m. The rectangular enclosure at Neatham was slightly larger, measuring 160 x 220m (Millett and Graham 1986). Evidence retrieved from Alfoldean during the excavations of 2005 suggests that the bank and ditch dated to no later than AD 90 (Mark Corney pers. comm.), whilst similar evidence has also been obtained from Hardham (Winbolt 1927) and Iping (James Kenny pers. comm.).

The size and scale of the earthworks clearly indicates that the enclosing ramparts were considered necessary and that the *mansiones*, and whatever else lay close by, needed protection. But from what? This area of West Sussex and eastern Hampshire was, we can assume, relatively free of revolt, rebellion and military instability by the final years of the first century AD. Why then did the planners, road builders and administrative officials of the *civitas* feel it necessary to enclose the four sites with defensive ramparts? The solution may all lie in the nature of the *mansiones*, for the creation of defences helped to define a strong control point on the official highway. Not everyone would presumably have had the access, permission or inclination to travel the State road and those that did could expect to have their movements observed and recorded. Alfoldean and Hardham were also placed where Stane Street crossed the river Arun, ensuring that river users were also under the watchful eye of the State. The sites could also have been where specific resources, such as grain, new recruits for the army and tax money for central government, were protected and contained *en route* to London. Other key resources, such as iron, a substance whose movements were controlled in the first and second century by the military, may also have been safely stored here, in the equivalent of an official depot or warehouse.

Apart from possessing a specific range of policing duties (keeping the roads clear of bandits and other potential lawbreakers), Alfoldean, Hardham and Iping could also have performed a more insidious function. Repair to the highway would, we may presume, have been a fairly constant activity and, once a road such as Stane Street had been constructed by the military, the likelihood is that responsibility for its upkeep would have devolved to regional, tribal (*civitas*) authorities. In order to fund maintenance and repair works, the local authorities would have to have been continually raising money. To do this they could increase local levels of taxation (not a popular move as any aspiring politician today is acutely aware) or impose a less obvious form of income generation, or 'stealth tax', by charging those making use of the highway.

Throughout history fees or tolls have been collected at fixed points along major thoroughfares in order to generate revenue for central or local government authorities. Such tolls could be used to pay for the upkeep of a national or regional army, to supplement taxes or, more usually, to fund road maintenance projects. In seventeenth- and eighteenth-century England, specific authorities were permitted to collect a fee for road use, cash being collected at monitored points, such as toll houses, which possessed a gate or other means of blocking the highway. Today in Britain, the stealth tax on road use has returned, tolls being charged on new motorways, bridges and tunnels. Often the point of cash collection is represented by a formidable array of electronic barriers controlled by automatons from behind heavily fortified bunkers of reinforced glass, concrete and steel. The Roman equivalent of these government-sanctioned zones of highway robbery was undoubtedly the enclosed *mansio*.

It is possible that another significant roadside settlement developed at Hassocks, to the north of Brighton. The zone of Roman activity here comprises a large cremation cemetery, recorded from the western margins of the modern town. Unfortunately the site has been extensively damaged by a large sand extraction pit, the cutting of which began late in the nineteenth century. Over 150 Romano-British burial urns are known to have been recovered from the area of the pit, although the probability is that many more have been lost or destroyed during the extraction process. The bulk of deposition seems to have been between the mid-first and later third century AD, burial perhaps coming to an end after AD 270. It is not clear whether the termination of cremated deposits reflects a change in burial rite, with inhumation (and Christianity?) becoming more popular, or because settlement refocused elsewhere (Lyne 1994, 79).

The quantity of remains recovered at Hassocks certainly suggests an important area of settlement activity at the intersection of the Greensand Way across the Weald and the London to Brighton road. It is conceivable that this settlement and burial activity may have focussed around an enlarged, possibly enclosed *mansio* dating to the late first or early second century. Given that neither the Greensand Way nor the London to Brighton road were major highways, at least in the sense of Stane Street; however, the evidence recovered from Hassocks may relate less to a State-sponsored *mansio*, such as Alfoldean, and more to a settlement or small town growing organically in order to meet the needs of travellers and to successfully exploit the economic possibilities of the new road network.

The *mansiones* of Hardham, Alfoldean and Iping, together with the area of roadside activity from Hassocks, represent a frequently overlooked element of Roman rural settlement in Sussex. The archaeological evidence recovered to date hints at major zones of habitation at all four sites, combined with evidence of trade, exchange, burial, agriculture and industrial production. Certainly, Alfoldean and Hardham sat at the epicentre of a landscape filled with all the natural resources required to successfully sustain an industrial economy, such as timber, iron ore and clay (necessary for the manufacture of pottery, tile and brick). The position of both sites was critical: at points in the landscape where the two major routes of Stane Street and the river Arun crossed. Linked to the official communications network of the road and river, the importance of Hardham and Alfoldean is self-evident.

Could it be that places such as these grew to fulfil 'some of the same objectives behind the creation of *civitas* capitals' (Luke and Wells 2000, 97-8), namely as administrative, judicial and market centres? Established at semi-regular intervals (*c.*10-12km) along the major highways north from Chichester, Alfoldean and Hardham would have been ideally suited to serve the rural community. These sites may have been established to provide protection, facilities and refreshment for official travellers on the imperial highway, as well as collecting a toll for road use, but by the later second century AD they seem to have spawned successful and thriving, semi-autonomous communities.

It may be instructive to consider the proposed sequence provided for the *mansio* enclosures of Sussex. The Roman centres at Alfoldean and Hardham appear to have had their origins in the mid-first century, possibly as early as the AD 50s. As artificial constructs of the State, these two sites, at least, would owe their origins to the *civitas* of *Noviomagus*. At this time, dedications were being set up in the city centre to the emperor Nero, whilst Tiberius Claudius Togidubnus oversaw the finishing touches to a fine classical temple to Neptune and Minerva. The later creation of large enclosure circuits around Hardham, Alfoldean and Iping in the AD 90s, probably relate less to Togidubnus, and more to his successor Gaius Sallustius Lucullus. Could it be that the establishment of *mansiones* along the roads to London and Silchester was part of a deliberate attempt to fast-track the Romanising process by creating a regular series of brand, spanking new officially administered market centres?

The *mansiones* would further facilitate the necessary infrastructure of government whilst the creation of fixed toll points along the roads would help to generate the cash necessary to fund larger and more ambitious building projects across the region. Alternatively, the establishment of elaborate earthwork circuits around Alfoldean, Iping and Hardham at the end of the first century could relate to the time immediately following the dispatch of Lucullus by the emperor Domitian. After this, whatever client or 'friendly' status the region may previously have enjoyed would have gone and the kingdom of the Regini could be more fully integrated into the province of Britannia.

At some point in the late third century, the earthwork enclosure at Alfoldean was levelled, a similar event also possibly occurring at Hardham and Iping. This 'slighting' may have been a deliberate act intended to create better access to, and freedom of movement along, the highway of Stane Street. Perhaps the fixed toll and highway monitoring points were no longer considered helpful, or it may be that the political institutions that created the entire *mansio* system were no longer powerful. No clear evidence as to the end of the *mansio* building itself has yet been provided, but it could also have been demolished in the third century. The civilian settlement seems to have lasted a little longer, but by the early fourth century, its importance was diminishing.

8

VILLAS AND RURAL SETTLEMENT

The establishment of an efficient inland communications network, coupled with the development of palatial structures at Fishbourne, Southwick and elsewhere across Sussex must have had a profound effect upon the indigenous population. To those living beyond the new urban centre of *Noviomagus,* a basic lifestyle choice would have presented itself: continue the basic rhythms of life as before, unaffected by the imposition of Roman central government, or adapt and adopt the trappings of the new social elite. It was essential that those who wished to succeed under Roman rule displayed their wealth in new and more complex ways. In short they needed to become 'Roman'.

Legal niceties of citizenship aside, the adoption of Roman culture, customs and fashions was a necessary prerequisite for success in the new province and those infected early by Rome were more likely to benefit in the new order. Being Roman gave one the opportunity to enter in to a 'new world of consumer goods, personal prestige and self-advancement' (Johnston 2004, 7). Those members of the native aristocracy who publicly clung onto the old ways would, at best, have found themselves increasingly marginalised. At worst, such conservative elements would have been treated with suspicion and contempt. A good way to clearly (and unambiguously) demonstrate 'Roman-ness' and loyalty to the new regime would have been to live in an increasingly Roman manner. Timber-framed, straw-covered roundhouses with daub walls were out and rectangular, tiled roofed structures with solid floors were in.

Some archaeologists and historians have noted their dislike of the term 'villa' due to its connotations of 'luxury holiday' or 'retirement home' combined with its apparent inappropriateness when comparing British sites with those grand Roman villas found across Italy and the Mediterranean. Personally, I have no such qualms.

A villa in the context of Roman Britain was a place where the *nouveau riche* spent their hard-earned (or more dubiously acquired) cash. The majority of villas in Britain were at the centre of a working, successful agricultural estate it is true, profits generated from selling farm surplus presumably providing the necessary cash for home improvement, but a villa is as far away from a 'normal' working farm as one could expect.

Villas possessed elaborate bathing suites, ornate dining rooms and a generally high level of internal décor. Farms possessed more basic, functional accommodation with easy access to pigsties, cow sheds and ploughed fields. In this respect, the Roman villas of Sussex can perhaps be better compared with the grand estates, country houses and stately homes of the more recent landed gentry of England, Scotland and Wales. These houses represented monumental statements of power designed to dominate the land and impress all who passed by. As the home of a successful landowner wishing to attain a certain level of social standing and recognition, the stately home or country house was the grand, architectural centrepiece of a great agricultural estate where the owner could enhance his or her art collection, develop business opportunities, dispense the law and dabble in politics. In this, the Roman villa was probably little different.

The Roman villa is an easy enough type-site to identify archaeologically in Britain. Villas were high-status, Romanised houses and, as such, can clearly be distinguished from the type of 'normal' rural buildings that proceeded them. Villas possessed a broadly rectangular plan, comprising a range of rooms connected by a corridor or veranda. Walls, especially those in public areas, were often decorated whilst the provision of solid floors allowed the opportunity to invest in mosaic pavements depicting scenes from classical mythology. Architectural details, such as ornate columns, glazed windows and tiled roofs embellished the whole whilst major structural 'add-ons' such as the integrated bathing suite and underfloor heating system, were often brought in as and when finances allowed.

Of course we will never be able to answer, with any certainty, the question 'Who lived in the villas?'. This is a shame, as it is the one question that will always be asked. No known inscriptions (funerary or otherwise) outlining the background, life and career path of villa owners in Britain has survived, and those fragments of information that have been found serve only to tantalise and infuriate in equal measure. One such example is from a fourth-century mosaic found in a villa at Thruxton in Hampshire. Here, preserved in an inscribed panel, a personal name was found, presumably that of the owner himself: Quintus Natalius Natalinus. Sadly little can be usefully made of this discovery, other than to note, as many have done, that the name Natalius 'was not a real Roman name but an artificially constructed one, showing that the villa owner was a native' (Henig 2002, 109). Interestingly Natalinus recorded in the mosaic that he was *et bodeni* (of the Bodeni), which may be a link to the Bodunni (invariably and incorrectly cited as the Dobunni in most modern works), a British tribe whose *civitas* capital was at Cirencester.

A qualification to the original question on villa ownership 'Was it a Briton or Roman who lived here?' is, however, easier to answer, for although the *ethnic* origins of the owner cannot be determined, we can confidently state that they were all *culturally* Roman. Ethnicity is almost impossible to establish within the archaeological record (unless one is fortunate to find a tombstone which spells out the birthplace of the deceased) and the owner of a Romanised house in Sussex could just as easily have originated from Egypt, Gaul, Spain, Italy or anywhere else in the empire, having retired from the army or arriving in the hope of being able to make money in the new province, rather than having been born and raised in Britain. In building a Roman house for themselves, complete with all the trappings of a classical lifestyle (including baths, painted plaster on the walls and mosaics on the floors) villa owners were demonstrating their Roman-ness; their desire to fit in and be seen to be successful. Their ancestry or tribal background was subsumed and, to all intents and purposes, replaced by Roman attitudes, culture and beliefs. The villa owners worshipped Romanised gods, spoke (or made an attempt to understand) Latin, the universal language of empire, traded and paid tax in Roman coins and gave Roman names to their offspring. Archaeologically speaking, such people were no longer identifiably 'British' or 'Celtic', but wholly and indisputably Roman.

Unfortunately, though a large number of villa sites have been archaeologically examined in southern Britain since the early nineteenth century, few excavations were conducted with any kind of scientific rigour. In fact, the majority of investigations conducted into Roman villas in Britain were, until the mid-twentieth century, little more than elaborate exercises in treasure hunting in which the basic plan of the most substantial of structural features was made and only the most spectacular of artefacts recorded. Context, dating and sequence of evolution from Iron Age to Roman and Roman to post-Roman was often not considered during the course of such examinations and, as a consequence, much vital evidence was either overlooked or lost. This situation has thankfully been in decline since the mid-twentieth century with many detailed excavations of villas and their surrounding estates having been conducted, especially across Sussex.

Roman villas can take a variety of different forms, as one would expect from a type of structure that appears to have developed organically, without direct imposition from the State. Away from the planned rigidity displayed in the elite power-houses of Fishbourne and Southwick, the earliest Romanised rural houses of Sussex were comparatively modest. As centres of successful agricultural estates, however, their importance should not be underestimated. The appearance of Roman-style houses across the rural landscape of Britain perhaps tells us more about the relative success of Roman culture in the island, than anything else. Towns and forts were directly imposed from the top; forts being the product of direct military subjugation whilst towns were considered necessary to effectively administer demilitarised zones. Together with the road network and newly established harbour installations, forts and towns represented the essential infrastructure of control necessary for the effective government and exploitation of newly conquered territory. Villas and other Romanised elements of rural settlement are something completely different for these represent evidence for the relative success of Rome's attempts to win the hearts and minds of the indigenous population.

Four basic types of villa building are identifiable from Sussex: the Cottage House, Corridor House (sometimes with wings), Aisled Building and Courtyard House. Cottage or 'Strip' Houses represent the first form of Romanised rural buildings, comprising little more than a cluster of four or five squared rooms set in a line and covered by a single roof. Absence of surviving door sills often prevents us from understanding how each room in a Cottage or Strip House was originally accessed, although in order to maintain some level of internal privacy each room may have been provided with access to a porch or veranda. Corridor Houses represent an advancement in domestic planning, allowing increased privacy together with the possibility of being able to create 'a hierarchy of rooms' (Johnston 2004, 17), dividing public and private space as well as separating the house owner from his or her family, servants or employees. Corridor Houses often developed from simpler Cottage or Strip designs, whilst later developments sometimes included wings, at either end of the main corridor, constructed in order to accommodate a bathing suite or heated rooms.

Aisled Buildings represent a distinctive form of design, comprising a large, rectangular structure containing two parallel lines of posts, usually running the entire length of the building. These posts would originally have supported the roof, dividing the internal space of the structure into a central nave and two side aisles. One end of the building, or hall, is generally given over to more private, Romanised, forms of accommodation. Aisled structures are seldom in complete isolation, generally being found close to villas of the Cottage or Corridor variety. The fourth type of villa, the Courtyard House, represents the final evolutionary phase of Romanised rural building, with three or four ranges of domestic activity developing from a primary phase Cottage or Corridor House.

COTTAGE AND CORRIDOR HOUSES

At Beddingham, in East Sussex, a villa dating from the late first century (66) has been examined by David Rudling, excavations conducted between 1987 to 1992 revealing a sequence of development lasting until the mid-fourth century (Rudling 1998, 52-9). The primary phase of occupation here seems to have commenced some time around AD 50, although coins of the British kings Cunobelinus and Eppatticus combined with an abraded sherd of late Republican amphorae may hint at earlier activity (Rudling 1998, 52). The primary structure identified on site was the footprint of a *c*.9m-diameter timber roundhouse. Little was recovered from within the roundhouse, ploughing having removed all primary deposits, though pottery found within the fill of a number of postholes appears to indicate a 'pre-Flavian but

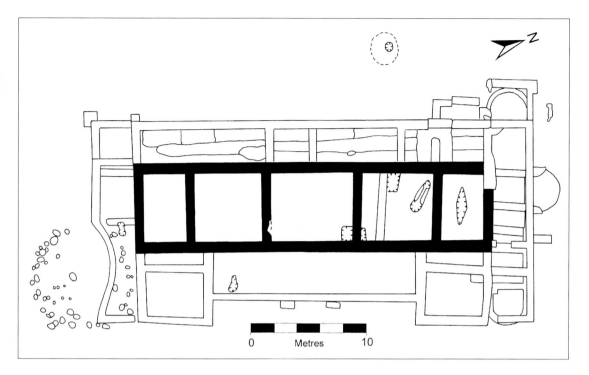

66 Beddingham: plan of the main domestic range, a winged Corridor Villa, showing all phases. The earliest phase of construction, a five-room Cottage House of the late first century, is outlined in black. At the bottom left of the drawing (the south-eastern quadrant) is the posthole circle of an earlier roundhouse or shrine. *Redrawn from Rudling 2003*

post-Conquest date' (i.e. between AD 43 and 69) for its construction (Rudling 1988, 52). The circular building possesses clear affinities with a range of house structures found across southern Britain in the Late Iron Age and Early Roman period, although the apparent lack of domestic features and deposits when combined with the observation that the space left by the building was respected long after it had been abandoned, has led Rudling to speculate that it may originally have functioned as a shrine (Rudling 1998, 52; Rudling 2003, 118).

The first stage of *Romanitas* evident at Beddingham was the construction of a rectangular building with mortared flint foundations, comprising five adjoining rooms with a drainage ditch to the rear. This type of construction represents one of the more simple forms of Romanised rural building, the Cottage House. The larger middle room of the phase 1 building may have functioned as the principal dining or reception area, with more private accommodation to the north or south (Rudling 1998, 53). Scattered *tesserae* suggest the former presence of, presumably rather simple, mosaic floors.

From the early years of the second century AD, significant additions were made to the basic Romanised house. A bathing suite, comprising at least three major phases of building and including a heated floor and an immersion bath, was established

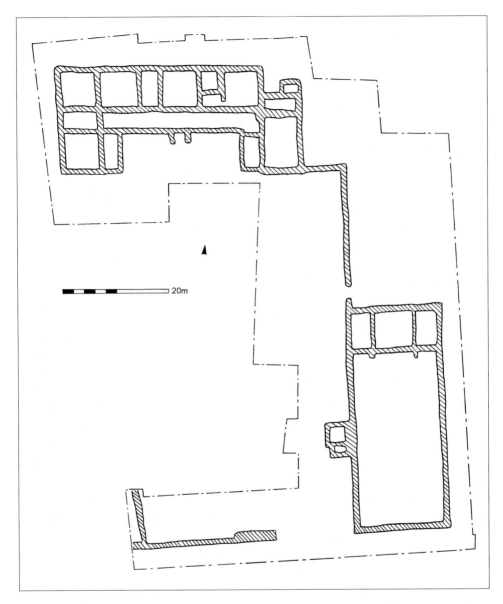

67 Barcombe: plan of the main domestic range, a winged Corridor Villa (north) and Aisled Building (east), both replacing earlier timber phases of construction. *Redrawn from Rudling 2003*

along the northern edge of the original house some time after AD 100. This suite appears to have gone out of use by the early third century, possibly being replaced by a detached bathhouse to the immediate north-east of the domestic range (Rudling 1998, 55). By this time changes were occurring within the villa itself, with the addition of a corridor on the eastern side, subdivision of internal space and the creation of new wings along the northern and southern ends.

Two circuits of ditch enclosed the villa at Beddingham, the Roman equivalent perhaps of the farm wall defining the limits of domestic space as well as protecting the resources of the farmyard. The innermost ditch seems to date from the late first to early second century, making it a possible contemporary of the primary phase timber roundhouse. In the mid-second century, as the villa began to take on its enlarged appearance, a second ditch was cut in order to enclose a more significant area. Unfortunately, little of the interior area defined by either ditch has been fully investigated to date, although a small, square masonry structure, measuring 3.6 x 3.7m, with a later apsidal space added to its western edge, has been located in the south-western quadrant. This building, which possibly dates to the third century, has, like the timber roundhouse, been interpreted as a shrine (Rudling 1998, 55-6).

Excavations at Barcombe, to the north-west of Beddingham, between 2001 to 2005 have produced a villa of similar size and sequence (*67*). Here the primary phase of occupation appears to have comprised a series of timber roundhouses, two of which were overlaid by the later Romanised house. Roundhouse 1, which was sealed by a deposit of baked clay which has produced an archaeomagnetic date of between AD 140 and 200, was of similar form and structure to the roundhouse discovered beneath the southern margins of the Beddingham villa, though here preservation was significantly better with traces of the outer wall or gulley surviving. At some point Roundhouse 1 was replaced by a rectangular, timber-framed building with flint footings, itself replaced, possibly in the third century, by a simple winged Corridor House (Rudling 2003, 121). This structure seems to have formed the northern domestic range of a larger, enclosed farmyard that included an extensively plough-damaged Aisled Building (see below). As at Beddingham, the original ground level at Barcombe had been lowered through agricultural attrition, though a few scattered fragments of flooring and many *tesserae* attest the former presence of mosaics and tessellated pavements.

A villa of Corridor style has also been found and excavated by Alec Down at Chilgrove, to the north of Chichester (*68*). The primary timber phase building, given the name 'Chilgrove 1' in order to distinguish it from another site located 1400m to the north-east, was constructed late in the first century AD, possibly replacing a farmstead of the Late Iron Age (Down 1979, 53-6). In the mid-to-late third century the building was rebuilt in a more grand style, later stages of development commencing early in the fourth century. The villa, in its final phase, comprised a range of rooms accessed from a single north-east to south-west aligned corridor, a modest bath suite being established at its southern end (*69*). Partial examination of the surrounding area suggested a farm wall or stockyard and outbuildings, at least one of which may have been of aisled construction.

The bath suite at Chilgrove 1 possessed a hot room (*caldarium*: room 1a) with an apsed immersion bath, heat deriving from a furnace or *praefurnium* (room 4), a warm room (*tepidarium*: room 1b) and a cold room (*frigidarium*: room 3), with a cold plunge (Down 1979, 64-6). The *frigidarium* underwent a variety of modifications during its use, and may, in its primary phase, have served as an *apodyterium* or changing area. rooms within the domestic range appear to have been well appointed with wall plaster,

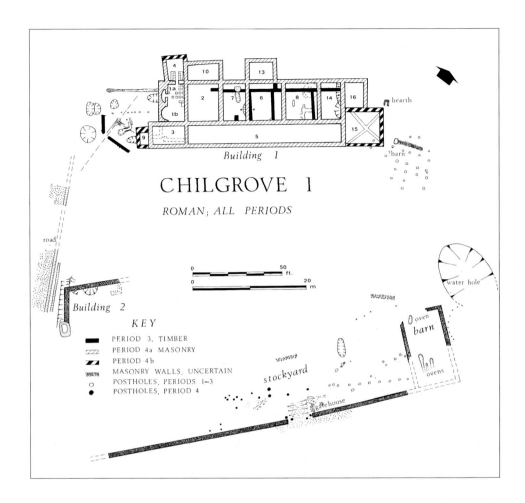

CHILGROVE 1

ROMAN; ALL PERIODS

KEY
- ▬ PERIOD 3, TIMBER
- ▨ PERIOD 4a MASONRY
- ▧ PERIOD 4b
- ▦ MASONRY WALLS, UNCERTAIN
- ○ POSTHOLES, PERIODS 1–3
- ● POSTHOLES, PERIOD 4

Above: 68 Chilgrove 1: ground plan showing all phases of the Corridor Villa in its farmyard setting. © *Chichester District Council*

Left: 69 Chilgrove 1: imaginative recreation, drawn by C. de la Nougerede, of the Corridor Villa under construction in the early fourth century AD. Note that a clerestory is depicted. © *Chichester District Council*

mosaics being recorded from room 6 (the central and no doubt principal public room of the house) and room 15 at the northern end. The intricate design of the room 6 floor comprised a central roundel surrounded by interlaced squares forming an octagon, itself enclosed within a square (*colour plate 11*). Unfortunately, the mosaic had been badly damaged by ploughing so that, although one can reasonably surmise the complete form of the geometric design, it is not possible to identify the nature and affiliation of the centrepiece. The floor of room 15 had originally been heated via a cross-flue hypocaust. Unfortunately, the collapse of the mosaic into the underfloor heating system meant that little of its design remained available for study.

AISLED BUILDINGS

The eastern range of the villa complex investigated at Barcombe (see above) comprised a large rectangular, north–south aligned Aisled Building. The northern end of the structure had been divided into a large central room and two narrow side rooms, a form which reflected the structural nature of the side aisles and central nave. The north-western room in this range, possessed a small area of red *tesserae* which was the only fragment of floor level to survive the depredations of the plough (*70*) (Chris Butler pers. comm.).

70 Barcombe: the last fragment of a red tessellated floor preserved within the north-western room of the Aisled Building. Better than anything else, this photograph highlights the very grave risk that ploughing presents to the long-term survival of buried archaeological remains. *Author*

Another simple form of Aisled Building in Sussex has been located on the western banks of Fishbourne Channel, 500m to the south-west of the main palace (71). The structure, excavated in 1983, replaced a rectangular timber building, possibly an earlier form of aisled hall or store established close to the margins of the Chichester Harbour. Dating evidence for the primary phase of building work at the site was scarce, though the excavator, David Rudkin, has postulated a date in the last quarter of the first century AD (Rudkin 1986, 57). By the mid-second century, the first structure had been replaced by a larger, north–south aligned, aisled masonry building which measured 32 x 16m. Two parallel sets of 10 piers divided the internal space into a 7m-wide central nave and two smaller side aisles.

A later phase of internal subdivision at the northern end of the Fishbourne hall created a roughly square room, measuring 7m x 5m across the nave, two narrower spaces, or corridors, being created by walling off the side arcades. Little survived of the original ground level within the building, although the narrow room in the north-eastern corner seems to have been floored with coarse gravel. Later still, extensions were punched through the north wall of the aisled hall whilst at the south a porch was added to the main entrance. The rest of the interior space contained a variety of features which included a T-shaped corn drier (or malting oven), five hearths and a V-shaped gulley (possibly a soakaway). In the south-eastern corner of the structure lay a large rectangular pit which the excavators interpreted as a form of underfloor heating, probably for use in grain drying rather than for domestic or bathing purposes (Rudkin 1986, 61).

At West Blatchington, near Hove (72), a third Aisled Building was unearthed during a dramatic rescue excavation conducted between 1947 and 1949 in advance of a major housing development. Unfortunately, the full nature and extent of the site could not be determined due to the difficult conditions the excavators found themselves working under, although that anything at all could be salvaged from the site is a testament to the skill and determination of excavation directors, N.E.S. Norris and G.P. Burstow, and their team of enthusiastic volunteers. At the north-western margins of the area investigated, a rectangular building with flint footings was found (Norris and Burstow 1950). The structure, which measured 32m in length x 15m in width, seemed to date from the third century possibly replacing an earlier roundhouse, containing high-status Roman pottery of the second century, to the south-east (Norris and Burstow 1950, 41). Internally, the building had been divided in two discrete zones, the larger comprising an aisled hall (room I), its roof supported by two rows of four parallel piers. As at Barcombe and Fishbourne, the northern block, where two equally sized rooms (II and III) linked by two smaller rooms (rooms IV and V) were constructed, appears to have been designed specifically for domestic accommodation. Although the basic form of the north range continued the alignment of the central posts forming the aisled hall, Norris and Burstow felt that it did not represent a later addition or modification, being part of the original design (Norris and Burstow 1950, 39).

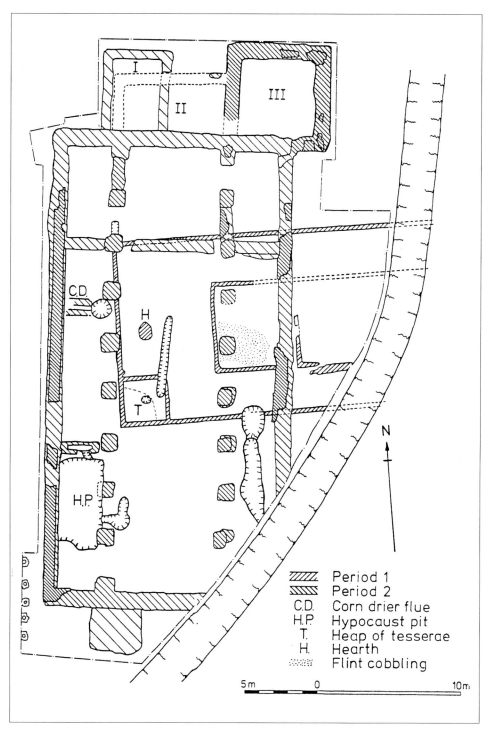

71 Fishbourne Creek: all phases of activity within and around the Aisled Building as excavated by David Rudkin in 1983. © *Chichester District Council*

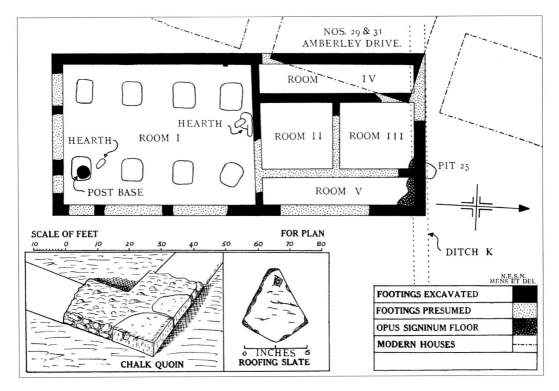

72 West Blatchington: ground plan of the Aisled Building as exposed between 1947 and 1949.
© *Sussex Archaeological Society*

Little of the original floor levels survived within the West Blatchington Aisled Building, but enough was preserved in the northern corners of rooms III and V to suggest the former presence of *opus signinum* (waterproof mortar) floors (Norris and Burstow 1950, 38). The whole had originally been roofed in slates of Upper Greensand and tile. The nature of internal décor within the domestic range remains something of a problem, due to the poor level of preservation. Ploughing across the site in the early nineteenth century is known to have dredged up 'the painted stucco of the walls', 'a small portion of a stucco floor' and 'flue tiles of a bath' (Douglas 1818, quoted in Norris and Burstow 1950, 5). Unfortunately, it is not known whether these discoveries relate to the Aisled Building as exposed in 1948, or, what is actually far more likely, a separate bathhouse or a Corridor Villa to the north.

An Aisled Building and associated structures similar to that recorded at Barcombe (and hinted at West Blatchington) was also investigated at Batten Hanger, near Elsted in West Sussex, between 1988 and 1991. The rectangular, east–west aligned Aisled Building, measuring 40m x 15m, had been constructed just over 10m to the north of a long and, presumably residential, building. The Aisled Building had been reduced in size, by the creation of more private space at its western end, probably at some point in the early half of the third century AD. This new space comprised three central rooms with a corridor running along their northern and southern sides. Later still, the northern corridor was subdivided into three by the construction of internal partition walls. This alteration, although increasing the number of usable rooms, clearly did not expand upon the amount of residential space available to the occupants (Magilton 1991, 27).

Significant alteration to the remainder of the hall, to the east of the domestic range, occurred at the same time as the alterations to the northern corridor, with the insertion of a tiny bath suite against the north wall. The bath suite, although measuring only 9 x 4m in size, possessed, in its primary phase, a changing room (*apodyterium*) with a simple mosaic floor leading into a heated room (*caldarium*) with a hypocaust and a hot immersion 'tub'. A second small bath, presumably the cold plunge, was added to the north wall of the changing room (Magilton 1991, 27). In the south-eastern corner of the Aisled Building, a new room was inserted consisting of a red tessellated floor set over a channelled hypocaust.

Aisled Buildings such as those represented at West Blatchington, Batten Hanger and Fishbourne are not uncommon in Roman Britain and may reflect a form of house in which a family and its animals could be contained under one roof (Smith 1997, 36). In such a scheme, any modification to the original ground plan could indicate a gradual desire to become more 'Roman' due to an increase in disposable income, political necessity or simple peer pressure. Certainly the form taken by such Aisled Buildings seems to reflect a more agricultural origin than some of the more grand and luxurious of Corridor and Courtyard Villas. The basic division recorded at Batten Hanger, West Blatchington and Fishbourne between large hall and smaller private rooms beyond, is not that dissimilar to the division between human and animal living space recorded from within certain medieval long houses, such as those noted at Hound Tor in Devon. If an Aisled Building had not originally been designed to accommodate livestock, it is possible that it may have served broader 'communal purposes like eating and cooking', the smaller rooms behind indicating 'the desire of the owner and his family for privacy and seclusion from everyday domestic activity' (Cunliffe 1973, 84).

Alternatively, when found in close association with more usual Corridor or Courtyard Villas, such as at Batten Hanger and Barcombe, Aisled Buildings may have been specifically designed for administrative purposes (as an estate office) or as a place for semi-public assemblies and meetings, akin to the late first-century aisled halls noted from the Fishbourne and Southwick palaces. It could even be that those Aisled Buildings or basilical halls provided with private internal space were intended to function as a residential building for a farm manager and their family. In such a model, the provision of a discrete set of rooms at one end of the hall or barn (for meetings, animals, farm equipment or the storage of foodstuffs) could relate to the upgrading of office space or the subsequent improvement of domestic accommodation for those who saw to the day-to-day running of the estate.

At Batten Hanger, the emphasis on domesticity finally overcame whatever other purpose the aisled hall may originally have served. The bathhouse, constructed into the external wall of the north arcade, had a soakaway or pit, into which excess water from the heated bath would drain, cut into the floor of the former hall. This arrangement would seem to suggest that, by the time the bathhouse was established, the roofed interior of the Aisled Building had become an open yard (Magilton 1991, 27). In contrast, the relatively meagre level of internal sophistication evident within the structure found next to Fishbourne Channel, may indicate that, even by the end of the third century, its functions were still primarily agricultural (Rudkin 1986, 61).

CHILGROVE 2

It is worth looking at two developed examples of Sussex villa, namely Chilgrove 2 and Bignor, in more detail at this stage. Both sites have been well examined and both provide an excellent example of the sequence of villa evolution from simple Cottage House combined with Aisled Building to a far more extensive range, demonstrating the sometimes complex relationship between the two types of building.

The villa complex of Chilgrove 2, excavated by Alec Down, lies some 1400m to the north-east of Chilgrove 1, and around 200m to the east of the main Roman road linking Chichester in the south to Silchester. The primary phase of building activity at Chilgrove 2, in the late first and early second century AD, appears to have been a timber house set out within a rectangular ditched enclosure or farmyard. At some point, possibly in the second century, a simple, four room, north-east to south-west aligned Cottage House (Building 1), measuring approximately 18 x 6m, with a veranda along its eastern side, was built. The first stage of a larger, possibly Aisled Building or barn (Building 2) seems to have been started at the north-eastern edge of the domestic range at this time (73).

By the late third century, the Cottage House of Building 1 had been modified in stone. The veranda was formalised into a covered corridor, although the extension of room 1 to the south-east across the line of the corridor shortened it by just over 2m. The enlarged room 1, now subdivided into 1a and 1b, probably became the main focus for the building. In the first quarter of the fourth century, the structure to the north of Building 1 was replaced by a rectangular masonry Aisled Building, measuring 15 x 24m. To the south of Building 1, a new bathhouse was built (Building 3), comprising a cold room (*frigidarium*: room 11) with apsidal immersion bath, a warm room (*tepidarium*: room 10b) and a hot room (*caldarium*: room 10a) with hypocaust. The function of the remaining rooms in the suite is uncertain, although 14 appears to have been a corridor and 12 may have been a changing room or *apodyterium*. A rectangular building, interpreted by Down as a barn (Down 1979, 92), was set out in the eastern corner of the farmyard. By the mid-fourth century (74), four rooms were inserted into the area of the Aisled Building, three rooms at the south-western end (rooms 6, 7 and 8), two of which possessed tessellated floors (rooms 6 and 7), whilst the fourth (room 9) was added inside (and to the east of) the south-facing entranceway.

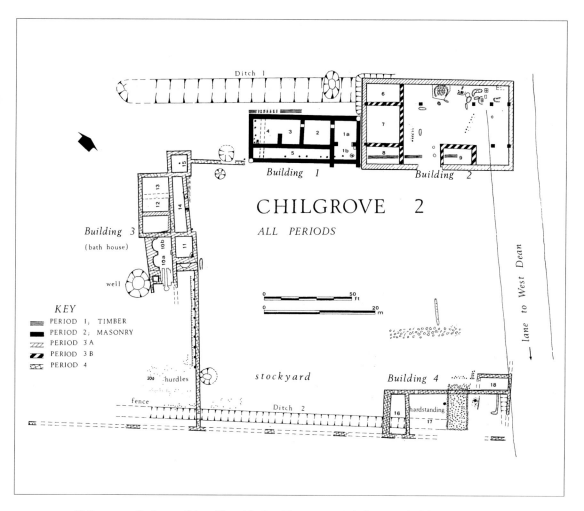

73 Chilgrove 2: all phases of the villa, with Corridor House, Aisled House, bathhouse and stockyard. © *Chichester District Council*

The floor in the south-western corner of the Aisled Building (room 6), where it survived, was of plain red tile *tesserae*. The pavement recorded in the larger room next door (room 7) however, is worth noting in detail, as it represents one of the most curious, and to date inexplicable, designs yet recovered from any Roman villa in Britain (*colour plate 12*). The floor, which may date to the first quarter of the fourth century (Down 1979, 85), consisted of red tile *tesserae* 'unrelieved except by nine circular motifs executed mainly in slightly smaller *tesserae* of white (chalk) and greensand' (Smith in Down 1979, 111). The circles, which varied between 0.29m to 0.44m, lay in two rows, a row of seven forming a line across the room parallel to, and at a distance of 2.5m from, the western wall of the room, and two set 1.1m from the east wall. From north to south the row of seven circles comprised:

74 Chilgrove 2: imaginative recreation, drawn by C. de la Nougerede, of the Corridor Villa, Aisled Building, bathhouse and stockyard in the early to mid-fourth century AD. Note that both the bathhouse and the main domestic range are depicted with clerestories. © *Chichester District Council*

(i)   'four white *tesserae* in a cruciform' enclosed by two concentric circles;

(ii)   an open circle;

(iii) an open circle with a single white tessera at its centre;

(iv) an apparently irregular group of white *tesserae* enclosed by a double circle 'those of the inner circle being staggered in relation to those of the outer';

(v)   a solid white circle enclosed by a circle 'with dentils projecting all round' except on the east where 'a short white tail projected';

(vi) a 'saltire cross' enclosed by two concentric circles, the outer with four short rays projecting westwards;

(vii) four concentric circles, 'the innermost formed of only four *tesserae*' (Smith in Down 1979, 111-2).

From north to south, the second set of two circles at the eastern end of the room comprised:

(i)   three white *tesserae* in a partial cruciform enclosed by two concentric circles (similar to the arrangement of the first circle in the western row);

(ii)   an open circle with a circle (composed of four white *tesserae*) at its centre.

The excavators were at a loss as to the meaning of the arrangement. Alec Down noted that 'the temptation to indulge in uncontrolled incursions into the realms of fantasy must be firmly resisted' (Down 1979, 92), whilst D.J. Smith commented that 'it seems futile even to comment further upon it' (Smith in Down 1979, 112). The bizarre nature of the floor, to the modern eye, certainly begs attention and, despite the warnings of the excavation team, a few observations may be considered helpful.

If the designs were meant to simply subdivide the room, possibly as a way to segregate space for furniture within what may have been the main room of the estate office (in the manner of a modern car-parking bay), it seems strange that so distinctive and unusual a motif was chosen. It *is* conceivable, that the design was intended as a form of astrological chart, perhaps depicting seven planets or stars, the remaining two in the eastern row representing the sun and moon. Perhaps the sequence was intended to convey a solar or lunar cycle. Possibly the western seven represent the seven days of the week, or seven deities within the Roman pantheon or local (Celtic) family. Possibly they also could have related to a particular religious practice or game, the rules of which are now lost. It may be that they were specific to administrative or managerial activities conducted within the room, each symbol representing a particular activity, job, family or worker on the estate. Unless a parallel is ever supplied, we are unlikely ever to be sure of the meaning behind this distinctive floor, but the point is that, without speculation, the design simply becomes another forgotten element of the distant past. It is perhaps unfortunate that the wall plaster in the room, which may conceivably have provided an answer (especially if the motif had been continued up from the floor) did not survive and whatever originally sat (or stood) in the niche preserved in the eastern wall of the room, remains wholly unknown.

To the immediate south-west of room 7 in the Aisled Building, lay a similar red tessellated floor in the adjoining room of Building 1, what is thought to be the main domestic range. The floor here is also curious for, whilst the remaining pavements recorded from the building (rooms 2, 3 and 5) are apparently of undecorated red tile *tesserae*, that in room 1a possesses a strange set of figures or markings (75). D.J. Smith, who examined the floors in detail, observed that the arrangement of greensand *tesserae* in the western corner suggested 'a childish attempt to depict a horse with a rider', whilst the design, as it unravelled to the north, was 'an inexplicable jumble' (Smith in Down 1979, 111). It has to be said that it is quite unlikely that a villa owner would commission, pay for and be happy with 'a childish' floor design in what was the largest and (we may presume) most important social space in the

75 Chilgrove 2: part of the curious design in the tessellated floor of room 1a in the main domestic range. © *Chichester District Council*

domestic range. The design, though it may appear 'inexplicable' to the modern eye, must have possessed some meaning to the floor maker and also to the villa owner. Was it a signature, akin perhaps to the bird on the Boy and Dolphin mosaic at Fishbourne (see below) or did it possess some deeper religious connotation? Alec Down saw it as belonging to 'a native tradition which was never completely overlaid by Romanisation' (Down 1979, 92) We will probably never know the real meaning behind the figures, but their proximity to the curious designs in room 7 of the Aisled Building is intriguing.

BIGNOR

The Roman building at Bignor is justly famous as one of the best-preserved villas in the country. To enter the independently thatched cover buildings and gaze at the impressive mosaic floors today is undeniably uplifting. The site is, of course, not just important because of the visitor experience that it represents, but because this is one of the largest and best understood of Roman rural 'power houses' that we possess in the UK.

Discovered in 1811, the complex at Bignor was extensively examined by John Hawkins and Samuel Lysons between 1811 and 1818. During this time, a series of reports on the excavation were published (e.g. Lysons 1817; 1819; 1821) and a set of highly detailed engravings (76) were composed by Lysons with the help of Richard Smirke and Charles Stothard. Although clearly less objective than the archaeological elevations and technical drawings of today, these coloured engravings are highly atmospheric and provide a wealth of information concerning the state of the villa at the time it was first uncovered. Protective buildings were erected over the mosaics by the Tupper family, who owned the site, and, by 1815, the villa had become a popular tourist attraction. Fortunately the Tuppers have never lost interest in Bignor and today it still stands as one of the foremost Roman buildings in Britain.

Originally interpreted by Lysons and others as a monumental, single-period piece of construction, excavations conducted across Bignor villa in the late twentieth century by Samuel Winbolt, Shepherd Frere, Margaret Rule, Fred Aldsworth and David Rudling (Aldsworth and Rudling 1995) have demonstrated that the ground plan that we see today is the result of at least four discrete phases of building activity (77). The earliest phase is perhaps the least well understood, the series of 'diagonal walls' exposed by Lysons beneath the northern range of the main complex (Aldsworth and Rudling 1995, 181) possibly representing a range of rooms set around a large central courtyard. The plan is similar to the Mediterranean-style domestic range evident in the Proto Palace at Fishbourne (see chapter 6) and artefacts recovered from the area certainly hint at some form of late first-century activity. Whatever this structure represents, its full extent and nature remain, at the present time at least, unknown.

76 Bignor: the bathhouse of the southern wing under excavation in the early nineteenth century, taken from Samuel Lysons' 1815 account published in the *Reliquiae Britannico-Romanae*, looking east. In the foreground are the *pilae* of the hot room (*caldarium*), whilst the immersion bath of the cold room (*frigidarium*) and the Medusa mosaic of the changing room (*apodyterium*), artistically overlain with fragments of columns, can be seen in the background. *Reproduced with kind permission of the Tupper family, Bignor villa, West Sussex*

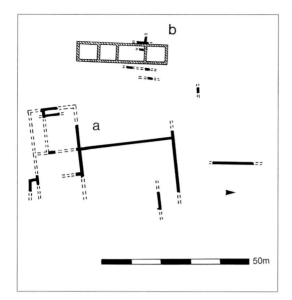

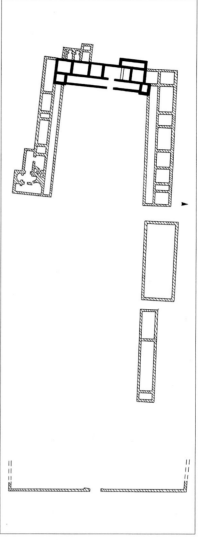

Above: 77 Bignor: ground plan of the earliest phases. The poorly understood primary phase building (A) may represent a late first-century courtyard house akin to the Proto Palace phase at Fishbourne. The main domestic range of the Romanised Cottage House (B) began much later, in the early to mid-third century. *Redrawn from Aldsworth and Rudling 1995, 183*

Right: 78 Bignor: ground plan of the late third- and early fourth-century redevelopment. The winged Corridor Villa, itself a modification of the Cottage House, has here been incorporated into a larger Villa, wings being extended along the northern and southern sides. Baths have been added to the south range, and further domestic accommodation in the north. Note the construction of an Aisled Building and smaller rectangular structure along the northern side. *Redrawn from Aldsworth and Rudling 1985, 184*

The first identifiable masonry element of the villa complex at Bignor began life in the early to mid-third century, and probably no earlier than AD 225 (Aldsworth and Rudling 1995). This relatively simple four-roomed rectangular building (representing a Cottage-style Villa akin to the primary phase of Beddingham: see above) is still visible at the centre of what became the west wing (rooms 27-30). Gradually additional enclosed spaces were added on to the structure, so that by the end of the primary phase (referred to as 'Period II': Aldsworth and Rudling 1995), a larger building comprising rooms 27 (with 31), 28, 29, 30, 33, 40 and 41, linked by a north–south aligned corridor (34) had developed (*78*). The Cottage-style House had become a winged Corridor Villa.

During the second main phase of constructional activity (Period III [i]), possibly commencing at the very end of the third or beginning of the fourth century AD, extensive wings were added to the north and south of the Corridor Villa. A bath suite was begun within the southern half of, what was now, the western range (rooms 36-39) in around AD 300, but these never seem to have been completed. A new and more spacious bathing complex was instead built at (and not possibly integrated with) the eastern end of the southern range. This suite was continually modified and updated over time, but, in its earliest phase, comprised a substantial *praefurnium* or furnace room (51), an *alveus* or hot bath (room 52a), a *caldarium* or hot room (52) and a *tepidarium* or warm room (54).

The evolution of the north wing throughout Period III is not without interest, Fred Aldsworth and David Rudling observing that the range had twice been extended 'perhaps in response to a growing family'. The room extensions noted appear to have been conducted in blocks of three (rooms 13, 14 and 15; rooms 16, 17 and 24; rooms 21, 22 and 23), something that was felt significant as the three-room house 'is frequently encountered as a basic unit of accommodation in villas in southern England, and often these comprise a small room flanked by two larger ones of similar size.' (Aldsworth and Rudling 1995, 185)

The expansion of the north wing through rooms 16-24 (Period III [ii]) in order to accommodate more domestic space, necessitated the demolition of a large, free-standing, rectangular masonry structure (identified as 11, 18, 23 and 65 in Lyson's original scheme). The significance of this structure should not be lost on us, for this was an Aisled Building that may, like the halls already cited, have served either as a barn, a place for assemblies and audiences (akin to the late first-century basilical halls of Fishbourne and Southwick), the residence of the estate manager or, more probably, the main estate office. A second, free-standing rectangular building comprising rooms 66, 67 and 68, continued the basic alignment of the northern range, and is usually interpreted as a shed or series of pens for livestock. Analysis of the faunal remains recovered during the 1985 and 1990 examination of the farmyard area seem to indicate the predominance of cattle over sheep/goat and pig. The meat diet on site derived almost exclusively from domesticated animals, with only a limited amount of hunted foods, comprising 'a small number of red deer, a wild boar and unidentified bird species', appearing in the archaeological record (Aldsworth and Rudling 1995, 173).

As the north wing expanded eastwards through the fourth century, out over what is assumed to have been the farmyard, walls were added to form a fully enclosed space complete with an east-facing gate. A fresh series of outbuildings (room 69 and rooms 70-4), comprising a monumental aisled hall, were added to the internal corners of this wall, presumably replacing those lost during alterations to the north wing. The final ground floor plan of the main domestic range at Bignor is that of a fully enclosed Courtyard Villa, the eastern end of which comprised an ambulatory, or apsidal-ended corridor which linked the northern and southern ranges (79). The ambulatory here may have been similar in design to that which ran the entire length

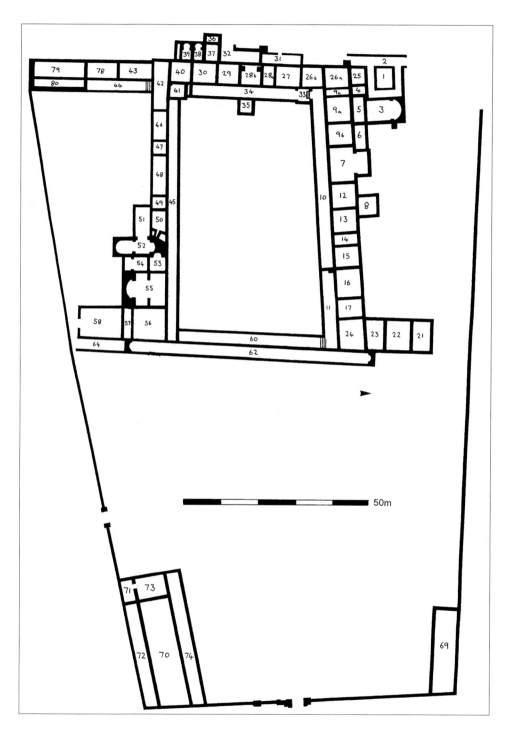

79 Bignor: ground plan of the final phase in the fourth century. The northern range has been extended over the Aisled Building, a replacement being constructed to the south-east. An ambulatory, linking the north and south wings, has now been built. *Redrawn from Aldsworth and Rudling 1995, 184*

of the west wing in the first century palace at Fishbourne: something interpreted as an enlarged exercising area or a space along which 'the owner and his advisers' could walk discussing matters of a private nature (Manley 2003, 130-1). Whether the apsidal ends of the Bignor ambulatory were internally lined with seating, as at Fishbourne, remains unknown (Aldsworth and Rudling 1995, 141).

BIGNOR VILLA: PRIVATE AND PUBLIC ACTIVITIES

In a villa such as Bignor, if it did originally function as a 'power house', the grand architectural centrepiece of what was by the fourth century AD a great agricultural estate (*colour plate 13*), then we should expect the very clear demarcation of space for two very different social activities, namely private and public. Public activities would include forms of local jurisdiction such as 'the settlement of disputes between members of a kin-group, dependants and tenants, and the punishment of misdemeanours; and decisions about tenancies and inheritance' (Smith 1997, 178). Private activities would include the entertainment of friends, family, social equals and superior officials.

Zones set aside for entertainment and social climbing are usually clear enough to identify within the archaeological record of most Roman villas, for such rooms usually possess the most ornate and exquisite elements of interior décor. At Bignor, the latter phase villa possessed room 7, a large area containing a hexagonal stone water basin (*piscina*), probably with a fully functioning fountain (*colour plate 14*). The mosaic that surrounded this water feature is a fine piece of craftsmanship depicting, in the main roundel, Ganymede, a prince of Troy, in the moment of being kidnapped by Jupiter (Zeus) who appears in the form of an eagle (*colour plate 15*). Ganymede is naked, apart from his boots, red cap and long flowing cape, and carries a shepherd's staff (*pedum*) in his left hand, as he was tending his father's sheep on the slopes of Mount Ida when the abduction occurred. Though Ganymede was later to serve as a cup-bearer to Jupiter, this was not the prime motive behind the kidnapping, the story remaining popular within certain circles of Greek and Roman society 'because it gave legitimacy to the love of an adult male for a young boy' (Witts 2005, 31). Around the stone pool dance a number of scantily clad women, dressed only in voluminously baggy trousers, holding plates or tambourines. These joyous figures have been interpreted as maenads, the followers of Bacchus, the Roman god of wine, perhaps reflecting Ganymede's new career as cup-bearer to the gods.

Room 7 has variously been interpreted as an entrance hall, reception area or atrium, though it is clear that it is more probably have been used as a formal dining room or *triclinium*. Benches or dining couches could easily have been set out around the Ganymede roundel, over the enlarged tessellated border or the flanking geometric designs, without obscuring the central work. Beyond, the pool and fountain would have made a suitable distraction when polite conversation faltered (and could even have provided a topic of discussion). Around the pool, in emulation of the mosaic figures, after-dinner entertainment may even have been provided 'by real-life dancers' (Witts 2005, 31). Absence of an obvious form of underfloor heating in room 7 may indicate that dining was a form of entertainment conducted here in the warmer months of summer.

The provision of a public space is perhaps more difficult to identify at Bignor. People seeking an audience with a social superior at the palaces of Fishbourne and Southwick late in the first century AD would have been directed to a grand public space, discretely isolated from the rest of the domestic range. At both these sites, the audience chamber comprised a large basilical hall that could be independently accessed from the outside, without the need for entering through staterooms or more private areas behind (chapter 6). Here the palace owner, or delegated representative, could 'hear petitions and grant requests' and 'receive the homage of inferiors' (Smith 1997, 178). Given the size, scale and degree of opulence displayed at Bignor in the late third and early fourth century, we really should expect something similar.

Bignor was clearly a significant centre of local power or 'seat of lordship' and, as such, required a formal space where the landowner could publicly enact their duties. Of all the rooms recorded within the plan of the villa, the most suitable public spaces would appear to be found in the apsidal-ended room 3 in the northern range and the aisled hall comprising rooms 70-74 in the east. Room 3 is sometimes interpreted as a winter *triclinium*, on the basis of its design and presence of an underfloor heating system or hypocaust. The room was, however, contemporary with room 7, the *triclinium* with Ganymede mosaic and *piscina*, only 10m to the south-east. Two dining rooms within such a small space would seem wastefully extravagant, even if one was intended only for winter use (and if room 7 was only for summer use, why was it in the north wing where the absence of natural light would have been significant?). Claims that rooms 3 and 7 were used by different members of the same household seem like special pleading.

A clue to the intended use of room 3 may be derived from its position in the villa. Room 3 is situated at the north-western margins of Bignor and could be entered independently from outside the complex along its south-western side. As with the earlier basilical halls of Fishbourne and Southwick, this arrangement means that room 3 possessed a significant degree of structural independence from the rest of the domestic range (Smith 1997, 179). Delegates to Bignor could therefore be swiftly ushered in and out, without disturbance to the household beyond. Room 2, through which access to the apsed room was gained, was a peristyle or 'cloister-walk' set around a small open courtyard (room 1), an ideal place to keep visitors as they awaited an audience. Rooms 25, 4, 5 and 6 to the immediate south of room 3, have the appearance of officials' lodgings or other important administrative rooms (c.f. the northern half of the east range at Fishbourne: see chapter 6). Room 6, at the eastern end of the range, possessed a pair of interconnected geometric mosaics raised above a hypocaust (*colour plate 16*). Although today a visitor can walk from the Ganymede room into room 6, there would have been no direct access in antiquity.

As an audience chamber (*colour plate 17*), the existence of a hypocaust beneath the mosaic of room 3 would make a great deal of sense. Not only would the visitor be impressed by the level of extravagance represented by underfloor heating but also, perhaps rather more crucially, as the hall would have been in use all year round, heating was imperative. The owner or their elected representative would after all have required a certain degree of warmth and luxury as they sat in state to meet, greet, listen and decide.

Although much of the interior design of room 3 is now lost to us, the female face depicted in the upper roundel of the pavement here (*colour plate 18*) must rank as one of the most accomplished pieces of art in any mosaic recovered from Britain (if not the north-western empire). Despite being restored in 1929 (the repair being conducted using slightly darker *tesserae*), the work is awe-inspiring. The figure, naked except for a decorative neck pendant, semi-circular diadem and tiara composed of tiny crosses, gazes serenely out into the room, delicate tresses of hair flowing down her neck and onto her shoulders. Behind her head, a sky-blue halo or nimbus unequivocally indicates divinity. The chalice beneath, from which tendrils unravel, almost exactly mirrors those that surround the youthful Ganymede in room 7, an observation that may indicate not only that both floors were contemporary, but were designed by the same hand.

The identity of the female portrait has caused some debate in recent years (suggestions ranging from a likeness of the villa owner (or his wife) to Juno, partner of Jupiter, through to Mary, mother of Jesus), although there seems little reason to doubt Lyson's original view that she represents Venus. Venus is primarily known as the Roman goddess of love, but, as her other attributes included being the goddess of spring and of fertility (and also of gardens), she was popular amongst farmers, landowners and horticulturists across the empire and this may be why she was chosen to figure so prominently in the Bignor floor. Certainly the whole upper image depicted in room 3 is positively bursting with images of fertility, from the flowing acanthus scroll, with its lush tendrils supporting fruit and lotus flowers, to the cornucopia, or horn of plenty, resting below. Patricia Witts has also noted that the image of the female face in the mosaic 'is seen as if reflected in a mirror' balanced between the 'leafy swags' on which two peacocks delicately perch (Witts 2005, 139). Peacocks, the lotus flower and the mirror all possess very strong associations with Venus, something which provides 'a coherent theme to the imagery in the apse' (Witts 2005, 139).

Beneath the representation of Venus, a rectangular panel serves to formally separate the apse from the remainder of the room. The panel itself is decorated with a series of cupid gladiators, which may originally have been viewed as a sequence of events taken from a single story, rather like a modern cartoon strip (*80* and *81*). Five major scenes are depicted in the story which, if read from the left-hand side, starts with a cupid dressed as a *Samnite* or *secutor*, a gladiator wearing a visored helmet and a plated armour on his right arm and left leg and carrying a shield and sword. The *secutor* is advancing on a *retiarius*, a gladiator who fights primarily with a net and a trident (although the Bignor example also has an arm guard and a dagger or short sword). Behind them

80 Bignor: part of the cupid gladiator panel in room 3. Scene 1, from left, the *secutor* advancing on the *retiarius*, with the *rudarius* (stick raised) standing behind. In scene 2 the *secutor* advances on the fallen *retiarius* whilst the *rudarius* moves forward to get the non combatant back on his feet. *Reproduced with kind permission of the Tupper family, Bignor villa, West Sussex*

81 Bignor: the second half of the gladiator panel. Scene 3, the *retiarius* returns his opponent's helmet. Scene 4, the rearmed *retiarius* is led back to the fight by the *rudarius*. Scene 5, the *secutor* moves forward for the kill. Note that the helmet lies in the dust at his feet. *Reproduced with kind permission of the Tupper family, Bignor villa, West Sussex*

stands a *rudarius*, or umpire, carrying his staff (*rudus*) which acted both as a symbol of office and as a way of forcefully separating (and punishing) miscreants. Between the two combatants sits a block of stone with a central iron ring to which unwilling participants could be tied (*colour plate 19*).

In the second scene, the *secutor* has successfully disarmed the *retiarius*, who, having dropped his trident and sword, falls forward, possibly onto his left knee (this part of the panel is lost). The *secutor* appears intent on causing harm, but the action is being stopped by the *rudarius*, who is sprinting over with his staff raised above his head. The normal interpretation of this action is that the *rudarius* has spotted some misdemeanour and is chastising the *secutor*; far more likely is that he is about to strike the *retiarius* and force him to his feet so that the fight may continue. The third scene has the *secutor* being armed (or rearmed) by a figure who appears to be the now standing *retiarius* (although, in a continuity error he is shown without his arm guard). It has been suggested that this piece of the story is 'out of place', and actually depicts the start of play when both gladiators are being prepared for combat. An alternative, and far more likely view is that the scene is exactly where it should be and marks a lull in the fighting, presumably after the *rudarius*' intervention, when the *retiarius* is sportingly returning his opponent's helmet. The *secutor* certainly does not appear to appreciate the gesture and, shortly after, the rearmed *retiarius* is led back to rejoin battle by the *rudarius*.

The fifth and final scene shows the *secutor*, having once again disarmed the *retiarius*, advancing for the kill, the returned helmet lying contemptuously in the dust at his feet. The *retiarius*, wounded in both leg and chest, sits below the stone slab, his trident, which he seems unable (or unwilling) to pick it up, lying on the ground beside him. Propped up on his right arm, he faces the *secutor* and awaits destiny. This time the *rudarius* does not intervene.

The significance of the gladiatorial panel is not immediately clear, although some classical scholars have interpreted it as a 'charming' scene of cupids play-fighting which was intended merely to amuse. Although cupids often appear in Roman art performing a pastiche of real activities (Witts 2005, 119-20), the final scene of the Bignor mosaic, with the *retiarius* lying bleeding in the sand awaiting death, makes it clear that this is not the case here. Whatever their meaning, the appearance of cupids here seems utterly appropriate, especially if the divine female appearing in the upper roundel is indeed Venus, for, in addition to being the Roman goddess of love and fertility, she was also Cupid's mother. The panel is, as noted, telling a story, although the exact details of the tale are lost to us. Perhaps this was a recreation of a real fight witnessed at a local amphitheatre (at Chichester, Silchester or London), or maybe it was part of a now long forgotten myth or legend. Perhaps it was intended as a form of morality tale, the fate of the *retiarius* acting as a particular warning.

A large part of the lower half of the mosaic has been lost, *tesserae* scattering at some point when the floor collapsed into the hypocaust below. This is unfortunate, for the section destroyed would probably have contained a decorative centrepiece that could have helped explain the significance of the floor. A series of naked cupids, holding objects associated with Bacchus, still dance energetically around the missing area, whilst intricate geometric designs link the whole.

It is the suggested interpretation of room 3 as an audience chamber that helps to make sense of the mosaic design. The visitor, tenant or prospective petitioner would have entered the room from a door in the south-west. Directly facing them across the expanse of the room was the apse in which, we may assume, sat the owner, lord/lady of the estate or their delegated representative (*colour plate 17*). In front of them was positioned the face of Venus, surrounded by images of fertility and fruitfulness, a more than appropriate image for the controller of a large and (we may presume) prosperous estate. In front of Venus ran the panel of fighting cupids, formally separating the apse from the more public body of the room in which the visitor stood. As a place where justice was dispensed and disputes settled, the unfurling story of gladiatorial combat would have made perfect sense. In the absence of a permanent police force in Britain, the Roman criminal justice system was best served by the amphitheatre. Criminals were, as noted in chapter 5, often put to death in the most public of ways, their fate serving not just to entertain but also to remind the masses of the fate that would befall them should they ever transgress the law. Perhaps the cupid *retiarius* who appears so reluctant to fight, who attempts to win over his opponent (by handing him back his armour) and who eventually is killed, was meant to personify the punished law-breaker. His nemesis, the *secutor*, is every bit the hardened fighter and may, in this story, have represented the ultimate triumph of the system. It would have been an unsettling, and no doubt thoroughly sobering, design to find oneself confronted with.

BIGNOR VILLA: THE DOMESTIC RANGE

Beyond the world of the private and public at Bignor in the fourth century AD, lay the great domestic ranges of the villa household. Room 26b, at the junction between the north and west wings, contained, along with the 'Venus and Gladiators' mosaic of room 3 and the Ganymede mosaic of room 7, one of the finest floors in the entire complex. Sadly, only a few fragments of the design remain, but they provide a clear idea of how the whole must once have appeared. The mosaic originally possessed a depiction of the four seasons, although only 'Winter' remains intact at the north-eastern corner. Heavily muffled beneath a hooded cape, Winter appears as a gaunt female figure, a bare, dead branch slung over her left shoulder (*82*).

To the south, a small section of floor preserves the image of a dolphin. Above it lies a small triangular panel upon which the letters TER have been set, the E being reversed and combined (ligatured) with the R (*colour plate 20*). This is of particular interest as letters, words or phrases are rarely found on British mosaics. Unfortunately 'TER' in itself does not make an awful lot of sense and with only fragments of the

82 Bignor: Winter, heavily muffled beneath a hooded cape, a dead branch slung over her shoulder, the only surviving figure from the four seasons mosaic that originally graced room 26b of the villa. *Reproduced with kind permission of the Tupper family, Bignor villa, West Sussex*

complete mosaic in existence, we cannot be sure how many other panels (if any) originally contained letters. The most likely suggestion to date is that the fragment of text was intended to represent the first part of a personal name: presumably of the mosaicist rather than the owner, given the relatively insignificant position of the piece (Witts 2005, 80). Such a name could conceivably have been 'Terentius, Tertullus, Tertius or something similar' (Wilson 2002, 81).

Personifications of spring, summer and autumn would undoubtedly have graced the remaining corners of the room 26b mosaic, but we possess no idea as to the nature of the central roundel, long since destroyed. A possible clue may perhaps lie in a floor that lies to the immediate south-east, in what was room 33, at the northernmost limit of the Period III winged Corridor Villa. This floor, which was joined to the later phase through the construction of room 10, the north corridor (*colour plate 21*), may have been laid down around AD 300, and also depicts the four seasons with dolphins and survives in better condition than that in room 26b because, unlike the north wing, the earlier phase was deeply terraced into the slope of the hill. The centrepiece to the floor contains a representation of the Gorgon Medusa, a figure already noted as being popular in the mosaics of the palace at Fishbourne. With her writhing snakes for hair and gaze that could turn men into stone, Medusa may seem an odd choice for the centrepiece of a prestige Roman mosaic. It is possible, however, that she was chosen because of her protective powers against evil spirits, something which could prove invaluable to farmers who owed their prosperity to the fruits of the land.

Given the similarity of design between floors in rooms 26b and 33, it is possible that Medusa also originally appeared in the centre of the now largely destroyed 26b (she certainly appears one further time at Bignor, in the ornate floor of the changing room in the bath suite of the southern range: see below). The 'four seasons' appearing in room 33 is not, however, as competent or assured a piece of work as its immediate neighbour. The seasons themselves appear in black and white and are almost so schematic, that it is difficult to tell them apart. Winter appears in a hooded cape (as with the later floor in room 33) and we might infer that the figure to her right, with fractionally shorter hair than her colleagues, represents spring. A coloured engraving produced by Lysons and his colleagues at the time the room was first exposed, shows that the walls, which survived to almost a metre in height, were originally covered in painted plaster (*colour plate 22*). Five vertical panels were recorded by the excavation team of the early nineteenth century; the central panel being white with red on either side.

The bathhouse suite at the eastern end of the southern range has been extensively examined and a broad sequence of constructional phases established (*83*). In their final arrangement, the structure appears to have comprised a suite of rooms entered from the east–west corridor of the southern range, via a heated changing room or *apodyterium* (room 56). The floor of this changing or exercise room was covered with a geometric mosaic, comprising a series of interlocking squares, at the centre of which was a particularly fine representation of Medusa (*colour plate 23*). To the west of this, a door provided access, along a red and white tiled passageway in the northern half of room 55 (containing a cold immersion bath) to the first *tepidarium* or warm room (53). Passing from the tepidarium, the bather entered the *caldarium* or hot room (52) with its own *alveus* or warm immersion bath. Leaving this, the bather would pass through the second *tepidarium* (54) on their way to full immersion in the apsidal bath of the *frigidarium* or cold room (55), before returning to the *apodyterium* (Aldsworth and Rudling 1995, 105-37).

LATE DEVELOPMENT AT FISHBOURNE AND SOUTHWICK

As a number of farm estates began to prosper and invest more heavily in a Roman lifestyle throughout the second, third and fourth centuries AD, the grand palaces of the late first century appear to have been in a state of contraction and decline. This is perhaps unsurprising, given that sites like Fishbourne and Southwick represented imperial-style architectural statements, pieces of Italy 'transplanted into a distant, newly conquered province' (Wilson 2002, 70). They were centres of consumption where the earliest adherents to the Roman State spent their money swiftly and conspicuously. The first villas, in contrast, developed from successful farming estates. As centres of wealth generation, villas evolved more gradually, estate owners buying into Roman culture as and when their finances allowed.

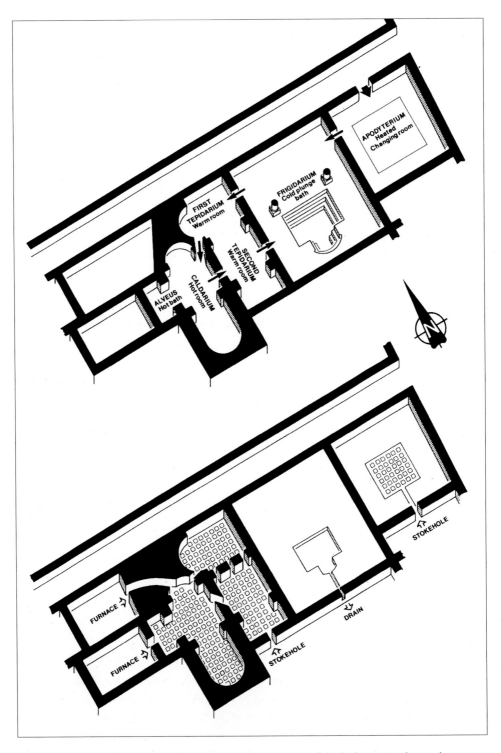

83 Bignor: a simplified ground and beneath ground floor plan of the bath suite in the southern range of the villa. *Reproduced with kind permission of the Tupper family, Bignor villa, West Sussex*

Unlike the villas, the palace sites do not appear to have possessed a way of sustaining their high levels of expenditure. Perhaps the money ran out too quickly, in a flurry of swift extravagance. Possibly the palace owners, after throwing themselves so swiftly into *Romanitas*, discovered that their accounts had been suddenly frozen. The Roman historian Dio Cassius provides one such example of the consequences of Roman financial mismanagement in Britain, during his introduction to the Boudican revolt of AD 60:

> An excuse for the war was found in the confiscation of the sums of money that Claudius had given to the foremost Britons; for these sums, as Decianus Catus, the *procurator* of the island, maintained, were to be paid back. This was one reason for the uprising; another was found in the fact that Seneca, in the hope of receiving a good rate of interest, had lent to the islanders 40,000,000 sesterces that they did not want, and had afterwards called in this loan all at once and had resorted to severe measures in exacting it. (Dio Cassius *Roman History* LXII, 2)

Maybe a similar, unexpected recall of loans financially crippled the owners of the Sussex palaces. Perhaps a change in imperial fiscal policy, following the overthrow of the Romano-British governor Gaius Sallustius Lucullus in the AD 90s, simply led to a decrease in the viability of grand palatial apartments and of the political will to maintain them.

Whatever the case, by the middle of the second century AD, a major phase of redevelopment at Fishbourne indicates the first serious attempt to escape the constraints of a single palace concept, and move towards more discrete units of occupation, similar to those of the villa estates developing elsewhere. The early second-century bath suite of Fishbourne, constructed through the remains of the great basilica was demolished and all the rooms to the east of room N15 in the north wing were removed right down to foundation level (*84*). The reasons for this particular alteration appear to have been practical, for the eastern end of the north wing seems to have fallen victim to the perennial scourge of mortgage advisors (and delight of jobbing builders) everywhere: subsidence. Colonnades, *hypocausts* and mosaics had, throughout the second century, begun to buckle and sink into the poorly backfilled remains of earlier phases of activity on the site; the pits, ditches and postholes of the primary fort.

A set of baths, intended to replace those torn down, were inserted into an extant courtyard belonging to the east wing of the old palace, close to the exercise hall, which may have continued in use. The new bathing suite was larger than the one it replaced, although the arrangement of *frigidarium* with cold plunge, *tepidarium* with apsed immersion bath and *caldarium* with bath was a fairly simple one. The scale of the suite, though nothing like the opulence of the earliest phases of building on site, demonstrate that the owners of the revamped palace were, by the mid-second century, clearly doing well for themselves.

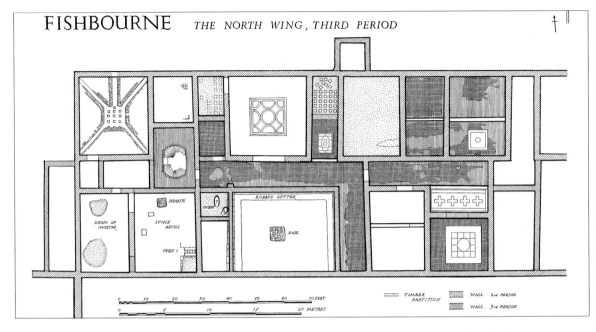

84 Fishbourne: the redesigned north wing of the former palace in the mid-second to late third century AD. © *Institute of Archaeology, Oxford and Sussex Archaeological Society*

Above left: 85 Fishbourne: the Cupid on a Dolphin mosaic from room N7; one of the finest preserved mosaics in Britain. © *Institute of Archaeology, Oxford and Sussex Archaeological Society*

Above right: 86 Fishbourne: a Cantharus, or decorated vase, from the top right hand corner of the Cupid on a Dolphin mosaic. © *Institute of Archaeology, Oxford and Sussex Archaeological Society*

The main area of domestic accommodation, centred within the western two-thirds of the old north wing of the Fishbourne palace, was modified at the time the baths were constructed. New corridors were built, small *hypocausts* inserted and new internal partitions set up across some of the larger internal spaces. At least four new floors were also added to the building, the most famous of which is the so-called 'Cupid on a Dolphin' mosaic in room N7 (*85, 86, 87* and *88*). The central roundel of this, one of the best preserved mosaics in Britain, continues the aquatic theme that runs through the interior décor of all phases of the site. Presumably this is due to the setting and connections of the developing palace site, but it may also be due in part to a continuation of the cult of Neptune as evidenced in the first-century dedication of the temple to Neptune and Minerva in nearby Chichester. Around the winged cupid (*colour plate 24*) swim sea-horses (literally horses with marine tails and fins: *89*) and sea-panthers (*colour plate 25*) whilst a small bird perched incongruously inside a leaf-scroll border (*90*) may represent the signature symbol of the mosaicist.

It has been noted (Black 1987, 51) that of the period 3 mosaics in rooms N5a, N8 and N13 at Fishbourne display 'a disproportionate amount of plain border on one side', whilst the southern panel of the floor in N11 possesses a wider border along two of its sides. This, it may be assumed, was in order to allow the positioning of major pieces of furniture, such as beds, without significant loss to the decorated floor motif below.

87 Fishbourne: detail of a vase and tendrils from the border of the Cupid on a Dolphin mosaic.
© *Institute of Archaeology, Oxford and Sussex Archaeological Society*

88 Fishbourne: detail of the top left-hand corner of the Cupid on a Dolphin mosaic. © *Institute of Archaeology, Oxford and Sussex Archaeological Society*

89 Fishbourne: detail of sea horse appearing at the top of the Cupid on a Dolphin mosaic. © *Institute of Archaeology, Oxford and Sussex Archaeological Society*

90 Fishbourne: a bird perched on a curled tendril in the upper left hand side of the Cupid on a Dolphin mosaic border. It has been suggested that this may represent the signature of the mosaicist. © *Institute of Archaeology, Oxford and Sussex Archaeological Society*

By the mid-to-late third century, the palace at Southwick had also undergone significant change to its ground plan. By then the main domestic range was no longer the unitary building emulating both Fishbourne and the *Domus Flavia*, being down-sized and subdivided to the point that it was beginning to resemble the more usual forms of Romanised farm house found across Sussex and the south-east. Only the northern range was maintained for domestic occupation, the bulk of the eastern and southern wings being demolished save for the outermost wall, which seems now to have served as a paddock, yard or other form of boundary (Black 1987, 104). An unmortared wall of 'flint and rubbish' continued the line of the yard round along the western perimeter (Winbolt 1932, 15). At some later, and unspecified, date, a possible corn-drier or malting floor (interpreted by the original excavators as a latrine) was inserted into the north-eastern corner of the complex and the secondary-phase bath suite at the western end of the north wing was torn down and replaced with a chalk-floored timber building (Black 1987, 104).

NON–VILLA SETTLEMENT

Those that did not become Roman seem to have remained culturally (and perhaps stubbornly) 'British' for some considerable time. It would be wrong to assume that everyone lived in a villa or Romanised house during the time that Britain was part of the Roman Empire, far from it. For the bulk of the population, being 'Roman' was probably well beyond their financial means and may well have conflicted with their feelings of identity and community. Villas tend to occur only in those areas of Sussex 'where the land is rich enough to support the required level of production' necessary to generate significant wealth, which 'in practical terms means excluding much of the Weald, with the exception of the very fertile Upper Greensand ridge, and the chalk Downs except for the southern valleys floored with rich silts.' (Cunliffe 1973, 96)

One might also add that villas would also only occur in those areas where the desire to be 'Roman' was considered important. Villa buildings, even the relatively moderate examples like those recorded from Batten Hanger and West Blatchington, were, with regard to rural settlement forms across Roman Britain, by far and away the exception. The majority of the rural population of Roman Britain saw no benefit in becoming Romano-British.

A good example of the limited effect that Roman culture had upon the rural communities of Sussex can be found within the agricultural settlements of the South Downs. Here the lifestyle, nature of food production and settlement type appears to change little from the Early Iron Age and into the Roman era. Sometimes the 'Roman' period farm can be shown to occupy the same plot as its prehistoric predecessor, although 'more often there is a slight shift of nucleus within a restricted territory' (Cunliffe 1973, 96). Good agricultural land would have remained profitable, diminishing the desire to move elsewhere. Fields were ploughed, animals tended, metal worked, pottery manufactured, food produced, babies born and houses built in the same, traditional manner. Occasionally Roman goods, such as the odd coin, brooch or cooking pot might appear; sometimes new building materials would necessitate a different structural form, but essentially the people in the farm would see no benefit in completely (and radically) changing their style of living.

A good example of the largely untroubled continuity of rural settlement from the Iron Age into the Roman period can be seen at Park Brow, to the north of Cissbury near Worthing. Here a range of domestic areas and associated field systems can be traced, beginning in the Later Bronze Age, stretching along both sides of a sinuous sunken lane or droveway. Excavations conducted in the 1920s across an area of settlement that spanned the Late Iron Age and Early Roman period revealed five rectangular timber buildings within an area of pits, associated postholes and boundary ditches (Wolseley *et al.* 1927). One of the five rectangular buildings had been set upon a terraced platform measuring 9.8m x 7.6m. The walls were of timber with wattle and daub infill, the interior of which had been keyed in order to receive a layer of red-painted plaster. Finds further suggested a roof of red tile whilst window glass and an iron door key suggest further elements of a more 'sophisticated' Roman lifestyle.

It is not sure, from the published excavation report, whether the Park Brow settlement represented a small, closely associated kin group or the successive development of individual, unrelated structures (Cunliffe 1973, 98; Rudling 1998, 47). One view, which has gained currency in recent years, is that such clusters of prehistoric of buildings were the product of a single phase of occupancy, each structure performing a different purpose. In such a model, an individual 'hut' would be the equivalent of a single room in a house or villa. A cluster of huts, as represented at Park Brow, would not therefore have functioned as a village or hamlet, but as a 'household', possibly for no more than a single extended family (Rivet 1964, 108).

Along the eastern slopes of Thundersbarrow Hill, above Shoreham, another Downland settlement has been investigated. The settlement, first excavated in 1932, seems to have developed alongside a pronounced drove or ridgeway (*91* and *92*), outside the remains of a disused hilltop enclosure of the Later Bronze and Early Iron Age (Curwen 1933). Artefactual remains suggested a largely unbroken period of settlement activity here from the late first century BC to the mid-fourth century AD and, although there can be no definite proof, 'it is tempting to see the Romano-British villagers as essentially the descendants of the hillfort community who first established themselves on the hill' (Cunliffe 1973, 101). A series of grain storage pits, corn-drying ovens/malting floors (*93*) and other features were examined during the course of the 1932 excavation, although little is known about the structural nature of domestic buildings. Linear field banks spread all around and up to the disused enclosure and, whatever their origin, these seem to have been broadly maintained into the Roman period.

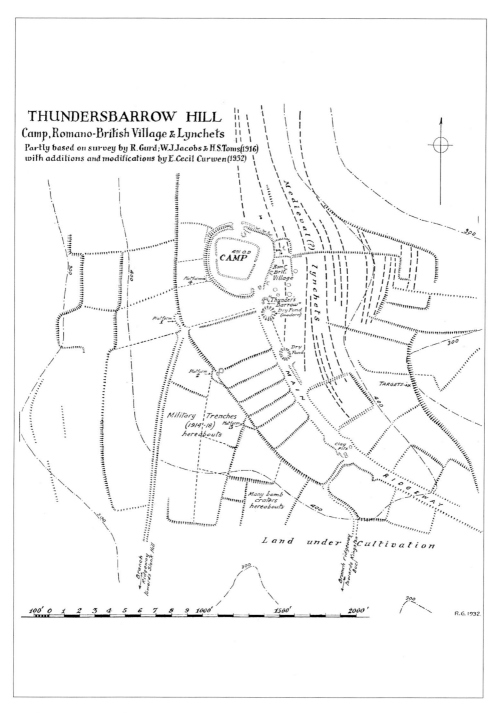

91 Thundersbarrow Hill: a plan of the prehistoric and Romano-British settlement as drawn by Robert Gurd in 1932. The area of Romano-British settlement lies to the immediate south-east of the prehistoric enclosure (here marked as 'camp'), whilst lynchets, field systems and property boundaries flank either side of the 'main ridgeway'. © *Sussex Archaeological Society*

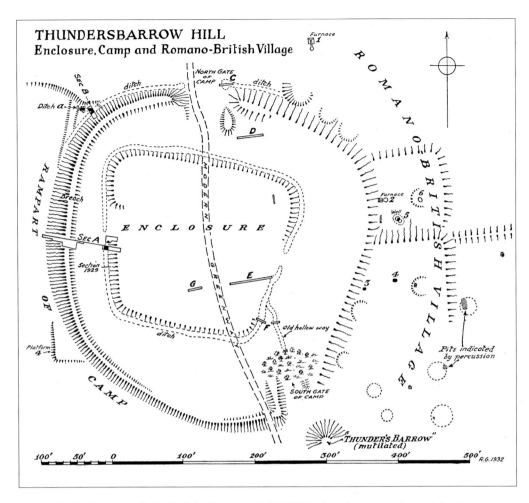

92 Thundersbarrow Hill: detail of the 'Romano-British Village' on the eastern slope of the Later Bronze and Early Iron Age hilltop enclosure , showing the relative position of hut platforms or pits and 'furnaces' or corn-drying/malting ovens. © *Sussex Archaeological Society*

Settlements of comparable nature to Park Brow and Thundersbarrow, and displaying a similar range of finds (including both local and Romano-British fine ware pottery), have also been investigated at Bullock Down, near Eastbourne (Rudling 1982), Bishopstone (Bell 1977), Slonk Hill, near Shoreham (Hartridge 1978), Boxgrove, near Chichester (Bedwin and Place 1995) and Wolstonbury and Devil's Dyke, near Brighton (Holleyman 1935; Burstow and Wilson 1936). The main elements of the economy at Bishopstone and Bullock Down were, as far as could be ascertained, purely arable, with 'associated field systems and marl pits' and animal pens as well as threshing floors, corn dryers/malting floors, storage pits, carbonised seed, animal bone (mostly sheep), pottery 'cheese presses', loom weights and spindle whorls all in evidence (Rudling 2003, 117).

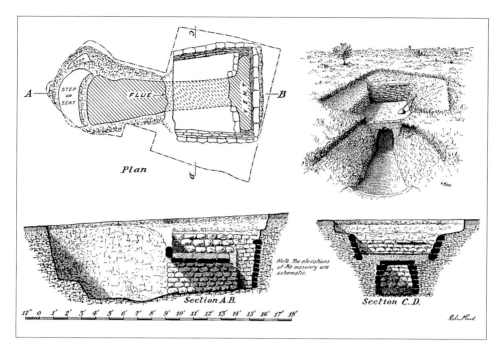

93 Thundersbarrow Hill: a grain-drying or malting oven, showing the furnace, flue and squared chamber, over which a floor would originally have been placed. The overall effect would have been not unlike that produced by a hypocaust. © Sussex Archaeological Society

Unfortunately, settlements such as these have received relatively little consideration within the context of Romano-British studies, especially when compared with the more monumental villa estates. This is unfortunate for, although they are perhaps less visually impressive than a site with stone walls, a mosaic or a bathhouse, they would appear to represent the norm as far as regards rural settlement of the period. However these so-called 'peasant' settlements of the Sussex Downs are interpreted, it is clear that, by the third century at least, contact with the Roman markets had begun to infect the minds of certain farming communities, albeit at a very low level. Farmers living at such sites may have had no desire to be seen as fully integrated members of Roman society, unlike the villa owners, but they were willing, on occasion, to buy into certain aspects of the Romano-British lifestyle.

THE DECLINE OF ROMAN RURAL SETTLEMENT

The picture of Roman villa settlement in Sussex throughout the late third and fourth century is one of developing prosperity and wealth. By the end of the fourth century, however, the situation appears to have changed, a marked decline being followed by abandonment and collapse (Rudling 1998, 51). Unfortunately the exact circumstances

94 Chilgrove 1: collapsed flue tiles and other structural debris in room 7. © *Chichester District Council*

95 Chilgrove 1: an imaginative recreation of the villa building in a state of disrepair, secondary reuse and robbing of architectural detail, drawn by C. de la Nougerede. © *Chichester District Council*

of this 'retreat from grandeur' are not always well understood. At Bignor, for example, the later phases of activity were cleared away by the nineteenth-century archaeologists, in order to swiftly reveal the mosaics and masonry beneath. More recent excavations at villa sites have attempted to better record and understand the final phases of *Romanitas*, but our understanding of the end of villa use remains incomplete.

The villa of Chilgrove 1 had reached its peak by the early fourth century. By the third quarter of the fourth century part of the main range had been damaged by fire (Down 1979, 68-71), burning beams and stone tiles covering the southern end of the main corridor (*94*). No further structural repairs were conducted to the villa after this time (*95*), the bath suite being dismantled, stripped of materials and backfilled (Down 1988, 92). The general absence of later fourth-century coins indicates a lack of elite or status activity across the domestic range, room 8 being subsequently reused as the site for an ironworking furnace (Down 1979, 68-9). A small set of corn driers or malting ovens located in one of the stockyard buildings (identified by Down as a barn) remained in use, possibly into the fifth century.

At Chilgrove 2, the Aisled Building underwent significant modification in the later fourth century, hearths and ovens, at least one of which was for baking bread, being constructed in the western end. The bathhouse was at this time in a state of disrepair, part of the structure having been used for corn drying (or malting). Shortly after AD 375, the Aisled Building was destroyed by fire, evidence for the collapse of the roof structure being found in room 7, where the roof beams fell upon the tessellation, 'discolouring the floor badly at the western end' (Down 1979, 96). Some attempt at salvage seems to have been conducted, two discrete piles of nails being found within the debris, but, as with Chilgrove 1, no attempt was made to rebuild.

At Beddingham, the apsed masonry 'shrine', located to the immediate west of the main domestic range, was 'hollowed out', during the late fourth or early fifth century, presumably by the construction of a Germanic-style *Grubenhauser* or Sunken Feature Building (Rudling 1998, 55-9). The fill of the cut contained a mixture of Early Saxon and Late Roman pottery, suggesting a form of settlement continuity. Whether this represents a settlement belonging to Saxon settlers, replacing a Romanised farming community, or a simple change in cultural identity, the descendants of the Romano-British landowners choosing to live in a more Germanic way (just as their Iron Age ancestors had once become more Roman), is impossible to say on present evidence.

The decline of villas with vast rural estates at the end of the Roman period may have been due to extreme political instability (see chapters 11 and 12), populations moving to more secure and defendable positions. Villa owners, as the wealthy elite of the province, may have been obvious targets for those seeking financial advancement through plunder; estates proving easy targets in the turmoil of central government collapse. The apparent termination of activity at a number of villa sites across southern England in the fourth century could also have derived from the political fallout of the period, certain prominent villa owners perhaps falling victim to the 'purges and show trials' that follow rebellion and counterrevolution (Henig 2002, 98-9).

Alternatively, the decline of the Romanised villa could, at least in part, mirror the decline of the stately home and country house in Britain during the late nineteenth and early twentieth century. Here, the combination of agricultural depression and devastating global conflict meant that the income and manpower necessary to maintain great estates became increasingly difficult to obtain. Domestic and agricultural staff recruited into the armies of the First and Second World Wars were either slaughtered on the field of battle or recruited into munitions factories and centres of alternative urban employment. Heirs to the estate were killed in the frontline whilst surviving relatives found that on their return taxation had increased. In some instances, both the land and house were requisitioned by the military. The solution to spiralling debt, in many cases, was to downsize: sell off the land, dismantle the house and move to a more manageable property.

9

RELIGION AND BELIEF

Whichever way you approach it, getting to the summit of Chanctonbury Ring is quite an achievement. The route from the north, against the wooded slopes of the great chalk escarpment, is the most direct, but can also be the most tiring. Emerging from the trees and onto the well-worn footpath is, however, an exhilarating experience. As you stride onto the chalk ridge, with the Weald spreading out behind you, Chanctonbury looms menacingly to your right. The tight clump of beech, once the most recognisable feature on the South Downs, has crowned the summit since 1760. As well as being distinctive, the trees have the effect of making Chanctonbury a curiously unsettling place. As a child, before the great storm of 1987 devastated the plantation, entering the darkened spaces between the trees was like crossing over into another world. The wind died suddenly away, the light began to fade and noises became muffled and distorted.

Occasionally there was evidence of recent human activity amongst the gnarled tree roots of the Ring. Sometimes this was simply charcoal, ash, cigarette stubs and baked bean tins. Sometimes it was mutilated animal carcasses and nodules of chalk arranged into curious five-sided shapes. The hill has always possessed strong associations with witchcraft, something that can make visiting the Ring an eerie experience. Despite the damage caused in 1987, there remains a curious stillness about the place. Ghost stories abound and folklore tells of strange encounters with 'the other'. A low earthwork bounds the trees, the remains of a Late Bronze or Early Iron Age enclosure. At the centre of this lies the undoubted cause of Chanctonbury's unease: the buried remains of a Roman temple.

CLASSICAL RELIGION

Religion and religious belief infused every aspect of Roman life from daily business, to sporting activities, travelling, education, feasting or simply relaxing by the pool.

The chief Roman deities were collectively known as the pantheon and each god or goddess had a particular name, legend or background story and clearly defined set of attributes. This meant that requests, prayers or dedications could be directed to specific gods. Jupiter, for example, as head of the Roman pantheon, was considered to be the most powerful of gods, father of the human race and protector of Rome itself. Jupiter was, perhaps not unexpectedly given his attributes of strength and power, highly popular within the Roman army and many altars set up outside forts on the northern frontier of Britain are dedicated to *Jupiter Optimus Maximus*, literally 'Jupiter Best and Greatest'.

Jupiter, in his guise as protector of Rome and chief Roman deity, is named in a prominent dedication recovered from Chichester (RIB 89). The piece (*96*), found in 1935 during the excavation of foundations for the Post Office building on the northern edge of West Street (Down and Rule 1971, 15) reads:

I O M
IN HONOREM DO
MV[S] DIVINAE S...

which may be translated as:

To Jupiter, Best and Greatest, in Honour of the Divine House, S...

The 'Divine House' is a reference to the imperial family of either Claudius (reigned AD 41-54) and Nero (AD 54-68), for Caesar, Augustus and later Claudius himself were all deified by the Roman senate, or to Titus (79-81) and Domitian (81-96), as their father Vespasian and later Titus himself were similarly honoured. The text provides no clue as to which 'Divine House' is being commemorated here, nor to which specific emperor is the dedication being made. The similarity of the reference to that found in the Togidubnus stone (RIB 91: see chapter 3), not to say the style of lettering evident, have suggested to some that the inscription dates from the reign of either Claudius or Nero (e.g. Collingwood and Wright 1965, 24-5). It is possible that the rest of the missing word following the 'S' on the last surviving line of the inscription was that of the donor, and that could have been Sallustius Lucullus (see chapter 4). If Lucullus had set up a third monumental dedication at the centre of Chichester (in addition to RIB 90 and RIB 2334), that would date the piece to the Flavian House of Vespasian, Titus and Domitian, and probably to the reign of Domitian himself. This was when the Briton was at the height of his powers, being appointed as governor of the province. Whilst an undeniably attractive hypothesis, in the absence of a more complete transcription, this can be no more than guesswork.

The Jupiter inscription had been carved on one side of a rectangular sandstone column base measuring 1.04 x 0.4 x 1.04m. Sculptured figures adorned the non-

96 Chichester: the inscribed front of the 'Jupiter Stone', probably part of a base for a Jupiter column originally set within the forum precinct of *Noviomagus.* © *Chichester District Council*

97 Chichester: the left side of the Jupiter Stone, showing two naked female figures. © *Chichester District Council*

inscribed face. On the left-hand side, two naked female figures, each with the right arm outstretched, right hands touching each other's left shoulder, stand in front of ornate foliage (*97*). The right-hand side of the stone is sadly damaged and only the raised right arm of a, presumably male, figure survives. The hand grips a staff and once again there is a background of ornate vegetation. The rear of the stone possesses the same type of foliage, though there is no clear evidence of any figures. A small sandstone fragment of a sculptured female, waist to knee wearing a chiton, was found at the same time as the block and this may have formed part of a lost scene from the damaged back panel. Collingwood and Wright have suggested the figure could represent the goddess Minerva (Collingwood and Wright 1965, 24).

The stone would appear to have formed the larger part of a base for a Jupiter column, probably set within the forum precinct of *Noviomagus* (see chapter 5). Such imposing monuments, with key gods adorning the base and a statue of Jupiter, usually on horseback or with thunderbolts, astride the top, are known from other important towns across the empire and from Britain at least one has been recorded from Cirencester (Collingwood and Wright 1965, 30-1). Such a dedication would only have been made by the wealthiest or most influential of townspeople, and Sallustius Lucullus (as noted above) or Togidubnus 'the Great' would surely be prime candidates.

As well as being the chief god of Rome, Jupiter was worshipped together with the goddesses Juno and Minerva in a group known collectively as the 'Capitoline Triad'. Juno, Jupiter's wife, was the foremost female deity, principally associated with childbirth, whilst Minerva, their daughter, was the goddess of warfare, crafts, wisdom and (sometimes) healing. Beneath the top three came a variety of other important State deities including Mars, Mercury, Neptune, Venus, Diana, Apollo, Ceres, Vesta, Saturn, Vulcan and Janus. Although the gods and goddesses that comprised the Roman pantheon could be worshipped anywhere, altars, statues and mobile shrines being set up wherever it was thought appropriate, specific temples, or houses of the god, were frequently established. Temples, dedications and altars, specifically to Jupiter, Juno, Minerva, or the Capitoline Triad as a whole, are commonly found at the centre of new urban developments across the Roman world, though other temple buildings can be found on the margins of towns, outside forts, close to ports or alongside prominent highways.

Classical temples were built to a standard design throughout the Roman world, with an enclosed room or *cella* that contained the cult statue of the deity in question. The *cella*, which was built according to the principle that its length should not exceed one and a quarter times its width, was normally approached through a double door surrounded by an ornate set of columns which in turn supported highly a decorated pediment (*98*). Temples were where members of the public could travel to make a dedication or to pray directly to their god or goddess. Usually the public did not enter the *cella*, for worship was not a congregational activity, the focus of religious fervour being at the front of the building, which explains why so many classical temples possess ornate façades. Temples were usually set within their own *temenos*, or sacred precinct, something which helped further distance the holy building from the real world beyond. Upon approaching a temple, the request, gift or prayer was either left on the main altar in front of the building, or passed directly to a priest who would then convey it inside. The *cella* therefore acted as a sort of celestial telephone, a hotline connecting the priest to the heavens; a transmitter for talking to god.

Few classical temples have been recorded from the British Isles. In Colchester, the Roman town of *Colonia Claudia Victricensis*, a temple was dedicated to the deified emperor Claudius and, though nothing remains above ground, the foundations of the great podium are still preserved beneath the Norman castle (Crummy 1997, 59-60). In Bath, the footprint of a classical temple has been found whilst significant

98 Chichester: although nothing survives of the temple to Neptune and Minerva above ground, it is likely that it followed the standard pattern of a classical style religious building, set on a high podium, with a decorated façade and high supporting columns. This modern building in Chichester provides a good example of what the temple may originally have looked like, although here the deity being worshipped is one associated with fast-food, his brand-logo a powerful modern example of imperial domination

amounts of the temple pediment, sawn up for use in later building projects, have also been discovered (Cunliffe and Davenport 1985). Although not proven, it seems likely that the temple at Bath was first established in the late first century by Tiberius Claudius Togidubnus (Henig 1999), the Romano-British king also recorded from dedicatory inscription found in Chichester. The Chichester inscription (RIB 91: see chapter 3) records the building of a classical-style '*Templum* to Neptune and Minerva', the exact position of which within the town has yet to be conclusively proved (see chapter 5).

The combination of Minerva, daughter of Jupiter and Juno, and Neptune does not appear to be a common one within the Roman world (de la Bédoyère 2002, 56), although their Greek counterparts, Poseidon and Athene (representing the combination of sea and land), were the co-guardians of Ancient Athens (Henig 2002, 48). Minerva's appeal as a member of the Capitoline Triad would appear clear enough and she seems to have been a popular deity in the north-western provinces of the Roman Empire, frequently appearing as the goddess of war adorned with a spear and classical Greek helmet. She also possessed healing attributes and, in Britain, was associated with the hot springs and early Roman temple complex at Bath (*Aquae Sulis*). Furthermore, her associations with arts and crafts may have made Minerva the deity of choice for the guild of smiths or artisans who are recorded as providing the Chichester temple 'from their own resources' (RIB 91). The choice of Neptune as co-deity for the Chichester temple may have resulted from a desire to placate the Roman god of the sea. Chichester's prosperity was based on direct contact with the world of Rome via the expansive natural harbours to the south-west and any budding entrepreneur here in the first century AD would certainly have wanted the sea on their side.

Apart from the key monuments of *Noviomagus*, many of the gods and goddesses of the Roman pantheon appear in Sussex on the coins in daily circulation. Stone portraits of specific classical deities are rare in Sussex, but at the villa of Chilgrove 2 in West Sussex, the base of a seated female figure has been found (Down 1979). The piece (*99*) may originally have derived from a *Lararium* or household shrine and is thought to represent the goddess Fortuna, the controller of human destiny (although it may alternatively represent a mother goddess or a figure of the *Dea Nutrix* or nursing goddess: cf. Green 1983, 52-3). Another portrait of Fortuna, this time in bronze, has been recovered from Hastings (Devenish 1978), whilst miniatures depicting Mercury, Neptune and Venus have been recovered from Bodiam, Maresfield, Chichester and Alfoldean respectively (Lemmon and Darrall Hill 1966; Down 1989, 218; Winbolt 1924). Images of the gods also appear upon the mosaics of well-to-do town houses and rural villas, but, as has been pointed out (Rudling 1988, 228), the choice of image within mosaic floors does not necessarily indicate that a particular deity was being worshipped. The use of classical legends within the interior décor of villas may indicate nothing more than the owner's desire to be seen and acknowledged as a fully integrated member of Roman society.

In Sussex and eastern Hampshire, the key figure from classical mythology to appear upon mosaic floors is that of the unfortunate Medusa. Medusa figured on at least two important floors at Bignor, a third-century 'four seasons' mosaic from the northern end of the west wing and a fourth-century floor in the southern baths. At Fishbourne, a second-century pavement again shows Medusa in the central panel, whilst she also features strongly in floors recovered from Brading in the Isle of Wight and Bramdean in Hampshire. In Greek mythology, Medusa (the 'queen') was the daughter of the marine god Phorcys and the sea monster Keto. Together with her two sisters Stheno (the 'mighty') and Euryale (the 'forceful'), the three women were known as 'the Gorgons'. In her youth Medusa was famed for her beauty and for her golden hair. Seduced by Neptune in the temple of Minerva, Medusa was cursed by the outraged goddess who transformed her into a hideous monster. Later, after helping arrange the assassination of Medusa, Minerva took the severed head of the Gorgon and wore it thereafter on her armour.

The dual actions of Neptune and Minerva, the key deities named in the inscription of Togidubnus in Chichester, had together created then dispatched Medusa the monster. Would it be too much to argue that the reason why the Gorgon appeared in mosaics around *Noviomagus*, the capital of the Regini, was because of her associations with Neptune and Minerva and the continued popularity of Togidubnus' temple throughout the second and third centuries AD? In this respect it might be interesting to note the classical temple recovered and reconstructed, from a mass of jumbled

99 Chilgrove 1:
the lower half
of a statuette,
presumed to be
of Fortuna.
© *Chichester
District Council*

fragments, from the Roman city of *Aquae Sulis* (modern-day Bath). Here, the central pediment of the temple contained a startling image: a 'craggy face, penetrating gaze and luxuriant moustache' which would originally have stared out and down towards the pilgrims, devotees and worshippers. Closer inspection shows that the snaky hair is literally that, a writhing mass of serpents.

Some recent writers have attempted to identify the face in the Bath temple with the Roman sea deities Neptune or Oceanus, but the wings evident in the hair, just behind the ears, make the identification of the figure certain: this is Medusa, albeit a male, moustached Medusa. Perhaps the sculptor commissioned to generate the piece was unfamiliar with the iconography of the Gorgons and wrongly provided her with male attributes. Given the prominence given to the piece, however, this seems unlikely. More probably we are seeing here a deliberate attempt to portray the fusion between Neptune and Minerva to create the Medusa of legend. Anyone seeing the face should automatically have made the connection, the head of Medusa appearing on the shield of Minerva as an early form of brand or logo. To those who did not make the association, additional attributes signifying Minerva, namely an owl, were added, as were Victory and a Victor's wreath.

The pediment formed the centrepiece to the main temple in Bath, dedicated to Sulis Minerva, a conflation of the Roman goddess and (we may presume) the local British deity of the hot spring. The structure seems to have been set out and constructed between AD 75 and 90, making it a contemporary of Fishbourne and, most probably, of the temple of Neptune and Minerva in Chichester, both sites possibly having been sponsored by Togidubnus himself (Henig 1999). Given the similarity in dates and the observation that the Roman deities marked out at Bath (Neptune and Minerva) were the same as those cited for the classical *templum* in Chichester, we must wonder whether the iconography of both was also similar. Is there, somewhere beneath the streets of modern Chichester, a male, moustached Gorgon still waiting to be rediscovered?

THE IMPERIAL CULT

The possible presence of a second classical-style temple in Sussex is hinted at from a range of stone discoveries made in the Broadbridge area of Bosham, to the west of modern Chichester. We have already noted the monumental head of Nero from Bosham (chapter 6), but one further discovery from the area needs mentioning here. The find is that of a white marble head of a man, measuring nearly 0.3m in height (*100*). The head is in excellent condition, suffering only minor damage to the nose and ears (some of which has been repaired in recent times), the whole having been set into a more modern bust of green marble. The circumstances of discovery are unfortunately vague, the Reverend K.H. MacDermott noting in a letter to the British Museum in 1910 that it had been found 'in an old garden' and that, at the time of writing it was 'standing in a flower pot – surrounded by pebbles' (MacDermott quoted in Painter 1965, 179).

MacDermott observed that the head had originally been unearthed during the cutting of foundations for a house 'some 50 or 60 years ago' and had then been left as part of a garden rockery (MacDermott quoted in Painter 1965, 180). The British Museum acquired the piece in 1961 and has since largely ignored it, believing it to be either a hoax (Jones *et al.* 1990) or perhaps a late import into the British Isles (possibly a piece collected by an early antiquarian during a 'Grand Tour' of Italy or North Africa: Toynbee 1962, 123). Had this been the only Roman stone portrait retrieved from the Bosham area, one might be forgiven for taking the cynical view and believing that it represents a modern import or deliberate fake. Sadly for this theory the head is only part of a larger group of statuary recovered from this part of Sussex and there is indeed every reason to believe that it is genuine. The neglect shown to it by the British Museum, and its subsequent omission from all works on the Roman province, is quite simply scandalous.

J.M. Toynbee dated the head to the very early days of the empire (late Augustan or early Tiberian) and suggested that it was likely to represent 'a member of the ruling house', possibly Germanicus (Toynbee 1962, 123). Germanicus Julius Caesar

100 Bosham: a white marble head of the emperor Caligula. One of the most important archaeological discoveries of Roman Britain, it has sadly been long forgotten and ignored by the academic community.
© *Sussex Archaeological Society*

(15 BC to AD 19), adopted grandson of the emperor Augustus and brother of Claudius, had been marked out for greatness from an early age. A favourite of Augustus, Germanicus served well in the Roman military, being appointed commander of the army in Germany after the emperor's death in AD 14. In AD 19, however, Germanicus' rise to power came to an abrupt end: whilst serving in Syria as heir designate to the second emperor Tiberius, he died. A portrait of the popular brother of the emperor Claudius, 'conqueror of Britain' would make perfect sense in the context of Late Iron Age and Early Roman Britain. It would also be explicable from the perspective of Sussex, for we have already noted that the British king Togidubnus set up a dedication in Chichester in which he honoured the 'Divine House' of the imperial family (RIB 91).

This is all well and good, but unfortunately the Broadbridge head is not that of Germanicus. Neither is the portrait another well-respected younger member of the early imperial household, such as Lucius or Gaius, the much-honoured grandsons of the emperor Augustus. In fact there is only one plausible candidate for the identity of the piece and we have already met him at the start of this book. It is Gaius Caesar Augustus Germanicus, the son of Germanicus Julius Caesar, who ruled as the third emperor of Rome and who is better known to history as Caligula.

Portraits of Caligula are comparatively rare across the Roman world. Although he was not officially consigned to *damnatio memoriae* following his assassination (as both Nero and Domitian would later be), Claudius was none the less keen to remove all likenesses of his predecessor (and nephew) quickly, quietly and efficiently. The historian Dio Cassius records that:

> when the senate desired to dishonour Gaius, he personally prevented the passage of the measure, but on his own responsibility caused all his predecessor's images to disappear by night. (Dio Cassius *Roman History* LX, 4, 5)

Those that were not buried or hidden were defaced, vandalised and generally disfigured, apparently from 'spontaneous demonstrations against his memory' (Varner 2004, 24). A bronze figure of the emperor from a private collection in Switzerland has been attacked by someone wielding a hammer intent on gauging out the eyes, whilst a marble portrait of Gaius from Aquileia in Italy had been broken apart with some force (Varner 2004, 23-4). More frequently an image of the deposed *princeps* was covertly reworked with a chisel into the face of another member of the imperial household. The Broadbridge head has not been greatly damaged and, with the exception of a break to the nose (later repaired) it survives in fine condition, suggesting it must have been concealed shortly after Caligula's assassination; possibly even before Claudius set foot in Britain late in AD 43.

The discovery of one marble portrait of the Julio-Claudian house from Sussex would be important enough, but from the same general area we have already noted a monumental likeness of the emperor Nero Claudius Drusus Germanicus (chapter 6) whilst a life-size image of the younger Nero has also been recovered from the footings of Fishbourne palace to the east. A larger than life upper torso of a Roman military statue (almost certainly an emperor) has, furthermore, been found within the exterior makeup of Bosham Manor house whilst a bronze thumb from a life-sized figure has also been located nearby (Kenny 2004, 17). Both the Bosham and Fishbourne heads of Nero clearly demonstrate the ferocious nature of *damnatio memoriae*, whereby the face of the emperor has been mutilated, decapitated and smashed almost to the point of being unrecognisable. Although we cannot be sure of the identification of the torso and bronze thumb, it is possible a similar process of deliberate destruction is evident in both cases.

Although the exact context of these imperial pieces remains obscure, it is worth noting that the examples cited are not only all from the first or early second century AD, but are also derived from a very restricted geographical area. What was going on in this area of the Sussex coast? Was this area of the county, on the eastern margins of Chichester Harbour and to the immediate west of the Roman town of *Noviomagus* (Chichester) a centre of the Imperial Cult?

The Imperial Cult was a process of worship that centred upon the emperor as a god. Generally speaking, emperors did not claim to be divine in their own life, although many, such as Augustus, Tiberius, Claudius and later Titus and Domitian, were keen to stress the god-like status of their immediate forbears. A leader descended from a father whom the senate had deified (or who could demonstrate that they had a god in the family), would obviously strengthen both their earthly status and their claim to rule. Most of the early emperors benefited from the deification of their immediate predecessor, unless, of course, that predecessor had been so awful (as in the case of Nero and Domitian) that the senate decreed *damnatio memoriae*; an eradication of memory.

The Imperial Cult was also a vital element in the unification and control of newly acquired provinces, providing a focal point of personal devotion to the emperor and his household. From a military perspective, within frontier garrisons, far removed from the centre of Roman life, a dedication or oath of allegiance to the emperor proved an essential way of reaffirming loyalty to the Roman State that went beyond blood, race, friends or tribe. A similar attempt at fostering 'a sense of belonging' through a public affirmation of loyalty can be seen in the citizenship ceremonies that many nation states advance to this day. In Britain, at the time of writing, the 'Citizenship Ceremony' considers an oath or affirmation of fidelity to the sovereign as a key condition to the process of naturalisation. Whether or not existing citizens consider that 'Her Majesty Queen Elizabeth the Second, her Heirs and Successors' have a right to power is ultimately irrelevant, for the key factor in the ceremony is to present a figure to whom allegiance can be directed. To the first century AD Briton, a prominent display of fidelity to the emperor could help fast track citizenship and secure a place in the new order.

In Britain, the Imperial Cult appears to have first focused upon the *numen* (the genius, spirit or creating force) of the emperor Claudius. At *Colonia Claudia Victricensis*, modern-day Colchester, a classical temple to Claudius was erected following the removal of the military garrison there in the AD early 50s. Nothing of the temple superstructure survives, though the foundations suggest a substantial building set within a large sacred precinct (Crummy 1997, 59-60). *Colonia Claudia Victricensis*, previously a major tribal centre or *oppidum* of the Catuvellauni tribe (known as *Camulodunum*), appears to have been the main focus of the Roman advance under the emperor Claudius following the destabilisation of the south-east during AD 43 (see chapters 1 and 2). We have already noted that the centre was first heavily garrisoned, by the *XX Valeria* legion, before becoming a colony town for retired soldiers. *Verulamium* (St Albans), *Calleva* (Silchester) and *Noviomagus* (Chichester), the other key tribal *oppida* of the south-east, do not appear to have suffered so heavily from direct contact with the Roman military and, as already surmised, it would appear that these centres were positively rewarded by the Roman State for their loyalty, support and co-operation.

Given what has already been noted about the events surrounding the 'invasion' of AD 43 and the role played by Togidubnus and later Sallustius Lucullus, it would perhaps seem surprising if their preferred town of *Noviomagus* had not possessed a cult or religious centre dedicated to the imperial family. The presence of monumental imperial sculpture from the Bosham area, some 4.5km west of Chichester, is intriguing and may hint to a focus of activity here. Further evidence may come from a series of masonry structures and associated features discovered around Bosham Harbour from the early nineteenth century. These features include a possible temple building, measuring approximately 23 x 15m, with a central pool or *piscina*, a 'large excavation in the form of a basin' allegedly containing 'tiers of seats', at least one mosaic and a timber palisade (possibly part of an original enclosure: Black 1985, 255).

The rather vague nature of the original account (Mitchell 1866) makes full understanding and interpretation of the site almost impossible, though the range of structures allegedly discovered is intriguing. There can be little doubt that the main structure described (and reconstructed by Ernest Black from the original account: *101*) was that of a temple or religious building, but more problematical is the 'large excavation'. The account recorded by Mitchell certainly *sounds* like the remains of a theatre or amphitheatre, especially if it had indeed contained remains of tiered seating, but Mitchell himself did not see the structure, he merely recorded the observations of someone remembering what members of his family had seen.

Throughout the Roman empire, theatres, and less frequently amphitheatres, were intimately associated with religion and religious sites, the theatre indicating 'the presence of large gatherings and the obvious popularity of the deity concerned' (Wacher 1995, 56). Across south-eastern England, a series of temple and theatre/ amphitheatre relationships have been observed, most prominently at Colchester (both from inside the town and at Gosbecks to the south-west), *Verulamium* (St Albans), Frilford and Canterbury. At Frilford, in Oxfordshire, a series of religious structures were set within a sacred precinct (*temenos*). Close by lay an amphitheatre, a 45m-diameter arena space, cut into the natural clay. Spoil derived from the excavation of the arena floor was thrown up to form an external bank, some 11-12m wide, which provided a secure base for tiers of fixed timber seating (Burnham and Wacher 1990, 178). At Gosbecks, in an area which seems, prior to the Roman invasion, to have been the focus of tribal power within the *oppidum*, the presence of a theatre and temple may indicate that the basic 'functions of State' continued here well into the Roman period (Hawkes and Crummy 1995, 178). At *Colonia Copia Felix Munatia Lugdunum* (modern-day Lyon) in Gaul, tribal representatives gathered in an amphitheatre adjoining a sanctuary containing dedications to Rome and

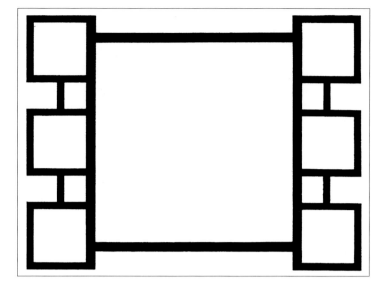

101 Bosham: a speculative recreation, by Ernest Black, of the Roman building excavated early in the nineteenth century, based on an account made in 1866. *Redrawn from Black 1985*

to Augustus (Drinkwater 1983, 111-4). The city was particularly revered within the Julio-Claudian house as the birth-place of Claudius and, on his return from Britain in AD 43 or 44, the emperor stopped here as part of his carefully planned procession back to Rome. Could the Broadbridge site represent a rural theatre/ temple complex akin to those of Frilford, Gosbecks and Lyon, with dedications made to the imperial family, designed and paid for by the local tribal authority? At present we may only speculate, but, given the discoveries made to date, the possibility would seem very real.

NATIVE CULTS

Iron Age religious practice was not recorded in any great detail by Roman and Greek historians, most of whom viewed it as being wholly alien to classical sensibilities. Julius Caesar, a first-hand witness to prehistoric society in Britain and Gaul, did not produce any radical insight into the nature of indigenous religion. Perhaps this is unsurprising for Caesar, as we have already noted, was writing for a Roman audience and much of what he does tell us is infused with racial prejudice. Hence he speaks of headhunting, cannibalism and bloody human sacrifice in sacred groves. These are all emotive issues even today for mutilation, decapitation and the eating of human flesh are activities which, when reported by the media, are guaranteed to shock, terrify and repulse. The reality of Iron Age religious practice is lost somewhere in Caesar's text. Although headhunting and sacrifice may well have existed in Britain and Gaul, it is worth noting that they also did within polite Roman society albeit conducted under the guise of entertainment.

One term in particular that Caesar uses in relation to Iron Age religion that has resonance today is that of 'druid'. The word druid is powerful and emotive, conjuring up a wide range of diverse images within modern popular culture. Unfortunately Caesar does not provide a description of what the term druid actually means and for most people today it is has become a catchall phrase for priests, seers, teachers, shamans and holy men or women. Infuriatingly, despite being witnessing the priestly or druid caste in Gaul, Caesar supplies no information on belief systems (other than in very general terms) or the mythology surrounding certain deities. More dauntingly, especially for those anxious to demonstrate that druidism was firmly enmeshed within the British Isles, Caesar refers only once, and almost in passing, that 'it is thought that the druidic system was invented in Britain and thence imported to Gaul.' (*Gallic Wars* V, 13)

Generally speaking, Rome was happy to tolerate all belief systems that it encountered during its campaigns of expansion, incorporation and conquest. The absorption of local, non-Roman cults, gods and goddesses into the imperial system was conducted primarily because of the deeply superstitious nature of the Roman mind in which it was felt important to get the indigenous spirits of conquered peoples on the side of the new government. Toleration was also useful from the practical viewpoint that a society whose religious beliefs are not persecuted is far less likely to rebel. The only notable occasions where the Roman State objected to a particular religion is when the practice in question was judged to possess a political dimension. Two examples of this were druidism in Gaul, which was believed to have instigated uprisings against Rome, and Christianity, which rejected the earthly powers of the emperor.

The non-acceptance of indigenous religious practice has always proved a major sticking point in processes of domination and cultural change. A conquering power must accept all local religions, or modify them only gently, if they hope to succeed and maintain control. The founders of European empires carved out in the Americas, Australia and Africa were intolerant of the indigenous religions they encountered and repeatedly tried to stamp them out or at least replace them with the standard European perspective on divinity. This led unfailingly to resistance, revolt and protracted war, the effects of which can be seen to this day. In its tolerance and acceptance of indigenous practice, the Roman State often managed to absorb pre-Roman deities and combine them with accepted Mediterranean examples. Thus in the city of *Aquae Sulis* (Bath) we hear of the goddess Sulis Minerva. Minerva being the Roman deity associated with wisdom, craft, war and healing, whilst Sulis, it would appear, was her local Iron Age equivalent: the goddess of the hot spring.

Conflation with classical gods and goddesses is often the only process through which the particular names of Iron Age deities have survived to the present day. British society did not write the names of their gods on altars, on walls or on the countless pieces of metalwork they deposited in springs, bogs and other watery places. They did not record the nature of their religious practice and neither did they build, as far as we can tell, monumental temple structures in which particular deities could reside. It is only through later Roman altars and religious dedications, all nicely inscribed in Latin, that we encounter the unfamiliar sounding Celtic names of indigenous gods, goddesses and spirits of the place. Hence at Lydney, in Gloucestershire, we hear of Mars Nodens (Wheeler and Wheeler 1932), a Romano-British god of healing, whilst at Colchester in Essex we find Mars Medocius (Collingwood and Wright 1965, 62: RIB 191) and in Carlisle one Mars Belatucadrus (Collingwood and Wright 1965, 316: RIB 948).

In Chichester, an inscription discovered from a pit cut through the backfilled remains of the early 'military' ditch, may provide us with evidence for just such a conflation between native and Rome. The fragmentary text, derived from the site of Needlemakers, just outside the area of the east gate, has been reconstructed as:

...BVS DOMEST...
...VS ARK...
...P

which may be translated as:

To the Mother Goddesses of the Homeland....us the Treasurer (*arkarius*) set this up at his own expense

Mother goddesses were popular figures within the native belief systems of Britain, Gaul and Germany, being specifically associated with fertility. The *Deae Matres* usually, though not exclusively, appear in triplicate and in sculptured form are often to be seen 'nursing infants or holding baskets of fruit, loaves or other fertility symbols such as fish' (Green 1983, 51). Dedications to mother goddesses occur throughout Britain, and are to be especially found within the chief cities and frontiers of the province. The concept of dedicating to the mother goddess appears to have generally been related to the Celtic world beyond Rome, although examples exist elsewhere through the empire.

It is a great shame that, in its current fragmentary state, we cannot read who the treasurer was, what he was treasurer of, nor which 'homeland' to which the mother goddesses being cited was specific. The concept of mother goddess may have been popular in the immediate vicinity of *Noviomagus*, a female statuette made of Oolitic Limestone thought to represent the 'Celtic Mother Goddess' being found near East Gate in the 1970s (Magilton 1992, 73-4), whilst the lower half of a seated female figure, usually thought to represent Fortuna but which may alternatively be mother goddess, was found to the north of Chichester, in the villa of Chilgrove 2 (Down 1979). The nature of the Chichester Needlemakers inscription strongly suggests that it belonged to the earliest years of Roman activity at *Noviomagus*, and it could have been contemporary with the dedications, already noted from the town, to Nero and to Neptune and Minerva. The shrine to the *Matres Domesticae* may originally have lain close to its findspot, outside the east gate, on the road to London (Down 1988, 71).

Unlike Roman State religion, there does not seem to have been a universal pantheon of gods and goddesses within Iron Age Britain, rather deities may have been specific to particular tribes, clans or family groups. Spirits were furthermore, as far as it is possible to tell, associated with natural features in the landscape, such as a spring, river, mountain, hill or forest. The process of acceptance into the Roman world would have meant that any local Iron Age deity would have received a brand new stone-built house within which the spirit of the place could reside. Such houses or temples would have been sited on or close to the point at which earlier practices had been conducted. Discovery of Iron Age deposits (metalwork, pottery, and cremation burials) beside or beneath a Roman temple building could therefore imply the presence of a significant focus of earlier worship.

An excellent example of a native cult centre preserved beneath the remains of a later Roman religious complex may be seen at Hayling Island, in Hampshire. Although the site does not lie within the modern administrative borders that define Sussex, its position, at the eastern margins of Chichester Harbour, when combined with its date, recorded artefactual assemblage and structural form, all clearly tie the site to the social and political developments occurring around Chichester in the Later Iron Age and Early Roman period. The primary phase of construction at Hayling Island appears to have been a round structure, measuring over 10m in diameter, defined by settings of internal posts and external gullies, possibly during the middle of the first century BC (Woodward 1992, 21-3; King and Soffe 1994; Davenport 2003, 104).

The Hayling Island building, which clearly resembled the form of a domestic structure, was set within a roughly square enclosure, the ditch of which had been filled at specific places with a range of artefacts which seem to reflect 'the trappings of an Iron Age warrior and his horse-drawn vehicle' (Woodward 1992, 21). Other assemblages included pottery vessels (possibly containing offerings), the bones (and meat) of sheep and pig and a wide range of Iron Age coins. Extensive cross-channel contacts with central and north-eastern Gaul are evidenced from the coins, whilst the British series seem to emphasise links with Hampshire and Dorset (Davenport 2003, 103). In the late first century AD at about the time of the great developments at Fishbourne and in Chichester, the site was redeveloped, the stone foundations of the new complex following the same basic plan of its predecessor (a circular building within a square enclosure), albeit on a significantly grander scale.

At Lancing Down in West Sussex, the excavation of a Roman temple building in 1980 revealed further evidence of Late Iron Age religious practice in the form of a small, roughly square-shaped, timber building (*102*), set within a shallow, oval-shaped enclosure gulley or *temenos* (Bedwin 1981). Around the temple, to the south and west, a series of Iron Age and early Roman cremations, together with a single inhumation, were also located. The timber structure, which clearly dated to the Later Iron Age, was very similar in basic form, albeit on a vastly smaller scale, to the later Roman temple (see below), something which may suggest continuity in religious practice

102 Lancing Down: view, looking north-west, of the small, roughly square-shaped, timber building (centre of shot), with the *temenos* or enclosure gulley in the foreground, and the masonry corner of the later Romano-Celtic temple in the background. © *Sussex Archaeological Society*

from the Late Prehistoric to the Roman period. Whether structures like the small, square Iron Age building (which may be interpreted as a shrine) found at Lancing Down would have been used in a manner reminiscent of a Late Roman temple, with a priest conducting ceremonies outside and conveying prayers, messages and requests to the cult statue within the sacred, non-public inner space, is unknown. Given the size of the Lancing structure it is, however, unlikely that this would or could have functioned as a place of congregational worship; more likely it was a building designed to house a particular idol, entity or religious identity.

Timber structures of similar size, if not shape, to that found on Lancing Down have been located during the course of excavations conducted at Westhampnett, prior to the construction of the A27. The Westhampnett buildings, of which at least four have now been investigated, lay to the immediate east of, and on higher ground than, a large Late Iron Age cremation cemetery and associated pyre structures. The nature of the evidence suggests that all buildings were probably formed by edge-set planks bedded within linear foundation trenches and possibly covered in daub. The area to the west of the buildings comprised a range of pyre-related pits and trenches and at least 161 individual cremation deposits, the largest single cremation cemetery for its period yet recorded in England. The deposits were positioned along the southern and eastern edges of a wide and apparently empty circular space, older people being set down close to the centre, younger people towards the outer edge. The majority of cremations were unurned, though they may have originally been held within a leather or textile container that has not survived. Urns that were associated with cremations were often highly decorated, whilst a range of metal forms, especially brooches, suggests a date range of between 90 and 50 BC for the bulk of deposition activity.

Other evidence of Late Iron Age religious practice in Sussex may be seen at Muntham Court near Worthing. Here, excavations in the late 1950s revealed a complex mass of postholes, pits and other features, all apparently dating to the Late Iron Age and Roman period. The floor of a circular timber structure, measuring approximately 11m in diameter, had been cut by three shallow pits, each of which contained an ox skull 'resting on the other bones of the skeleton' (Burstow and Holleyman 1957; Bedwin 1981, 192). The discovery is suggestive of the primary phase central structure recorded from Hayling Island, but in the absence of a detailed account for Muntham Court, it is difficult to take this analogy further. Other finds associated with this building were a copper alloy cheek piece from a horse bit, a bronze buckle from a Roman cavalry harness, a harness stud, an enamelled fish brooch and a bronze pommel, possibly for a ceremonial mace or sceptre. Found with these was a tiny clay model of a human leg, possibly indicative of a desire to cure illness or of the presence here of a specific healing cult. A 'well' or shaft close by was traced to a depth of over 80m, the fill containing 'the skeletons of many dogs' (Bedwin 1981, 192). Finds, including a range of coins, seem to indicate a date in mid-third to early fourth century AD for the bulk of deposition (Rudling 2003, 122).

Further evidence to suggest the veneration of earlier sites, if not a broad continuity of worship, may be seen from the treatment of a number of prehistoric mounds. At Slonk Hill, near Shoreham, two round mounds dating to the Bronze Age were remodified and surrounded by a rectangular enclosure ditch, possibly creating a sacred precinct or *temenos*, in the second or third century AD (Hartridge 1978). By the fourth century, the enclosing ditch appears to have been backfilled and a set of posts, measuring around 11m square, were set around the easternmost round mound, through the remains of the external quarry ditch. A small group of fourth-century coins were added to a posthole at this time and the leg bones of lambs and piglets were also placed within the fill of a cut made into the uppermost fill of the western barrow ditch (Hartridge 1978; Rudling 2003, 122). At Money Mound, Lower Beeding, over 150 coins, dating from AD 69-388) were buried within the structure of an Early Bronze Age round cairn (Beckensall 1967).

ROMANO-CELTIC TEMPLES

The deliberate fusion of Iron Age deities and spirits of the place with their Roman counterparts probably meant that, for many Britons, the worship of the old gods could continue, albeit within the more substantial masonry structures built under the new administrative order. At sites like Hayling Island in Hampshire and Lancing Down in West Sussex, we have already noted that not only do religious structures of the Later Iron Age lie directly beneath their Roman counterparts, but the form taken by the later buildings appears to represent a more monumental version of the original structure. Romanisation of native belief systems therefore probably meant little more than the deliberate reshaping of the primary shrine using more permanent building materials. No doubt altars and cult statues were also added and deposition of artefacts continued, though the coins, objects and animal remains were all now derived from a much wider geographical area.

As with the classical pantheon, images of native deities from Sussex are rare. A number of stone heads of 'Celtic' style, with enlarged eyes and a distinctly non-Roman feel, have been found to the east of the county, but the identification of such pieces is fraught with difficulty. A fragment of a carved face with large almond-shaped eyes and traces of a moustache was retrieved from a rockery of an Eastbourne nursing home in around 1900. Although removed from its archaeological context, the piece, now in Seaford Museum, was found with fragments of masonry disturbed from the Eastbourne villa (chapter 6) and may presumably have derived from the same source. Stylistically it belongs to the period late first century BC – third century AD, though nothing certain is known about its origins.

A second head, allegedly found near Wilmington in East Sussex, and currently on display in Barbican House Museum in Lewes, similarly possesses no context and, although cited as a 'Celtic' piece, may derive from any period from the Late Iron Age

103 Piltdown: a carved stone head, possibly that of a Celtic or Romano-British deity. *Author courtesy of the Sussex Archaeological Society*

to the nineteenth century. A third head carved into a large block of stone found in a bog near Piltdown in east Sussex (*103*) has also been interpreted as that of a Celtic or Romano-British deity (Holden and Tebbutt 1983). Despite the connotations surrounding the place name 'Piltdown', there is no suggestion that the head itself is a fake, though nothing can, unfortunately, be said concerning a specific date or place of origin. Pieces such as this may have been designed to sit within a temple or shrine or to be placed close to the spot where a specific deity was thought to reside, but in the absence of any useful archaeological information surrounding their discovery, little more can really be said.

Similar problems exist regarding another type of archaeological discovery thought to have intimate connections with Romano-British religious practice: the bronze boar. Miniature depictions of boars cast in bronze have been found from a variety of locations in Sussex, notably Muntham Court and Washington in West Sussex and Brighton, Itford, Lewes and Woodingdean in the East (Rudling 2001, 116-8). Unfortunately, with the exception of the Muntham Court example, the majority of such discoveries are unstratified and, ultimately, undatable, being retrieved as chance surface finds. Stylistically the bulk appear to be Romano-British, but whether they were votive offerings, religious icons, good luck talismans or children's toys, remains to be seen. The Muntham Court example is, however, of some additional interest, as it seems to depict a slain or dying boar. Given its association with the circular shrine or temple from Muntham Court (see above), it is possible that it was intended as an offering given prior to a hunting trip or it may have related to a specific hunting or healing cult (Green 1983, 60-1).

One particular type of structure that appears to be intimately associated with religious practice in north-western Europe (and specifically in northern Gaul, Germany and southern Britain) is the so-called Romano-Celtic temple. The main defining characteristics of this category of building are a central room or *cella*, usually, though not exclusively, square, with a concentric corridor, walkway or ambulatory (*porticus*) creating the effect of 'a square within a square'. As with more classical forms of temple structure, it is assumed that the central *cella* contained the cult statue and was off-limits to all but the professional religious specialists, whilst the encircling ambulatory was for more general access, providing a form of shelter from the elements, a secluded walkway for processions or a sacred space for meditation and the deposition of offerings. The area directly in front of a number of Romano-Celtic temples appears to have been set aside for an altar, upon which specific offerings and dedications could be left and prayers made.

On Lancing Down, the Roman temple comprised a Romano-Celtic 'square-within-a-square' building of chalk, flint and mortar (*104*). First examined in 1828, the central *cella* of the Lancing temple was seen to measure 5.5m internally, with an entrance facing due east. Buttresses were apparently noted on all of the external corners of the outer ambulatory, though none were observed during the partial re-examination of 1980 (Bedwin 1981, 44). Another Romano-Celtic temple has been identified in Sussex at Ratham Mill, near Funtington, from an aerial photograph taken in 1963 (King and Soffe 1983). This structure appears unusual, however, comprising three concentric squares, the inner measuring 4m, the middle 8.5m and the outer 15.5m across. Although unexcavated, it is possible that the inner square represented the remains of a plinth designed to support a cult statue, though it must be admitted that the dimensions would appear rather excessive. Alternatively one, or both, of the inner squares could represent a differential phase of constructional activity, possibly dating back to the Later Iron Age.

On Bow Hill, near Chichester, a series of postholes forming 'a roughly square building' measuring 5.5m across may indicate the presence of another Romano-Celtic-style temple building (Carlyon-Britton quoted in Bedwin 1981, 191); certainly the evidence recovered seemed to indicate an 'inner room' and an 'open veranda'. Unfortunately the site, excavated between 1926 and 1931, was never fully published, and all details and artefacts now appear to be lost (Bedwin 1981, 192). Coins suggested a broad date range of between AD 97 and 395 for the use of the structure whilst building debris indicated the former presence of a tiled roof and painted wall plaster.

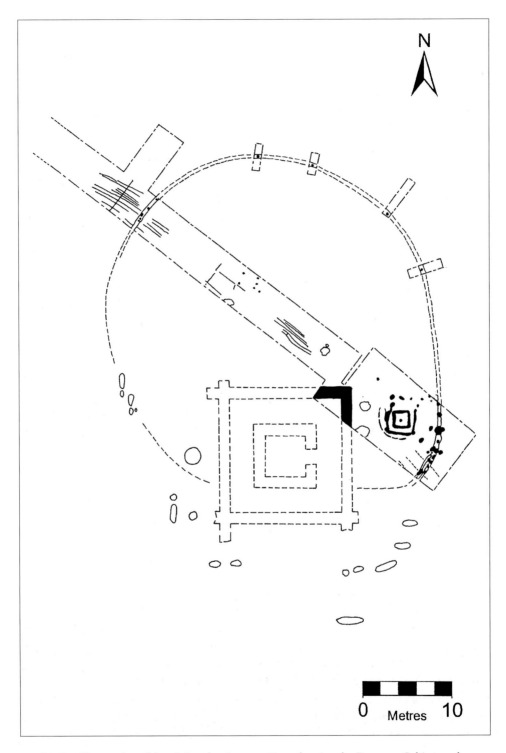

104 Lancing Down: plan of the 1828 and 1980 excavations showing the Romano-Celtic temple, smaller timber structure, *temenos* boundary and associated features. *Redrawn from Bedwin 1981, 39*

CHANCTONBURY RING

Probably the best evidence for Romano-Celtic religious practice in Sussex comes from the temple complex recorded from the summit of Chanctonbury in West Sussex. Chanctonbury, as noted at the start of this chapter, is probably best known for its landmark status: a tight clump of beech trees set on a high peak of the South Downs (*105*) with extensive views north across the Weald and southwards to Cissbury and the sea.

The trees have proved critical to the discovery and recording of the prehistoric and Roman archaeology of Chanctonbury. In 1909 and 1977, in preparation for the planting at the centre of the hill, the foundations of a stone-built temple and other associated structures were unearthed (Mitchell 1919; Bedwin 1980). Later, following the Great Storm of 16 October 1987, 75 per cent of the total tree coverage was blasted asunder, leaving the summit of Chanctonbury a tangled mass of shattered stumps and branches. As the great clump was brought down, root uplift tore at the buried archaeological remains, dragging masonry, tile and, in one case, a human torso to the surface. The fieldwork that followed the storm, between 1987 and 1991, pre-empted the additional planting of trees (Rudling 2001) and helped better elucidate the phasing, nature and extent of Roman cult practice across the hill.

The first major period of prehistoric activity on the summit of Chanctonbury appears to have been the establishment of two round barrows in the Early Bronze Age and the construction of a single entrance, univallate hillfort in the seventh century BC, at the end of the Later Bronze Age. Few features associated with the main phase of

105 Chanctonbury Ring: the wind-disrupted tree-clad hill in 1988. The Romano-Celtic temple complex lies on the summit. *Author*

hillfort construction and use have been found during excavations conducted within the enclosure, so the purpose to which the site was originally put remains something of a mystery. The pattern of limited or 'intermittent' usage, as demonstrated by the restricted range of pottery types retrieved, seems to have continued on the site throughout the Iron Age and into the first century AD (Rudling 2001, 111).

The first serious evidence of Roman interest in the site appears in the form of pottery and coins from the second half of the first century though the first structural remains do not appear to be any earlier than the first half of the second century AD. The highest point of the hill was occupied by a Romano-Celtic temple (Temple 1), comprising a central, rectangular *cella,* measuring 7 x 9.2m, surrounded along its north, west and southern sides by an ambulatory or *porticus.* The absence of a porticus wall along the eastern side may have been due to later stone robbing, or it may alternatively represent the main entranceway into the building. David Rudling, the director of excavations between 1987 and 1991, has suggested that the greater width of the internal walls when compared with those of the ambulatory, could indicate a deliberate attempt to increase the weight-bearing capacity, and therefore the height, of the *cella*, adding that 'it is likely that the *cella* was a tall tower-like structure which rose above the level of the lean-to porticus thus allowing clerestory windows for the provision of light.' (Rudling 2001, 112)

Temple 1 appears to have originally been roofed in red tile and fragments of red, green and yellow painted wall plaster suggest that 'at least some of the temple walls were decorated' (Rudling 2001, 113). Quantities of loose tile *tesserae* found 'near the inner wall' during the course of the 1909 excavations (Mitchell 1910, 135) may indicate the former presence of a red tessellated floor (possibly in the ambulatory) whilst some 4,000 smaller white and red *tesserae* located in 1977 may relate to a destroyed mosaic (Rudling 2001, 113).

Temple 2 at Chanctonbury lay some 20m to the south of the Romano-Celtic shrine. First partially explored in 1909, when it was noted as being of 'peculiar shape' (Mitchell 1910, 137), the full nature of this structure remained unknown until more completely exposed in 1990 and 1991 (*106*). The building consisted of a polygonal *cella* with a rectangular, north-east facing entrance chamber. The full number of sides comprising the polygonal room remains unknown, due to the limited areas available for study, but Rudling estimates it as being somewhere between nine and eleven (Rudling 2001, 113). The entrance chamber, which seemed to have been aligned upon the original eastern entrance of the Later Bronze Age enclosure, sat at a strange angle to the remainder of the building and may represent a later addition or modification. It had originally been floored with greensand *tesserae*. Nothing is known about the internal nature of the polygonal *cella*, though Rudling notes that the absence of *tesserae* retrieved during the excavation may indicate that it did not originally possess a mosaic. Temple 2 appears to have been roofed in red tile, whilst the discovery of plaster from the exterior may indicate that 'just the external wall facings were painted' (Rudling 2001, 114).

106 Chanctonbury: the polygonal *cella* of Temple 2, looking south–west, under investigation in 1990. *Author*

Parallels for the polygonal plan of Temple 2 are not hard to find, structures of the same basic diameter, albeit more clearly circular, being found on Hayling Island in Hampshire and at Wanborough in Surrey. At Wanborough, an 11.5m-diameter shrine, had been placed only 10m from a more regular square Romano-Celtic temple, whilst at Hayling Island a 14m-diameter *cella* was set within a square *temenos* (Rudling 2001, 114-5). Both Wanborough and Hayling Island possessed east-facing entrance chambers and both appeared to have replaced earlier timber structures of the Late Iron Age or Early Roman period. In Sussex, a second circular or polygonal shrine may have been excavated at Huddlestone, near Pulborough in the early nineteenth century (Martin 1859), although the accounts are somewhat garbled. The nature of religious activity within Temple 2 remains unknown (as does the deity in question), although the very large quantity of pig skull fragments found during the course of the 1990-1 excavations (4,961 pieces representing a minimum of 84 individuals) may indicate that 'the offering of heads of pigs was a major aspect of ritual concerning the cult.' (Rudling 2001, 116)

The date and possible sequence of religious activity at Chanctonbury is unfortunately unclear. Pottery evidence retrieved during the course of the three main phases of exploration (1909, 1977 and 1987-91) seem to indicate 'more intense activity around Temple 1 during the third-century than at temple 2' which may relate more to the mid-to-late second century (Rudling 2001, 118). The polygonal shrine could perhaps represent the earlier monumentalising of a native cult site, the more regular structure of Temple 2 indicating a secondary (and more significant) Romanising influence. On present evidence, however, this cannot be proven and the two structures could easily have co-existed. The coin evidence recovered from Chanctonbury extends to the emperor Gratian (AD 367–383) but there are few pieces of fourth-century pottery to accompany these and it is possible that major cult activity on the hill had ceased by the late third century AD (Rudling 2001, 118).

EASTERN CULTS

From the early third century AD, a variety of exotic deities from the eastern provinces of the Roman Empire (chiefly Egypt, Syria and Judea) and beyond started to make their appearance in Britain. Amongst the Roman army the most popular eastern deity was the Persian god Mithras, though within non-military social circles other religions, such as that based around the figure of Jesus Christ, were starting to develop. The popularity accorded to the majority of eastern cults, Christianity included, was due to the fact that they gave hope of a salvation and of a war between the forces of good and evil in which good would ultimately prevail. The chief difference between Christian and non-Christian doctrine, however, was that the cult of Christ was open to all levels of society, regardless of status, wealth (or lack of it), sex, social standing (free or slave) or ethnic origin. At a time when the Roman Empire was undergoing severe stress from economic turmoil, internal political conflict and mass population pressure from beyond the frontiers, Christianity offered redemption and peace to everyone. Mithraism offered salvation, but only to the freeborn males initiated into the faith.

The key distinctive aspect of eastern cults was that their places of worship were congregational. To pray at a Mithraic temple or early Christian church meant to enter the building and communicate directly with a higher power, unlike the classical temples where only the professional priest could enter the innermost sanctum of the divine. Congregations were composed of adherents and believers who had been admitted into the faith through teaching, baptism or some other initiation rite (which in some of the more extreme examples could include castration). Christianity was, for much of its early history, an underground religion, persecuted by the Roman State for a variety of reasons, chief among which was the belief that Christians refused to fully acknowledge the divine nature of the imperial family. Christians were also monotheists, and did not look kindly upon the pantheon of deities revered across the empire.

Many Christians were executed for their beliefs and, as a consequence, the iconography of recognition and worship took on a variety of secret symbols and messages, decipherable only by fellow believers. One of the oldest of such 'Christograms' is the combination of the Greek letters X (*chi*) and P (*rho*) taken from the first elements of the Greek word ΧΡΙΣΤΟΣ meaning 'Christos' (*chi-rho-iota-sigma-tau-omicron-sigma*). It is not known what impact Christianity had upon the population of Late Roman Britain. Certainly the religion was practised by some in the province, as both the archaeological (artefacts, wall paintings and mosaics) and historical sources (such as the martyrdom of Alban in the third century) clearly demonstrate.

Evidence recovered from a variety of non-Christian religious sites in Britain however, shows that, although Christianity became the State religion of Rome from the early fourth century, rural 'pagan' temples in Britain flourished well on into the latter half of the century (Millett 1990, 195-6). In Sussex, the decline of Chanctonbury Ring temple complex appears to sit at odds with the national picture, for here cult activity seems to have been decreasing from the late third century AD. Perhaps interest in the old gods was fading as the new deities from the East and from the Germanic north began to make their appearance felt. Perhaps the cost of maintaining and repairing distant rural shrines simply became too expensive; centres of worship devolving to the towns, villas or other rural settlements. Perhaps Christianity really was beginning to have an influence after all. At Wiggonholt, in a tributary of the river Arun near Pulborough, a large lead 'container' was dragged to the surface during dredging work conducted in 1943 (Curwen 1943). Panelling around the upper half of the vessel depicts a clear and repeating *chi-rho* motif, explicitly identifying the object's Christian associations. Taken out of context, the artefact is difficult to interpret, but it may represent a baptismal font or container for holy water. Could the presence of a Christian community in the area of Pulborough during the Late Roman period have tolerated the continued usage of the nearby Chanctonbury site? We may never know for sure, but some of the evidence recovered during the 1977 and 1987-91 investigations on the hill suggested that the temples had been subjected to 'episodes of destruction and/or robbing' (Rudling 2001, 118).

10

TRADE AND INDUSTRY

There was throughout the prehistoric and Roman periods, a huge network of trade and exchange across southern Britain, exporting goods to northern France, Belgium and the Netherlands, whilst simultaneously importing continental goods, ideas and people. Julius Caesar noted that certain coastal areas of southern Britain had, prior to 55 and 54 BC, been settled by 'Belgic immigrants' from northern Gaul who had come 'to plunder and make war' (*Gallic Wars* V, 12). Of course the major focus of Caesar's commentaries, as already noted, was to demonstrate the ferocity of the northern barbarians and their threat to the stability of empire, but there may well be an element of truth embedded within his writings. Caesar was a first-hand witness to the events, peoples and activities of northern Gaul and southern Britain, and would, of course, have been in an excellent position to judge similarities between communities on either side of the English Channel. Most of western Europe was affected in no small way by mass population movements (or folk migrations) throughout the first century BC, and it is quite likely that these movements would also have had an effect on those inhabiting the British Isles. New peoples bring new ideas, new fashions, new belief systems and fresh ways of doing things.

As with other periods in the past, however, mass migration need not be equated with full-scale military invasion, new groups displacing the old by force. Assimilation and peaceful integration were also significant driving forces behind cultural change. Sudden change, following any attack or invasion, is almost always reserved for those who hold power. If there was a movement of Belgic peoples into Britain during the first century BC, as Caesar suggested, then it may only have been the indigenous ruling elite that was affected. They would either have died on the battlefield, been moved to other areas of power or they would have modified their beliefs to find their place within the new order. For the bulk of the population, change was a far more gradual and insidious process.

TRADE

For many thousands of years the channel represented a vital link to (not protection from) the continental landmass of Europe. It is sometimes difficult to appreciate that for much, if not all, of later prehistory, the English Channel was the primary trade corridor to the outside world, sea fare being far more reliable and dependable than transportation of goods inland. In the days before an organised road, canal, rail or air network, the best way to move goods from A to B was by water, along the rivers, across the tidal estuaries and over the open sea. In the Iron Age, those communities living on the coast of Sussex would probably have had far more in common with those living on the opposite side of the English Channel. Language, religion, fashion and general outlook towards life would all have been closely similar; only in recent years has the desire to create fixed, impermeable boundaries helped to create segregated national identities, stalling the natural development of language and culture. The channel was an important trade link and it is in areas situated close to the sea that we find our best evidence for the importation of foreign artefacts in the Late Iron Age and Early Roman period.

The most obvious evidence of trade with the continent and with the newly expansive empire of Rome comes from the discovery of objects clearly originating from, or influenced by, Mediterranean culture. One of the most startling of new artefacts to appear within Late Iron Age society was the coin. The appearance of coins in the archaeological record does not mean that overnight Britain had become a monetary economy; rather coins appear to have been used as a way of using precious metals, given as payment or as a gift, to pass on a political message or a statement of allegiance. Coins represent, in very basic terms, a small fragment of metal (gold, silver or bronze) stamped with the name of a particular member of the local ruling elite. Sometimes they also contained an official title, line of descent, name of the royal seat of power and sometimes they also carried obvious symbols of wealth and power (ears of corn, horses, bulls, boars and ships). The coin was therefore a potent symbol of authority and dynastic intent and the propaganda statements that they carry provide the archaeologist with the first and only (albeit fragmentary) historical account of the Britons written by the British themselves.

Quite why coins were first adopted by the political elite of Late Iron Age Britain remains a mystery but, by the end of the first century BC, they had rapidly become the propaganda weapon of choice. If the symbols used on the reverse of the coin in question were obviously Roman (perhaps copied direct from Mediterranean originals) or the language used was Latin (such as the use of the term *Rex* for king), this could, in turn, imply an economic, political or military link with the Roman State. Coins appear in Sussex from the mid-first century BC and seem to have continued in production well after the Roman invasion of AD 43, something that may point towards a degree of continuity in tribal authority within the new Roman province. Proof of the production of coins, in the form of clay mounds designed to generate blanks prior to the stamping of an official design, has been found in Sussex, most notably at Boxgrove at the eastern edge of the Chichester Entrenchments.

Another good early indicator of the success of trade with Rome, and of the impact that contact had upon the population of Sussex, comes from the discovery of a distinctive form of pottery container known as the amphora. Amphorae are outwardly rather strange looking objects, comprising a long thin neck, prominent handles, slightly globular body and pointed base. Amphorae are singular items and were distinct from anything that had appeared in Britain before. The impact of such vessels upon Late Iron Age society should not be underestimated, for whoever had an amphora in their possession, house, or grave was evidently someone of great wealth and power. They would also be seen to possess a certain degree of prestige for whomsoever possessed an amphora could claim wider links with the world of the Mediterranean.

It is not the vessel itself that was important of course, though its distinctive form evidently helped, but the contents. Like the champagne bottle of today, the amphora was the visible container of status produce, in this case wine, olive oil and fish sauce (known as *garum*). Evidence that the native population of Sussex was accessing such prestige consumables may be found from the amphorae recovered from Late Iron Age contexts at Boxgrove, Carne's Seat and Oving (Bedwin and Orton 1984; Bedwin and Holgate 1985). Together, these sites suggest that a major focus of trade was in the natural harbours to the south and west of modern Chichester. Late Iron Age pottery and late first century BC to early first century AD Roman amphorae and fine ware have also been recovered in considerable quantities to the north-east of Pulborough. Here, the association of artefacts with a range of rectangular enclosure ditches (Cunliffe *et al.* 1996, 17, 135-6; Wells pers. comm.) may indicate the presence of an important trading post established at the northern limits of the tidal range of the river Arun in the latter years of the reign of the Roman emperor Augustus (Cunliffe *et al.* 1996, 17).

Amphorae containing previously unknown luxury commodities were brought to Britain by people seeking to exchange them for personal profit and, later on, for materials to help bulk out the official coffers of the Roman State. A list of the major trade items available in Britain is mentioned by the Greek historian, geographer and philosopher Strabo in his work the *Geography*, a 17-volume treatise covering all aspects of the known world in the early years of the first century AD. With regard to Britain, Strabo observed that the principal exports were 'grain, cattle, gold, silver, and iron' together with 'hides, slaves and hunting dogs' (Strabo *Geography* IV, 5). From the point of view of Sussex, the major export would presumably have been Wealden iron (see below), although given the relative economic prosperity of certain Iron Age communities, grain and cattle hides were presumably also top of the list.

The possibility that certain Britons grew rich on profits generated by the slave trade should also not be discounted. The trafficking of people represents one of the worst forms of criminal activity, a major violation of human rights which sadly remains a common practice in certain areas of the world today. In the Iron Age, slaves were undoubtedly generated through war, prisoners being deprived of all freedoms and exported directly into the developing world of Rome. The Roman economy was fuelled by slave labour and, when the senate and people of Rome were not directly involved in conquest, large numbers of slaves could still be acquired through trade with societies based beyond the frontiers of empire. Despite this, we do not know the extent of such activity in Late Iron Age and Early Roman Britain, for they did not leave much of an impact in the archaeological record.

INDUSTRY

Sussex was, and remains, a fertile land for agriculture, and food production must have been one of the major factors in the economy of the region during the Roman period. Aside from farming (chapter 7) other key elements in the economic infrastructure of the area which have left some trace in the archaeological record were the production of iron and salt, the manufacture of pottery and tile and the quarrying of stone.

Wealden mudstone (romantically known as 'Sussex marble') may be found within a number of early, prestigious building projects such as the palace complex and Proto Palace at Fishbourne, whilst Horsham sandstone seems at times to have been used as a material for roofing purposes. Large amounts of flint were also quarried from the Sussex chalk for incorporation in the building projects of the second, third and fourth centuries AD, most notably in villas, temples and for coastal defence. Although flint is visible in a wide variety of archaeological contexts from Roman Sussex, there is, as yet, no clear understanding of the circumstances under which this material was attained. Presumably there were many well-organised centres of extraction in existence throughout the Roman period, but little detailed work has yet been conducted upon the identification and analysis of such an industry. The open cast pits, adit mines and shafts which must have existed, still lie undiscovered and forgotten.

The problems surrounding a lack of identification and an absence of detailed analysis also bedevils any study concerning the production of salt. Salt was almost certainly one of the most important commodities throughout the Later Prehistoric and Roman periods. Today, salt is more commonly thought of as either a popular seasoning or an evil ingredient, found in all processed foods, which adds significantly to the rise of ill health and obesity within modern society. In the days before decent systems of refrigeration, however, salt was a vital element in the preservation of foodstuffs, especially meat, and one only has to consider aphorisms such as 'salt of the earth' or 'worth one's salt', to see how ancient societies judged the importance of this colourless crystalline solid (Hathaway 2004). Salt would have been produced, in the main, by boiling large quantities of sea water and some evidence for this activity, in the form of hearths, boiling pits and fragments of clay vessels, known as *briquetage*, has been found in the area of Chichester and Portsmouth Harbours.

On the shore of Nutbourne Creek, at Chidham near Chichester, a series of steep-sided pits and clay-lined trenches filled with *briquetage* strongly suggest the presence of a Romano-British salt making site. Richard Bradley, who investigated the features (Bradley 1989, 18-21), postulated three discrete phases in the manufacture of salt here:

(i)   storage of seawater in a large, flat-bottomed settling tank or cistern

(ii)   natural evaporation of seawater in a shallow, rectangular trough

(iii)   the heating of concentrated brine in *briquetage* vessels placed within fire-heated trenches.

At Great Cansiron Farm, near Hartfield, another industrial site has been investigated, this time a relatively short-lived centre of Roman tile manufacture, excavated in the early 1980s (Rudling 1986). The main feature of the investigations was a kiln, comprising a stokehole, flue and large combustion chamber, which had been sunk into side of the hill (*107*). The entrance from the stokehole to the flue was lined with reused tile, the lower courses of which had been partially vitrified by the former heat of the fire. One of these tiles had been inscribed with the numbers CCXX (220) and CCXIII (213), a piece of graffiti which may originally have related to a batch total or manufacturing output in a single firing period (Rudling 1986, 211-2). A group of eight unused roof tiles (*tegulae*) lay stacked against the south-eastern edge of this entrance, where they had apparently been left by the last person to use the kiln (Rudling 1986, 198). A layer of charcoal and ash led directly from the stokehole, through the flue (or 'fire tunnel') to the combustion chamber beyond. A section of the flue roof survived intact, as did two of the five cross walls that originally spanned the upper level of the combustion chamber.

Unfortunately, little remained of the oven that would have sat above the chamber at Hartfield, though two flat tiles found on the northernmost cross wall may represent part of the original floor. The oven itself was probably a relatively temporary affair, comprising walls of clay brick, reused tile or turf, which were removed after every firing. An archaeomagnetic date for a sample taken from the combustion chamber, provided a range of between AD 100-130 (Rudling 1986, 198). To the immediate north-west of the kiln was a rectangular depression bordered by four large postholes which the excavator, David Rudling, interpreted as a drying shed for the pre-fired tile forms (Rudling 1986, 199). To the south-east, a roughly square area of baked clay and broken tile was viewed as the remains of a possible workman's hut.

107 Hartfield: the tile kiln under investigation in 1983. The tiled entrance from the stokehole to the flue is in the foreground, with the cross walls of the combustion chamber behind. *Author*

Five main categories of tile form were identified from the excavations at Hartfield: box flue, *imbrex*, *tegula*, *voussoir* and flat (Rudling 1986, 204-8). *Imbrices* and *tegulae* represent the standard form of Roman roofing tile, whilst the flat examples may have been either for the roof or for flooring purposes. *Voussoir* and box flue are hollow tiles, essentially 'square pipes', designed to carry hot air through a wall or, in the case of the *voussoir*, an arch (Brodribb 1987). Some of the box flue tiles had been impressed with a roller pattern prior to firing, the design intending to act as a key for the later application of plaster. The recorded die pattern at Hartfield is a distinctive one, categorised as 'Lowther's Die 5A' (*108*), a form also found at Beddingham villa in East Sussex, Beddington villa in Surrey and from a variety of sites in Essex, Hertfordshire and eastern Hampshire (Rudling 1986, 209). The discovery of this die pattern may indicate that the kiln site was, in the late first and early second century, a temporary base for a 'mobile brick-yard' supplying products to a variety of building sites across the south-east of England (Rudling 1986, 209-11).

The obvious destination for tiles manufactured at Hartfield would have been a large ironworking area situated just over 500m to the west (Swift in Rudling 1986, 193), a site also dated to the final years of the first century AD. The presence of *voussoir* and box flue amongst the produce of the Hartfield kiln may further suggest that 'the ironworking establishment probably has a bath-house complex' (Rudling 1986, 227) perhaps similar to those recorded from the ironworking sites of Beauport Park and Garden Hill (see below).

Unlike the manufacture of tile, the production of pottery in Sussex has a long history going back to the initial phases of the Neolithic, or New Stone Age, in the fourth millennium BC. By the end of the Iron Age, the variety of pottery forms and the overall scale of production had changed significantly, it being possible to divide Sussex into two broad ceramic zones on the basis of the archaeological evidence. Pottery found to the west of the river Adur is generally characterised by 'sand tempered, sometimes wheel-turned, wares of good quality', whilst vessels to the east are predominantly handmade and heavily tempered with flint or 'grog', ground-up pieces of fired pottery (Lyne 2003, 141). This clear divide in ceramic style and manufacturing process may reflect the political differences apparent within Late Iron Age society, those communities living within or around the *oppidum* and later *civitas* (tribal) town of *Noviomagus* benefiting from increased trade opportunities with Rome. In East Sussex, the apparent lack of a clear social and political focus when combined with the increased levels of iron production into the Early Roman period may have resulted in 'little technological improvement' in native British wares (Lyne 2003, 141).

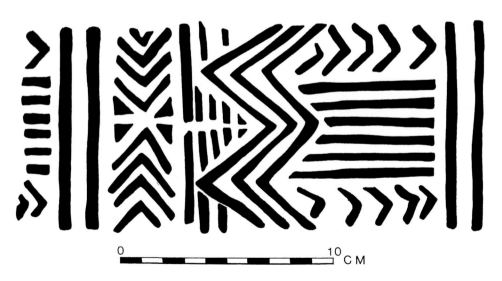

108 Hartfield: a reconstruction of roller stamp die 5A, also found on stamped tiles at Beddingham villa in East Sussex, Beddington villa in Surrey and from sites in Essex, Hertfordshire and Hampshire. *Redrawn from Rudling 1986, 210*

During the late first century AD, a variety of pottery kilns appear to have been producing a distinctive range of ceramic forms, which included cooking pots, bowls and beakers, in the Hardham/Wiggonholt and Littlehampton areas of West Sussex. Malcolm Lyne has recently described production at these centres as the 'Arun Valley' industry, and many of the end products seem to have turned up in Chichester (Lyne 2003, 142). This industry may have been grinding to a halt by the early third century AD.

Few Roman pottery production sites in Sussex have been well investigated or recorded, but at Wickham Barn to the north of Lewes, excavations conducted by Chris Butler and the Mid Sussex Field Archaeological Team between 1995 and 1996 have revealed two pottery kilns and a variety of associated features dated to between AD 250 and 350. A number of structures identified during the course of the investigations possibly indicate a form of temporary accommodation, workshops and/or drying sheds (Butler and Lyne 2001, 69). Potting appears largely to have been an outdoor activity, kilns being protected from the elements by nothing more than timber windbreaks. Wickham Barn has been interpreted as an independent rural workshop, possibly run by a farmer potter (Butler and Lyne 2001, 68), which distributed its wares to a variety of sites linked by the Greensand Way (27 per cent of the total ceramic assemblage from Barcombe villa, 3km to the east, was derived from Wickham Barn, whilst at Hassocks, 11km to the west, the total was 24 per cent). Few examples of 'Wickham Ware' made it further west than the river Arun (and certainly not as far as the river Adur) whilst no examples have yet been found in the area of the coastal fortress of Pevensey (Butler and Lyne 2001, 71).

IRONWORKING

One of the major sources of iron in Britain during the Iron Age and early Roman period was the Weald of Sussex, Surrey and Kent. The material was probably a major source of income to the rulers of the area during later prehistory and, in much the same way as the twentieth-century leaders of Saudi Arabia and Kuwait became fabulously wealthy through the sale of 'black gold' to the west, no doubt certain dynasts of prehistoric Sussex grew fat on the proceeds of trade. By the end of the first century BC, iron was one of the major trade commodities of southern Britain, a fact not lost on Julius Caesar who noted that 'iron is found on the coast' though he added the curious footnote 'but in small quantities' (Caesar *Gallic Wars* V, 12). Strabo, writing shortly after the time of Caesar observed that prior to Britain's formal incorporation into the Roman Empire, that the principal metal exports were 'grain and cattle, gold, silver and iron.' (Strabo *Geography*, IV, 5)

The combination of location and raw materials present in the Weald, conspired to make this area a metalworkers dream. There was an excellent source of iron ore, present in significant amounts at the base of the Wadhurst Clay, whilst associated deposits of sandstone made for ideal smelting furnaces. On the surface, the densely packed trees of the Wealden forest formed an abundant source of raw material both for burning and for building. Our understanding of how the exploitation of the Weald was organised in the Iron Age is unfortunately only poorly understood, much early evidence having been erased by the more intensive industrial processes of later Roman and medieval periods. What limited information exists, however, seems to indicate that by the third century BC at least, the iron ore of the Weald was being exploited to a fairly significant degree.

Taking direct control of the exploitation of metaliferous deposits in Britain had no doubt been a primary objective of the Roman State as its army moved through southern England in the years immediately following AD 43 and 44. How the exploitation of iron was organised in the wake of Roman absorption, however, remains unclear. As long ago as 1974, Henry Cleere observed that evidence of Roman ironworking in the Weald appeared to be clustered into two discrete areas: 'a western group, orientated on the major north–south highways, and an eastern group, with a primary outlet by sea' (Cleere 1975; 1978, 61). The eastern zone probably came under the jurisdiction of the British Fleet, the *Classis Britannica*, for their stamped tiles are found in abundance here, especially at sites such as Beauport Park, Bardown and Bodiam (Cleere 1978, 62). The western group, which included sites at Broadfields, Oldlands and Great Cansiron, may well have been controlled by private businesses, civilian entrepreneurs who used the new road network to export their product to the markets in London and beyond (Cleere 1978, 61).

THE WEALD AS AN IMPERIAL ESTATE

The involvement of the *Classis Britannica* in the working of iron raises a number of issues. Iron was a vital commodity to the military, especially when on campaign or engaged in major engineering projects, and they would have required a constant supply from a reliable source. The presence of the fleet in the eastern Weald may underlie the perceived importance of iron; the *Classis Britannica* was less of a 'navy' in the modern sense, for their role seems to have been more in terms of providing support rather than representing an effective fighting force. In the Weald, the fleet was presumably a crucial part of the transport infrastructure, moving iron from the areas of extraction to the more secure military depots established along the Kent coast. From there, iron could be directly exported into Gaul, and the heart of empire, or taken northwards to the frontier outposts of Britain. We do not know how directly, if at all, the military involved themselves in the day-to-day administration of mining and smelting activities. At areas such as Beauport Park, where some 1,600 stamped tiles belonging to the fleet were found from the on-site bathhouse, the *Classis Britannica* may simply have been involved in the construction of major works and the shipping out of finished product rather than overseeing production.

The production of iron in the Weald appears to have greatly accelerated, away from its small-scale prehistoric beginnings, towards the end of the first century AD (Cleere 1978; Cleere and Crossley 1985, 81). The dramatic increase in the number of working sites from just before AD 100 could be taken to indicate some form of direct State control (cf. Cleere 1978, 62-3), or at least that the Roman government had suddenly realised the potential of the British ironfields and decided to act upon it. What had caused this dramatic increase in the amount of extraction, processing and smelting activity?

The end of the first century AD was a time when Rome's advance into the British Isles reached its greatest extent, forts being established in the highlands of Scotland, the Roman fleet investigating the Orkneys and beyond (Tacitus *Agricola*, 38). Could the increase in ironworking have been in response to a sudden increase in demand from the army for weapons, armour and basic equipment needed to fuel their campaigns? Perhaps. Cleere, amongst others, has noted that although the Roman State automatically owned the mineral rights in all provinces of the empire, in practice the emperor only took direct control of the exploitation of precious metals, 'other types of mining being left in private hands in return for royalty payments' (Cleere 1978, 62). It is highly likely, therefore, that the iron industry of the Weald was, by the mid-first century AD, largely in the hands of private companies.

Examples of both individuals (*conductores*) and limited companies (*collegii*) making it big in the world of metals can be found from an early date across Britain. In the latter half of the first century, for example, a private company, apparently known as the *Socii Lutudarenes*, seems to have prominently established itself in the Peak District, whilst at the same time a certain Tiberius Claudius Trifernus was striking out in the lead-rich area of the Mendips (Birley 1979, 149). Given Trifernus' first names, it would seem likely that he was either a newly enfranchised citizen who owed it all to the emperor Claudius, as per Togidubnus and Catuarus (see chapter 2), or perhaps a freedman (ex-slave) of the imperial family who was in Britain to make his fortune. Trifernus is of particular interest to Sussex, for lead ingots bearing his name have been found close to the late first-century civilian development at Pulborough (chapter 6), presumably having been brought up the river Arun (the *Trisantona flumen*) from the coast (Black 1987, 12-13).

It would not be surprising if the metal-rich soils of the Sussex Weald had been exploited by a whole patchwork of private companies and successful entrepreneurs in the same way as the Mendips and Peak District appear to have been. A complicating factor in the exploitation of Wealden iron however, is the shadowy existence of the Iron Age aristocracy here. We have already noted (chapter 1) a host of Later Iron Age dynasts issuing coins in the Hampshire/Surrey/Sussex/Kent region prior to AD 43 who styled themselves as Roman kings. In the early AD 40s, certain rulers of the region, including Amminus and Verica had run into the protective arms of Caligula and Claudius (chapter 2), whilst Togidubnus, Catuarus and Lucullus are all examples of ethnic Britons who achieved power and status within the new Roman order (chapter 3). If Rome did not authorise regime change in central southern Britain and instead rewarded the existing aristocracy, actively promoting their interests to the point of acknowledging positions of authority such as Great King (Togidubnus) and Propraetorian Legate (Lucullus), then did it also permit them to maintain and develop the mining rights (at a price) of the Sussex Weald?

Perhaps, given that we assume that Tiberius Claudius Togidubnus, ruler of 'many states' including Chichester, the tribal town of *Noviomagus*, was approaching very old age by the last quarter of the first century (if he had not already died), then it could be that the increase in metal extraction in the Weald then was a result of the old tribal lands (and resources) passing directly into the hands of the emperor. It is also possible, given what we have established about Gaius Sallustius Lucullus, governor of Britain at some point in the AD 90s (chapter 3), that a dramatic rise in Wealden iron production was the direct result of his desire to Romanise the people of his homeland and more efficiently exploit their natural resources. It is also conceivable that the unambiguous involvement of the *Classis Britannica* in the transportation of iron away from the eastern Weald in the final years of the first century was a direct result of the military take-over of territory confiscated following the execution of Lucullus by Domitian sometime before AD 96.

The State-sanctioned murder of Lucullus would surely have resulted in the emperor taking control of the condemned man's wealth, home and territory, ostensibly to hold for the benefit of the senate and people of Rome. For some time now it has been suggested that the Weald may have been administered as an Imperial estate (e.g. Cleere 1978, 62), the lack of high-status occupation sites (such as villas) here throughout the Roman period being suggestive of direct military control. Take-over of land in the AD 90s would fit in with the theory that the emperor was taking a direct interest in the region and its resources, rather than allowing a native king or range of middlemen to control the production of iron. We shall probably never know for sure, but the hypothesis is a tempting one.

BEAUPORT PARK

Struggling through the dense vegetation that covers the site of Beauport Park today it is hard to believe that this was once the industrial heart of Roman Britain and the third largest ironworking complex in the whole of the empire. Forlorn, overgrown and, in parts, mutilated by a golf course, the site has changed out of all recognition. Bracken covers the slumping heaps of slag; the greens, bunkers and fairways of a surreal modern sport replacing the furnaces, ore roasting pits and hearths.

It was the slag heaps and cinder mounds that first drew antiquarians, archaeologists and others to the site at Beauport Park. In 1869, the Reverend S. Arnott mentioned the presence of 'a large cinder bank' at here and, within a matter of months, this was being extensively quarried for nearby road making activities (Brodribb and Cleere

1988, 217). Ernest Straker, in his book *Wealden Iron*, calculated that the equivalent of some 1500-2300 cubic metres of Roman-British cinder had been removed from Beauport Park every year for at least 10 years by the local Highway Surveyor (Straker 1931, 329). Certainly, by 1878, the antiquarian James Rock observed that only a small part of the original 'cinder bank' recorded by Arnott had survived and that destruction of this archaeological feature continued unabated. 'At the time of my visits, men were working very carefully on the face of the "cliff" which crumbled so readily at every stroke of the pick, that they had difficulty in keeping their footing.' (Rock 1879, 169).

In his article, entitled 'Ancient Cinder-Heaps in East Sussex', published in *Sussex Archaeological Collections* for 1879, Rock pondered on the possible date for the great cinder-heap. That it was Roman there was no doubt, but could it be more precisely identified? A major problem here was the way in which the site was being investigated, not carefully using due archaeological process, but swiftly with teams of poorly paid labourers. 'Occasionally a piece of pottery is found' Rock observed 'but rolling down with the cinders is usually broken very small ere it reaches the bottom of the bank' (Rock 1879, 169). This was evidently not the most satisfactory of recovery techniques, and had the result that the context of discovery was lost almost immediately. We must however be thankful that Rock was there at all and took an interest. Without him, we would be very much the poorer with regard to dating industrial activity at Beauport Park. Of the finds recorded, Rock paid particular attention to the coins, noting 'I have in my possession two coins of bronze, which were also found among the cinders – one of Trajan, the other of Hadrian. Both are in good preservation, especially the later. These would seem to fix the date of the cinder-heap at a somewhat early period of the Roman occupation.' (Rock 1879, 169).

Additional coin evidence recovered from the later examination of the site has broadly confirmed the early Roman hypothesis, the series running from the emperor Domitian (AD 81-96) to Decius (AD 249-51) whilst the pottery suggests that exploitation here probably commenced in the last quarter of the first century (Brodribb and Cleere 1988, 243). Rock also mentioned a bronze ring, a bronze spoon found 'at the bottom of the cinder-heap' and numerous fragments of pottery, including fine red Samian ware (Rock 1879, 170). A small and rather corroded iron statuette of a Roman horseman allegedly found at Beauport Park, which for many years was thought to represent the 'earliest known example of cast-iron in Europe' (Dawson 1903, 5), has since been shown to be a modern forgery (Russell 2003, 61-70).

It is difficult to estimate quite how many people would have been involved at any one stage in the industrial process at Beauport Park, although we may be reasonably sure of the range of tasks necessary to complete the cycle of iron production. Prospectors would first have been required to locate a good source of ore through the successful identification of a surface outcrop. An adit mine, shaft or open cast pit would then have been cut down into the natural clay and, once a suitable quantity of ore had been extracted, the material would have been washed in order to clear away all traces of soil still adhering. Next came the ore roasters, whose job it was to dry the ore and break it into more manageable pieces, and the smelters and forgers who refined the material and created finished artefacts. Before the blast furnace, iron was smelted in bloomery hearths (usually attaining temperatures of just over 900 degrees centigrade) which reduced the material 'to a pasty mass of sponge iron' (Downes 1956, 193). 'Bloom' iron, containing about less than one per cent of carbon, is tough and malleable and can easily be worked in a blacksmith's forge, where it is referred to as 'wrought iron'. Add to these processes the charcoal burners, who provided the necessary fuel for smelting, and the support, transport and administrative infrastructure necessary to keep the industry functioning successfully, and you have an active population at the site numbering something in the hundreds if not thousands.

Fieldwork conducted by Gerald Brodribb across Beauport Park seems to indicate that an area of some 8ha was originally utilised by the Romano-British workforce whilst the total estimated volume of slag generated at the site has been calculated at around 100,000 tons. Beauport Park must have been a bustling, noisy and thoroughly unhealthy place during the early Roman period, with a mass of roasting pits, furnaces, hearths and cooking fires belching smoke, not to say a variety of pollutants, into the atmosphere. Despite this, we know comparatively little of the people on the frontline of iron production. As low status workers, their existence was probably hard and generally unrewarding. Smelters, forgers and ore roasters may have been housed in meagre accommodation close to the place of actual production, whilst the charcoal burners and ore gatherers may, by analogy with later periods, have been semi-itinerant. Whatever the case, apart from the furnaces and slag heaps, the workforce has left little trace in the archaeological record. Fieldwork has recovered a small amount of domestic pottery, the fragmentary remains of footwear, amongst which were shoes which were 'likely to have been worn by women or adolescents', and at least one glass baby-feeding bottle (Brodribb and Cleere 1988, 241).

One aspect of iron production at Beauport Park that has left a significant footprint in the landscape however, is a rather splendid little bathhouse (*109*). Discovered in 1969 by Gerald Brodribb, the building was excavated and covered with a temporary roof of corrugated iron, with a view to long term consolidation and display. Sadly, at the time of writing, the future of the site looks bleak and, despite the best efforts of the Beauport Park Archaeological Trust, the structure looks set to be buried once and for all. Stone-built, as all bathhouses were, the example here is particularly well preserved, seemingly complete except for the roof with masonry surviving to a height of over 2.1m. Its loss is one of the most unfortunate stories in Sussex archaeology.

Probably built in the second quarter of the second century AD, the bathhouse at Beauport Park originally comprised four rooms: a cold room (*frigidarium*) with attached plunge bath, a warm room (*tepidarium*) and two hot rooms (*caldaria*). The structure was modified in the early third century, following an apparent period of disuse (Brodribb

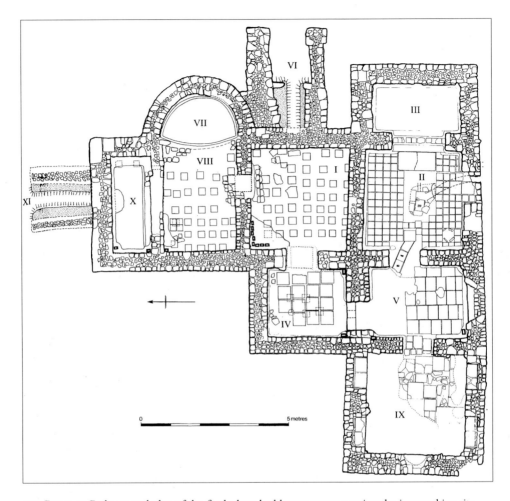

109 Beauport Park: ground plan of the final-phase bathhouse accompanying the ironworking site. *Reproduced with the kind permission of Henry Cleere*

and Cleere 1988, 234-6), with the addition of an undressing room (*apodyterium*), a new furnace (*praefurnium*), two new plunge baths and another hot room (*caldarium*). The new work, which was of lesser standard than the earlier construction, appears to have been commemorated with an inscription, part of which was found close to the main entrance during the initial stages of excavation in 1970 (Brodribb and Cleere 1988, 261). The surviving piece of the inscription (RIB 66a) read:

...G...
...E NOVO...
...VSSIT VIL...
C A BASSI...
TI...

This, highly fragmentary, text may be translated as:

...for the Emperor...
...I am renewing...
...by this command, vilicus...
...administered through the agency of Bassus...
...this inscription.

If correct, this would suggest that the original baths were expanded, repaired or rebuilt by a man called Bassus (or Bassianus) on the express orders of an (unnamed) *vilicus* or foreman of the ironworks (Brodribb and Cleere 1988, 261-2). Following a second period of abandonment in the mid-third century, in which fixtures and fittings were forcibly removed, and a brief period of 'squatter occupation', the shell of the bath building was buried in a catastrophic collapse of the nearby slag heap.

No evidence of an accompanying fort, barrack block or other military style structure has yet been found at Beauport Park, and it is quite possible that the bathhouse originally stood alone. There can be no doubt, however, that it was primarily a military installation, designed purely for military use; a little piece of luxury for the soldiers of the *Classis Britannica*, rather than to clean the general workforce. In this it may be compared to a modern shower-block, portacabin or mobile toilet established at the margins of a building site for the exclusive use of visiting officials, executives or supervisors. The charcoal burners, ore gatherers, forgers and blacksmiths *et al.* would not be allowed access to the bathing facilities and would, more than likely, have been expected to bathe in the stream and urinate in the open (or in buckets provided for the task).

A range of structures and features similar to those discovered at Beauport Park has been found at Bardown, near Ticehurst and Garden Hill near Hartfield. At Garden Hill, a small area of Late Iron Age settlement, comprising at least two roundhouses associated with ironworking, set at the north-eastern end of stone-revetted hillfort (*110*), was replaced in the later first century with a host of rectangular timber buildings, ore roasting and iron smelting furnaces and at least one forging hearth (Money 1977). At some point in the second century, a large timber building and associated stone bathhouse were added. The bathhouse was considerably smaller than the example recorded from Beauport Park, but possessed a *frigidarium* (with plunge bath), *tepidarium* and *caldarium* (Money 1977, 345-6). Early in the third century, the bath block was stripped and partially demolished.

At Bardown, a series of early second-century timber-framed post-built structures were found in association with quarry pits, forges, ore roasting hearths a probable charcoal burning hearth and an extensive area of slag dumping (Cleere 1970). At least one of the timber structures recorded has been interpreted as 'a standard military-style barrack block' (Cleere 1970; Cleere and Crossley 1985, 303-4). The main area of ironworking seems to have been discontinued by AD 200 (Cleere and Crossley 1985, 70).

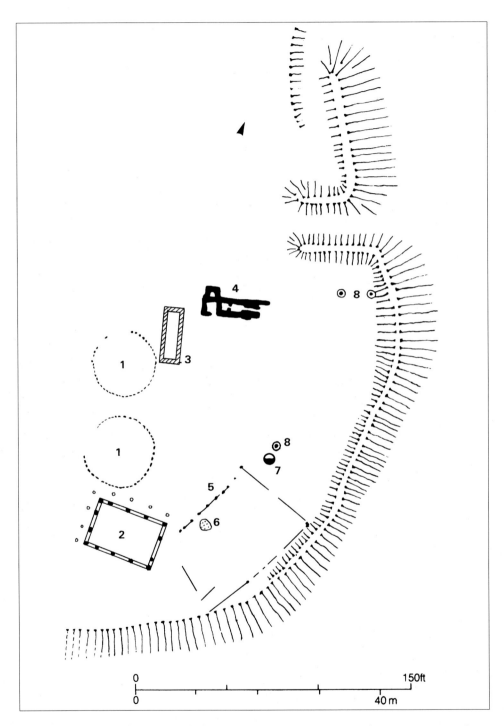

110 Garden Hill: simplified plan of settlement and ironworking activity in the Late Iron Age and Romano-British period: 1 = Late Iron Age roundhouses; 2 = timber building (isled?); 3 = rectangular Romanised timber house; 4 = bathhouse; 5 = enclosure; 6 = ore roasting hearth; 7 = forging hearth; 8 = smelting furnaces. *Redrawn from Cleere and Crossley 1985, 76 and 77*

THE END OF WEALDEN IRONWORKING

The termination of such a prominent Briton as Gaius Sallustius Lucullus may have proved lucrative in the short term for Domitian, opening up the ironfields of Sussex, Surrey and Kent for large-scale exploitation, but the consequences of the death of the last prominent member of the Romanised native aristocracy, would surely have had serious repercussions to the long-term political stability of the province. The seeds of discontent planted by the last Flavian emperor were to bear fruit in the centuries that followed.

With regard to the ironworking sites of the Weald, production seems to have continued profitably well on through the second and early third centuries AD. By the mid-third century however, the sites in the eastern Weald associated with the *Classis Britannica* seem to have been in the process of shutting down. It is possible that the Wealden ironworks may no longer have been thought of as being cost effective, production shifting to the Forest of Dean in the far west (Cleere and Crossley 1985, 84-5). Alternatively the silting up of the river estuaries and routes to the sea, may have made shipping of iron products more difficult and increasingly less viable.

The reasons behind the closure of fleet-controlled sites in the eastern Weald may alternatively have more to do with the fate of the *Classis Britannica* itself, than the relative prosperity of the Weald, for by the third century AD, the British Fleet seems to have been in terminal decline. At this time the *Classis Britannica* was no longer appearing on stone inscriptions or producing stamped tiles and nor, it would seem, was it in possession of a major base, its headquarters at Dover being dismantled by AD 215 (Philp 1981). The disappearance of the Fleet suggests major reorganisation of military units in Britain. Part of this reorganisation may have been due to the reshaping of political command systems in the face of increased external security threats, but also it may be due, at least in part, to the internal problems, insurrections and revolts that wracked the north-western empire (and particularly Britain) during the third and fourth centuries.

11

ANDERITUM

Driving through the small, but undeniably picturesque, villages of Pevensey and Westham in East Sussex, one is suddenly confronted by a solid and intimidating mass of brick and stone (*111, 112*). The walls that comprise the outer bailey of Pevensey castle are formidable. Chunky bastions, embedded with distinctively blood-red Roman tile, protrude menacingly out into the road, threatening the unwary motorist. The smaller buildings of the medieval and modern village seem to cower apologetically in the shadows.

The castle has brooded over nearly 2000 years of British History. The outer walls belong to a Roman fortress, a stronghold built to secure a prominent naval base. In AD 491 the first Saxon overlord of Britain, Aelle, laid siege to the fort and brutalised its inhabitants. In 1066, William the Bastard spent his first night on English soil here, secure behind the ramparts whilst his half-brother Odo, Bishop of Bayeux, held Pevensey against the crown in 1088. In 1147, king Stephen besieged Pevensey and in 1264, the supporters of Henry III, fleeing from the battlefield at Lewes, took shelter here from Simon de Monfort. In 1588 cannons were placed inside the perimeter wall in order to thwart the Spanish Armada and in 1940 the castle became an important command post for the Home Guard, the fifth Canadian Infantry Brigade and the US Army Air Corps.

Despite its history of violence and war, the Roman walls of Pevensey are in surprisingly good condition. Staring up at the solid masonry, one cannot help but be both impressed and mystified, for why is such an impressive defensive position here? Sussex, as we have seen over the past 10 chapters, was an early and apparently stable part of the Roman province of Britannia. Palaces and a town had been constructed, a road network established and villas, farming communities, villages and metalworking sites had flourished. The area was, furthermore, a very long way from the permanently militarised frontier of northern and western Britain. What had happened to cause the construction of fortress Pevensey so far 'behind the lines', in the heart of what was very friendly territory?

111 Pevensey: the imposing outer circuit of the Late Roman fortress. Roman masonry and tile bonding courses are clearly visible in both the wall and the projecting tower. *Author*

FORTRESS PEVENSEY

Pevensey is one of at least 11 fortresses built by Rome along the eastern and south-eastern seaboard of Britain. From Brancaster on the Norfolk coast, the sites consist of Caister, Burgh Castle, Walton, Bradwell, Reculver, Richborough, Dover, Lympne, Pevensey and Portchester. Collectively these sites are known as 'Saxon Shore Forts' and it is usually thought that they were constructed to protect the British Isles from the threat of Germanic invasion. The forts possess a range of strong, state of the art defensive elements including thick walls, projecting towers and recessed entrances. Within this group, the masonry circuit of Pevensey is unusual for it defines an irregular oval (*113*), enclosing over 3.6ha. The stereotypical footprint of a Roman military installation, especially in the first, second and third centuries AD, is often referred to as being akin to a 'playing-card'; that is a rectangle with the corners rounded off. The forts constructed by along the southern coast of Britain are far more varied in shape and overall design than those of the early empire, but none approach the dramatic curving form apparent at Pevensey.

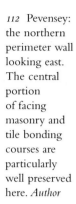

112 Pevensey: the northern perimeter wall looking east. The central portion of facing masonry and tile bonding courses are particularly well preserved here. *Author*

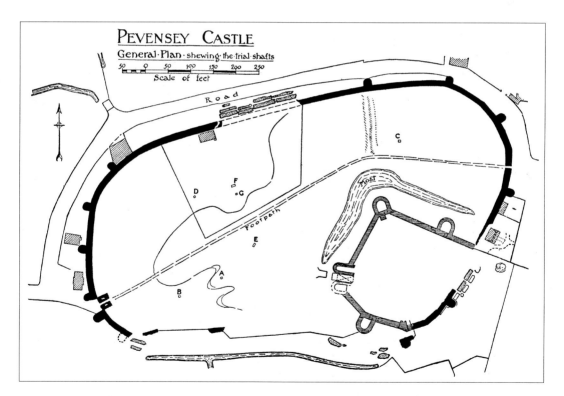

113 Pevensey: a plan of the Roman fortress compiled by Louis Salzman for his report on the 1906-7 excavations. Note the collapse of the circuit along the northern side and the near total loss of masonry along the southern edge. The later Norman castle sits in the south-eastern corner.
© *Sussex Archaeological Society*

The reason why the Sussex fortress adopted this apparently anomalous design may have been strategic, or it may simply have been due to the limited area available for construction. Pevensey occupies a low ridge that originally formed a promontory, presumably one guarding an important harbour approach. Extensive land reclamation projects conducted throughout the medieval period, combined with the natural forces of coastal accretion, have left modern Pevensey entirely landlocked. This was obviously not the case in the Roman period and the need to enclose maximum space in an area surrounded by marsh and open water would have given early military planners very little option other than to construct their fort as an oval.

The full nature and extent of the harbour that Pevensey protected remains unknown. It was clearly important, possibly due to its access to the interior of the Weald, but it was not the most hospitable of locations to be billeted. The eastern, or 'harbour gate' of Pevensey opened out onto a 'marshy embayment', navigation of which was undoubtedly difficult, being possible only 'along the courses of a number of deep-water channels. Some of these would have been blind-ended tidal creeks, whilst others would have been the tidal lower reaches of rivers, carrying fresh-water run-off from the gentle slopes to the west, north and east that defined the marsh' (Pearson 1999, 100). To the west, the strongly defended 'land gate' opened out onto a road which, as Ivan Margary has suggested, probably linked fortress Pevensey to the Lewes–London highway

Around two-thirds of the fortress wall of Pevensey remains upright today, significant areas of the southern perimeter from the imposing west gate to the start of the medieval castle at the east, having collapsed. Just over 50m of a section of the northern perimeter, from the north postern gate heading east, has also fallen, possibly following a deliberate attempt to slight the outer defences during the siege of 1264. The surviving Roman walls average 4.2m at the base, thinning, via a series of internal offsets, to around 2.4m as they approach parapet level. The masonry survives to a maximum height of over 8m although the wall walk and battlements (had they originally existed) have now gone.

The construction of the outer perimeter was conducted in a series of separate sections, each discrete stretch butting against, or being poorly bonded into, the adjacent segment. Such a constructional technique is thought to relate to the use of individual building groups, each working together with the defined objective of completing the fortress walls as quickly and efficiently as possible. Nowhere is this more obvious than in the north-western quadrant of Pevensey, where the join between work parties can clearly be seen. Here, in at least three short sections, the green sandstone and tile/brick bonding courses of the wall do not tally, whilst the squared putlog holes for scaffolding (erected during the construction phase) are at varying heights between the adjoining segments.

The wall circuit had been built over a plinth of large stone blocks and a foundation of piled timbers overlain by a thick deposit of heavily compacted chalk and flint (*114*). The outer and inner faces of the perimeter wall were originally faced with regular-shaped blocks of ashlar, large areas of which have been removed for a variety of post-Roman building projects (including the construction of the medieval castle in the south-eastern quadrant). The interior face has suffered particularly badly (*115*), the wall core of flint and

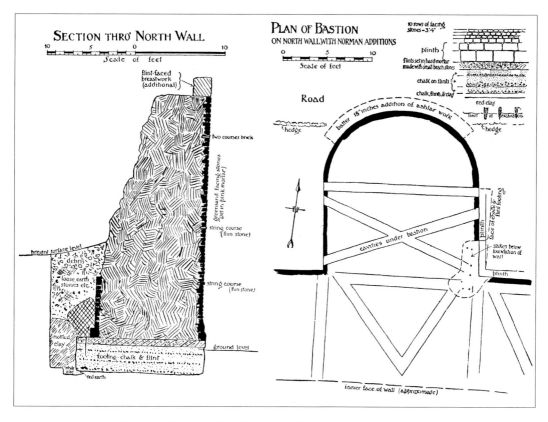

114 Pevensey: section through the north wall, showing the extent of later stone robbing, and plan features preserved beneath one of the bastions, showing the nature of the timber beams used in the foundation level. © *Sussex Archaeological Society*

115 Pevensey: the inner edge of the fortress wall close to the west gate. Here the extent of later stone robbing is clearly evident, the flint and rubble core being completely exposed above modern ground level

Above left: 116 Pevensey: excavations conducted against the north wall, revealing the well-preserved original Roman face, undisturbed by later stone robbers. © *Sussex Archaeological Society*

Above right: 117 Pevensey: the best-preserved of all projecting towers, in the northern perimeter of the fort. A round-headed window of possible Roman origin, blocked in 1940, is still visible in the upper courses of the masonry. It may represent all that is left of an internal room or chamber set above parapet level

118 Pevensey: inside the west gate, the two solid flanking towers project out, whilst in the foreground, the lower courses of the recessed, rectangular guard chambers are visible at either side of the modern tarmac path

rubble being completely exposed above modern ground level. Excavations conducted against the north wall, to the east of the collapsed section, however, have revealed the well-preserved original Roman face (*116*), undisturbed by later stone robbers.

Eleven solid, U-shaped projecting towers, or bastions, survive in the circuit of fortress Pevensey today, while the remains of at least two more lie in rubble beyond the eastern and southern perimeter. The towers, which measure 5m in diameter and project to just under 6m from the wall-line, appear to have been integral to the design of the fort, as they are all fully bonded into the masonry of the outer face. One tower situated in the northern perimeter survives to a height of well over 9m, and is thought to retain many of its original Roman features, including a large, round-headed window, blocked during the refortification of Pevensey during the Second World War (*117*). The presence of such an opening would suggest that this bastion, and presumably the others in the sequence, possessed an internal room or chamber above parapet level. Doubts have recently surfaced, however, as to the antiquity of the feature, Pearson commenting that 'the upper storey is in fact more probably of medieval age' (Pearson 2002, 35).

External towers were an addition to the architectural repertoire of the Roman military, who were not used to fighting a defensive war. Prior to the third century, the Roman army had usually been on the offensive, advancing deep into enemy territory and fighting set-piece battles in the field. The provision of projecting towers in the walls of the Roman Shore Forts marks a significant change in tactics and implies the presence of an organised and determined enemy, well versed in the art of siege warfare. Such an enemy, if attacking Pevensey fortress, would be in possession of scaling ladders, battering rams and siege engines, all items which the defenders would wish to keep well away from the outer face of the perimeter wall. Bastions could therefore provide excellent covering fire against anyone attempting to advance towards the fort, or hide in the shadow of its external face.

With the exception of Pevensey, the Roman Shore Forts of Britain possess towers that evenly subdivide the space between the main gates and the corners of the fort. The irregular nature of Pevensey's perimeter meant that in order to avoid creating a 'dead-space', where an enemy could successfully evade the defender's attention, bastions were placed at more frequent intervals where the wall curved dramatically. The impressive solidity of the towers at Pevensey could further suggest the presence of artillery. There were two forms of artillery available to the later Roman army, the bolt-or arrow-firing *ballista*, and the larger stone hurling catapult known as the *onager* (or 'wild ass'). Both forms, if used defensively from the walls of a military installation, would require secure and solid foundations. The bastions at Pevensey may well, therefore, have acted as the Roman equivalent of a modern gun emplacement.

The west (land) gate at Pevensey represents the ultimate in Roman defensive military architecture (*118*). Here, two solid flanking towers project out at either side of the entrance gap, forming a small courtyard or 'killing-zone', within which a potential attacker would face the concentrated firepower of the defending army. The gate itself is formed by a single, narrow passage, measuring 2.4m in width, set between two recessed, rectangular 'guard chambers'. The eastern (harbour) entrance is less well understood, having been modified by the builders of the medieval castle, but it seems to have comprised a single, 2.8m-wide gate, unprotected by projecting towers or internal chambers.

A narrow passageway set within the northern perimeter, to the immediate west of the collapsed section of wall at Pevensey, appears to represent a postern gate. Posterns occur in a variety of the Roman Shore Forts, such as at Richborough, Lympne and Burgh Castle, where they are usually accompanied by a tower or guard turret. The Pevensey example does not seem to have possessed any form of external defence, its only security measure apparently being its narrow, twisted route through the wall. A second curving postern seems to have existed in the southern perimeter (an area of masonry now collapsed) in a position almost directly opposite to that in the north (Maxfield 1989, 159). Quite why the Roman military architects felt it necessary to include postern gates in the walls of Shore Forts remains a mystery. It may be that they were intended to act as points where, as a last resort, defenders could sally forth to fight an enemy pressing up against the wall, but their inclusion would seem to significantly weaken an otherwise impressive defensive circuit.

A survey conducted by Andrew Pearson of the materials used in the wall and the work hours required to complete the building, has suggested that fortress Pevensey took some 160,000 days to finish. This calculation could equate with a team of around 570 working flat out for a year, just over 280 for two years or 115 in five years (Pearson 1999, 110). Building Pevensey was clearly a major undertaking that involved a complex support network supplying the necessary building materials as well as food and drink for the workforce. It could have been completed in a single season, but the will of the relevant authority to see the project completed swiftly must have been considerable (Pearson 1999, 114).

Given the impressive nature of the enclosing masonry, it may seem surprising that we know next to nothing about how the interior space of Pevensey fort was used. Excavations conducted in the north-western quadrant during the early years of the twentieth century, revealed a complex mass of timber slots, hearths, pits and postholes (Salzman 1908; 1909). Presumably these related to barrack blocks or other forms of military accommodation, although it is not known how many were in use at any one time. The apparent absence of substantial internal buildings is not a trait peculiar to Pevensey, however, for few of the Shore Forts possess what could be described as a logical or well-ordered layout. Headquarters buildings (*principia*) occur at some of the earlier forts in the sequence (such as at Reculver and possibly Richborough), but nowhere do we see the ordered layout and regular street grid apparent in the fortresses of the first and second century AD. These earlier military installations were filled with barracks, officers quarters, storage facilities, stables, administrative offices, hospitals, workshops and, in the better appointed examples, latrines and bathhouses. We should not be surprised to find that Pevensey and the other Shore Forts were equally packed, but the evidence, to date, has sadly not been forthcoming.

DATING PEVENSEY

Pevensey is a site whose date of construction just keeps getting earlier and earlier. Throughout much of the twentieth century it was thought that the fortress dated from the very late fourth century, possibly representing one of the final pieces of Roman military architecture set up in Britain. This supposition was derived from a series of discoveries made at the time of the first scientific investigation of the Roman fortress during the early years of the twentieth century (Salzman 1908).

In 1907, a prominent Sussex antiquarian by the name of Charles Dawson, presented a series of Roman bricks found at Pevensey to the Society of Antiquaries in London. The bricks had all been stamped with the same Latin inscription: 'HON AVG ANDRIA', which may be translated as 'Honorius Augustus Anderida' (Dawson 1907). The first part of the text is part of a Roman name, that of Flavius Honorius Augustus. Honorius was emperor of the western half of the Roman Empire between AD 395 and 423, his brother Arcadius ruling jointly in the East from Constantinople. His reign was not a successful one and his uninspired form of leadership, especially during the invasion of Italy by the Visigoths, managed to seriously destabilise Roman power in the West. From the perspective of Britain, Honorius' reign was critical for it was he who severed all official links with the province of Britain in AD 410. The discovery of his name on brickwork derived from Pevensey would therefore imply that either the fortress was built very late in the history of Rome in Britain, or that this was the last official period of garrison strengthening authorised by the Roman State within the province of *Britannia*.

Such re-strengthening could plausibly have happened in or around AD 396, when Honorius' chief of staff, the general Flavius Stilicho, led a campaign to bring Britain back into Rome's sphere of influence following a period of political instability. Honorius' imperial court poets praised Stilicho's efforts in a variety of sycophantic (and probably inaccurate) verses. One such poet, Claudius Claudianus (known to history simply as Claudian) gushed enthusiastically that in AD 398 'with the Saxons subjugated the sea is now more peaceful, with the Picts broken Britain is secure' (*Against Eutropius* I, 391–3 quoted in Ireland 1986, 163). A speculative construction (or reconstruction) of the fortress at Pevensey could of course fit easily within such a military campaign. In three short abbreviated words, therefore, the stamped bricks recovered by Dawson supplied an approximate date, an imperial sponsor and a name for fortress Pevensey. Unfortunately for all concerned, the bricks were forgeries.

Doubts concerning the provenance and authenticity of the artefacts had sporadically surfaced throughout the late 1960s. The 'spidery' nature of the lettering was unusual and the fabric of the bricks did not tally with any of those preserved elsewhere within the walls of the Roman fortress (Peacock 1973, 139). In the early 1970s, the bricks were subjected to thermoluminescence dating, a process which can provide an estimate of when particular ceramics were originally fired. The results were conclusive: the bricks had been manufactured 'no earlier than between AD 1900–1940 (Peacock 1973, 139).

The culprit for the forgery is still strongly debated, but in truth it is likely to have been none other than the discoverer, Charles Dawson himself (Russell 2003, 97-107).

With the Honorius bricks out of the picture, dating of Pevensey rested solely upon the discovery of a single coin of Constantine I, allegedly found in a void beneath one of the external towers (Bushe-Fox 1932). The coin was minted between AD 330 and 335, providing a useful *terminus post quem* or date after which the fort had presumably been built. Such a date, though considerably earlier than the one first suggested by Dawson in 1907, still placed Pevensey at the very end of the sequence of building on the Saxon Shore, the other forts all apparently dating to before the AD 290s.

Excavations conducted by Michael Fulford of Reading University in 1994 finally resolved some of the mystery surrounding the constructional date of the fortress. Here, beneath the foundations of a section of wall preserved at the eastern end of the fort, were discovered a mass of timber posts, driven into the geological natural in order to provide a solid base for the masonry above. A dendrochronological (tree ring) date for the timbers (all of which appear to have been of oak) provided 'a *terminus post quem* of 270 for their felling, with a probable range of 280-300' (Fulford and Tyres 1995, 1011). Two coins minted by the British usurpers Carausius (AD 286-93) and Allectus (AD 293-6) found in the upcast of the original foundation trench, tie the date after which the walls were constructed as AD 293. Pevensey can now be seen to be more or less contemporary with both the construction of town walls around Chichester (see chapter 5) and the fortress of Portchester in Portsmouth Harbour, where the current 'cut-off' date after which the fort must have been built is AD 286 (Cunliffe 1975, 41).

THE EMPIRE OF CARAUSIUS

Throughout the second and early third century AD, Britannia was a prosperous, successful and thriving province. In AD 286, however, it ceased to be an official part of the Roman world. The reason for this sudden termination of imperial authority was down to one man: Marcus Aurelius Mausaeus Carausius.

Carausius was a naval official who had been given the task of policing the sea lanes and clearing the English Channel of pirates. From the mid-third century, communications between Britain and Gaul had become difficult due to the presence of increasingly hostile maritime bandits operating from bases beyond the control of Rome. To the Roman historians, these pirates were known as the 'Saxons', a particularly violent Germanic tribe whose descendants today are known as the 'English'. We do not know how disruptive Saxon activity really was, but the Roman State clearly viewed them as a problem. Presumably their tactics were similar to the first Viking raiders who began infesting the seas around Britain over half a century later and would have entailed 'swift crossings, a night-time beaching and then a high-speed dash on foot or horseback inland looking for targets of opportunity like a villa, a roadside *mansio*, or travellers, before a hasty retreat and disappearing into the darkness with the tide.' (de la Bédoyère 2001, 93)

119 Fishbourne: a group of smashed pots, scattered by debris falling during the final fire, lie on the floor of room N12. © *Institute of Archaeology, Oxford and Sussex Archaeological Society*

That inland targets were hit during the course of Saxon raids seems evident enough from the written accounts that survive, the historians Eutropius and Aurelius Victor (both writing in the fourth century AD), noting that provincial 'booty' was being carried off by the pirates (Aurelius Victor *Lives of the Caesars* 39, 20). The archaeological evidence too seems to indicate some significant disruption along the coastal regions of Britain, especially in Sussex. At Fishbourne, the final phase of domestic activity, within what was formerly the northern wing of the palace, ended violently. In the later years of the third century, a fire ripped through the north range, causing extensive damage (*119*).

> Everywhere over the floors lay a thick blanket of broken and discoloured roof tiles, rafter nails and charred roof timbers, in some places up to a foot thick. The roof was ablaze long enough for the lead fittings to melt and drip onto the mosaics, forming large puddles of the molten metal; then, with the rafters weakened by the flames, the roof collapsed, some of the debris falling into the molten lead. The timbers continued to burn, discolouring the mosaics and tessellated floors with streaks of grey and blue, the heat being intense enough to refire the tiles from which the *tesserae* were made and occasionally to vitrify fragments of the roof tiles. (Cunliffe 1998, 141)

A similar fate seems to have befallen the rich villa building at Preston Park in Brighton, the excavators noting that 'burnt wood and charcoal, charred flints, superficially discoloured *tesserae*, blackened walls, and perhaps the condition of the coins, gave sufficient evidence that the house had been destroyed by fire.' (Toms and Herbert 1926, 13). Further afield, around the area of clay floor No. 5, the nature of discoloured tiles and building material implied that the outbuildings at Brighton had also been burnt down in the conflagration (Toms and Herbert 1926, 8).

Along the coast to the east, a fire also claimed the coastal villa complex of Eastbourne. Here, the sunken bath in the northernmost range investigated was 'filled with ashes and wood' associated with which was 'part of a burnt human skull and burnt bones' which lay 'as if the person had perished in the flames' (Page 1905, 24). The date for the catastrophic fires at Fishbourne and Brighton have been put at the end of the AD 290s (Cunliffe 1998, 142) and 'shortly after AD 270' (Toms and Herbert 1926, 13) respectively. Although the ultimate cause of these destructive episodes will probably never be known with any certainty, it is possible that they were not unconnected with the Saxon inland raiding that Carausius was meant to put a stop to (see below for an alternative interpretation).

Carausius seems to have had some success against the Saxons, but soon he found himself on the wrong side of the law. Word got back to Maximian, the emperor of the West (for at this time the empire was divided between two rulers) that the commander of the British Fleet was 'deliberately letting the barbarians in so as to catch them as they passed through with their booty and in this way enrich himself' (Eutropius IX, 21). Whether or not there was any truth in the rumour, it must have been patently clear to Carausius that he was about to be offered a one-way ticket to the circus in Rome. Unsurprisingly, he decided that his best interests, and indeed his only chance of survival, lay in open rebellion. Late in AD 286 he formally severed all ties with Rome and set up his own government in Britain and northern Gaul.

If Carausius had been corrupt, allowing pirates to raid deep into Roman territory simply in order to boost his own profit margin, it is unlikely that he would have received much backing from the British or Gallic elite for the rebellion. As it was, he appears to have been able to muster widespread support from military and civilian officials on both sides of the English Channel, something that suggests a significant degree of alienation and disenchantment with the imperial system. What Carausius offered the people of Britain and Gaul, we will never know; perhaps it was the opportunity of having a leader who understood regional issues and grievances, not one who was based hundreds of miles away in Italy. Perhaps he offered greater security from external threats. Perhaps he offered tax cuts to landowners and better financial incentives to the military.

The loss of Britain was a substantial blow not just to the prestige of the emperor, but, more importantly, to the whole Roman economy and plans were soon drawn up by Maximian to bring Carausius to heel. Initial efforts to defeat the usurper were, however, unsuccessful, an unhappy truce lasting until AD 293 when Carausius was (literally) stabbed in the back by Allectus, his finance minister. Three years later, in AD 296 the praetorian prefect of north-western Gaul, Asclepiodotus, landed unopposed (and under cover of a dense fog) with a large army somewhere in the Solent estuary. Allectus' troops were swiftly defeated, the remnants being destroyed by a second invading army, this time led by the junior emperor Flavius Valerius Constantius (later Constantius I), who landed somewhere near London.

If the villa/palace sites of Fishbourne, Brighton and Eastbourne had not already been destroyed, then it is possible that they perished during the chaos and confusion of Allectus' downfall. As the Roman State performed its own version of regime change, wealthy villa estates could well have been perceived as legitimate targets or have been sacked by the defeated army as it fled to the coast. As the last remnants of the rogue State were swept away, important landowners, especially those who were known (or suspected) to have sided with the breakaway government would have faced execution, imprisonment or confiscation of property. Whatever the cause of the fires that ripped through Fishbourne, Brighton and Eastbourne, it is clear that none were repaired, sites instead being robbed of their metal, tile, brick and stonework. Perhaps total rebuild would, in these cases, have proved too expensive and time-consuming. Maybe there was no longer the political will to retain and reconstruct these wealthy estate centres or maybe the coastal districts were simply no longer wholly safe.

Given the history of events as outlined here, the construction, date and nature of Pevensey fortress all conveniently falls into place. This was not a fortress designed to protect Britain from a Germanic invasion, for the Saxon pirates, whom we know were raiding coastal districts and intercepting shipping at the time the Shore Forts were being built, could easily have bypassed the installations, their target being unprotected villas and poorly protected cargo vessels. They were not, at least at this time, intent on invasion, conquest or bringing the government of Britain to its knees. Even if they had been, the defensive capabilities on show at Pevensey appear wildly excessive. Saxon pirates had no siege engines, battering rams or catapults. They were not equipped for a protracted and bitter war and did not possess the resources (or the desire) to take well defended positions. If they were, we would expect to see a similar range of strongpoints constructed along the shore of Belgium and Gaul, protecting Roman interests there, but we do not. The Shore Forts in their most defensive form appear peculiar to Britain.

The Shore Forts were not therefore part of an impregnable defensive chain, designed to protect the entire eastern seaboard of the province from a mass invasion by Saxon and Germanic pirates. Instead, they represent garrisoned harbours from which, we may presume, naval units could patrol and monitor the sea lanes, mobile units moving swiftly to areas where landings were detected. As strongly defended masonry installations, the forts sat in prominent locations along the coast, acting as a warning and deterrent to those wishing to access the major harbours and river estuaries. The impressive range of defensive features displayed at sites like Pevensey and Portchester clearly illustrate that these fortresses were designed specifically in order to defend and protect key harbours from a dangerous, very well trained, excellently equipped and utterly ruthless enemy: namely the Roman army.

From AD 286 onwards, the government of Carausius would have been expecting an attack. Whilst their supporters held on to territory in Gaul, the nature of the threat was relatively small, but it would never diminish altogether. Rome would not allow Britain to proclaim its own unilateral declaration of independence; it was a rogue State which needed to be swiftly brought back into line before other provinces decided to go the same way. Michael Fulford and Ian Tyres have observed that 'in taking the steps they did, Carausius and Allectus by no means overestimated the strength of their enemy', and it is interesting to note that when invasion did come, led by the Prefect Asclepiodotus in AD 296, it bypassed the defensive system altogether, landing in the Solent to the west of Portchester (Fulford and Tyres 1995, 1013).

The loss of Boulogne, Carausius' last foothold in continental Europe, to the forces of the Maximian in AD 293 was a significant blow to the usurper's prestige and it may well have been the event that triggered his assassination. Political disputes and leadership contests in the ancient world were not settled by the ballot box, they were settled by the sword, and in AD 293 it was Carausius' successor (and killer) Allectus who took control of Britain. In fact, it is conceivable that it is to Allectus that we should look when we consider the defences of Pevensey, for the loss of territory in Gaul had left the British coast particularly vulnerable to attack (Fulford and Tyres 1995, 1013). The years AD 293-6 must have been particularly tense, as both sides prepared for the inevitable.

NAMING PEVENSEY

The original form of the Roman name for fortress Pevensey has been heatedly discussed by academics for well over 100 years. The most commonly quoted variant is *Anderida*, although as long ago as 1979 Rivet and Smith observed that though the traditional form, this was 'not likely to be right' (Rivet and Smith 1979, 251). The earliest reference to '*Anderida*' appears to have been in the writings of William Camden, the sixteenth-century English antiquarian. Camden's *magnum opus* was *Britannia,* a county by county survey of the topography and landscape history of Britain, first published in 1586. To Camden, *Anderida* was a site of great antiquity at Neweden in Kent, though historians that followed him suggested that it could more plausibly be identified with Pevensey (Coates 1991, 250). No one seemed at all bothered that the version Anderi-*da*, was not found in any of the original source material relating to Roman Britain. Some credence to the -*da* form was provided by the discovery of stamped bricks at Pevensey with the name *Andria* (Dawson 1907), though these have now been shown to be twentieth-century forgeries (Peacock 1973; Russell 2003, 97-107).

The *Notitia Dignitatum*, a set of military dispositions originally compiled in the late fourth and early fifth century AD and irregularly updated thereafter, records the name of fortress Pevensey as being either *Anderidos* or *Anderitos* (depending on which copy you read), whilst the early eighth-century document known as the *Ravenna Cosmography*, cites the place name *Anderelio*. Further clues to the original form of the name may be found within the pages of the *Notitia Dignitatum*. Here, references to military units that may have once served at Pevensey (or who may plausibly have been recruited from the immediate locality) are cited as the *Anderetiani*, the *classis Anderetianorum* the *milites Anderetianorum* (Rivet and Smith 1979, 250). If the identification with Pevensey is correct, it would suggest, at the very least, a name closer to *Anderetia* rather than *Anderida*.

Rivet and Smith considered the name to have derived from a combination of the elements *ande-*, meaning great or big, and the British *ritu-*, meaning a ford (Rivet and Smith 1979, 251). Coates agreed, observing that the 'British neuter singular' form of the name would originally have been something akin to *Anderitu* (Coates 1991, 250). This seems a reasonable supposition and would in turn mean that the Romano-British name for fortress Pevensey would have been *Anderitum*, the sense of a 'great ford' perhaps having derived from one of the many rivers or watery inlets that originally separated the site from the mainland.

A form of *Anderitum* survived in the name later given to the Wealden forest which in AD 477, according to the *Anglo-Saxon Chronicle*, was called *Andredesleag*. Later references to the forest cite *Andred* and *Andredesweald* whilst the Hampshire section of the late eleventh-century Domesday calls part of the New Forest *Andret*. The application of the name for fortress Pevensey to the entire Wealden forest from East Sussex to Hampshire may seem strange though it may reflect the perceived regional importance of the fort (cf. Rivet and Smith 1979, 252). It is possible that *Anderitum* was, by the fifth century at least, the home of a dominant political and military force exacting tribute over the people of the Weald. Possibly the name was used to cover so large an area because the resources of the Weald, most notably iron, would have to pass through *Anderitum* before being redistributed elsewhere in Britain or the continent. Alternatively, perhaps Pevensey was simply a well-known Late Roman site and its name was used as a catch-all term for the strange and impenetrable Weald to the north of the developing Saxon kingdom of Sussex.

THE GARRISON

Following the events of AD 286-96, when Britain was part of the breakaway empire of Carausius and Allectus, military occupation at both Pevensey and Portchester in Hampshire seems to have ceased, with a number of internal buildings at Portchester apparently being demolished (Cunliffe 1973, 36). The abandonment of these strongholds at this critical time is perhaps not surprising, for if the forts had been established to deter an invasion by the forces of the Roman Empire, then they had both spectacularly failed.

By the mid-fourth century, the situation in the English Channel had deteriorated significantly. Piratical activity was on the increase and raids on both ships and inland settlements were becoming more daring. All coastal fortifications appear to have been recommissioned and repaired with naval units placed on a constant state of readiness. In AD 367 matters came to a head. The emperor Flavius Valentinianus (Valentinian I) was in the middle of conducting an expedition against the Alamanni, a Germanic people terrorising northern Gaul, when he received terrible news:

> indicating that Britain had been plunged into the depths of distress by a conspiracy of the barbarians, that Nectaridus, Count of the coastal district, had been killed, and that Duke Fullofaudes had been surrounded and captured in an enemy ambush. (Ammianus Marcellinus *Res Gestae* XXVII, 8)

The situation was indeed grave. The 'barbarians', comprising the piratical Franks and Saxons together with the Scots and Attacotti (from Ireland) and the Picts (from what is now Scotland), had launched a simultaneous attack on Britain 'causing much devastation' with their 'vicious acts of pillage, arson and the murder of all prisoners' (Ammianus Marcellinus *Res Gestae* XXVII, 8). The geographical extent of the barbarian horror is unknown, although the death of Nectaridus, officer in charge of the 'coastal district', suggests that a major theatre of conflict had been within the strongly fortified maritime regions of the south and east.

Repairs to the infrastructure of Romano-British government were conducted by one of Valentinian's senior military officers, Flavius Theodosius (later to become emperor Theodosius I). According to the Roman historian Ammianus Marcellinus, writing in the late fourth century, Theodosius restored order, recalled deserters, defeated those barbarian warbands still roaming the province and 'completely restored the cities and forts which ... had suffered repeated damage' (Ammianus Marcellinus *Res Gestae* XXVIII, 3). Presumably Pevensey and Portchester were both repaired and updated by Theodosius, whilst the walls of *Noviomagus* may also have been upgraded at this time with the addition of projecting towers (Down 1988, 100).

It is not known when, or indeed if, *Anderitum* was ever completely abandoned by the Roman military. The *Notitia Dignitatum*, compiled in the late fourth and early fifth century AD, records that the last official garrison was the *praepositus numeri Abulcorum*. A detachment of the *Abulci* is noted by the *Notitia* as forming part of the Gallic field army, but little is known of their ethnic affiliation. Contemporary Roman sources note that they were considered to be an elite and thoroughly efficient body of troops (Johnson 1979, 70).

The difficulties of using the *Notitia* as an objective source for identifying the respective garrisons of the *Litus Saxonicum* (Saxon Shore) have been well illustrated by Richard Reece in his study of the coin assemblage from *Portus Lemanis*, modern-day

Lympne in Kent. Here the coins appeared to run out in AD 348, whilst the remaining aspects of the excavated material culture strongly indicated complete abandonment of the site around AD 350. The *Notitia*, however, confidently stated that in around AD 395, *Lemanis* was still fully functioning, being garrisoned by a unit named as the *numerus Turnacensium*. This apparent conflict between historical and archaeological datasets was neatly resolved by Reece who observed that:

> the entry in the Notitia is only evidence that one bureaucrat in the later fourth-century Roman military machine had a reason for placing a number of troops in this fort of the Saxon Shore. The reason may be no more than incompetence or inertia, both military characteristics. (Reece in Cunliffe 1980, 263)

Historically we know little about the later use of *Anderitum* beyond what is stated in the official record of the *Notitia Dignitatum*. It is unclear whether the *numeri Abulcorum* were ever officially withdrawn, either by Stilicho in AD 398 to reinforce troops serving in mainland Europe (possibly joining other units of the *Abulci* serving in Gaul) or by a British usurper, such as Constantine III (whose brief reign lasted from AD 407 to 411), as part of an ill-fated campaign to become emperor. The *Notitia* records at least three units possessing variants of the name *Anderitum* serving on the continent in the early fifth century AD: the *Classis Anderetianorum* based in Paris, a *milites Anderetianorum* at Mainz under the command of an officer known as the *Dux Mogontacensis* (Rivet and Smith 1979, 250; Johnson 1979, 70; Pearson 2002, 148) and the *Anderetiani* serving in the Gallic field army (Rivet and Smith 1979, 250). All three may, as already noted, well have served at fortress Pevensey at a formative stage in their history, but the reasons for transferring them to Gaul and Germany (and the crucial question of when this occurred) are not answered in the pages of the *Notitia*.

The citing of a *Classis Anderetianorum* is interesting for it implies that at some stage the fortress at Pevensey had possessed its own fleet. It is possible, of course, that this represented a naval unit derived from the former *Classis Britannica* or British Fleet, that is known to have been heavily involved in the Wealden ironworking industry. The *Classis Britannica*, as already noted (chapter 10), appears to have been little more than an official haulage company, overseeing the efficient transportation of British iron oversees, than a 'navy' in the modern sense. The British Fleet had been in control of maintaining supply lines to and from Britain; they do not appear to have been well equipped, or even specifically designed, to protect the province from sustained seaborne attack.

By the mid-third century, *Classis Britannica* involvement in both the ironfields of southern Britain and the supply depots of the coastal fringe, was in severe decline, their headquarters at Dover had been demolished and they appear to have been written out of all official documentation. Perhaps the *Classis Britannica* disappeared during part of a major review of military dispositions in Britain; a reorganisation of the island's defensive capabilities conducted by Carausius or one of his immediate predecessors.

If the fleet had been revamped in order to successfully confront a new foe, then it is likely that hardware, equipment, expertise and soldiery would all have been recycled. Perhaps the new system of coastal defence, from either Saxon or Roman, required the provision of discrete (and elite) military units, each with their own style of fighting and each operating from different strategic points on the coast.

It is possible, if the fortress garrison had been established at Pevensey for some time, intermingling with the local population, that the soldiers would have become so enmeshed in society that it would have proved difficult, if not impossible, to transfer them elsewhere. If any garrison was left in place to guard the harbour area at *Anderitum* at the time that Britain finally revolted against the authority of Rome in AD 409, one thing was sure: they could expect no further pay or supplies from central government, such as it was. If they had lived and trained at *Anderitum* for some significant time, investing in the resources of the region and mixing freely with the populace, it would be unlikely, even in the turmoil of governmental collapse, that they would wish to surrender everything and totally abandon the site.

In the early years of the fifth century AD, the fortress of Pevensey remained a more than serviceable stronghold possessing state of the art military capabilities. The harbour it protected was a vital point of access to the iron and timber resources of the Weald. Whoever controlled *Anderitum* probably controlled a significant block of south-eastern England and the English Channel. Whether it was the remnants of the *numeri Abulcorum*, mutating into a locally based militia controlling a variety of resources and protection rackets or a roaming warband or mercenary unit that saw the opportunities of being based in a prominent and easily defensible position, it would appear that *Anderitum* remained a key player in the regional politics of post-Roman Britain.

12

FRIENDS, GERMANS, COUNTRYMEN

In AD 409 the authorities in Britain rebelled against Rome, forcibly ejected all imperial officers and set up their own government. Zosimus, a historian writing in Constantinople during the reign of the Eastern emperor Anastasius I (AD 491-518), observed that, this having been achieved, the Britons 'took up arms and, braving the danger on their own behalf, freed their cities from the barbarians threatening them' (Zosimus *New History*, VI, 5, 2). The Roman emperor of the West, Flavius Honorius Augustus, was too busy dealing with internal security measures (including rebellion, civil war and the mass migration of Germanic tribes across the Rhine) to worry about what was happening the other side of the English Channel. Belatedly acknowledging the inevitable, Honorius 'wrote letters to the cities in Britain bidding them to take precautions on their own behalf' (Zosimus *New History*, VI, 10, 2). Over 460 years after Julius Caesar had first set sail from Gaul, Rome was no longer interested in the affairs of Britain. What happened next has been a matter of heated academic debate for well over three centuries.

ON THE DESTRUCTION OF BRITAIN

The view of post-Roman Britain propounded by the sixth-century historian Gildas is one of anarchy, violence, moral decline and collapse into barbarism:

> The townships and high wall are abandoned; once again the citizens are put to flight; once again are scattered with less hope of recovery than usual; once again they are pursued by the enemy; once again massacres yet more cruel hasten upon them. The pitiful citizens are torn to pieces by their foes like lambs by butchers. (Gildas *On the Destruction of Britain* 19)

The wretched Britons in Gildas' work *On the Destruction of Britain* struggle desperately to survive their grim surroundings. The 'miserable remnants' of society send a final, desperate plea to a 'man of high rank' amongst the Romans whom Gildas calls Agitius (usually taken to be Aetius, chief military leader of the western empire from the 420s to AD 454). The plea conforms to Gildas' apocalyptic perspective by stating:

> The barbarians drive us to the sea; the sea drives us back to the barbarians; between these two forms of death we are either slaughtered or drowned. (Gildas *On the Destruction of Britain*, 20)

Unfortunately, Gildas is not one of the most objective of historians. He was writing for a very particular reason and his work clearly represents a robust piece of moral sermonising. The Britons he describes are greedy and corrupt and their cities are fifth-century versions of the biblical Sodom and Gomorrah, models of decadence and decay. The barbarian invaders, be they Saxon, Angle, Jute or Frank (from across the North Sea), Scot or Pict (from Ireland and southern Scotland respectively), are seen as a divine punishment; a cleansing force sent by God to purge his immoral flock. However one views this particular form of history, there can be no denying that it is dramatic stuff.

Gildas' sermonising has coloured our view of the final phases of Roman Britain. The picture he paints is one of terror and unimaginable cruelty: towns and villas ablaze whilst all around the Britons are exterminated on an epic scale. Only recently have historians and archaeologists attempted to distance themselves from the Gildas mindset, observing that either the catastrophes he recorded simply did not happen or have been vastly exaggerated. The view that has steadily emerged throughout the 1980s and '90s is one of 'permissive acculturation', whereby the process of transition from Roman Britain to Saxon England was more ordered and calm. The Romano-Britons changed into Germano-Britons because it was something they desired. Saxon, Angle, Pict, Jute and Briton co-existed in relative peace; fashions, ideas and languages mutated through trade and exchange, not war and aggression.

This new orthodoxy strikes me as somewhat akin to the Nazi and Soviet apologists who repeatedly argue, in the face of a battery of evidence to the contrary, that the concentration camps and gulags simply did not exist or were not quite as bad as usually claimed. Thankfully, the horrors of the past cannot easily be swept away by those possessing a distorted political agenda. Whatever is said about post-Roman Britain, it is clear from the writings of the contemporary Romans, Byzantines, Britons and Saxons that the fifth century was, like it or not, a time of danger, hatred, prejudice, uncertainty and extreme violence.

The effect that the fifth-century AD collapse of governmental infrastructure would have had on the population of Roman Britain can only be surmised. Within the space of a generation the political and military system that had held the provinces of Britain together, providing a modicum of stability, had gone. The army, merchants, administrators, businessmen and women and tax collectors had all disappeared. There can be no doubt that anyone brought up within the last decades of the fourth century AD would have found the sudden absence of *Romanitas* both alien and deeply unsettling.

The shocking consequences of a sudden removal of central government authority at a regional level were unfortunately (and sadly) highlighted during the final phases of writing this book, late in 2005, when the full force of hurricane Katrina hit the U.S. city of New Orleans. In a matter of hours familiar surroundings were destroyed and the comforting routines of life swept away together with all systems of local government and law enforcement. Within days, the horrors of this natural disaster were compounded by the instinct of a small minority to both profit and survive. Significant parts of the city became no go areas as armed gangs took control. Shops were looted, people murdered and homes destroyed. Aid agencies entering the city were reportedly shot at with all manner of projectiles and the police department were soon actively returning fire rather than rescuing the needy.

When the infrastructure of government collapses at a national level, the results can be positively terrifying. Military commanders, disenfranchised politicians, small-time criminals and chancers, all previously constrained by the legal niceties of a functioning justice system, are suddenly set free. In Russia and Germany, a democratic deficit, born of severe economic and political malaise, triggered social catastrophe during the first four decades of the twentieth century. More recently in states such as Chechnya, Somalia and Afghanistan, the catastrophic disintegration of central authority has effectively given power to a series of increasingly brutal warlords. Each emergent warlord has claimed their own territory, generating their own brand of fanatical acolytes in the process. Warlords form alliances or fight neighbours as and when the situation demands. Sometimes battle-lines are drawn on the basis of religious, cultural or ethnic grounds; more frequently the divide between factions is blurred. To an outsider the situation seems unfathomable, it being difficult to take sides or to determine 'good' from 'evil'. In situations such as this there can be no 'just cause' to support; only continually unfolding acts of violence in a bloody cycle of revenge.

The power vacuum of AD 409 may have had a similar effect on the relative stability of life in Britain. The basic rhythms of life were unsettled and the familiarity of daily existence was swept away, seemingly for good. New forces were at work at home and abroad, the consequences of which would undoubtedly have been distressing: a deep sense of psychological shock from which it would be difficult to emerge undamaged. The removal of imperial authority could, when combined with a profound economic recession, have torn at the fault lines of British society. Add to this the arrival of the warlike English, Scots and Picts and the resulting social and political fallout would last for generations. Rich country estates were abandoned and natural strongpoints in the landscape were refortified. Towns became the political centres of a new and potentially unstable military elite.

The fracturing of the political map of Britain seems to have created multiple independent states each with a defendable stronghold, a town wall, Saxon Shore Fort or recommissioned hillfort, at its heart. Each of these territories would have possessed its own distinctive leader, resources, land and political agenda. On occasion such fledgling states may have formed alliances for the mutual good against the Germanic invaders. Sometimes these petty kingdoms may have invited the newcomers in as mercenaries, friends or allies; sometimes they lived in peace; sometimes they fought amongst each other. In time, there would have been no simple, clear-cut struggle pitting Briton against Saxon, only a grubby war of attrition in which ethnic origin, cultural background, religious belief or tribal affiliation no longer possessed any meaning.

THE *ANGLO-SAXON CHRONICLE*

The Saxon perspective of the period is not preserved in anything like the gory detail of Gildas. One useful document however, is a compilation of stories explaining the origin of certain English kingdoms referred to as the *Anglo-Saxon Chronicle*. The *Anglo-Saxon Chronicle* was a piece of historical revisionism designed to present a single and coherent official version of the history and origins of Wessex and, by default, of the first Saxon kings in Kent, Sussex and the south-west of Britain. It appears to have been compiled in or around AD 892 from a variety of disparate sources and was designed to legitimise the Wessex dynasty whilst simultaneously defining Saxon ethnicity in the face of sustained Danish attack. The story is presented in clear-cut terms: a war of Briton against Saxon. The blurring of ethnic, social and political backgrounds is not discussed nor examined.

There are only three specific early references to Sussex contained within the *Chronicle*, but these are important as they provide a date and a setting for the first English settlers in the region. Unfortunately there is no attempt to provide a detailed or historically accurate account of Germanic first contact, and only those events considered essential to a ninth-century compiler are cited.

In 477 Aelle and his three sons, Cymen, Wlencing and Cissa, came to Britain in three ships, at the place called Cymensora, and there slew many Welsh, driving some of them to flight to the wood called Andredsleag

In 485 Aelle fought the Welsh on the bank near Merecredesburna

In 491 Aelle and Cissa besieged Andredescester and killed all who were inside, so there was not one Briton left

The details are frustratingly vague: just three sentences covering the political turmoil of some 14 years. Perhaps we are fortunate that Sussex is mentioned at all, for many other areas of Britain are simply ignored in the pages of the *Chronicle*. The reason that Sussex, or *Sud Seaxum* (the kingdom of the South Saxons) was mentioned in any detail was purely because it was one of the three early Saxon territories which, by the late ninth century, comprised the kingdom of Wessex. It was also the seat of power of Aelle, one of the foremost of early Saxon leaders in Britain.

AELLE

The story of Aelle as presented in the *Anglo-Saxon Chronicle* is cursory: he came, saw and conquered. There is no reference given to his status, nor any indication of his importance within society beyond a regional level. As a Saxon, Aelle presumably hailed from the ethnic homeland of the Saxon people, situated somewhere between the rivers Ems, Weser and Elbe on what is now the north-western coast of Germany. We know nothing of his background, his reasons for crossing the North Sea, the number of people in his entourage nor of his relations with the self-proclaimed leaders of Britain. According to the eighth-century historian Bede, Aelle was the founder of the kingdom of Sussex and a man of critical importance: the first Saxon to hold the office of *Bretwalda*, or Lord of Britain.

Bretwalda is a title that seems to have conferred ultimate power over all the English peoples south of the river Humber. Though the *Anglo-Saxon Chronicle* is brief in its treatment of Aelle, there can be little doubt that in the later half of the fifth century, he was the pre-eminent king of the Germanic people. Sadly, Aelle's *curriculum vitae* does not survive and there is nothing in either the *Anglo-Saxon Chronicle* nor the writings of Bede which explain his primacy. Perhaps he was the elder statesman of Saxon society; perhaps he was the most respected politician or, following his exploits in Sussex, the most bloodied warrior. Whatever the case, it is apparent that, as *Bretwalda*, he was the champion of the whole English movement against the Britons of the south (Stenton 1971, 19).

The *Chronicle*'s account of Aelle's entry into Britain is presented as a brief but straightforward origin myth, whereby the primary dynast arrives with a small following after a difficult sea crossing, and overcomes significant opposition to establish a kingdom. It is presented in terms not dissimilar to the classic myth of Aeneas, the legendary father of the Roman people, who led a band of refugees to Italy following the events of the Trojan War. Similar accounts to that of Aelle are also credited in the *Anglo-Saxon Chronicle* for the founders of the kingdom of Kent, Hengist and his son Horsa, who arrived in AD 449, for Cerdic and Cynric arriving in AD 495, for Port, Bieda and Maegla arriving in 501 and for Stuf and Wihtgar arriving in 514. The exploits of Aelle as he forged the kingdom of Sussex may have come down to the compilers of the *Chronicle* via a saga, now lost, or through oral tradition, but either way the primary source for the early history of the South Saxons is unlikely to have been wholly objective.

The basic sequence provided by the chroniclers of Aelle's 'landing, fighting and total liquidation of the enemy' is probably correct, but the dates provided should not be strongly adhered to. Whether anything can usefully be said concerning the chronology of early Saxon settlement in the *Chronicle* is uncertain. Some have argued that by comparing the known historical and archaeological evidence, that the time sequence provided has been distorted by at least two decades (e.g. Down 1988, 104). This would mean that the initial landings by Aelle took place in the mid-to-late 450s rather than 477, and the storming of *Andredescester* occurred around AD 471. Whilst such a suggestion may appear plausible, there is unfortunately nothing that can said to either definitively support or refute it.

Problems also exist with the secure placement of Aelle's activities in Sussex. Some historians have identified *Cymensora* or *Cymens Ora* with Selsey Bill (e.g. Stenton 1971, 17-18), noting that having established a foothold here, the Saxon warband would have drifted eastward across the Sussex coastal plain. It is worth pointing out, however, that archaeology cannot support the suggestion of an early Saxon presence in the area around either Selsey or Chichester, the best evidence for fifth-century Germanic activity in the county deriving from areas further to the east, at Highdown near Worthing and between the rivers Ouse and Cuckmere. Identification with Selsey rests solely with a mention of a *Cumeneshora* in a charter noting the gift of land on the Selsey peninsula to Bishop Wilfred in AD 683. Modern analysis of the document has, however, demonstrated sufficient doubt concerning the authenticity of the piece (Welch 1983, 256). The fact that the Britons opposing Aelle's landfall were driven into the Wealden forest, if taken at face value, may further invalidate a West Sussex landing, whilst simultaneously strengthening a location further to the east (Down 1988, 104-8).

It may be interesting to note that the Early Anglo-Saxon cemetery and associated settlement found at Highdown, a reused Later Bronze Age hillfort near Worthing, appears to sit in splendid isolation from the remaining fifth-century Saxon areas of activity recorded from East Sussex. If, as the archaeological evidence seems to indicate (see below), burials at Highdown began as early as the fourth century AD, it could be that the site was first a Roman cemetery which later became a focus for Saxon burial. This could in turn indicate that 'the Saxon community was here settled under the direct supervision of an existing Roman community' (Welch 1983, 217), possibly a mercenary force based within the circuits of the prehistoric fort. An alternative explanation could be that an existing population here were, from a very early date, more forward thinking in terms of fashion, changing from Romano-Britons to Germano-Britons on the basis of established trade links across the North Sea. Highdown could easily have been an early base for a trading enclave between Briton and Saxon at which two distinct cultures first met. Given the site's position, on a strategic high point overlooking and commanding the Sussex coastal plain, the suggestion of a militarised outpost in which Germanic mercenaries (possibly elements of the former Roman field army) were settled in order to protect both the coastal and land approaches to western Sussex (Welch 1983, 220-1) would perhaps appear plausible.

Identification of *Merecredesburna*, where Aelle fought a battle against 'the Welsh' is also problematic. Most historians have followed the interpretation, first suggested by John Morris in 1966, that the name meant the 'river of the frontier agreed by treaty' (Morris 1966, 256-7; Morris 1973, 94). This would fit the suggestion that, having forced his way into Britain, Aelle had signed some form of non-aggression pact with the British leaders, which allowed him land on which to settle. Which of Sussex's many water courses formed the 'river of the frontier' is a matter for speculation. It is possible it was the Arun, a plausible frontier if Aelle's immediate enemy was centred upon the Roman town of Chichester. Alternatively it may have been a more easterly river, especially if one notes that the bulk of fifth-century Saxon activity occurs between the rivers Ouse and Cuckmere, to the west of Eastbourne. If this block of the downs represents a territory ceded to Aelle and his followers 'by treaty', then, by implication the 'river of the frontier' could have been here.

ANDREDESCESTER

The battle of *Merecredesburna* may have been fought as Aelle attempted to expand his territorial claim, or it could have been a defensive struggle against a revitalised local resistance. Either way the next target of his campaign is clear enough for the site of *Andredescester* mentioned in the *Chronicle* entry for AD 491 can only be *Anderitum*: the Roman fortress at Pevensey. Though strongly fortified, *Anderitum* would be the obvious place for Aelle to concentrate his forces. As an important and strongly defended port, the inhabitants of the fortress could effectively block good access to the resources of the Weald (the forest of *Andredsleag*), whilst simultaneously disrupting Saxon communications along the English Channel. Worse, the proximity of the fortress to the east of the river Cuckmere, must have represented an ever-present threat to the security of Aelle's fledgling kingdom.

What was the population of *Anderitum* like at this time? Although their combat status is unknowable, any force deployed here may originally have descended from elements of the last 'official' garrison of the fort, the *praepositus numeri Abulcorum* (themselves possibly of Germanic origin: see chapter 11). We should not, however, view a fifth-century garrison as being representative of the Late Roman military system. By the time Aelle came to prominence, whatever force inhabited the fortress probably did so with its families, dependants and livestock. The garrison of *Anderitum* could therefore perhaps more realistically be described as a form of citizen militia; a force dominating both local resources and regional politics. Perhaps the Roman fortress was home to a prominent war band, followers of a Germano-British leader possessing de facto military control of the region (something that may be reflected in the Saxon name for the Weald, the *Andredsleag*). A modern parallel could be drawn with a warlord in early twenty-first-century Afghanistan, controlling large swathes of land from the crumbling remains of a Soviet airbase, or with the warlords of Somalia or Chechnya who rose to power as the infrastructure of central government collapsed.

If Aelle and his English subordinates wished to benefit from the resources of Britain, then they needed to curtail the influence of *Anderitum*. We have no way of knowing how the fortress was taken, but the *Anglo-Saxon Chronicle* was clear enough about the aftermath, Aelle executing all he found 'so there was not one Briton left'. This action has frequently been taken to be representative of a wider Anglo-Saxon attitude towards the British population, as if the conflict was one of near total 'ethnic cleansing'. This is a dangerous view to take, for the case of *Andredescester* was probably atypical. Here was an enemy stronghold whose very existence threatened the survival of one of the first Saxon kingdoms in Britain. If Aelle and his people were to survive and thrive, then the power of *Anderitum* had to be dramatically terminated. As with the campaigns of Julius Caesar against the Gauls, some 500 years earlier, the invader had to make it clear that any centre of population that did not immediately capitulate could expect no mercy. The unfortunate inhabitants of *Andredescester* were not spared and, as a consequence, the role of the fortress in the politics of the south-east was forever silenced.

CISSECEASTER

What role did *Noviomagus,* the market town of the Regini play in all this? As the administrative centre and the major focus of Romano-British population in the area, one might expect the town to have played a prominent role in the early years of Saxon colonisation. In fact we hear nothing about the city in any of the surviving literary sources (which, to be fair, are rather scanty) whilst the archaeological detail provides little on which to generate theories. This could mean that the town had been largely abandoned and therefore did not play a significant part in the politics of the fifth century. Alternatively, *Noviomagus* may have performed a vital and important part, its relative strength in opposition to the Germanic newcomers ensuring that it was effectively written out of the later *Anglo-Saxon Chronicles*, the entries of which preferred to document English successes.

Archaeologically speaking there is little to guide us, excavations conducted across the city of *Noviomagus* throughout the twentieth century providing few clues as to what happened behind the security of the walls in the fifth, sixth or even seventh century. Coins, our best source of dating evidence, do not appear to have reached the town in any great number before the end of the fourth century and a dark layer of organic silt, interpreted as the product of decaying buildings and unchecked vegetational growth, begins to develop thereafter (Down 1988, 101-2).

Perhaps archaeologists have simply overlooked evidence for sub- or post-Roman activity, which may have left a less significant a footprint than the substantial structures of the first and second century AD. Given the quality and quantity of excavation conducted within Chichester since the late 1950s by Alec Down and others, this may, however, seem somewhat unlikely. Perhaps later activity in the medieval period and after, when Chichester once again became important, has erased all traces of post-Roman occupation. Perhaps excavations have simply been in the wrong parts of town, for the focus of fifth- and sixth-century settlement could have shifted to those areas as yet largely untouched by archaeological investigation (such as the Cathedral and Bishop's palace in the south-eastern quadrant of the city). It is of course possible, as already noted, that *Noviomagus* was abandoned by its inhabitants, following the disintegration of the governmental system that had created it back in the first century AD. If this had occurred, we may have expected the population to have moved either to places with better forms of protection, or to those areas more connected to patterns of fifth- and sixth-century trade and exchange.

One possible clue as to what happened to the city and of its status in the eyes of both Briton and Saxon may be found the modern name of 'Chichester'. The earliest variant of this name first appears in the *Anglo-Saxon Chronicle* in the entry for AD 895. In that year a marauding Danish army, having previously attacked *Exanceaster* (Exeter) 'went up plundering in *Sud-Seaxum* at *Cisseceaster*; but the townsmen put them to flight, and slew many hundreds of them, and took some of their ships'. In 1086, the Domesday Book, the great land survey commissioned by William the Bastard, noted that the town was by then called *Cicestre*.

The name 'Chichester' itself is unusual for, whilst it possesses the standard ceaster element derived from the Latin term *castrum*, meaning fort (and found in a number of towns with a Roman origin such as Winchester, Silchester, Cirencester and Gloucester), the first element ''Cisse' appears to have no parallel. Other Roman cities derived their modern name from the combination of the word *Castrum* with an abbreviated form of the original Latin name. Hence *Venta Belgarum* became *Venta-castrum* or Winchester, *Durnovaria Durotrigum* became Durnovaria-castrum or Dorchester and *Calleva Atrebatum* became Calleva-castrum or Silchester (Millett 1990, 222). Most towns seem to have discarded their tribal affiliation, presumably because by the fifth century such terms no longer possessed any meaning. By the end of Roman rule, towns were probably acting more independently as the focal point of separate states or petty kingdoms. Each town would have had their own leaders, their own territory, their own frame of reference and their own distinctive agenda. Set in this context it is interesting that *Noviomagus Regnensium* did not, as one would expect, mutate into *Noviomagus-castrum*, *Nov-ceaster*, *Magus-Ceaster* or even *Noviomagus-ceaster* but, crucially, *Cisse-ceaster*.

Cisseceaster is usually translated as Cissa's *Castrum / Castra* or 'the fortress of Cissa'. As Cissa is specifically cited in the *Anglo-Saxon Chronicle* as being a son of the Saxon warlord Aelle, this in turn would imply that the town had at some point become a Germanic stronghold. Unfortunately the archaeological record has to date produced no evidence of an early Saxon presence in Chichester. Perhaps the nomenclature may indicate wishful thinking on behalf of Cissa who 'claimed suzerainty over the town' (Down 1988 106), even if that may not have been formally acknowledged by any of its inhabitants.

It is possible, of course, that we have been looking at the problem from the wrong angle. It has already been noted that the *Anglo-Saxon Chronicle* was created in the ninth century by a Saxon hierarchy determined to establish a credible and unified identity in the face of Danish incursions. Genealogies were fabricated and dynasties legitimised through the judicious rewriting of history. As part of this process a number of mythical characters were created, presumably to give credence to specific geographical names. James Graham Cambell, writing in 1982, noted that on at least nine separate occasions, the *Anglo-Saxon Chronicle* provides a place name that is directly associated 'with that of one of the *dramatis personae*' (Cambell 1982, 26). Hence the entry for AD 501 notes:

> This year Port and his two sons, Beda and Mela, came into Britain, with two ships, at a place called Portsmouth. They soon landed, and slew on the spot a young Briton of very high rank;

whilst in 514 they:

> came the West-Saxons into Britain, with three ships, at the place that is called Cerdicsore and Stuff and Wihtgar fought with the Britons, and put them to flight.

In the context of the *Anglo-Saxon Chronicle*, it would appear that Port and Wihtgar have been generated in order to explain the names Portsmouth (ultimately derived from the Latin term *Portus*) and the Isle of Wight (which evolved from the Roman name *Vectis*). In a similar vein, two of Aelle's sons, Cymen, Wlencing could be artificial creations deduced from the Sussex place names *Cymensora* (where Aelle first landed) and Lancing (Myres 1986, 137). Such observations naturally create concern over the name Cissa, which should perhaps also be viewed in the same suspicious light as Cymen and Wlencing. Hence, rather than assuming that Chichester was named *after* Aelle's third son (as the *Anglo-Saxon Chronicle* would like to have us believe), it would perhaps be more prudent to believe that 'Cissa' was wholly fabricated from an existing name for the West Sussex town.

This is all well and good, but does it leave us any closer to understanding the real origin of the name Cisse-ceaster? Is it possible to know whether the Cisse element was a name given to the town by its (non-Saxon) inhabitants and, if so, was it a personal name, a tribal affiliation or a geographical term?

A possible solution may lie in the terms of ethnic reference used by both Saxons and Britons. To the Saxons, the indigenous population they encountered in Britain were 'Welsh' (*wylisc* or *wealh* in Old English), an all encompassing term meaning 'foreigners'. Hence when the *Anglo-Saxon Chronicle* records the landing of Aelle at *Cymensora* in Sussex in 477, it is the 'Welsh' that he drives into the Weald. The Britons, perhaps understandably, did not view themselves as foreign and preferred the term *combrogi* (Morris 1973, 41-3). *Combrogi* may be loosely translated as 'us', 'fellow-countrymen' or simply 'the people' and it has survived in the modern names Cymru (Wales) and Cumbria. In Latin the equivalent word is *cives*, a term that the sixth-century historian Gildas regularly uses to describe his countrymen and distinguish them from the barbaric Saxons. Is it stretching credulity too far to suggest that the origin of *Cisseceaster* lies in such a term? Did *Noviomagus Regnensium*, the 'New Market town of the People of the Kingdom' evolve into *Cives Castrum*, the 'Fortress of Fellow Countrymen'? We may never know for certain, though it is worth pointing out that this solution is just as credible as any theory that the modern name was derived from the mythical son of the first Saxon king of Sussex.

DE–ROMANISATION

Within this period of uncertainty and change, one thing is abundantly clear: Romano-British culture did not survive. In Britannia, Rome's most northerly province, it is apparent that 'to an extent unparalleled elsewhere, the indigenous people failed to transmit the ways of the ancient world to the people who came to settle on their soil.' (Moorhead 2001, 124)

This can be taken as evidence of the relative success of 'barbarism' over 'civilisation', but the archaeological evidence seems to favour a more subtle reason to explain the failure of Mediterranean culture to have any lasting impact upon the British Isles. In part, the disappearance of *Romanitas* in Britain was due to the fact that the Germanic peoples settling in Kent, Sussex and beyond in the later half of the fifth century had not been greatly exposed to the systems of empire and were probably less likely to be infected by them. Perhaps more importantly, certain elements within British society seem to have felt no compunction to live as Romans and had been establishing their own distinctive form of culture before the first Saxons appeared on the scene. The collapse of Roman life and the arrival of the Saxons, Picts and Scots was not a simple example of cause and effect.

The process of de-Romanisation is apparent at all levels of British society from as early as the early third century AD. It can be detected in the decline, alteration and gradual disappearance of key aspects of Roman life. Throughout the third and fourth centuries AD there were fewer trade items originating from the Mediterranean entering Britain and more products generated from within Britain's Gallic and Germanic neighbours. Towards the end of the fourth century, town life (as opposed to 'life in towns') decreased in significance and rich rural estates imploded. Roman art forms (sculpture, wall painting, mosaics) lost their popularity, coin supply and use came to an end and monumental buildings of stone were no longer considered essential. It may be that Roman fashion was outdated, conservative and seen to be the preserve of the unpopular business magnate, tax collector or imperial official; the type of person that the British elite later rallied against (in the great revolt of AD 409).

By the fourth and fifth centuries AD we can see the populations of the eastern seaboard of Britain becoming gradually more 'Germanised' in that more objects of Germanic and Scandinavian origin appear in settlements and cemeteries and new forms of Germanic religion, building and burial appear. A whole new way of speaking, thinking and conceptualising the landscape developed. The western seaboard of Britain, an area largely unaffected by migration from or trade with the Germanic world, became more 'Celtic' in outlook, presumably through contact with Ireland and north-western France. More Celtic-style artefacts appeared in settlements and cemeteries whilst Christianity survived and the Celtic language flourished.

GERMANISATION

As the fifth century progressed, a series of new and distinctive burial types appeared at sites such as at Alfriston, Bishopstone and Selmeston, located between the rivers Ouse and Cuckmere in East Sussex, and at Highdown, on the margins of Worthing in the West. The primary rite at all these sites was inhumation, but the range and nature of artefactual associations is unlike much of what went before.

At Alfriston, a cemetery dating from the mid-fifth to the early seventh century was investigated between 1912 and 1913 (Welch 1983, 188). Status amongst the male burials appears to have been through association with weapons, the most prestigious deposits possessing an axe or, on occasion, a sword. Lower-status burials were accompanied by spears, shields or knives (Welch 1983, 188-211). Female graves contained a diverse range of status indicators including distinctively Germanic brooches, necklaces and dress pins.

At Highdown the picture is broadly similar, though there is a greater range of exotica included with the inhumation deposits. One of the burials, recorded as 'grave 82' contained a New Forrest Ware Beaker belonging to the early half of the fourth century, something which could indicate the resting place of a Romanised Britain rather than a Germanic settler (Welch 1983, 215). Other intriguing discoveries from Highdown include an ornate glass goblet, probably manufactured in the eastern Mediterranean (Egypt or Syria) in or around AD 400, which was recovered from grave 49 (*colour plate 26*). The vessel depicts a lively hunting scene, in which a hound pursues two hares, and a Greek inscription which may be interpreted as 'use me and good health to you' (Welch 1983). Late Roman glassware was also found within graves 32 and 79, in the form of a series of cone beakers, at least one of which might also be of possible Egyptian manufacture.

It is difficult to see whether the graves containing Roman glassware and pottery at Highdown were those of the Late Romano-British population who were steadily becoming Germanised, or the burials of Germanic settlers adopting the status indicators of their Romano-British predecessors. If the people buried here were Germanic migrants, then the artefacts in question could plausibly be interpreted as either loot taken by force from a rural estate or perhaps as part payment for military (mercenary) service from the grateful indigenous population. The problem lies with the inescapable fact that ethnic origin is something which, at present, is impossible to determine with any certainty from skeletal remains. Culturally, we must conclude that certain graves recorded from Highdown were Roman, whilst others demonstrated more Germanic affiliations. Perhaps, more than anything else, the Highdown cemetery serves to demonstrate the cultural melting pot that was fifth-century Sussex.

Similar problems with regard to the interpretation of ethnicity and understanding cultural affiliation surround the so-called Patching hoard (*colour plates 27* and *28*), which comprised 23 gold coins, 25 silver coins (or fragments), 2 gold rings and over 50 small pieces of silver bullion. It is not known whether the find was an isolated deposit or had originally been associated with other finds or features (although none were found in a later trial excavation of the site: White *et al.* 1999). The coins span an overall period of 137 years, from AD 337 (Constans I) to AD 465 (Libius Severus), although the bulk were minted between AD 367 (Gratian) and 455 (Valentinian III). Together they represent the last identifiably Roman piece of archaeology yet recovered from Sussex (if not the whole of Britain); but what did it all mean?

The main obstacle to understanding the full significance of the Patching find is the nature of the material itself. The problems that bedevil a study of Romano-British hoards have recently been summarised by Richard Reece:

> There are two ways of looking at hoards ... and they can be summed up as with excitement or depression. In the first case there is expectation, and the certainty that here is something out of the ordinary! This is the exclamation made by people who look at a hoard in admiration for a few minutes and then go on to the next sensation. The second way evokes more of a groan; here is yet another group of coins which demand a large amount of hard and not very exciting work in order to make a record of them, and here is another chance for fantasies to be weaved and wrong-headed prejudices to be given yet another airing. This is the exclamation often made by people whose job it is to examine and record hoards. (Reece 2002, 67)

The trouble is that a coin hoard buried in antiquity and found 'out of context' or without recorded associations, ultimately has no archaeological value, for it tells us nothing as to why it was buried in the first place, nor why the person who buried it never returned to claim their prize (Reece 1988, 55). It is tempting to link the discovery of buried Late Roman coins with the political and social upheavals of the fifth century AD, for one only has to go to the *Anglo-Saxon Chronicle* to note:

In 418 the Romans collected all the gold-hoards there were in Britain; some they hid in the earth, so that no man might find them, and some they took with them to Gaul.

Could this be a reference to the panic burial of personal wealth by the Romano-British elite in the face of overwhelming barbarian advance? Possibly, possibly not. Whether comments made in the ninth-century *Anglo-Saxon Chronicle* can be stretched to fit the archaeological discoveries of Late Roman Britain, is a matter for debate. We know nothing about the circumstances surrounding the deposition of the Patching hoard at some time in the latter half of the fifth-century AD. It could easily represent the last collection of Roman coins (a soldier's wage or official's pay) buried for safekeeping, a stash of valuables looted from a villa estate in Gaul by a Saxon warrior, payment by the people of *Noviomagus* to a group of Germanic mercenaries, a bribe or 'payoff' made to a raiding party or an offering made to the local gods. Anything is possible and nothing is proven. All we can realistically say is that, for whatever reason, the owner of the coins never came back to retrieve them. The chief interest in the find lies in its exceptionally late date (for Britain anyway), the *terminus post quem*, the date after which it must have been deposited, being in the later AD 460s. Somehow, and by some unknown means (official or otherwise) a series of imperial coins appeared in Sussex and were buried, half a century after Britain had ceased to be a functioning part of the Roman empire.

Cemeteries and hoards are dramatic archaeological finds in their own right, human burials supplying useful information on the size and relative health of past populations, but the contemporary settlements provide better information on the structure of society. At Bishopstone, in East Sussex, some 22 buildings, only part of a small village or hamlet occupied from the late fifth century, was investigated in the 1970s (Bell 1977). Here, the most distinctively Germanic structure was the Sunken Feature Building or *Grubenhauser*. As the name implies, a Sunken Feature Building (or SFB) comprised a small, roughly square or oval timber and thatch hut built over a floor set below ground level. When SFBs were first examined during the early half of the twentieth century, they confirmed archaeologists' suspicions that their Anglo-Saxon forebears had grubbed around in dank, semi-waterlogged holes in the ground.

More detailed (not to say enlightened) examination of SFB structures has indicated that the *Grubenhauser* may well have been used more specifically for a range of craft activities (such as weaving) rather than forming basic domestic accommodation (Gardiner 1988, 267-70). SFBs were seldom built in isolation, the Bishopstone examples were associated with a series of more 'regular' post-built structures, interpreted as halls (Bell 1977). Rectangular in shape, these timber halls possessed entrances set in the middle of both of the longer walls, though their full original height and nature of internal partitioning, remains unknown.

The first Germanic settlers on the Sussex coast arrived to find a landscape of fields which 'were either still being cultivated by the Sub Roman population or had very recently been abandoned' (Gardiner 1988, 287). Unlike the Iron Age to Romano-British transition, evidence of continuity in settlement and agricultural practice from the Roman to Early Saxon period is either rare or difficult to interpret. Part of the problem is that the Germanic attitude towards agricultural production is largely unknown. Some fields would almost certainly have gone out of use, for the demands on food production imposed on Britain by the Roman State in order to feed its military and civil population had been immense. In contrast, the local food demands of a post-Roman or Germanic population would probably have reduced pressure on the land significantly. Whether the basic rural population of Sussex remained unaltered, exchanging Romano-British masters for a largely Germanic aristocracy is, in the absence of useful data, unknown.

It is possible that, for the bulk of the population living in Sussex during the fifth century AD, after the arrival of Aelle and his followers, the basic rhythms of life would have continued much as before. Fields were ploughed, crops grown, children and livestock reared whilst progressively more Germanic customs, belief systems, words and names were gradually adopted. Only for the ruling elite of Late and post-Roman society, would the arrival of the Saxon warbands have caused major turmoil. For the surviving descendants of Tiberius Claudius Togidubnus and Gaius Sallustius Lucullus, if they were still around, the choice would have been relatively simple: resist (and possibly die on the battlefield), migrate westwards (out of harm's way) or to stay put and modify their outlook and allegiance so as to find a place in the new order. Whatever choices the remnants of the British ruling elite made, it was clear that, by the end of the fifth century AD, the land bordering the coast of central south-east Britain belonged to the Saxons.

GAZETTEER

What follows is a short listing of the visible Roman remains in Sussex. Grid references, directions and access details are provided. ★ indicates good preservation. ★★ indicates excellent preservation. There are also, in addition, a good range of museums displaying Late Prehistoric to Early Saxon material, the best being in Lewes (Barbican House), Chichester (Little London and Guildhall Museum, Priory Park), Arundel, Horsham, Eastbourne, Hastings, Worthing, Battle and Littlehampton. Excellent 'on-site' museums exist at Bignor Roman villa and at Fishbourne. At the time of writing, the Museum at Fishbourne is undergoing re-development and it is hoped that the entire reserve collection of Chichester Museum will soon be on display there. Brighton Museum, which used to house one of the best archaeological collections in the county (if not the country), has for many years been closed. It is hoped that soon the archive will find a permanent home, possibly in Hove.

ALFOLDEAN
(TQ 117330)
The line of Stane Street, the Roman road that in its final incarnation linked Chichester with London, is still closely followed by large sections of the A29 north from Billingshurst. At Alfoldean, the modern road bisects the slight earthwork remains of an enclosed *mansio*. There is a lay-by placed to the south of the modern bridge and roundabout, from which the nature of both the road and its surroundings may be appreciated, but be careful, this is a notoriously dangerous stretch of road and the low bank of the *mansio* is on private land. Private. No access.

BEAUPORT PARK
(TQ 786140)
Closed at the time of writing and about to be backfilled, the *Classis Britannica* bathhouse at Beauport Park is worth mentioning due to sheer quality of preservation (with walls surviving up to 2.2m in height). Sadly hopes to erect a cover building and museum have proved unsuccessful and there are no immediate plans to reopen the site.

**BIGNOR
(SU 988146)

The villa at Bignor is best reached from the A29, between Arundel and Pulborough, where it is well signposted. A minor road from Bury leads through the picturesque hamlet of Bignor to the gates of the villa estate, where there is a car park. A series of nineteenth-century thatched cottages cover the main mosaics, which include the stunning Venus and Cupids, Ganymede, Medusa and Winter floors. The north corridor has one of the longest mosaics preserved in Britain. The rest of the villa beyond the cover buildings is marked out in the grass. There is a small, but well-stocked shop, a museum and a café. Privately owned. Open From March to October. There is a small admission charge.

*BIGNOR HILL
(SU 970128)

Just to the west of the Bignor villa entrance (signposted from the A29 from Bury), a minor road diverts off up onto the Downs. There is a small (and discrete) National Trust parking area at the top of Bignor Hill. To the south-east, a wooden sign points the line of Stane Street north-east to London and south-west to Chichester. From the crest of Bignor Hill running south towards Eartham, the line of Stane Street is impressively preserved as a raised *agger* with flanking ditches just visible in the undergrowth. National Trust. Open Access.

BOSHAM
(SU 803039)

Holy Trinity church in Bosham is worth seeing for the majesty of its Anglo-Saxon architecture, historical associations (the church is depicted in the Bayeux Tapestry) and setting by Chichester Harbour. Claims have been made that the west wall of the nave is predominantly Roman, with herringbone setting of stones and brick bonding course. As yet, this is unproven. The 'Roman arch base' preserved beneath the chancel would appear to be Saxon.

CAMP HILL
(TQ 471290)

A small but still impressive section of the London to Lewes Roman road is visible on Camp Hill in the Ashdown Forest north of Uckfield. The raised *agger* is visible as an earthwork on the western side of the B2026, just south of its junction with the B2188, next to a small (and often packed) car park.

CHANCTONBURY RING
(TQ 139120)

Whilst there is absolutely nothing to see of the two Romano-Celtic temples that once stood on the top of Chanctonbury, the earth rampart of the Later Bronze Age enclosure, which may have acted as the *temenos* or precinct wall, survives, and the view across the Weald is simply breathtaking. The South Downs Way footpath runs next to the site. There is a small car park at the foot of the Downs to the north, accessed via a minor road from the A283 between Steyning and Washington. Expect a long walk.

★CHICHESTER
(SU 860047)

Chichester is quite simply one of the finest towns in Britain, but unfortunately little of Roman *Noviomagus* is visible beneath the Georgian and medieval street plan. At the time of writing, there are ambitious plans to excavate and display the Roman baths within a new museum complex, which should then form the centrepiece of any visit. The present museum, at 29 Little London, is small but well worth a visit. Finds on display include the monumental stone head of Nero. The museum is open all year round (except Mondays). Entrance is free. Other pieces of the Roman town, including the Jupiter stone, are on display in the Guildhall Museum in Priory Park. Open March – September. Entrance is free.

In the portico of the Assembly Rooms in North Street, to the north of the market cross, the famous Togidubnus inscription recording a temple to Neptune and Minerva is preserved. A small fragment of geometric mosaic is on display beneath the floor of the south aisle in the cathedral. A fragment of tessellated floor and assorted architectural stone may be seen in the main entrance to the Little London car park, leading off from Little London Mews. The amphitheatre survives as a low oval bank and shallow depression, to the south of Whyke Lane. A modern path (open access) runs next to a children's play area, neatly bisecting the site.

The city walls are worth inspecting, especially now that the entire circuit (even where the wall itself has vanished) may be explored via the 'Chichester Walls Walk'. The walk is well signposted and is best started from the former area of the North Gate, where pedestrianised shopping ends and the A286, A259 and B2178 coincide, travelling in a clockwise direction through Priory Park. Though the earth rampart behind the wall is in reasonable shape, very little evidence of Roman stone may be seen, but a good idea of the size and scale of Roman Chichester may be gained by walking the perimeter. To the south of the Bishop's palace, two bastions, on the line of the Roman originals, are preserved in the south-western circuit. These may be viewed at all reasonable hours.

★CHICHESTER DYKES
(SU 841067)

The Late Iron Age ramparts that form the Chichester Dykes or Entrenchments are well preserved in places, but difficult to access. The best and most visible segment of the earthworks can be seen in Brandy Hole Copse, on the northern fringes of Chichester. Parking immediately next to the Copse is not advisable, although a lay-by for Public

Parking exists off the B2178 to the west. The entrenchments can be examined as they run through the copse and in the woodland to the south and west. Local Nature Reserve. Open Access.

**FISHBOURNE
(SU 841047)
The remains of Fishbourne palace, which constitute one of the most important Roman sites in Britain, are well signposted from the A27 to the south-west of Chichester. An excellent cover building and museum has existed on site since the late 1960s and, at the time of writing, is undergoing major refurbishment, redisplay and repair. Mosaics on display include the world famous Boy on a Dolphin and the black and white geometric floors of the north wing, the earliest Roman decorated floors visible in Britain. Finds include decorative wall plaster, the stone portrait of a young Nero and the Catuarus ring. Parts of the east wing are marked out in the grass. The gardens are partially recreated and there is a small garden museum. There is well-stocked souvenir and bookshop, education centre and café. Sussex Archaeological Society. Open all year round with restricted hours December to February. There is an admission charge.

HARDHAM
(TQ 030175)
The slight earthwork remains of an enclosed *mansio*, badly mutilated by a railway cutting, lie to the west of the modern A29, Arundel to Pulborough road, on the original line of Stane Street. Parking is possible in Hardham. Whilst the site is on private land, a public footpath bisects the site.

HOLTYE
(TQ 460380)
A disappointing section of road surface, metalled with cinder and iron slag, first exposed in 1939 and now very overgrown, may be found via a public footpath leading from the A264 Tunbridge Wells to East Grinstead road, 90m east of the White Horse Inn.

**PEVENSEY
(TQ 644048)
One of the best-preserved and most impressive Roman fortresses in northern Europe. The site lies to the north-east of Eastbourne. The A27/A259 Polegate to Bexhill road passes to the north. Most of the northern circuit is standing, although the southern has fallen in places. Ten bastions, one preserved up to window level, a postern gate and the spectacular west gate are visible today. The evocative remains of an important medieval castle sit in the south-eastern quadrant. The site is owned and maintained by English Heritage. The Roman walls may be viewed at any time. There is a small admission charge, with more restricted hours, to view the castle. There is a car park to the east of the castle, in the village of Pevensey.

THUNDERSBARROW HILL
(TQ 229084)

The low ramparts of a Late Bronze Age/Early Iron Age enclosure may be seen, especially to the west of a footpath running from Southwick Hill in the south that bisects the site. An extensive area of Romano-British settlement lies on the eastern slopes of the hill on private land, surrounded by a series of low field banks and lynchets. The site is best appreciated in low sunlight when the earthworks appear more pronounced.

WESTHAMPNETT
(SU 900069)

Large pieces of Roman box flue and hypocaust tile are built into the outer, south-facing chancel wall of St Peter's church at Westhampnett, to the east of Chichester. It is not known whether these pieces derived from a site in Chichester itself or from Fishbourne palace or perhaps even from an unknown villa in the immediate vicinity.

GLOSSARY

Adit	A horizontal mine shaft
Agger	A cambered embankment carrying a road
Ambulatory	Covered portico surrounding the inner shrine of a temple
Amphorae	Large pottery storage vessels, often contained wine, oil and *garum*
Apodyterium	The changing room in a bathhouse
Arkarius	A treasurer
Atriarius	A porter
Ballista	A Roman torsion-powered crossbow-like catapult
Balneum	A bathhouse that was smaller and less luxurious than the heated *thermae*
Barbaricum	The lands beyond Roman imperial frontiers
Basilica	A covered hall in a town designed for administrative and judicial purposes
Berm	A flat area between a ditch and rampart
Bonding course	A layer of brick, tile or stone running through the thickness of a wall
Box flue	A hollow, box-shaped tile built into the wall of a room heated by a hypocaust so that hot air may pass out of the building
Bretwalda	Lord of Britain. A Saxon title that conferred ultimate power over all the English peoples south of the river Humber
Briquetage	Clay vessels used in salt manufacture
Caldarium	The hottest room in a bathhouse
Calida piscina	A heated pool in a bathhouse
Cantharus	A decorative, handled vase appearing in mosaics
Cella	Central shrine within a temple
Censitores	Magistrates responsible for maintaining the census and certain aspects of finance

Chi-rho	A secret Christian symbol comprising the first two letters of the word 'Christ' in Greek
Civitas	A town based loosely on a pre-existing Celtic tribal territory. An independent administrative centre governed under the supervision of the Roman provincial administration
Classis Anderetianorum	A naval unit stationed at Pevensey but later moved to Paris
Classis Britannica	The British Fleet. Heavily involved in the production and transportation of Wealden iron
Client Kings	Iron Age leader owing their position to Rome
Collegii	A limited company
Colonia	A settlement of retired military personnel, who received an allotment of land on discharge from the Roman army
Colossus Neroni	An immense statue depicting Nero as the sun god Sol, which stood in the great atrium of the *Domus Aurea* in Rome
Conductores	Officers assisting or working for the provincial *procurator*
Dado	A painted plaster border around the lower part of a wall
Damnatio memoriae	Damnation of memory. Official Roman condemnation of a person resulting in the destruction or obliteration of the person's name and image
Dea Nutrix	Nursing mother goddess
Deae Matres	The trinity of mother goddesses who ruled fertility and creativity
Decurion	A member of the *civitas* council (*ordo*) who looked after affairs within the local region
Denarius	Silver Roman republican coin
Dendrochronology	Dating large samples of wood by matching the pattern of annual rings to a dated reference sequence; the final ring provides a *terminus post quem* for the cutting of the tree and for any structure or artefact made from its wood
Domus Aurea	The 'Golden House' of the emperor Nero in Rome
Domus Flavia	The palatial home of the emperor Domitian in Rome
Duoviri aediles	A pair of magistrates annually elected from their number to deal with buildings and finance
Duoviri iuridicundo	A pair of magistrates annually elected from their number to hear all petty legal cases
Exedrae	Relaxation rooms in a bathhouse
Forum	Open courtyard in front of a basilica designed as the prestige economic heart of a town
Frigidarium	Coldest room in a bathhouse, usually with a cold immersion pool
Garum	Pungent fish sauce

GLOSSARY

Gladius	Roman sword, often refers to military double bladed short sword
Guilloche	A decorative, intertwining band in a mosaic
Herringbone	A type of construction with the stone or brick laid in zig-zags
Hippodromos	A race course
Hypocaust	Roman method of underfloor heating whereby the floor is raised on *pilae* enabling hot air to pass underneath
Hypocauston	A small room with a furnace which has the function of indirectly heating rooms adjacent to them
Imbrex	A semi-circular roof tile linking two flat roof tiles (*tegulae*)
In situ	Something found in its original position
Insula	A block of buildings in a town bordered by streets on all sides
Laconium	A room of intense dry heat in a bathhouse
Lararium	Household shrine
Latrine	A lavatory or toilet
Legatus Augusti pro praetore	Provincial governor, imperial legate with authority of *praetor*
Ligatured	Where two letters in an inscription or mosaic are joined together to save space or in order to correct a mistake
Lintel	A horizontal slab or beam above a door
Litus Saxonicum	The Saxon Shore
Mansio	Inn or guesthouse used especially by government officials
Matres Domesticae	Mother goddess of the home
Medianum	A suite of rooms accessed directly from a hallway
Milites Anderetianorum	A military unit stationed at Pevensey but later moved to Mainz
Mosaic	Floor composed of coloured *tesserae*
Municipium	A chartered town of elevated status with a mix of Roman and native laws, Magistrates of which became Roman citizens upon their retirement
Natatio	An open-air pool
Notitia Dignitatum	A set of military dispositions originally compiled in the late fourth or early fifth century AD
Numen	Spirit of the Emperor, worshipped at the Imperial Cult Centre
Numeri Abulcorum	The last official garrison of Pevensey according to the *Notitia Dignitatum*
Numerus Turnacensium	The garrison of Lympne as recorded in the *Notitia Dignitatum*
Onager	Wheel-mounted siege engine with ammunition ejected from an arm powered by twisted ropes

Oppidum(a)	Large Late Iron Age settlement with some town-like qualities, often highly defended
Opus sectile	A floor composed of large pieces of cut stone
Opus signinum	Waterproof pink mortar
Ordo	A council in charge of administration within the *civitas* made up of about 100 *decurions*, who were wealthy local landowners.
Palaestra	An exercise yard in a bathhouse
Pediment	A triangular gabled end of a temple roof
Pharos	A lighthouse
Pilae	Pillars of stone (or brick) supporting the floor above a hypocaust
Pilaster	A column partially incorporated in a wall
Pilum	A military spear
Piscina	Public swimming bath
Plinth	Projecting masonry at the foot of a wall
Podium	Raised platform on which a temple is constructed
Polis	City state (Greek)
Portal	A door or entrance way
Portico	A roofed space, open or partly enclosed, forming the entrance of the façade of a temple or house
Postern	Minor gate in the wall of a fort
Praefurnium	A furnace room
Praetor	Senior Roman magistrate, commanded minor military forces during the Republic
Precinct	Enclosed area
Princeps	First Citizen (official title of a Roman emperor, first used by Augustus 23 BC)
Principia	Headquarters building in a fort
Proconsul	Acting consul or official having consular rank
Procurator	Financial administrator in the provincial government
Propraetorean legatus	Most senior ranking official within a province
Putlog hole	Square hole in a wall designed to hold scaffolding during construction
Quaestores	A magistrate who was primarily a government official in charge of financial administration
Retiarius	Gladiator armed with a net and a trident
Rex	The Roman word for 'king'
Romanitas	Being Roman, Romanisation
Rudarius	Gladitorial umpire
Saltire	An equal-armed cross in a mosaic
Samian	High quality red-slip pottery

GLOSSARY

Sarcophagus	A lead or stone coffin
Secutor	Gladiator armed with a shield, sword and helmet
Socii Lutudarenos	A private company operating in the Peak District
Stibadium	A curved dining couch
Stucco	Plaster
Stylobate	The masonry at ground level on which a column rests
Sudatorium	A room of dry heat in a bathhouse
Tegula	A flat roof tile with raised edges
Temenos	Sacred precinct around a temple
Templum	Temple
Tepidarium	A warm room in a bathhouse
Terminus ante quem	A solid, datable layer (such as a floor) which provides a date earlier than itself for all layers below it
Terminus post quem	A datable object providing the date on or after which the layer of soil that contains it was deposited
Tessellated floor	An undecorated floor composed of plain *tesserae*
Tesserae	Small cubes of coloured stone used to form a mosaic
Therma	A large and luxurious bathhouse
Thermoluminescence dating	A dating technique recently applied to archaeology. It is based on the principle that almost all natural minerals are thermoluminescent. Energy absorbed from ionising radiation frees electrons to move through the crystal lattice and some are trapped at imperfections. Later heating releases the trapped electrons, producing light
Triclinium	A dining room
Vicus	Civilian settlement outside a fort
Vilicus	A foreman
Voussoir	A thick, wedge-shaped stone forming part of an arch

APPENDIX 1

ROMAN EMPERORS OF THE FIRST CENTURY AD

JULIO–CLAUDIAN DYNASTY

Reign	Common name	Personal name	Imperial name
27 BC–AD 14	Augustus	GAIVS OCTAVIANVS	CAESAR AVGVSTVS
14–37	Tiberius	TIBERIVS CLAVDIVS NERO	TIBERIVS CAESAR AVGVSTVS
37–41	Caligula	GAIVS IVLIVS CAESAR GERMANICVS	GAIVS CAESAR AVGVSTVS GERMANICVS
41–54	Claudius	TIBERIVS CLAVDIVS DRVSVS	TIBERIVS CLAVDIVS CAESAR AVGVSTVS GERMANICVS
54–68	Nero	LVCIVS DOMITIVS AHENOBARBVS	NERO CLAVDIVS CAESAR DRVSVS GERMANICVS

YEAR OF THE FOUR EMPERORS AD 69

Reign	Common name	Personal name	Imperial name
68–69	Galba	SERVIVS SVLPICIVS GALBA	SERVIVS GALBA CAESAR AVGVSTVS
69	Otho	MARCVS SALVIVS OTHO	MARCVS OTHO CAESAR AVGVSTVS
69	Vitellius	AVLVS VITELLIVS	AVLVS VITELLIVS GERMANICVS AVGVSTVS

FLAVIAN DYNASTY

Reign	Common name	Personal name	Imperial name
69–79	Vespasian	TITVS FLAVIVS VESPASIANVS	VESPASIANVS CAESAR AVGVSTVS
79–81	Titus	TITVS FLAVIVS VESPASIANVS	TITVS CAESAR VESPASIANVS AVGVSTVS
81–96	Domitian	TITVS FLAVIVS DOMITIANVS	CAESAR DOMITIANVS AVGVSTVS

APPENDIX 2

THE FAMILY TREE OF LUCULLUS

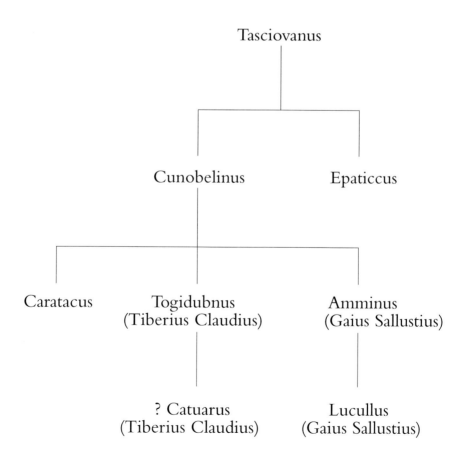

Tasciovanus

Cunobelinus   Epaticcus

Caratacus   Togidubnus   Amminus
              (Tiberius Claudius)   (Gaius Sallustius)

              ? Catuarus   Lucullus
              (Tiberius Claudius)   (Gaius Sallustius)

BIBLIOGRAPHY

Alcock, J. 2006 *Life in Roman Britain*. Stroud: Tempus.

Aldsworth, F. and Rudling, D. 1995 Excavations at Bignor Roman Villa, 1985-1990, *Sussex Archaeological Collections* **133**, 103-188.

Allen, D. 1976 Did Amminius strike coins? *Britannia* **7**, 96-108.

Applebaum, S. 1966 Peasant economy and types of agriculture. *In:* C. Thomas (ed), *Rural Settlement in Roman Britain*. London: Council for British Archaeology. 99-107.

Ashe, G. 2000 *Kings and Queens of Early Britain* (second edition). London: Methuen.

Ball, L. 2003 *The Domus Aurea and the Roman architectural revolution*. Cambridge University Press.

Barber, L. 1994 The excavation of a Romano-British site at Moraunt Drive, Middleton-on-Sea, West Sussex, 1992. *Sussex Archaeological Collections* **132**, 87-100.

Barber, L., Gardiner, M. and Rudling, D. 2002 Excavations at Eastwick Barn. *In:* D. Rudling (ed), *Downland Settlement and Land-use, The Archaeology of the Brighton Bypass,* UCL Field Archaeology Unit Monograph No.1. London: Archetype Publications. 107-40.

Barrett, A. 1979 The career of Tiberius Claudius Cogidubnus, *Britannia* **10** 227-42.

Barrett, A. 1989 *Caligula: the corruption of power*. London: Batsford.

Beckensall, S. 1967 The Excavation of Money Mound. *Sussex Archaeological Collections* **105**, 13-30.

Bedwin, O. 1980 Excavations at Chanctonbury Ring, Wiston, West Sussex 1977, *Britannia* **11**, 173-222.

Bedwin, O. 1981 Excavations at Lancing Down, West Sussex 1980. *Sussex Archaeological Collections* **119**, 37-56.

Bedwin, O. and Holgate, R. 1985 Excavations at Copse Farm, Oving, West Sussex. *Proceedings of the Prehistoric Society* **51**, 215-45.

Bedwin, O. and Place, C. 1995 Late Iron Age and Romano-British occupation at Ounces Barn, Boxgrove, West Sussex; excavations 1982-1983. *Sussex Archaeological Collections* **133**, 45-101.

Bedwin, O. and Orton, C. 1984 The excavation of the eastern terminal of the Devil's Ditch (Chichester Dykes), Boxgrove, West Sussex, 1982. *Sussex Archaeological Collections* **122**, 63-74.

Bell, M. 1976 The Excavation of an early Romano-British site and Pleistocene Land Forms at Newhaven, Sussex, *Sussex Archaeological Collections* **114**, 218-305.

Bell, M. 1977 Excavations at Bishopstone. *Sussex Archaeological Collections* **115**.

Birley, R. 1979 *The People of Roman Britain*. London: Batsford.

Black, E. 1983 The Roman Villa at Bignor in the Fourth Century, *Oxford Journal of Archaeology* **2**, (1), 93-107.

Black, E. 1985 The dating of relief-patterned flue tiles. *Oxford Journal of Archaeology* **4**, 353-76.

Black, E. 1986 Romano-British Burial Customs and religious Beliefs in South East England. *The Archaeological Journal* **14**, 201-39.

Black, E. 1987 *The Roman Villas of South-East England,* British Archaeological Report British Series **171**.

Black, E. 1993 The Period IC bath-building at Fishbourne and the problem of the Proto-palace, *Journal of Roman Archaeology* **6**, 233-237.

Black, E. 1994 Villa-owners: Romano-British Gentlemen and Officers. *Britannia* **25**, 99-110.

Black, E. 1995 Cursus Publicus: the infrastructure of government in Roman Britain. *British Archaeological Research Report* **241**.

Black, E. 1997 Afterthoughts. *In:* R.M. & D.E. Friendship-Taylor (eds), *From Round 'house' to Villa,* Fascicle 3 of the Upper Nene Archaeological Society, 59-61.

Bogaers, J. 1979 King Cogidubnus in Chichester: another reading of *RIB* 91, *Britannia* **10**, 243-54.

Bradley, R. 1989 Chidham: Iron Age and Roman salt production. *The Archaeology of Chichester and District 1989.* Chichester: District Council.

Bradley, R. 1992 Roman Salt Production in Chichester Harbour: Rescue Excavations at Chidham, West Sussex, *Britannia* **23**, 27-44.

Brandon, P. 1978 *The South Saxons*. Chichester: Phillimore.

Brodribb, G. 1979 A Survey of Tile from the Roman Bath House at Beauport Park, Battle, E. Sussex. *Britannia* **10**, 139-56.

Brodribb, G. and Cleere, H. 1988 The *Classis Britannica* Bath-house at Beauport Park, East Sussex. *Britannia* **11**, 217.

Brown, A. (ed) 1995 *Roman Small Towns in Eastern England and Beyond*. Oxbow Monograph **52**.

Burnham, C. 1987 The Morphology of Romano-British 'Small Towns', *Archaeological Journal*. **144**, 156-90.

Burnham, C. 1986 The origins of Romano-British small towns *Oxford Journal of Archaeology* **5**, 185-203.

Burnham, C. and Wacher, J. 1990 *The Small Towns of Roman Britain*. London: Batsford.

Burstow, G. and Holleyman, G. 1956 Excavations at Muntham Court, Findon, interim report 1954-1955, *Sussex Notes And Queries* **14**, 196-8.

Burstow, G. and Holleyman, G. 1957 Excavations at Muntham Court, Findon, Sussex, *The Archaeological News Letter* **6** (4), 101-2.

Burstow, G. and Wilson, A. 1936 Excavation of the ladies golf course, the Dyke, Brighton. *Sussex Archaeological Collections* **77**, 195-201.

Bushe-Fox, J. 1932 Some notes on Roman coast defences. *Journal of Roman Studies* **22**, 60-71.

Butler, C. and Lyne, M. 2001 *The Roman pottery production site at Wickham Barn, Chiltington, East Sussex.* British Archaeology Research Report **323**.

Cambell, J. (ed) 1982 *The Anglo Saxons.* London: Book Club Associates.

Cleere, H. 1970 *The Romano-British industrial site at Bardown, Wadhurst.* Sussex Archaeological Society Occasional Paper 1.

Cleere, H. 1975 The Roman iron industry of the Weald and its connexions with the Classis Britannica. *Archaeological Journal* **131**, 171-99.

Cleere, H. 1978 Roman Sussex – the Weald. *In:* P. Drewett (ed), *Archaeology in Sussex to AD 1500,* Council for British Archaeology Research Report. **29**, 59-63.

Cleere, H. and Crossley, D. 1985 *The Iron Industry of the Weald.* Leicester University Press.

Coates, R. 1991 Anderida: not the Roman name of Pevensey. *Sussex Archaeological Collections* **129**, 250-1.

Collingwood, R. 1929 Town and country in Roman Britain, *Antiquity* **3**, 261-76.

Collingwood, R. and Wright, R. 1965 *The Roman Inscriptions of Britain. 1: Inscriptions on Stone.* Oxford: Clarendon.

Collingwood, R. and Wright, R. 1995 *The Roman Inscriptions of Britain. 1: Inscriptions on Stone* (revised second edition) Oxford: Clarendon.

Creighton, J. 2000. *Coins and Power in the Late Iron Age Britain.* Cambridge University Press.

Creighton, J. 2001 The Iron Age-Roman Transition. *In:* S. James and M. Millett (eds), *Britons and Romans: advancing an archaeological agenda,* Council for British Archaeology Research Report. **125**, 4-11.

Crickmore, J. 1984 *Romano-British urban defences.* British Archaeological Report British Series **126.**

Crummy, P. 1997 *City of Victory: the story of Colchester – Britain's first Roman town.* Colchester: Colchester Archaeological Trust.

Cunliffe, B. 1971 *Excavations at Fishbourne 1961-1969, Vol.* 1: *The Site.* Society of Antiquaries of London Research Reports **26**.

Cunliffe, B. 1971b *Excavations at Fishbourne 1961-1969, Vol.* 11: *The Finds.* Society of Antiquaries of London Research Reports **27**.

Cunliffe, B. 1973 *The Regni.* London: Duckworth.

Cunliffe, B. 1975 *Excavations at Portchester Castle. Volume I: Roman.* Society of Antiquaries of London Research Reports **32**.

Cunliffe, B. 1980 Excavation at the Roman Fort at Lympne, Kent 1976-78. *Britannia* **11**, 227-88.

Cunliffe, B. and Davenport, P. 1985 *The temple of Sulis Minerva at Bath. Vol 1: the site.* Oxford.

Cunliffe, B. 1988 *Greeks, Romans and barbarians: spheres of interaction*. London: Batsford.

Cunliffe, B. 1991. *Iron Age communities in Britain* (third edition.). London: Routledge.

Cunliffe, B. 1998 *Fishbourne Roman palace*. Stroud: Tempus.

Cunliffe, B., Down, A. and Rudkin, D. 1996 *Chichester Excavations 9, Excavations at Fishbourne 1969-1988*, Chichester: District Council.

Curwen, C. 1933 Excavations on Thundersbarrow Hill, Sussex. *Antiquaries Journal* **13**.

Curwen, C. 1943 A Roman lead cistern from Pulborough, Sussex. *Antiquaries Journal* **23**, 155-7.

Dark, K. and Dark, P. 1997 *Landscape of Roman Britain*. Stroud: Sutton.

Davenport, C. 2003 The late Pre-Roman Iron Age of the West Sussex coastal plain: continuity or change? *In*: D. Rudling (ed), *The Archaeology of Sussex to AD 2000*. University of Sussex. 101-10.

Dawson, C. 1903 Sussex ironwork and pottery. *Sussex Archaeological Collections* **46**, 1-62.

Dawson, C. 1907 Note on some inscribed bricks from Pevensey. *Proceedings of the Society of Antiquaries* **21**, 411-13.

de la Bédoyère, G. 1989 *The finds of Roman Britain*. London: Batsford.

de la Bédoyère, G. 1991 *The buildings of Roman Britain*. Stroud: Tempus.

de la Bédoyère, G. 1999 *The Golden Age of Roman Britain*. Stroud: Tempus.

de la Bédoyère, G. 2001 *Eagles over Britannia: the Roman army in Britain*. Stroud: Tempus.

de la Bédoyère, G. 2002 *Gods with thunderbolts: religion in Roman Britain*. Stroud: Tempus.

de la Bédoyère, G. 2003 *Roman towns in Britain*. Stroud: Tempus.

Devenish, D. 1978 Romano-Gaulish figurine from Hastings. *Sussex Archaeological Collections* **116**, 404-5.

Down, A. 1974 *Chichester Excavations 2*. Chichester: District Council.

Down, A 1978 Roman Sussex – Chichester and the Chilgrove Valley. *In:* P.L. Drewett (ed), *Archaeology in Sussex to AD 1500*, Council for British Archaeology Research Report **29**, 52-8.

Down, A. 1978 *Chichester Excavations 3*. Chichester: District Council.

Down, A. 1979 *Chichester Excavations 4. The Roman Villas at Chilgrove and Up Marden*. Chichester: District Council.

Down, A. 1981 *Chichester Excavations 5*. Chichester: District Council.

Down, A. 1988. *Roman Chichester*. Chichester: Phillimore.

Down, A. 1989 *Chichester Excavations 6*. Chichester: District Council.

Down, A. and Magilton, J. 1993 *Chichester Excavations 8*. Chichester: District Council.

Down, A. and Rule, M. 1971 *Chichester Excavations 1*. Chichester: District Council.

Downes, R. 1956 *Charles Dawson on trial: a study in archaeology*. Unpublished manuscript. Sussex Archaeological Society. Lewes.

Drinkwater, J. 1983 *Roman Gaul: the three provinces, 58 BC – AD 260*. London: Croom Helm.

Dudley, C. 1981 A re-appraisal of the evidence for a Roman villa in Springfield Road, Brighton, following further discoveries on the site. *In:* E. Kelly and C. Dudley, Two Romano-British Burials. *Sussex Archaeological Collections* **119**, 65-88.

Esmonde-Cleary, S. 1992 Small towns, past and future, *Britannia* **13**, 341-4.

Esmonde-Cleary, S. 1987 *Extra-Mural Areas of Romano-British Towns*. British Archaeology Report British Series **169.**

Faulkner, N. 2000 *The Decline and Fall of Roman Britain*. Stroud: Tempus.

Finch Smith, R. 1987 *Roadside settlements in lowland Britain*. British Archaeological Report British Series **157.**

Francis, L. 1991 Civilised Britain AD 43 http://www.reshistoriaeantiqua.co.uk

Frere, S. 1982. The Bignor Villa, *Britannia* **13**, 135-95.

Frere, S. 1987. *Britannia: A history of Roman Britain* (third edition). London: Pimlico.

Fulford, M. and Tyres, I. 1995 The date of Pevensey and the defence of an *Imperial Britanniarum. Antiquity* 69, 1009-14.

Gardiner, M. 1988 The Early Anglo-Saxon period, 410-650 AD. *In:* P. Drewett, D. Rudling, and M. Gardiner, *The South East to AD 1000*. London: Longman. 178-245.

Gilkes, O. 1993 Iron Age and Roman Littlehampton. *Sussex Archaeological Collections* **131**, 1-20.

Gilkes, O. 1998 The Roman villa at 'Spes Bona', Lansgstone Avenue, Langstone, Havant. *Proceedings of the Hampshire Field Club & Archaeological Society* **53**.

Gilkes, O. 1999 The bathhouse of Angmering Roman villa. *Sussex Archaeological Collections* **137**, 59-69.

Green, M. 1983 *The gods of Roman Britain*. Aylesbury: Shire.

Green, M. 1986 *The gods of the Celts*. Gloucester: Alan Sutton.

Green, M. (ed) 1995 *The Celtic World*. London: Routledge.

Greep, S. (ed) 1993 *Roman Towns: The Wheeler Inheritance: A Review of 50 Years' Research*, Council for British Archaeology Research Report **93.**

Guy, C. 1981 Roman circular lead tanks in Britain. *Britannia* **12**, 271-6.

Hamilton, S. 1998 Using elderly databases: Iron Age pit deposits at the Caburn, East Sussex and related sites. *Sussex Archaeological Collections* **136**, 23-39.

Hamilton, S. and Gregory, K. 2000 Updating the Sussex Iron Age. *Sussex Archaeological Collections* **138**, 57-74.

Hamilton, S. and Manley, J. 1999 The End of Prehistory *c.*100 BC-AD 43. *In:* K. Leslie and B. Short (eds), *An Historical Atlas of Sussex*. Chichester: Phillimore.

Hartridge, R. 1978 Excavations at the Prehistoric and Romano-British site on Slonk Hill, Shoreham, Sussex. *Sussex Archaeological Collections* **116**, 69-141.

Hathaway, S. 2004 *A study of the salt production in Poole Harbour from 700 BC to AD 450*. Bournemouth University.

Haverfield, F. 1895 Manuscript materials for Romano-British epigraphy. *Archaeologia Oxoniensis* **6**, 15-22.

Hawkes, C. and Hull, M. 1947 *Camulodunum*. Reports of the Research Committee of the Society of Antiquaries of London **14**.

Hawkes, C. and Crummy, P. 1995 *Camulodunum 2*. Colchester Archaeological Report **11**.

Henig, M. 1984 *Religion in Roman Britain*. London: Batsford.

Henig, M. 1998 Togidubnus and the Roman Liberation. *British Archaeology* **37**, 8-9.

Henig, M. 1999 A new star shining over Bath. *Oxford Journal of Archaeology* **18**, 419-25.

Henig, M. 2002 *The Heirs of King Verica, Culture & Politics in Roman Britain*. Stroud: Tempus.

Henig, M. and Nash, D. 1982 Amminus and the kingdom of Verica. *Oxford Journal of Archaeology* **1**, 243-6.

Hill, J. 1995 *Ritual and rubbish in the Iron Age of Wessex*. British Archaeological Report British Series **242** Oxford.

Hind, I. 1989 The invasion of Britain in AD 43 – An Alternative Strategy for Aulus Plautius. *Britannia* **20**, 1-21.

Hodgkinson, J. 1999 Romano-British iron production in the Sussex and Kent Weald: a review of current data. *The Journal of the Historical Metallurgy Society* **33**, (2), 68-72.

Holden, E. and Tebbutt, C. 1983 A Sussex Celtic head re-discovered. *Sussex Archaeological Collections* **121**, 202-3.

Holleyman, G. 1935 Romano-British Site on Wolstonbury Hill. *Sussex Archaeological Collections* **76**, 35-45.

Holmes, J. 1962 The defences of Roman Chichester. *Sussex Archaeological Collections* **100**.

Horsfield, T. 1824 *The History and Antiquities of Lewes and its Vicinity*. Lewes: J.Baxter.

Horsfield, T. 1835 *The History, Antiquities, and Topography of the County of Sussex*. Lewes: J.Baxter.

Ireland, S. 1986 *Roman Britain: a sourcebook*. London: Routledge.

Jackson, K. 1970 Romano-British names in the Antonine itinerary. *Britannia* **1**, 68-82.

Johnson, S. 1976 *The Roman Forts of the Saxon Shore*. London: Paul Elek.

Johnston, D. (ed) 1977 *The Saxon Shore*, Council for British Archaeology Research Report **18**.

Johnston, D. 2004 *Roman villas*. Princes Risborough: Shire.

Jones, B. and Mattingly, D. 1990 *An Atlas of Roman Britain*. Oxford: Blackwells.

Jones, M., Craddock, P. and Barker, N. (eds) 1990 *Fake?: the art of deception*. London: British Museum.

Kelly, E. and Dudley, C. 1981 Two Romano-British burials. *Sussex Archaeological Collections* **119**, 65-8.

Kenny, J. 2004a Bosham: the facts and the fiction. *Past Matters 2004*. Chichester: District Council.

Kenny, J. 2004b Chichester city walls. *Past Matters 2004*. Chichester: District Council.

King A. and Soffe G. 1994 The Iron Age and Roman temple on Hayling Island. *In:* A. Fitzpatrick and E. Morris (eds), *The Iron Age in Wessex: recent work*. Salisbury: Trust for Wessex Archaeology, 114-16.

Knight, J. 2001 *Roman France: an archaeological field guide*. Stroud: Tempus.

Lemmon, C. and Darrall Hill, J. 1966 The Romano-British site at Bodiam. *Sussex Archaeological Collections* **104**, 88-102.

Luke, M. and Wells, J. 2000 New evidence for the origins, development and internal morphology of the Roman roadside settlement at Alfoldean. *Sussex Archaeological Collections* **138**, 75-101.

Lyne, M. 1994 The Hassocks Cemetery. *Sussex Archaeological Collections* **132**, 53-85.

Lyne, M. 2003 The pottery supply to Roman Sussex. *In*: D. Rudling (ed) *The Archaeology of Sussex to AD 2000*. University of Sussex, 141-50.

Lysons, S. 1817 An Account of the Remains of a Roman Villa, discovered in Bignor, in Sussex *Archaeologia* **18**, 203-21.

Lysons, S. 1819 *Reliquiae Britannico-Romanae Vol. 111, Remains of a Roman Villa Discovered in Bignor in Sussex*.

Lysons, S. 1821 An Account of Further Discoveries of the Remains of a Roman Villa at Bignor in Sussex *Archaeologia* **19**, 176-7.

Magilton, J. 1991 Elsted: the Roman villa at Batten Hanger. *The Archaeology of Chichester District 1991*. Chichester: District Council, 27-32.

Magilton, J. 1992 A mother goddess statuette from Fishbourne. *The Archaeology of Chichester District 1992*. Chichester: District Council, 73-4.

Magilton, J. 1996 Roman Roads in the Manhood Peninsula, *The Archaeology of Chichester and District 1995*. Chichester: District Council, 31-4.

Magilton, J. and Rudkin, D. 1999 Roman Chichester and Fishbourne. *In:* K. Leslie and B. Short (eds), *An Historical Atlas of Sussex*. Chichester: Phillimore. 26-7, 145.

Manley, J. 2000 Measurement and metaphor: The design and meaning of Building 3 at Fishbourne Roman Palace, *Sussex Archaeological Collections* **138**, 103-13.

Manley, J. 2002 AD 43 – *The Roman Invasion of Britain: a reassessment*. Stroud: Tempus.

Manley, J. 2003 Inside/outside: architecture and the individual at Fishbourne Roman palace. *In*: D. Rudling (ed), *The Archaeology of Sussex to AD 2000*. University of Sussex. 127-40.

Manley, J. and Rudkin, D. 2003 Facing the palace. *Sussex Archaeological Collections* **141**.

Margary, I. 1948 *Roman Ways in the Weald*. London: Phoenix House.

Margary, I. 1953 Recent discoveries by the Ordnance Survey of Roman roads in Sussex. *Sussex Archaeological Collections* **91**, 1-19.

Margary, I. 1965 *Roman Ways in the Weald* (revised edition). London: Phoenix House.

Martin 1859 Some recollections of apart of the 'Stane Street causeway' in its passage through West Sussex. *Sussex Archaeological Collections* **11**, 126-46.

Mason, D. 2003 *Roman Britain and the Roman navy*. Stroud: Tempus.

Maxfield, V. (ed) 1989 *The Saxon Shore: A Handbook*. Exeter: University Press.

McDermott, W. and Orentzel, A. 1979 *Roman portraits: the Flavian – Trajanic period*. Columbia: University of Missouri Press.

Middleton, A., Cowell, M. and Black, E. 1992 Romano-British relief-patterned flue tiles: a study of provenance using petrography and neutron activation analysis. *In:* S. Mery (ed), *Earth Sciences and Archaeological Ceramics, Experimentations, Applications, Documents et Travaux, IGAL, Cergy*, No. **16**, 49-59.

Middleton, A. 1997 Tiles in Roman Britain. *In:* L Freestone and D. Gaimster (eds), *Pottery in the making*. London: British Museum Press, 158-63.

Millett, M. 1990. *The Romanization of Britain*. Cambridge University Press.

Millett, M. 1995. *Roman Britain*. London: Batsford.

Millett, M and Graham, D. 1986 *Excavations on the Romano-British small town at Neathan, Hampshire, 1969-1979*. Hampshire Field Club Monograph **3**.

Mitchell, H. 1866 On the early traditions of Bosham. *Sussex Archaeological Collections* **18**.

Mitchell, G. 1910 Excavations at Chantonbury Ring, 1909, *Sussex Archaeological Collections* **53**, 131-37.

Money, J. 1977 The Iron Age hillfort and Romano-British ironworking settlement at Garden Hill, Sussex: interim report on excavations, 1968-1976. *Britannia* **8**, 339-50.

Moorhead, J. 2001 *The Roman Empire divided*. London: Longman.

Morris, J. 1973 *The age of Arthur*. London: Weidenfeld and Nicolson.

Myres, J. 1986 *The English settlements*. Oxford University Press.

Norris, N. and Burstow, G. 1950 A prehistoric and Romano-British site at west Blatchington, Hove. *Sussex Archaeological Collections* **89**, 1-54.

Orwell, G. 1948 *Nineteen Eighty-Four*. London: Penguin.

Page, W. (ed) 1905 *The Victoria history of the county of Sussex: volume 1*. Haymarket; James Street.

Painter, K. 1965 A Roman marble head from Sussex. *Antiquaries Journal* **45**, 178-82.

Peacock, D. 1973 Forged brick-stamps from Pevensey. *Antiquity* **47**, 138-40.

Peacock, D. 1987 Iron Age and Roman Quern Production at Lodsworth, West Sussex. *Antiquaries Journal* **67**, 61-85.

Pearson, A. 1999 Building Anderita: late Roman coastal defences and the construction of the Saxon Shore Fort at Pevensey. *Oxford Journal of Archaeology* **18**, 95-117.

Pearson, A. 2002 *The Roman Shore Forts*. Stroud: Tempus.

Petrie, F. 1917 Neglected British History. *Proceedings of the British Academy* **8**, 251-78.

Philp, B. 1981 *The excavation of the Roman forts of the Classsis Britannica at Dover 1970-77*. Kent Archaeological Monograph 3.

Praetorius, C. 1911 Report on the villa at Borough Farm, Pulborough. *Proceedings of the Society of Antiquaries of London* **23**, 121-9.

Reece, R. 1988 *My Roman Britain*. Cirencester: Cotswold Studies.

Reece, R. 2002 *The coinage of Roman Britain*. Stroud: Tempus.

Rivet, A. 1964 *Town and Country in Roman Britain*. Second edition. London: Hutchinson.

Rivet, A. and Smith, C. 1979 *The Place Names of Roman Britain*. London: Batsford.

Rock, J. 1879 Ancient cinder heaps in East Sussex. *Sussex Archaeological Collections* **29**, 168-74.

Rudkin, D. 1986 The excavation of a Romano-British site by Chichester Harbour. *Sussex Archaeological Collections* **124**, 51-77.

Rudkin, D. 1988 Fishbourne Roman palace: a second interim account of excavations in the west wing. *The Archaeology of Chichester and District 1988*, 28-31.

Rudkin, D. 2002 Military forces, *Sussex Past & Present* **98**, 9.

Rudling, D. 1979 Invasion and Response: Downland Settlement in East Sussex. *In:* B.C. Barnham and R.B. Johnson (eds), *Invasion and Response: The Case of Roman Britain,* British Archaeological Report British Series **73**. 339-56.

Rudling, D. 1982 The Romano-British Farm on Bullock Down. *In:* P. Drewett, *The Archaeology of Bullock Down, Eastbourne, East Sussex: The Development of a Landscape,* Sussex Archaeological Society Monograph **1**, 97-142.

Rudling, D. 1984 Excavations in Tarrant Street, Arundel, West Sussex. *Bulletin of the Institute of Archaeology (University of London)* **21**, 45-7.

Rudling, D. 1985 Excavations on the site of the Southwick Roman Villa, 1965 and 1981. *Sussex Archaeological Collections* **123**, 73-84.

Rudling, D. 1986 The Excavation of a Roman Tilery on Great Cansiron Farm, Hartfield, East Sussex. *Britannia* **17**, 191-230.

Rudling, D. 1988 A Colony of Rome, AD 43-410. *In:* P. Drewett, D. Rudling, and M. Gardiner, *The South East to AD 1000.* London: Longman. 178-245

Rudling, D. 1997. Round 'house' to Villa: The Beddingham and Watergate Villas. *In:* R.M. and D.E. Friendship-Taylor (series eds), *From Round 'house' to Villa,* Fascicle 3 of the Upper Nene Archaeological Society.

Rudling, D. 1998. The development of Roman villas in Sussex. *Sussex Archaeological Collections* **136**, 41-65.

Rudling, D. 2001 Chanctonbury Ring revisited, The excavations of 1988-1991. *Sussex Archaeological Collections* **139**, 75-121.

Rudling, D. 2003 Roman rural settlement in Sussex: continuity and change. *In:* D. Rudling (ed), *The Archaeology of Sussex to AD 2000.* University of Sussex. 111-26.

Rudling, D. and Gilkes, O. 2000 Important archaeological discoveries made during the construction of the A259 Rustington bypass. *Sussex Archaeological Collections* **138**, 15-28.

Rudling, D. and Butler, C. 2002 Barcombe Roman Villa. *Current Archaeology* **179**, 486-9.

Rudling, D. and Gilkes, O. 2000 Important archaeological discoveries made during the construction of the A259 Rustington Bypass 1990. *Sussex Archaeological Collections* **138**, 15-28.

Russell, M. 2003 *Piltdown man: the secret life of Charles Dawson and the world's greatest archaeological hoax*. Stroud. Tempus.

Salway, P. 1984 *Roman Britain*. Oxford University Press.

Salzman, L. 1908 Excavations at Pevensey, 1906-1907. *Sussex Archaeological Collections* **51**, 99-114.

Salzman, L. 1909 Excavations at Pevensey, 1907-8. *Sussex Archaeological Collections* **52**, 83-95.

Sauer, E. 2000 Alchester, a Claudian 'Vexillation Fortress' near the Western Boundary of the Catuvellauni: New Light on the Roman Invasion of Britain. *Archaeological Journal* **157**, 1-78.

Scott, E. 1993 *A Gazetteer of Roman Villas in Britain*. Leicester Archaeology Monographs No.1.

Scott, L. 1938 The Roman Villa at Angmering. *Sussex Archaeological Collections* **79**, 3-44.

Scott, L. 1939 Angmering Roman Villa. *Sussex Archaeological Collections* **80**, 89-92.

Sear, F. 2000 *Roman architecture*. London: Routledge.

Segala, E. and Scortino, I. 1999 *Domus Aurea*. Rome: Soprintendenza Archeologica di Roma.

Smith J. 1997 *Roman villas: a study in social structure*. London: Routledge.

Southern, P. 1997 *Domitian: tragic tyrant*. London: Routledge.

Stenton, F. 1971 *Anglo-Saxon England*. Oxford University Press.

Stevens, L. and Gilbert, R. 1973 *The Eastbourne Roman Villa*. Eastbourne: Crain Services.

Straker, E. 1931 *Wealden iron*. London: Bell.

Sutton, T. 1952 The Eastbourne Roman Villa, *Sussex Archaeological Collections* **90**, 1-12.

Tebbutt, C. 1981 Wealden bloomery iron smelting furnaces. *Sussex Archaeological Collections* **119**, 57-63.

Todd, M. 1970 The small towns of Roman Britain, *Britannia* **1**, 114-30.

Tomlin, R. 1997 Reading a 1st-century Roman gold signet ring from Fishbourne, *Sussex Archaeological Collections* **135**, 127-30.

Toms, H. and Herbert, G. 1926 Roman villa at Preston. *Brighton and Hove Archaeologist* **1**, 3-27.

Toynbee, J. 1962 *Art in Roman Britain*. London: Phaidon.

Varner, E. 2004 *Mutilation and transformation: Damnatio Memoriae and Roman imperial portraiture*. Brill: Leiden.

Vincent, A. 2000 *Roman Roads of Sussex*. Midhurst: Middleton Press.

Wacher, J. 1962 A survey of Romano-British Town Defences of the early and middle second century. *Archaeological Journal* **119**, 103-13.

Wacher, J.S. (ed) 1966, *The civitas capitals of Roman Britain*. Leicester University Press.

Wacher, J. 1974 *The Towns of Roman Britain*. London: Batsford.

Wacher J. 1995 *Towns of Roman Britain* (second revised edition). London: Routledge.

Waldron, T., Taylor, G. and Rudling, D. 1999 Sexing of Romano-British baby burials from the Beddingham and Bignor villas. *Sussex Archaeological Collections* **137**, 71-9.

Webster, G. 1993 *The Roman invasion of Britain*. London: Routledge.

Wells, H. 1898 *The war of the worlds*. London: Penguin.

Welch, M. 1983 *Early Anglo-Saxon Sussex*. British Archaeological Report British Series **112**.

Wheeler, R. and Wheeler, T. 1932 *Report on the excavation of the prehistoric, Roman and post Roman site in Lydney Park, Gloucestershire*. Society of Antiquaries Research Report **9**.

White, G. 1936 The Chichester amphitheatre: preliminary excavations. *Antiquaries Journal* **16**.

White, D. 1961 *Litus Saxonicum: the British Saxon Shore in Scholarship and History*. Madison (WI): Department of History, University of Wisconsin.

White, S., Manley, J., Jones, R. Orna-Ornstein, J., Johns, C. and Webster, L. 1999 A Mid-Fifth-Century Hoard of Roman and Pseudo-Roman Material from Patching, West Sussex. *Britannia* **30**.

Wilson, A. 1947 Angmering Roman Villa. *Sussex Archaeological Collections* **86**, 1-21.

Wilson, A. 1957 *The archaeology of Chichester city walls*. Chichester Papers **6**.

Wilson, R. 2002 *A guide to the Roman remains in Britain*. London: Constable.

Winbolt, S. 1923 Alfoldean Roman Station: first report, 1922. *Sussex Archaeological Collections* **64**, 81-104.

Winbolt, S. 1924 Alfoldean Roman Station: second report (on 1923). *Sussex Archaeological Collections* **65**, 122-27.

Winbolt, S. 1927 Excavations at Hardham Camp, Pulborough. *Sussex Archaeological Collections* **68**, 122-27.

Winbolt, S. 1932 Roman villa at Southwick. *Sussex Archaeological Collections* **73**, 13-32.

Winbolt, S. 1935 Romano-British Sussex, in L.P. Salzman (ed), *The Victoria History of the Counties of England, A History of Sussex*, Volume **3**, 1-70.

Witts, P. 2005 *Mosaics in Roman Britain: stories in stone*. Stroud: Tempus.

Wolseley, G. Smith, R. and Hawley, W. 1927 Prehistoric and Roman Settlement on Park Brow. *Archaeologia* **76**, 1-40.

Woodward, A. 1992 *Shrines and Sacrifice*. London: Batsford.

INDEX

INDEX